Paris,
CAPITAL OF
MODERNITY

PARIS,
CAPITAL OF
MODERNITY

DAVID HARVEY

Routledge
Taylor & Francis Group
New York   London

First Routledge hardcover edition, copyright © 2003 by David Harvey.
First Routledge paperback edition, copyright © 2006 by David Harvey.

Published in 2006 by
Routledge
Taylor & Francis Group
270 Madison Avenue
New York, NY 10016

Published in Great Britain by
Routledge
Taylor & Francis Group
2 Park Square
Milton Park, Abingdon
Oxon OX14 4RN

© 2006 by David Harvey
Routledge is an imprint of Taylor & Francis Group

Printed in the United States of America on acid-free paper
10 9 8 7 6 5 4 3 2 1

International Standard Book Number-10: 0-415-95220-4 (Softcover)
International Standard Book Number-13: 978-0-415-95220-0 (Softcover)
Library of Congress Card Number 2003004067

Library of Congress Cataloging-in-Publication Data

Harvey, David, 1935-
    Paris, capital of modernity / David Harvey.
        p. cm.
    Includes bibliographical references and index.
    ISBN 0-415-94421-X (hardcover : alk. paper) - ISBN 0-415-95220-4 (pbk.: alk. paper)
    1. Paris (France)--Civilization--19th century. 2. France--History--Second Empire, 1852-1870. I. Title.

DC715.H337 2003
944'.36107--dc21   2003004067

informa

Taylor & Francis Group
is the Academic Division of Informa plc.

Visit the Taylor & Francis Web site at
http://www.taylorandfrancis.com

and the Routledge Web site at
http://www.routledge-ny.com

Contents

Part Three
Coda

Illustrations

TABLES

Modernity as Break

One of the myths of modernity is that it constitutes a radical break with the past. The break is supposedly of such an order as to make it possible to see the world as a tabula rasa, upon which the new can be inscribed without reference to the past—or, if the past gets in the way, through its obliteration. Modernity is, therefore, always about "creative destruction," be it of the gentle and democratic, or the revolutionary, traumatic, and authoritarian kind. It is often difficult to decide if the radical break is in the style of doing or representing things in different arenas such as literature and the arts, urban planning and industrial organization, politics, lifestyle, or whatever, or whether shifts in all such arenas cluster in some crucially important places and times from whence the aggregate forces of modernity diffuse outward to engulf the rest of the world. The myth of modernity tends toward the latter interpretation (particularly through its cognate terms of modernization and development) although, when pushed, most of its advocates are usually willing to concede uneven developments that generate quite a bit of confusion in the specifics.

I call this idea of modernity a myth because the notion of a radical break has a certain persuasive and pervasive power in the face of abundant evidence that it does not, and cannot, possibly occur. The alternative theory of modernization (rather than modernity), due initially to Saint-Simon and very much taken to heart by Marx, is that no social order can achieve changes that are not already latent within its existing condition. Strange, is it not, that two thinkers who occupy a prominent place within the pantheon of modernist thought should so explicitly deny the possibility of any radical break at the same time that they insisted upon the importance of revolutionary change? Where opinion does converge, however, is around the centrality of "creative destruction." You cannot make an omelet without breaking eggs, the old adage goes, and it is impossible to create new social configurations without in some way superseding or even obliterating the old. So if modernity exists as a meaningful term, it signals some decisive moments of creative destruction.

FIGURE 1 *Ernest Meissonier's painting of the barricade on the Rue de la Mortellerie in June 1848 depicts the death and destruction that stymied a revolutionary movement to reconstruct the body politic of Paris along more utopian socialist lines.*

Something very dramatic happened in Europe in general, and in Paris in particular, in 1848. The argument for some radical break in Parisian political economy, life, and culture around that date is, on the surface at least, entirely plausible. Before, there was an urban vision that at best could only tinker with the problems of a medieval urban infrastructure; then came Haussmann, who bludgeoned the city into modernity. Before, there were the classicists, like Ingres and David, and the colorists, like Delacroix; and after, there were Courbet's realism and Manet's impressionism. Before, there were the Romantic poets and novelists (Lamartine, Hugo, Musset, and George Sand); and after came the taut, sparse, and fine-honed prose and poetry of Flaubert and Baudelaire. Before, there were dispersed manufacturing industries organized along artisanal lines; much of that then gave way to machinery and modern industry. Before, there were small stores along narrow, winding streets or in the arcades; and after came the vast sprawling department stores that spilled out onto the boulevards. Before, there was utopianism and romanticism; and after there was hard-headed managerialism and scientific socialism. Before, water carrier was a major occupation; but by 1870 it had almost disappeared as piped water became available. In all of these respects—and more—1848 seemed to be a decisive moment in which much that was new crystallized out of the old.

FIGURE 2 *Daumier's* L'Emeute *(The Riot), from 1848, captures something of the macabre, carnivalesque qualities of the uprising of February 1848. It seems to presage, with grim foreboding, the deathly outcome.*

So what, exactly, happened in 1848 in Paris? There was hunger, unemployment, misery, and discontent throughout the land, and much of it converged on Paris as people flooded into the city in search of sustenance. There were republicans and socialists determined to confront the monarchy and at least reform it so that it lived up to its initial democratic promise. If that did not happen, there were always those who thought the time ripe for revolution. That situation had, however, existed for years. The strikes, street demonstrations, and conspiratorial uprisings of the 1840s had been contained and few, judging by their unprepared state, seemed to think it would be different this time.

On February 23, 1848, on the Boulevard des Capucines, a relatively small demonstration at the Foreign Ministry got out of hand and troops fired at the demonstrators, killing fifty or so. What followed was extraordinary. A cart with several bodies of those killed was taken by torchlight around the city. The legendary account, given by Daniel Stern and taken up by Flaubert in *Sentimental Education*, focuses on the body of a woman (and I say it is legendary because the driver of the cart testified that there was no woman aboard).[1] Before largely silent crowds gathered in the streets, according to Stern's account, a boy would periodically illuminate the body of the young woman with his torch; at other moments a man would pick up the body and hold it up to the crowd. This was a potent symbol. Liberty had long been imagined as a woman, and now it seemed she had been shot down. The night that followed was, by several accounts, eerily quiet. Even the marketplaces were so. Come dawn, the tocsins sounded throughout the city. This was the call to revolution. Workers, students, disaffected bourgeois, small property owners came together in the streets. Many in the National Guard joined them, and much of the army soon lost the will to fight.

Louis Philippe hastily appointed first Louis Molé and then Adolphe Thiers as prime minister. Thiers, author of voluminous histories of the French Revolution, had held that position earlier in the July Monarchy (1830) but had failed to stabilize the regime as a constitutional monarchy along British lines. Thiers is thought to have advised the King to withdraw to Versailles and marshal forces loyal to himself—and, if necessary, to crush the revolutionary movement in Paris (a tactic later deployed against the Paris Commune of 1871). The aged and demoralized King, if he heard, did not listen. He abdicated in favor of his eight-year-old grandson, leaped into a coach, and fled to England with the Queen, disguised as Mr. and Mrs. Smith. By then the city was in the hands of revolutionaries. Conservative deputies fled, and a brief attempt to set up a regency for the new King in the National Assembly was brushed aside. Across town, a provisional government was declared at the Hotel de Ville. A group of eleven, including Lamartine, a Romantic poet with republican and socialist sympathies, and Louis Blanc (a longtime socialist) were acclaimed to head a provisional government. The population invaded the Tuileries, the King's erstwhile residence, and sacked it, destroying furnishings and slashing paintings. Common people, even street urchins, took turns sitting on the throne before it was dragged through the streets to be burned at the Bastille.

FIGURE 3 *Daumier hilariously reconstructs the moment when the street urchins of Paris could momentarily occupy the throne of France, while joyously racing around the abandoned Tuileries Palace. The throne was subsequently dragged to the Bastille and burned.*

Many people witnessed these events. Balzac, although anxious to get on his way to Russia to be with his beloved Madame Hanska, could not resist a trip to the Tuileries to see for himself. Flaubert rushed to Paris to see events at first hand "from an artistic point of view," and wrote a lengthy, informative, and, some historians accept, accurate version of it into *Sentimental Education* twenty years later. Baudelaire was swept up in the action. But Georges-Eugène Haussmann, then subprefect at Blaye, near Bordeaux, and later the mastermind behind the transformation of Paris, was, like many others in provincial France, surprised and dismayed when he heard the news two days later. He resigned, and refused reappointment by a government he considered illegitimate.

The provisional government held elections in late April, and the Constituent Assembly met in May to officially proclaim the Republic. Much of provincial France voted right, much of Paris voted left, and some notable socialists got elected. More important, spaces were created in which radical organizations could flourish. Political clubs formed, worker associations sprang up, and those who had been most concerned about the question of work procured an official commission that met regularly in the Luxembourg Palace to look into social and political reform. This became known as "the workers' parliament." National workshops were created to offer work and wages to the unemployed. It was a moment of intense liberty of discussion. Flaubert brilliantly represented it thus in *Sentimental Education*:

> As business was in abeyance, anxiety and a desire to stroll about brought everybody out of doors. The informality of dress masked the differences of social rank, hatreds were hidden, hopes took wing, the crowd was full of good will. Faces shone with the pride of rights won. There was a carnival gaiety, a bivouac feeling; there could be nothing such fun as the aspect of Paris on those first days. . . .
>
> [Frédéric and the Marshal] visited all, or almost all, of [the clubs], the red and the blue, the frenetic and the severe, the puritanical and the bohemian, the mystical and the boozy, the ones that insisted on death to all kings and those that criticised the sharp practice of grocers; and everywhere tenants cursed landlords, those in overalls attacked those in fine clothes, and the rich plotted against the poor. Some, as former martyrs at the hands of the police, wanted compensation, others begged for money to develop their inventions or else it was a matter of Phalanstèrian (Fourièrist) plans, projects for local markets, systems to promote public well-being, and then there would be a flash of intelligence amid these clouds of foolishness, sudden spatters of exhortation, rights declared with an oath, flowers of eloquence on the lips of some apprentice lad wearing his sword sash next to the skin of his shirtless chest. . . . To appear reasonable it was necessary always to speak scathingly of lawyers and to make use of the following expressions as frequently as possible: every man must contribute his stone to the edifice . . . social problems . . . workshops.[2]

But the economy went from bad to worse. Debts remained unpaid, and bourgeois fears for their property rights as owners, rentiers, and employers fueled sentiments of reaction. ("Property was raised to the level of Religion and became indistinguishable from God," wrote Flaubert.) Minor agitations in April and May deepened the fears, and the last of these ended with several radical leaders under arrest. Retribution against the left was in the making. The national workshops were failing to organize productive work but kept workers from returning to their earlier employments. The republican government, with the right wing in a clear majority, closed them down in June. Significant elements within the populace rose up in protest. In Guedella's classic description: "The men were starving, and they fought without hope, without leaders, without cheers, shooting sullenly behind great barricades of stone. For four days Paris was alight with the dull glow;

FIGURE 4 *This rare and extraordinary daguerrotype of the barricades on the Faubourg du Temple on the morning of June 25, 1848, illustrates what the forces of order were up against as they sought to reoccupy Paris.*

guns were brought up against the barricades; a great storm broke over the smoking town; women were shot without pity, and on a ghastly Sunday a general in parlay with the barricades was shamefully murdered; the Archbishop of Paris, with a supreme gesture of reconciliation, went out at sunset to make peace and was shot and died. It was a time of horror, and for four summer days Paris was tortured by the struggle. Then the rebellion broke, and the Republic survived."[3] The National Assembly had dismissed the government (Lamartine among others) and placed its faith in Louis Cavaignac, a bourgeois republican general with much experience in colonial Algeria. Given command of the army, he ruthlessly and brutally put down the revolt. The barricades were smashed.

The June Days did not put an end to matters. Centrist republicans were now discredited, and the National Assembly was increasingly divided between a monarchist right and a democratic socialist left. In between there arose the specter of Bonapartism in the guise of the nephew, Louis Napoleon. Still officially exiled in England, he had been elected to a seat in the Assembly in June. He refrained from trying to take his seat but indicated ominously in a letter that "if France called him to duty he would know how to fulfill it." The perception began to take hold that he, and only he, could reestablish order. He was reelected in another election in September. This time he took his seat. With the new constitution creating a President on the American model, to be elected by universal suffrage, Louis set about campaigning for that position. In the election of December 10 he received 5.4 million votes against 1.4 million for Cavaignac and a derisory 8,000 for Lamartine. But the presidency was limited to four years and Louis did not command much support in the Assembly (only a smattering of Bonapartists were elected in 1849; the majority was conservative royalist). Louis began to display a capacity to keep law and order and suppress "the reds" while showing scant respect for the constitution.

Most of the socialist leaders (Louis Blanc, Alexandre Ledru-Rolin, Victor Considérant, etc.) had been driven into exile by the summer of 1849. Cultivating popular support particularly in the provinces (with the covert help of officials like Haussmann), and even more importantly among Catholics (by helping to put the Pope back into the Vatican against the revolutionaries in Italy) and within the army, Louis Napoleon plotted his way (with the unwitting help of the Assembly that foolishly abolished universal suffrage, reinstituted press censorship, and refused to extend the presidential term) to the coup d'état of December 2, 1851. The Assembly was dissolved, the main parliamentary figures (Cavaignac, Thiers, etc.) were arrested, the sporadic resistance was easily put down in Paris (though the death of a democratic-socialist representative, Baudin, on one of the few barricades was later to become a symbol of the illegitimacy of Empire). In spite of some surprising pockets of intense rural resistance, the new constitution (modeled on that of Year VIII of the Revolution) was confirmed by a huge majority of 7.5 million votes against 640,000 in the plebiscite of December 20. Louis Napoleon, to cries of "Vive l'empereur," rode triumphantly around the city for several hours before entering and taking up residence in the Tuileries Palace. It took a year of further cultivation of popular support for the empire to be declared (and again confirmed by a massive majority in a plebiscite). Republicanism and democratic governance had been tried, and had failed. Authoritarianism and despotism (though whether benevolent or not had yet to be determined) constituted the answer.[4]

Haussmann, with clear Bonapartist sympathies, resumed his prefectural role in January 1849, first in Var and then in Auxerre. Invited to Paris to receive a new assignment, he just happened to be at a soirée at the Elysée Paris on the evening of December 1, 1851. Louis Napoleon shook his hand, informed him of his proposed new appointment, and asked him to present himself early in the morning to the minister of the interior to receive his instructions. That evening Haussman discovered that the existing minister had no idea what he was talking about. At 5 o'clock the next morning Haussmann presented himself and found the Duke of Morny, half brother of Louis Napoleon, now in charge. The coup d'état was in process and Morny correctly presumed that Haussmann was with them. Haussmann was reassigned first to the frontier region with Italy (a delicate problem because of border difficulties) but then to his favored region of Bordeaux. And as the Prince-President toured the country in preparation for the declaration of Empire, he culminated with a major speech at Bordeaux ("The Empire is Peace," he proclaimed) in October 1852. Haussmann's ability to mobilize spectacle to imperial purposes during the Bordeaux visit was duly noted (along with his Bonapartist sympathies and energies).

FIGURE 5 *This photo by Marville (taken sometime in 1850– 1851) shows the demolitions already under way around the Rue de Rivoli and the Palais*

In June 1853 he was reassigned to Paris. On the day that Haussmann took his oath of office, the Emperor handed him a map, so the legend spun by Haussmann in his *Mémoires* has it, on which were drawn in outlines of four different colors (representing the urgency of the projects) the plans for the reconstruction of the street system of Paris. This was, according to Haussmann, the plan that he faithfully carried out (with a few extensions) over the next two decades.

We now know this to be a myth.[5] There had been considerable discussion about, as well as practical efforts (led by Rambuteau, who was prefect from 1833 until 1848) toward the modernization of Paris under the July Monarchy. During the 1840s innumerable plans and proposals were discussed. The Emperor, after being elected President in 1848, had already been party to urban renewal initiatives, and Berger, Haussmann's predecessor, had begun the task in earnest. The Rue de Rivoli was already being extended, as was the Rue Saint Martin; and there are LeSecq's and Marville's photos and Daumier's trenchant commentaries on the effects of the demolitions from 1851–1852, a year before Haussmann took office, to prove it.[6] Furthermore, the Emperor appointed a commission under Count Simeon in August 1853 to advise upon urban renewal projects. Haussmann claimed it rarely met and produced only an interim report marked by banal and impracticable recommendations. It in fact met regularly and produced an elaborate and extremely detailed plan that was delivered to the Emperor in December 1853. Haussmann deliberately ignored it, though what influence it had on the Emperor (who consulted rather more frequently with Haussmann than the latter admitted) is not known. Haussmann, furthermore, did both more and less than the Emperor wanted. The Emperor had instructed him to be sensitive to existing structures of quality and to avoid the straight line. Haussmann ignored him on both counts. The Emperor had little interest in the delivery of running water or in the annexation of the suburbs, but Haussmann had a passion for both—and got his way. Haussmann's *Mémoires*, upon which most accounts have hitherto relied, are full of dissimulation.

There is, however, something very telling about Haussmann's denials. They reveal far more than egoism and vanity (though he had plenty of both). They signal in part what it

FIGURE 6 *Daumier here takes up, as early as 1852, the issue of the displacement of populations by the demolitions. Interestingly, he never bothered with the issue again.*

FIGURE 7 *This lithograph by Provost depicts conditions in Les Halles in the early 1850s (it parallels a photograph taken by Marville; see De Thèzy, 1994, 365). The new Les Halles is on the right and the old system, in which merchants stored their goods under the overhanging eaves of the buildings, is on the left.*

was that Haussmann had to struggle against. He needed to build a myth of a radical break around himself and the Emperor—a myth that has survived to the present day—because he needed to show that what went before was irrelevant; that neither he nor Louis Napoleon was in any way beholden to the thinking or the practices of the immediate past. This denial did double duty. It created a founding myth (essential to any new regime) and helped secure the idea that there was no alternative to the benevolent authoritarianism of Empire. The republican, democratic, and socialist proposals and plans of the 1830s and 1840s were impractical and unworthy of consideration. Haussmann devised the only feasible solution, and it was feasible because it was embedded in the authority of Empire. In this sense there was indeed a real break in both thought and action after the disruptions set in motion by 1848 had done their work. Yet Haussmann also acknowledged, in an exchange of letters with the Emperor that prefaced the publication of the first volume of the *Histoire Générale de Paris* (published in 1866), that "the most striking of modern tendencies" is to seek within the past for an explication of the present and a preparation for the future.[7]

If the break that Haussmann supposedly made was nowhere near as radical as he claimed, then we must search (as Saint-Simon and Marx insist) for the new in the lineaments of the old. But the emergence of the new (as Saint-Simon and Marx also insist) can still have a not-to-be-denied revolutionary significance. Haussmann and his colleagues were willing to engage in creative destruction on a scale hitherto unseen. The

FIGURE 8 *Baltard's first design of 1852 for the new Les Halles (known as La Fortresse), here recorded in a photograph by Marville, was heartily disapproved of by the Emperor and Haussmann, and soon dismantled.*

FIGURE 9 *"Umbrellas of iron" is what Haussmann wanted, and eventually what Baltard gave him, in the classic modernist building of Les Halles from 1855.*

FIGURE 10 *The Palais de l'Industrie, as portrayed by Trichon and Lix, achieved an even grander interior space than Les Halles, illustrating again a radical transformation of scale made possible by new materials, architectural forms, and modes of organization of construction.*

formation of Empire out of the ruins of republican democracy enabled them to do this. Let me preview the sorts of shifts I have in mind.

Hittorf had been one of the main architects at work on the transformation of Paris under the July Monarchy. A new avenue to link the Arc de Triomphe and the Bois de Boulogne had long been mooted, and Hittorf had drawn up plans for it. The street was to be very wide by existing standards—120 feet. Hittorf met with Haussmann in 1853. The latter insisted there be 440 feet between the facing buildings with an avenue 360 feet wide.[8] Haussmann thus tripled the scale of the project. He changed the spatial scale of both thought and action. Consider another instructive example. The provisioning of Paris through Les Halles had long been recognized as inefficient and inadequate. It had been a hot topic of debate during the July Monarchy. The former prefect Berger, under orders from Louis Napoleon as President, had made it a priority to redesign it. Figure 7 shows the old system (soon to be demolished), where merchants stored their goods as best they could under the overhanging eaves of the houses. Louis Napoleon suspended work on Baltard's new building of 1852—known locally as "the fortress of Les Halles"—as a totally unacceptable solution (figure 8). "We want umbrellas" made "of iron," Haussmann told a chastened Baltard in 1853, and that, in the end, is what Baltard gave him, though only after Haussmann had rejected (thereby earning Baltard's perpetual resentment) several hybrid designs. The result was a building that has long been regarded as a modernist classic (see figure 9). In his *Mémoires*, Haussmann suggests he saved Baltard's reputation (when Louis Napoleon asked how an architect who produced something so awful in 1852 could produce such a work of genius two years later, Haussmann immodestly replied "different prefect!").

Then go to the Palais de l'Industrie, built for the Universal Exposition of 1855 (figure 10) and see a cavernous space that goes far beyond Baltard. Now compare these new spaces with the arcades that had been so important in the early 1800s (figure 11). The form and the materials are the same, but there has been an extraordinary change of scale (something that, incidentally, Walter Benjamin fails to register in his Arcades project in spite of his intense interest in the spatial forms of the city). The architectural historian Loyer, in his detailed reconstruction of architectural and building practices in nineteenth-century Paris enunciates the principle at work exactly: "One of capitalism's most important effects on construction," he writes, "was to transform the scale of projects."[9] While Haussmann's myth of a total break deserves to be questioned, we must also recognize the radical shift in scale that he helped to engineer, inspired by new technologies and facilitated by new organizational forms. This shift enabled him to think of the city (and even its suburbs) as a totality rather than as a chaos of particular projects.

FIGURE 11 *This Marville photo of an arcade—the Passage de l'Opéra—illustrates the dramatic shift in scale (though not in form) that occurred in construction between the 1820s, when many of the arcades were built, and Les Halles and the Palais de l'Industrie of the 1850s.*

In a seemingly quite different register, consider the radical break that Flaubert supposedly accomplished in his writing. Before 1848, Flaubert was a miserable failure; he agonized, to the point of nervous breakdown in the 1840s, over how and what to write. His explorations of Gothic and Romantic themes produced abysmal literature, no matter how hard he worked at polishing his style. Even his best friends (Maxime du Camp and Louis Bouilhet) considered the first draft of his *Temptation of Saint Anthony* a total failure, and in 1849 clearly told him so. Bouilhet then advised a shocked Flaubert that he should study Balzac and suggested, according to Steegmuller, "that if Flaubert were to write a novel about the bourgeois (a class that had always interested him and which he was wrong to believe unworthy of literary treatment), emphasizing their emotional rather than their material concerns and employing a good style of his own, the result would be something new in the history of literature." Two years later (after Flaubert's voyage to the Orient), Bouilhet suggested that Flaubert take up the tragic suicide of a provincial doctor's wife and treat it (a scene from provincial life, as it were) in the manner of Balzac.

Flaubert swallowed his pride (Balzac, he had early on concluded, had not the faintest idea of how to write) and dutifully worked on this from 1851 to 1856. *Madame Bovary*, when published, was (and still is) widely acclaimed as the first major literary sensation and masterpiece in Second Empire culture.[10] It is even sometimes depicted as the first great modernist novel in the French language. However that may be, Flaubert finally came into his own only after romanticism and utopianism were put to the sword in 1848. Emma Bovary commits suicide, the victim of banal romantic illusions, in exactly the same way that the revolutionary romantics of 1848 had, in Flaubert's view, committed suicide on the barricades (in the senseless way he was to depict in *Sentimental Education*). Wrote Flaubert of Lamartine: "The people have had enough of poets" and "Poets cannot cope." Flaubert downplayed his debt to Balzac (much as Haussman denied the influence of his predecessors), but he perceptively recognized the dilemma. "To accomplish something lasting," he wrote, "one must have a solid foundation. The thought of the future torments us, and the past is holding us back. That is why the present is slipping from our grasp."[11]

That apostle of modernity, Baudelaire, lived with this dilemma daily, careening from side to side with the same incoherence with which he slid from one side of the barricades to the other in 1848.[12] He had already signaled rejection of tradition in his Salon of 1846, urging artists to explore the "epic qualities of modern life," for their age was "rich in poetic and wonderful subjects," such as "scenes of high life and the thousands of uprooted lives that haunt the underworld of a great city, criminals and prostitutes." "The marvelous envelops us and saturates us like the atmosphere; but we fail to see it," he then wrote. Yet he dedicated his work to the bourgeoisie, invoking their heroism: "You have entered into partnership, formed companies, issued loans, to realize the idea of the future in all its diverse forms." Though there may be a touch of irony in this, he is also appealing to the Saint-Simonian utopianism that sought to harness the qualities of visionary poet and astute businessman to the cause of human emancipation. Baudelaire, caught in his own struggle against tradition and the "aristocrats of thought," and incidentally also inspired by the example of Balzac, proposed an alliance with all those among the bourgeoisie seeking to overthrow traditional class power. Both, he hoped, could nourish the other until "supreme harmony is ours."[13]

But that alliance was not to be. How, after all, could artists depict the heroism in those "uprooted lives" in ways not offensive to the bourgeoisie? Baudelaire would be torn for the rest of his life between the stances of flaneur and dandy, a disengaged and cynical voyeur on the one hand, and man of the people who enters into the life of his subjects with passion on the other. In 1846 that tension was only implicit; but 1848 changed all that. He fought on the side of the insurgents in February and June, and perhaps also in May. He was horrified by the betrayal wrought by the bourgeoisie's Party of Order but equally distressed at the empty rhetoric of Romanticism (as represented by the poet

Lamartine). Disillusioned, Baudelaire switched to the socialist Pierre Proudhon as hero for a while, then linked up with Gustave Courbet, attracted by the realism of both men. In retrospect, he wrote, "1848 was charming only through an excess of the ridiculous." But the evocation of "excess" is significant. He recorded his "wild excitement" and his "natural" and "legitimate pleasure in destruction." But he detested the result. Even return to the secure power of tradition then seemed preferable. In between the high points of revolutionary engagement, he helped edit reactionary newspapers, later writing, "There is no form of rational and assured government save an aristocracy" (Balzac's sentiments exactly). After his initial fury at Louis Napoleon's coup d'état, he withdrew from politics into pessimism and cynicism, only to confess his addiction when the pulse of revolution began to throb: "The Revolution and the Cult of Reason confirm the doctrine of Sacrifice," he wrote.[14] He even came to express sporadic appreciation of Louis Napoleon as someone cast in the role of warrior-poet as King.

There is a contradiction in Baudelaire's sense of modernity after the bittersweet experience of creative destruction on the barricades and the sacking of the Tuileries Palace in 1848. Tradition has to be overthrown, violently if necessary, in order to grapple with the present and create the future. But the loss of tradition wrenches away the sheet anchors of our understanding and leaves us drifting, powerless. The aim of the artists, he wrote in 1860, must therefore be to understand the modern as "the transient, the fleeting, the contingent" in relation to that other half of art which deals in "the eternal and immovable." The fear, he says, in a passage that echoes Flaubert's dilemma, is "of not going fast enough, of letting the spectre escape before the synthesis has been extracted and taken possession of."[15] But all that rush leaves behind a great deal of human wreckage. The "thousand uprooted lives" cannot be ignored.

There is an eloquent evocation of this in his story of "The Old Clown" in *Paris Spleen*. Paris is there depicted as a vast theater. "Everywhere joy, moneymaking, debauchery; everywhere the assurance of tomorrow's daily bread; everywhere frenetic outbursts of vitality." The *fête imperiale* of the Second Empire is in full swing. But among the "dust, shouts, joy, tumult," Baudelaire sees "a pitiful old clown, bent, decrepit, the ruin of a man." The absoluteness of his misery is "made all the more horrible by being tricked out in comic rags." The clown "was mute and motionless. He had given up, he had abdicated. His fate was sealed" (figure 12). The author feels the "terrible hand of hysteria: gripping his throat,"

FIGURE 12 *Daumier's touching* The Clown *captures something of the sentiments expressed in Baudelaire's prose poem. With the crowd moving away from him and only a boy looking curiously on, he stares into the distance like some noble figure now left behind.*

and "rebellious tears that would not fall" blur his sight. He wants to leave money, but the motion of the crowd sweeps him onward. Looking back, he says to himself, "I have just seen the prototype of the old writer who has been the brilliant entertainer of the generation he has outlived, the old poet without friends, without family, without children, degraded by poverty and the ingratitude of the public, and to whose booth the fickle world no longer cares to come."[16]

For Marx, 1848 marked a similar intellectual and political watershed. Experienced from afar in exile in London (though he did visit Paris in March), the events of 1848–1851 in Paris were to be an epiphany without which his turn to a scientific socialism would have been unthinkable. The radical break often evinced between the "young" Marx of the *Economic and Philosophic Manuscripts* of 1844 and the "mature" Marx of *Capital* was, of course, no more radical than were Haussmann's or Flaubert's shifts, but it was nonetheless significant. He had been deeply affected by Romanticism and socialist utopianism in his early years, but was scathing in his dismissal of both in 1848. While there may have been a historical moment when utopianism had opened up new vistas for working-class consciousness, he wrote, it was now at best irrelevant and at worst a barrier to revolution. It is understandable, given the chaotic ferment of ideas produced in the 1840s in France (the subject of chapter 2, below) that Marx would have a strategic interest in boiling down oppositional thought to a much more rigorous and tougher synthetic science of socialism. But for the Marxist movement later to assume a radical break, as if nothing that happened before was relevant, has been a serious error. Marx took all manner of ideas from thinkers like Saint-Simon, Louis Blanqui, Robert Owen, and Etienne Cabet; and even when he rejected others, he shaped his conception as much through critique and opposition as through plucking thought out of thin air. His presentation of the labor process in *Capital* is shaped in response to Fourier's idea that unalienated labor is defined solely by passionate attraction and the joy of play. To this Marx replies that it takes commitment and grit to complete major projects, and that the labor process, however noble, can never entirely escape the arduousness of hard work and collective discipline. Marx in any case held—and this he took from Saint-Simon—that no social order can change without the lineaments of the new already being present in the existing state of things.

If we apply that principle rigorously to what happened in and after 1848, we would see not only Flaubert, Baudelaire, and Haussmann, but also Marx himself, in a very particular light. But the fact that Haussmann, Marx, Flaubert, and Baudelaire all came into their own so spectacularly only after 1848 gives support to the myth of modernity as a radical break, and suggests that it was the experience of those years which had something vital to do with subsequent transformations in thought and practice in a variety of settings. This, it seems to me, is the central tension to be addressed: How far and in what ways were the radical transformations achieved after 1848 already prefigured in the thought and practices of earlier years?

Marx, like Flaubert and Baudelaire, was greatly influenced by Balzac. Paul Lafargue, Marx's son-in-law, noted that Marx's admiration for Balzac "was so profound that he had planned to write a criticism of "La Comédie Humaine" ("The Human Comedy") as soon as he should have finished his economic studies."[17] The whole of Balzac's oeuvre, in Marx's judgment, was prescient about the future evolution of the social order. Balzac "anticipated" in uncanny ways social relations that were identifiable only "in embryo" in the 1830s and 1840s. In drawing back the veil to reveal the myths of modernity as they were forming from the Restoration onward, Balzac helps us identify the deep continuities that underlay the seemingly radical break after 1848. The covert dependency of both Flaubert and Baudelaire upon the perspectives he developed shows this continuity at work even on the terrain of literary production. Marx's explicit debt spreads the continuity across political economy and historical writing. If revolutionary movements draw upon latent tensions within the existing order, then Balzac's writings on Paris in the 1830s and 1840s stand to reveal the nature of such. And out of these possibilities, the transformations of the Second Empire were fashioned. In this light I examine Balzac's representations of Paris in chapter 1.

Daumier's art, of which I make considerable illustrative use here, exhibited similarly prescient qualities. Frequently compared to Balzac, Daumier produced incessant commentary on daily life as well as politics in Paris that forms an extraordinary source. Baudelaire once complained that viewers of Daumier merely looked at the joke and paid no mind to the art. Art historians have subsequently rescued Daumier from dismissal as a mere caricaturist and focused on the finer points of his art, though given his prolific output, the work is generally acknowledged as of uneven quality. But I am here more concerned with the subjects he chooses and the nature of the jokes that he (and others, such as Gavarni and Cham) shared with his audience. What Daumier so often does is to anticipate, and thereby render very visible, processes of change in an embryonic state. As early as 1844 he satirized the way the new dry goods stores were organized, and anticipated the experience of the department stores of the 1850s and 1860s. Most of his commentaries on clearances and demolitions (dismissed by Passeron as inferior art) are from 1852, before the more massive demolitions occurred. He had, then, an uncanny ability to see not only what the city was, but what it was becoming, well before it got there.[18]

This issue of how to see the city and how to represent it during phases of intense change is a daunting challenge. Novelists like Balzac and artists like Daumier pioneer ways to do it in interesting but indirect ways. It is a curious fact, however, that although there are innumerable studies and monographs on individual cities available, few of them turn out to be particularly memorable, let alone enlightening about the human condition. There are, of course, exceptions. I have always taken Carl Schorske's fin-de-siècle Vienna as the model to be aspired to, no matter how impossible to replicate.[19] An interesting feature of that work is precisely how it manages to convey some sense of the totality of what the city was about through a variety of perspectives on material life, on cultural activities, on patterns of thought within the city. The most interesting urban writing is often of a fragmentary and perspectival sort. The difficulty then is to see the totality as well as the parts, and it is on this point that fin-de-siècle Vienna works its particular magic. This difficulty is pervasive in urban studies and urban theory. We have abundant theories as to what happens *in* the city but a singular lack of theory *of* the city; and those theories of the city that we do have often appear to be so one-dimensional and so wooden as to eviscerate the richness and complexity of what the urban experience is about. One cannot easily approach the city and the urban experience, therefore, in a one-dimensional way.

This fragmented approach to the totality is nowhere more brilliantly articulated than in Walter Benjamin's study of Paris in his Arcades project.[20] This has been the focus of considerable and growing interest in recent years, particularly after the appearance of a definitive English translation of the Arcades study in 1999. My aim is, of course, quite different from Benjamin's. It is to reconstruct, as best I can, how Second Empire Paris worked, how capital and modernity came together in a particular place and time, and how social relations and political imaginations were animated by this encounter. Benjamin scholars should, I hope, find something useful in this exercise. I do, of course, make use of many of Benjamin's insights, and I do have some rough ideas as to how to read (and even, as already suggested by the examination of the scale of spatial form, to critique) him. The fascination of his Arcades project for me rests upon the way in which he assembled a vast array of information from all sorts of secondary sources and began to lay out the bits and pieces (the "detritus" of history, as he called it), as if they were part of some giant kaleidoscope of how Paris worked and how it became such a central site for the birth of the modern (as both techne and sensibility). He plainly had a grand conception in mind, but the study was unfinished (perhaps unfinishable) and its overall shape (if it was ever meant to have one) therefore remains elusive. But, like Schorske, Benjamin does return again and again to certain themes, persistent threads that bring together the whole and render some vision of the totality possible. The arcades (a spatial form) operate as a recurrent motif. Benjamin also insists (as do some other Marxist writers, such as Henri Lefebvre) that we do not merely live in a material world but that our imaginations, our dreams, our conceptions, and our representations mediate that materiality in powerful ways; hence his fascination with spectacle, representations, and phantasmagoria.

The problem for the reader of Benjamin is how to understand the fragments in relation to the totality of Paris. Some, of course, would want to say it just doesn't fit together and it is best to leave it at that; to superimpose thematics (be it Benjamin's arcades or my own concern for the circulation and accumulation of capital and the pervasiveness of class relations) is to do such violence to experience that it is to be resisted at all costs. I have much more faith in the inherent relations between processes and things than to be satisfied with that. I also have a much deeper belief in our capacities to represent and communicate what those connections and relations are about. But I also recognize, as any theorist must, the necessary violence that comes with abstraction, and that it is always dangerous to interpret complex relations as simple causal chains or, worse still, as determined by some mechanistic process. Resort to a dialectical and relational mode of historical-geographical inquiry should help avoid such traps.

A work of this kind (and this was as true for Schorske and Benjamin as it has been for me) necessarily depends heavily on archival work done by others. The Parisian archive has, however, been so richly mined, and the secondary sources are so abundant (as the lengthy bibliography attests), that it takes a major effort to bring innumerable studies done from different perspectives into a dynamic synthesis. Reliance upon secondary sources (many informed by a completely different framework of concepts and theory than that which animates my own) is in some ways limiting, and always poses the question of reliability and trustworthiness, to say nothing of their compatibility. I have frequently read these sources against the grain of their own theoretical framework, but the archival work on Paris has, from no matter what perspective, been carefully done (Gaillard's outstanding study,[21] on which I rely heavily, is an example), and I have striven to retain the integrity of substantive findings.

To put things this way is also to go against the grain of much contemporary academic practice, which concentrates on the discursive constructions that permeate supposedly factual accounts in order to understand the latter as cultural constructions open to critique and deconstruction. Such interrogations have been invaluable. From this standpoint, to speak of the "integrity" of findings is highly suspect, since integrity and truth are effects of discourse. It is useful to know, for example, that the statistical inquiry into Parisian industry of 1847–1848 was riddled with conservative political-economic presuppositions that, among other things, classified workers subcontracted at home as "small businesses" and which sought to foreground the importance of the family as guardian of social order.[22] And Rancière's challenge to the "myth" of the artisan distressed at the deskilling, degradation, and loss of nobility of work as a prime actor in class struggle has to be taken very seriously.[23]

But a work of synthesis, of the sort I am here attempting, must perforce construct its own rules of engagement. It cannot stop at the point of endless deconstruction of the discursive elaborations of others, but has to press on into the materiality of social processes even while acknowledging the power and significance of discourses and perceptions in shaping social life and historical-geographical inquiry. For this the methodology of historical-geographical materialism, which I have for several years been evolving (and to which the original Paris study published in 1985 so signally contributed) provides, I believe, a powerful means to understand the dynamics of urban change in a particular place and time.[24] I emphasize, however, my deep indebtedness to the long-standing tradition of serious scholarship that has mined the Parisian archive so well and reflected on its meanings for so long from so many diverse perspectives. The extraordinary facilities in the Bibliothèque Historique de la Ville de Paris (an institution that Haussmann set up) and the collection of visual materials (including Marville's photos, commissioned on Haussmann's watch to record what was being creatively destroyed) now assembled in the Photothèque des Musées de la Ville de Paris made the preparation of this work much easier as well as pleasurable.

The study of Paris in part II is a revised and extended version of the essay in *Consciousness and the Urban Experience* (published jointly by Johns Hopkins University

Press and Basil Blackwell in 1985). The coda, "The Building of the Basilica of Sacré Coeur," is slightly revised from the same volume; it had initially appeared in the *Annals of the Association of American Geographers* in 1979. The study on Balzac is a revised and extended version of earlier efforts separately published in *Cosmopolitan Geographies*, edited by Vinay Dharwadker (published by Routledge in 2001) and in *Afterimages of the City*, edited by Joan Ramon Resina (published by Cornell University Press in 2002). Chapter 2 and this introduction are wholly new.

Part One

Representations:
Paris 1830–1848

CHAPTER ONE

THE MYTHS OF MODERNITY
BALZAC'S PARIS

"Balzac has secured the mythic constitution of the world through precise topographic contours. Paris is the breeding ground of his mythology—Paris with its two or three great bankers (Nucingen, du Tillet), Paris with its great physician Horace Bianchon, with its entrepreneur César Birotteau, with its four or five great cocottes, with its usurer Gobseck, with its sundry advocates and soldiers. But above all—and we see this again and again—it is from the same streets and corners, the same little rooms and recesses, that the figures of this world step into the light. What else can this mean but that topography is the ground plan of this mythic space of tradition, as it is of every such space and that it can become indeed its key."

—WALTER BENJAMIN

Modern myths, Balzac observes in *The Old Maid*, are less well-understood but much more powerful than myths drawn from ancient times. Their power derives from the way they inhabit the imagination as indisputable and undiscussable realities drawn from daily experience rather than as wondrous tales of origins and legendary conflicts of human passions and desires. This idea, that modernity must necessarily create its own myths, was later taken up by Baudelaire in his critical essay "The Salon of 1846." He there sought to identify the "new forms of passion" and the "specific kinds of beauty" constituted by the modern, and criticized the visual artists of the day for their failure "to open their eyes to see and know the heroism" around them. "The life of our city is rich in poetic and marvelous subjects. We are enveloped and steeped as though in an atmosphere of the marvelous; though we do not notice it." Invoking a new element, "modern beauty," Baudelaire concludes his essay thus: "The heroes of the Iliad are pygmies compared to you, Vautrin, Rastignac and Birotteau" (all characters out of Balzac's novels) "and you, Honoré de Balzac, you the most heroic, the most extraordinary, the most romantic and the most poetic of all the characters you have produced from your womb."[1]

FIGURE 13 *Daumier's view of the new Rue de Rivoli (1852) captures something of Balzac's prescient descriptions of Paris, beset by "building manias" (witness the pickax being wielded in the background) and appearing as a "rushing stream," as "a monstrous miracle, an astounding assemblage of movements, machines and ideas" in which "events and people tumble over each other" such that "even negotiating the street can be intimidating."*

Balzac painted in prose, but could hardly be accused of failing to see the richness and the poetry of daily life around him. "Could you really grudge," he asks, "spending a few minutes watching the dramas, disasters, tableaux, picturesque incidents which arrest your attention in the heart of this restless queen of cities?" "Look around you" as you "make your way through that huge stucco cage, that human beehive with black runnels marking its sections, and follow the ramifications of the idea which moves, stirs and ferments inside it."[2] Before Baudelaire issued his manifesto for the visual arts (and a century before Benjamin attempted to unravel the myths of modernity in his unfinished Paris Arcades project), Balzac had already placed the myths of modernity under the microscope and used the figure of the flaneur to do it. And Paris—a capital city being shaped by bourgeois power into a city of capital—was at the center of his world.

The rapid and seemingly chaotic growth of Paris in the early nineteenth century rendered city life difficult to decipher, decode, and represent. Several of the novelists of the period struggled to come to terms with what the city was about. Exactly how they did so has been the subject of intensive scrutiny.[3] They recorded much about their material world and the social processes that flowed around them. They explored different ways to represent that world and helped shape the popular imagination as to what the city was and might become. They considered alternatives and possibilities, sometimes didactically (as did Eugène Sue in his famous novel *Les Mystères de Paris*), but more often indirectly through their evocations of the play of human desires in relation to social forms, institutions, and conventions. They decoded the city and rendered it legible, thereby providing ways to grasp, represent, and shape seemingly inchoate and often disruptive processes of urban change.

How Balzac did this is of great interest because he made Paris central—one might almost say the central character—in much of his writing. But "The Human Comedy" is a vast, sprawling, incomplete and seemingly disparate set of works, made up of some ninety novels and novellas written in just over twenty years between 1828 and his death (attributed to drinking too much coffee) in 1850, at the age of fifty-one. Exhuming the myths of modernity and of the city from out of this incredibly rich and often confusing oeuvre is no easy task. Balzac had the idea of putting his various novels together as "The Human Comedy" in 1833, and by 1842 settled on a plan that divided the works into scenes of private, provincial, Parisian, political, military, and rural life, supplemented by a series of philosophical and analytical studies.[4] But Paris figures almost everywhere (sometimes only as a shadow cast upon the rural landscape). So there is no option except to track the city down wherever it is to be found.

Reading through much of "The Human Comedy" as an urbanist (rather than as a literary critic) is a quite extraordinary experience. It reveals all manner of things about a city and its historical geography that might otherwise remain hidden. Balzac's prescient insights and representations must surely have left a deep imprint upon the sensibility of his readers, far beyond the literati of the time. He almost certainly helped create a climate of public opinion that could better understand (and even accept, though unwittingly or regretfully so) the political economy that underlays modern urban life, thus shaping the imaginative preconditions for the systematic transformations of Paris that occurred during the Second Empire. Balzac's supreme achievement, I shall argue, was to dissect and represent the social forces omnipresent within the womb of bourgeois society. By demystifying the city and the myths of modernity with which it was suffused, he opened up new perspectives, not only on what the city was, but also on what it could become. Just as crucially, he reveals much about the psychological underpinnings of his own representations and furnishes insights into the murkier plays of desire (particularly within the bourgeoisie) that get lost in the lifeless documentations in the city's archives. The dialectic of the city and how the modern self might be constituted is thereby laid bare.

BALZAC'S UTOPIANISM

The "only solid foundation for a well-regulated society," Balzac wrote, depended upon the proper exercise of power by an aristocracy secured by private property, "whether it be real estate or capital"[5] The distinction between real estate and capital is important. It signals the existence of a sometimes fatal conflict between landed wealth and money power. Balzac's utopianism most typically appeals to the former. What the literary theorist Fredric Jameson calls "the still point" of Balzac's churning world focuses on "the mild and warming fantasy of landed property as the tangible figure of a Utopian wish fulfillment." Here resides "a peace released from the competitive dynamism of Paris and of metropolitan business struggles, yet still imaginable in some existent backwater of concrete social history."[6]

Balzac often invokes idyllic pastoral scenes from the earliest novels (such as *The Chouans*) onwards. *The Peasantry*, one of his last novels, opens with a long letter composed by a Parisian royalist journalist describing an idyllic "arcadian" scene of a country estate and its surroundings, contrasted with "the ceaseless and thrilling dramatic spectacle of Paris, and its harrowing struggles for existence." This idealization then frames the action in the novel and provides a distinctive perspective from which social structures can be observed and interpreted. In *The Wild Ass's Skin*, the utopian motif moves center stage. Raphael de Valentin, seeking the repose that will prolong his threatened life, "felt an instinctive need to draw close to nature, to simplicity of dwelling and the vegetative life to which we so readily surrender in the country." He needs the restorative and rejuvenating powers that only proximity to nature can bring. He finds "a spot where nature, as light-hearted as a child at play, seemed to have taken delight in hiding treasure," and close by came upon:

> a modest dwelling-house of granite faced with wood. The thatched roof of this cottage, in harmony with the site, was gay with mosses and flowering ivy which betrayed its great antiquity. A wisp of smoke, too thin to disturb the birds, wound up from the crumbling chimney. In front of the door was a large bench placed between two enormous bushes of honeysuckle covered with red, sweet-scented blossoms. The walls of the cottage were scarcely visible under the branches of vine and the garlands of roses and jasmine which rambled around at their own sweet will. Unconcerned with this rustic beauty, the cottagers did nothing to cultivate it and left nature to its elvish and virginal grace.

The inhabitants are no less bucolic:

> The yelping of the dogs brought out a sturdy child who stood there gaping; then there came a white-haired old man of medium height. These two matched their surroundings, the atmosphere, the flowers and the cottage. Good health brimmed over in the luxuriance of nature, giving childhood and age their own brands of beauty. In fact, in every form of life

FIGURE 14 *Daumier often made fun of the pastoral utopianism of the bourgeoisie. Here the man proudly points out how pretty his country house looks from here, adding that next year, he plans to have it painted apple green.*

there was that carefree habit of contentment that reigned in earlier ages; mocking the didactic discourse of modern philosophy, it also served to cure the heart of its turgid passions.[7]

Utopian visions of this sort operate as a template against which everything else is judged. In the closing phases of the orgy scene in *The Wild Ass's Skin*, for example, Balzac comments how the girls present, hardened to vice, nevertheless recalled, as they awoke, days gone by of purity and innocence spent happily with family in a bucolic rustic setting. This pastoral utopianism even has an urban counterpart. Living penniless in Paris, Raphael had earlier witnessed the impoverished but noble life of a mother and daughter whose "constant labor, cheerfully endured, bore witness to a pious resignation inspired by lofty sentiments. There existed an indefinable harmony between the two women and the objects around them."[8] Only in *The Country Doctor*, however, does Balzac contemplate the active construction of such a utopian alternative. It takes a supreme act of personal renunciation on the part of the doctor—a dedicated, compassionate, and reform-minded bourgeois—to bring about the necessary changes in a rural area of chronic ignorance and impoverishment. The aim is to organize harmonious capitalist production on the land by way of a collaborative communitarian effort that nevertheless emphasizes the joys of private property. Balzac hints darkly, however, at the fragility of such a project in the face of peasant venality and individualism. But again and again throughout "The Human Comedy" we find echoes of this utopian motif as a standpoint from which social relations can be understood.

Balzac looked for the most part to the aristocracy to provide leadership. Their duties and obligations were clear: "Those who wish to remain at the head of a country must always be worthy of leading it; they must constitute its mind and soul in order to control the activity of its hands." But it is a "modern aristocracy" that must now emerge, and it must understand that "art, science and wealth form the social triangle within which is inscribed the shield of power." Rulers must "have sufficient knowledge to judge wisely and must know the needs of the subjects and the state of the nation, its markets and trade, its territory and property." Subjects must be "educated, obedient," and "act responsibly" to partake "of the art of governance." "Means of action," he writes, "lie in positive strength and not in historic memories." He admires the English aristocracy (as did Saint-Simon, as we shall see) because it recognized the need for change. Rulers have to understand that "institutions have their climacteric years when terms change their meaning, when ideas put on a new garb and the conditions of political life assume a totally new form without the basic substance being affected."[9] This last phrase, "without the basic substance being affected," takes us back, however, to the still point of Balzac's pastoral utopianism.

A modern aristocracy needs money power to rule. If so, can it be anything other than capitalist (albeit of the landed sort)? What class configuration can support this utopian vision? Balzac clearly recognizes that class distinctions and class conflict cannot be abolished: "An aristocracy in some sense represents the thought of a society, just as the middle and working classes are the organic and active side of it." Harmony must be constructed out of "the apparent antagonism" between these class forces such that "a seeming antipathy produced by a diversity of movement. . . . nevertheless works for a common aim." Again, there is more than a hint of Saint-Simonian utopian doctrine in all of this (though Saint-Simon looked to the industrialists rather than to the aristocracy for leadership). The problem is not, then, the existence of social differences and class distinctions. It is entirely possible for "the different types contributing to the physiognomy" of the city to "harmonize admirably with the character of the ensemble." For "harmony is the poetry of order and all peoples feel an imperious need for order. Now is not the cooperation of all things with one another, unity in a word, the simplest expression of order?" Even the working classes, he holds, are "drawn towards an orderly and industrious way of life."[10]

This ideal of class harmony fashioned out of difference is, sadly, disrupted by multiple processes working against it. Workers are "thrust back into the mire by society." Parisians have fallen victim to the false illusions of the epoch, most notably that of equality. Rich people have become "more exclusive in their tastes and their attachment to their personal belongings than they were thirty years ago." The aristocrats need money to survive and to assure the new social order; but the pursuit of that money power corrupts their potentialities. The rich consequently succumb to "a fanatical craving for self-expression."[11] The pursuit of money, sex, and power becomes an elaborate, farcical, and destructive game. Speculation and the senseless pursuit of money and pleasure wreak havoc on the social order. A corrupt aristocracy fails in its historic mission, while the bourgeoisie, the central focus of Balzac's contempt, has no civilized alternative to offer.

These failures are all judged, however, in relation to Balzac's utopian alternative. The pastoralism provides the emotive content and a progressive aristocracy secures its class basis. While the class perspective is quite different, Marx could nevertheless profess an intense admiration for the prescient, incisive, and clairvoyant qualities of Balzac's analysis of bourgeois society in "The Human Comedy" and drew much inspiration from the study of it.[12] We also admire it too because of the clarity it offers in demystifying not only the myths of modernity and of the city but also its radical exposure of the fetish qualities of bourgeois self-understandings.

PARIS AND ITS PROVINCES:
THE COUNTRY IN THE CITY

While Balzac's utopianism has a distinctively landed, provincial, and even rustic flavor, the contrast with actual social relations on the land and in the provinces could not be more dramatic. Innumerable characters in Balzac's works undertake (as did Balzac himself) the difficult transition from provincial to metropolitan ways of life. Some, like Rastignac in *Old Goriot*, negotiate the transition successfully, while a priest in *César Birotteau* is so horrified by the bustle of the city that he stays locked in his room until he can return to Tours, vowing never to set foot in the city again. Lucien, in *Lost Illusions* and *The Harlot High and Low*, never quite makes the grade and ends up committing suicide. Still others, like Cousin Bette, bring their peasant wiles with them and use them to destroy the segment of metropolitan society to which they have intimate access. While the boundary is porous, there is a deep antagonism between provincial ways and those of the metropolis. Paris casts its shadow across the land, but with diminishing intensity the further away one moves. Brittany as depicted in *The Chouans* is like a far-off colonial outpost, and Burgundy and Angoulême are far enough away to evolve autonomous ways of life. Here the law is locally understood and locally administered, and everything depends on local rather than national power relations.

The distinctive pattern of class relations in the provinces is brilliantly laid out in *The Peasantry*. Balzac here sets "in relief the principal types of a class neglected by a throng of writers" and addresses the "phenomena of a permanent conspiracy of those whom we call 'the weak' against those who imagine themselves to be 'the strong'—of the Peasantry against the rich." That the weak have many weapons (as James Scott in more recent times has argued) is clearly revealed. Balzac portrays "this indefatigable sapper at his work, nibbling and gnawing the land into little bits, carving an acre into a hundred scraps, to be in turn divided, summoned to the banquet by the bourgeois, who finds in him a victim and an ally." Beneath the "idyllic rusticity" there lies "an ugly significance." The peasant's code is not the bourgeois code, writes Balzac: "the savage" (and there is more than one comparison to James Fenimore Cooper's portrayal of the North American Indian) "and his near relation, the peasant, never make use of articulate speech, except to lay traps for their enemies."[13]

The struggle between the peasants and the aristocracy is fiercely joined, but the real protagonists in the action are a motley crew of local lawyers, merchants, doctors, and others hell-bent on accumulating capital by usurious practices, monopoly controls, legal chicanery, and the weaving of an intricate web of interdependencies and strategic alliances (cemented by opportunistic marriages). This group is locally powerful enough to defy or subvert the central authorities in Paris, to hem in aristocratic power, and to orchestrate events for their own benefit. The peasants are inevitably drawn into an alliance with local bourgeois interests against the aristocracy, even though they stand not to benefit from the outcome. The bourgeois lawyer Rigou, variously described as "the vampire of the valley" and "a Master of Avarice," holds oppressive mortgages and uses them to extract forced labor from a peasantry he controls with "secret wires." Cortecuisse, a peasant, borrowed money from Rigou to purchase a small estate, but never manages to pay more than the interest on the loan, no matter how hard he and his wife work. Constantly threatened with foreclosure, Cortecuisse can never go against Rigou's will. And Rigou's will is to use the power of the peasantry—in particular their chronic and ghastly impoverishment, their resentments, and their traditional rights to gleaning and to the extraction of wood—as a means to undermine the commercial viability of the aristocratic estate. Says one perceptive peasant:

> Frighten the gentry at the Aigues so as to maintain your rights, well and good; but as for driving them out of the place and having the Aigues put up for auction, that is what the bourgeois want in the valley, but it is not in our interest to do it. If you help divide up the big estates, where are all the National lands to come from in the revolution that is coming? You will get the land for nothing then, just as old Rigou did; but once let the bourgeois chew up the land, they will spit it out in much smaller and dearer bits. You will work for them, like all the others working for Rigou. Look at Courtecuisse![14]

While it was easier for the peasantry to go against the aristocracy and blame them for their degraded condition than to resist the local bourgeois upon whom they depended, the resentment of local bourgeois power was never far from the surface. For how long, then, could it be controlled, and did not the bourgeoisie in both Paris and the countryside have reason to fear it? Insofar as the countryside is a site of instability and class war, its threat to the Parisian world becomes all too apparent. While Paris may reign, it is the countryside that governs.[15]

Parisians of all classes lived in a state of denial and distrust of their rural origins. The complex rituals of integration of provincial migrants into the city can be explained only in

FIGURE 15 *In Daumier's view, the realities of rural life were far from idyllic. The bourgeoisie either encountered horrible accidents (usually provoked by untoward encounters with rural life) or else suffered from boredom.*

such terms. Having viciously picked apart the small-town provincialisms of Angoulême in the opening part of *Lost Illusions*, Balzac describes excruciating scenes as Lucien and Madame de Bargeton move to Paris to consummate their passion. Taken to the opera by the well-connected Madame d'Espard, Lucien, who has already spent much of the little money he has on clothes, is scrutinized variously as "a tailor's dummy" or as a "shopkeeper in his Sunday best." When it transpires that he is actually the son of an apothecary and really has no claim to his mother's aristocratic lineage, he is shunned altogether, including by Madame de Bargeton. The latter fares little better at first. In Paris she appears to Lucien as "a tall, desiccated woman with freckled skin, faded complexion and strikingly red hair; angular, affected, pretentious, provincial of speech and above all badly dressed." The butt of barbed comments from many at the opera, she is saved because everyone could see in Madame d'Espard's companion "a poor relation from the provinces, and any Parisian family can be similarly afflicted."[16] Under Madame d'Espard's tutelage, Madame de Bargeton is quickly initiated into Parisian mores, though now as Lucien's enemy rather than his lover.

Balzac frequently recounts scenes of ritual incorporation into Parisian life out of provincial origins, no matter whether it be of a merchant (like César Birotteau), an ambitious young aristocrat (like Rastignac), or a well-connected woman (like Madame de Bargeton). Once incorporated, they never look back, even if they are ultimately destroyed (like Birroteau and Lucien) by their Parisian failures. The avid denial of provincial origins and of provincial powers thereby evolves into one of the founding myths of Parisian life: that Paris is an entity unto itself and that it does not rely in any way upon the provincial world it so despises. It is in *Cousin Bette* that we see how costly such a denial can be: a woman of peasant origins uses her wiles to destroy the aristocratic family whose status she so envies. Paris depended crucially upon its provinces but avidly sought to deny that fact.

THE RUSHING STREAM

The contrast between the leisurely pace of provincial and rural life and the daily rush in Paris is startling. Consider the wide range of metaphors that Balzac deploys to convey this sense of what Paris is about. The city, he writes, "is endlessly on the march and never taking rest," it is "a monstrous miracle, an astounding assemblage of movements, machines and ideas, the city of a thousand different romances . . . a restless queen of cities." In "the rushing stream of Paris," events and people tumble pell-mell over each other. Even negotiating the street can be intimidating. Everyone, "conforming to his own particular bent, scans the heavens, hops this way and that, either in order to avoid the mud, or because he is in a hurry, or because he sees other citizens rushing along helter-skelter." This frenetic pace, with its compressions of both time and space, in part derives from the way Paris has become a "vast metropolitan workshop for the manufacture of enjoyment." It is a city "devoid of morals, principles and genuine feeling," but one within which all feelings, principles, and morals have their beginning and their end. What Simmel later came to define as the "blasé attitude" so characteristic of the city of modernity is spectacularly evoked:

> No sentiment can stand against the swirling torrent to events; their onrush and the effort to swim against the current lessens the intensity of passion. Love is reduced to desire, hate to whimsy . . . in the salon as in the street no one is *de trop*, no one is absolutely indispensable or absolutely noxious. . . . In Paris there is toleration for everything: the government, the guillotine, the Church, cholera. You will always be welcome in Parisian society, but if you are not there no one will miss you.[17]

The chaos of commodity markets compounds the confusions:

> The rue Perrin-Gasselin is one byway in the labyrinth . . . forming, as it were, the entrails of the town. It swarms with an infinite variety of commodities—various and mixed, stinking and stylish, herrings and muslin, silks and honey, butter and tulles—and above all a host of little shops, of which Paris no more suspects the existence than most men suspect what is going on in their pancreas.[18]

To find out how this Paris works, to get beneath the surface appearance, the mad jumble, and the kaleidoscopic shifts, to penetrate the labyrinth, you have "to break open the body to find therein the soul." But it is there, at the core, that the emptiness of bourgeois life becomes all too evident. While the dominant forces at work are interpreted in various ways, behind them loom figures like Giggonet the discounter, Gobseck the banker, and Rigou the moneylender. Gold and pleasure lie at the heart of it all. "Take these two words as a guiding light," and all will be revealed because, we are told, "not a cog fails to fit into its groove and everything stimulates the upward march of money." In Paris "people of all social statures, small, medium and great, run and leap and caper under the whip of a pitiless goddess, Necessity: the necessity for money, glory or amusement."[19] The circulation of capital is in charge.

In particular, "the monster we call Speculation" takes over. *Eugénie Grandet* records a key historical moment of conversion: the miser who hoards gold becomes the rentier who speculates in interest-bearing notes, thereby equating self-interest with monetary interest. Marx may have had Grandet in mind when he wrote: "The boundless greed after riches, this passionate chase after exchange value, is common to the capitalist and the miser; but while the miser is merely a capitalist gone mad, the capitalist is a rational miser."[20] So it is with Grandet. But it is speculation of all sorts that rules. The working classes speculate as "they wear themselves out to win the gold which keeps them spellbound, " and will even take to revolution, "which it always interprets as a promise of gold and pleasure!" The "bustling, scheming, speculating" members of the lower middle classes assess demand in Paris and reckon to cater for it." They forage the world for commodities, "discount bills of exchange, circulate and cash all sorts of securities" while making "provision for the fantasies of children," spying out "the whims and vices of grown-ups." They even squeeze out "dividends from diseases" as they offer spurious remedies for real and imagined ills.[21] César Birotteau, a perfumer, pioneers the use of advertising to persuade everyone of the superiority of his product, thus driving out all rivals. At an even grander level, speculation in house property and land rents reshapes the city:

> Paris may be a monster, but it is the most monomaniacal of monsters. It falls for a thousand fantasies. At one moment it takes to brick-laying like a lord enamoured of the trowel. . . . Then it falls into the slough of despond, goes bankrupt, sells up and files its petition. But a few days later, it puts its affairs in order, sallies forth in holiday and dancing mood. . . . It has its day to day manias, but also its manias for the month, the season, the year. Accordingly, at that moment, the whole population was demolishing or rebuilding something or other, somehow or other.[22]

Returns from real estate speculation may, however, be slow and erratic (it took eight years for the crafty bourgeois Crevel in *Cousin Bette* to realize the benefits of rising rents from neighborhood improvements, and those, like César Birotteau, who have not enough credit to wait, can lose all to unscrupulous financiers). We even witness something we now call "gentrification": "In building fine and elegant houses with a porter's lodge, laying footpaths and putting in shops, speculative builders, by the high rents that they charge, tend to drive away undesirable characters, families without possessions, and every kind of bad tenant. And it is in this way that districts rid themselves of their disreputable population."[23] Grand financiers stand ready not only to ruin honest bourgeois investors like Birotteau but also, as with Baron Nucingen, to swindle poor people out of their money. "Do you know what he calls doing a good stroke of business?" asks Madame Nucingen of a shocked Goriot:

> He buys undeveloped land in his own name then has houses built on it acting through men of straw. These men draw up the contracts for the buildings with all the contractors and pay them with long-dated bills. They hand over possession of the houses to my husband for a small sum, and slide out of their debt to the duped contractors by going bankrupt.[24]

The guiding strings of power in this new society lie within the credit system. A few clever financiers (Nucingen and Gobseck in Paris, Rigou in Bourgogne) occupy nodal points in networks of power that dominate everything else. Balzac exposes the fictions of bourgeois power and values. This is a world where fictitious capital—dominated by bits of paper credit augmented by creative accounting—holds sway, where everything (as Keynes much later was to argue in his *General Theory of Employment, Interest, and Money*, and as our own recent spate of financial scandals illustrates) dances to the tune of expectations and anticipations with only accidental relationship to honest toil. This fictive world

FIGURE 16 *Daumier represented Balzac's figure of the "bustling, scheming, speculating" members of the lower classes in an extensive series depicting Robert Macaire, a charlatan, opportunist, and braggart always out for quick success. He here offers to sell shares "to those prepared to lose money" and advises a salesman that he will realize a lot more profit if he grinds up his product into powder, or turns it into a lotion and sells it as a remedy for some ailment. When told the sack contains corn, he merely replies, "So much the better!"*

carries over into personal behaviors; to adopt all the trappings of wealth, particularly to assume the clothing of its outward signs (dress, carriage, servants, well-furnished apartments), and to go into debt to do it, is a necessary prelude to achievement of wealth. Fiction and fantasy, particularly the fictions of credit and interest, become reality. This is one of the key founding myths of modernity. And this is what all the sophisticated social facades and all the chaotic turbulence of "the rushing stream" conceal. Balzac peels away the fetishism (the idea that financial chicanery is accidental rather than structural) and exposes the fictions to reveal the utter emptiness of bourgeois values within. Dancing in this way to the tune of "her highness political economy" may even have revolutionary implications:

> The needs of all classes, consumed by vanity, are overexcited. Politics no less fearfully than morality must ask itself where the income is to come from to meet these needs. When one sees the floating debt of the Treasury and when one becomes acquainted with the floating debt of each household which models itself on the state, one is shocked to see that a half of France is in hock to the other half. When accounts are settled, the debtors will be far ahead

of the creditors. . . . This will probably signal the end of the so-called era of industry. . . . The rich bourgeoisie has many more heads to cut off than the nobility; and even if they have the guns they will find their adversaries among those that make them.[25]

In 1848 the truth of this became all too evident.

THE INFERNO AND ITS MORAL ORDER

Though the surface appearance is of atomistic and chaotic competition between individuals in a relentless struggle for gold, power, and pleasure, Balzac penetrates behind this chaotic world of appearance to construct an understanding of Paris as a product of constellations and clashes of class forces. In *The Girl with the Golden Eyes* he deploys an amazing mixture of metaphors to describe this class structure. Dante's vision (which seems to have inspired Balzac's overall choice of title, "The Human Comedy") of spheres in the descent into hell is first invoked: "For it is not only in jest that Paris has been called an inferno. The epithet is well deserved. There all is smoke, fire, glare, ebullience; everything flares up, falters, dies down, burns up again, sparkles, crackles and is consumed. . . . It is for ever vomiting fire and flame from its unquenchable crater."[26] Balzac rapidly shifts metaphors, and we find ourselves first ascending through the floors of a typical Parisian apartment building, noting the class stratification as we go up, then viewing Paris as a ship of state manned by a motley crew, and then, finally, probing into the lobes and tissues of the body of Paris considered as either a harlot or a queen.

But the class structure throughout is clear. At the bottom of the pile is the proletariat, "the class which has no possessions." The worker is the man who "overtaxes his strength, harnesses his wife to some machine or other, and exploits his child by gearing him to a cog wheel." The manufacturer is the intermediary who pulls on guiding strings (a language that Marx echoes when he comments on the invisible threads through which capital commands domestic industries in a unified system of production) to put "these puppets" in motion in return for promising this "sweating, willing, patient, industrious populace" a lavish enough wage "to cater to a city's whims on behalf of that monster we call Speculation." Thereupon the workers "set themselves to working through the night watches, suffering, toiling, cursing, fasting and forging along: all of them wearing themselves out in order to win the gold which keeps them spellbound." This proletariat, amounting to three hundred thousand people by Balzac's estimate, typically flings away its hard-earned wealth in the taverns that surround the city, exhausts itself with debauchery, explodes occasionally into revolutionary fervor, and then falls back into sweated labor. Pinned like Vulcan to the wheel (an image that Marx also invokes in *Capital*) there are nevertheless some workers of exemplary virtue who typify "its capacities raised to their highest expression and sum up its social potentialities in a kind of life in which mental and bodily activity are combined." Still others carefully harbor their incomes to set up as small retailers—encapsulated in Balzac's figure of "the haberdasher" who achieves a rather different lifestyle of respectable family life, sessions reading the newspaper, visits to the Opera and to the new dry goods stores (where flirtatious shop attendants await him). He is typically ambitious for his family and values education as a means to upward mobility.[27]

The second sphere is constituted by "wholesale merchants and their staffs, government employees, small bankers of great integrity, swindlers and cats paws, head clerks and junior clerks, bailiffs', solicitors' and notaries' clerks, in short the bustling, scheming, speculating members of that lower middle class that assesses demand in Paris and reckon to cater to it." Burned up with desire for gold and pleasure, and driven by the flail of self-interest, they, too, "let their frantic pace of life ruin their health." Thus they end their days dragging themselves dazedly along the boulevard with "worn, dull and withered" faces, "dim eyes and tottering legs."

The third circle is "as it were, the stomach of Paris in which the interests of the city are digested and compressed into a form which goes by the name of affaires." Here, "by some acrid and rancorous intestinal process" we find an upper middle class of "lawyers, doctors, barristers, business men, bankers, traders on the grand scale." Desperate to attract and accumulate money, those who have hearts leave them behind as they descend the stair in early morning, "into the abyss of sorrows that put families to the torture." Within this sphere we find the cast of characters (immortalized in Daumier's satirical series on Robert Macaire) who dominate within the whole corpus of Balzac's work and about whom he has so much critical to say. This is the class that now dominates even though it does so in self-destructive ways that encompass its own ruinous practices, activities, and attitudes.[28]

Above this lives the artist world, struggling (like Balzac himself) to achieve originality but "ravaged, not ignobly, but ravaged, fatigued, tortured" and (again like Balzac himself) "incessantly harassed by creditors," so that they succumb to both vice and pleasure as compensation for their long nights of overwork as they "seek in vain to conciliate mundane dalliance with the conquest of glory and money with art." "Competition, rivalry and calumny are deadly enemies to talent," Balzac observes (and we have to look no further than the corruption of journalistic talent as depicted in *Lost Illusions* for examples of what this might mean).[29] This now hegemonic middle class lives and works under the most appalling conditions, however:

> Before we leave the four social tiers on which patrician wealth in Paris is built, should we not, having dealt with moral causes, make also some sounding about physical causes? . . . Should we not point out a deleterious influence whose corruptive action is equal only to that exerted by the municipal authorities who so complacently allow it to subsist? If the air of the houses in which the majority of the middle-class citizens live is foul, if the atmosphere of the street spews out noxious vapors into practically airless back premises, realize that, apart from this pestilence, the forty thousand houses of this great city have their foundations plunged in filth. . . . Half of Paris sleeps nightly in the putrid exhalations from streets, backyards and privies.[30]

FIGURE 17 *Daumier captures Balzac's distinctive physiognomies of the different classes in this depiction of the affluent classes on the Boulevard des Italiens (top) and the "anxious" middle classes on the Boulevard du Temple (bottom).*

These were the living conditions that Haussmann was summoned to address more than twenty years later. But the working conditions of the middle-class were no better (as the depictions of the squalid offices of the publishers around the Palais Royale in *Lost Illusions* graphically illustrate). They "live in insalubrious offices, pestilential courtrooms, small chambers with barred windows, spend their day weighed down by the weight of their affairs."

All of this makes for a tremendous contrast with "the great, airy, gilded salons, the mansions enclosed in gardens, the world of the rich, leisured, happy, moneyed people" (typified by the exclusionary society centered on the Faubourg St. Germain). Yet, in Balzac's dyspeptic account, the residents of this upper sphere are anything but happy. Corrupted by their search for pleasure (reduced to opium and fornication), bored, warped, withered and consumed by a veritable "bonfire of the vanities" (as Tom Wolfe later dubbed it when writing of New York), curiously preyed upon by the lower classes who "study their tastes in order to convert them into vices as a source of profit," they live "a hollow existence" in anticipation of a "pleasure that never comes." This was the class in whom Balzac invested all his utopian hopes, but perhaps exactly for that reason it assumes the ugliest of actual personas: "pasteboard faces, those premature wrinkles, that rich man's physiognomy on which impotence has set its grimace, in which only gold is mirrored and from which intelligence has fled."[31]

Balzac summarizes thus: "Hence it is that the phenomenal activity of the proletariat, the deterioration resulting from the multiple interests that bring down the two middle classes described above, the spiritual torments to which the class of artists is subjected and the surfeit of pleasure usually sought by the grandees, explain the normal ugliness of the Paris population."[32] Thus are the "kaleidoscopic" experience and "cadaverous physiognomy" of the city understood.

The seeming rigidity of these class distinctions (as well as crucial distinctions of provincial origin and social history) is offset by the rapid shifts that occur as individuals participate in the high-stakes pursuit of money, sex, and power. Lucien, for example, returns to his provincial origins penniless, powerless, and disgraced at the end of *Lost Illusions*, only to reappear in Paris reempowered by his association with the archcriminal Vautrin, who orchestrates his liaison with the wealthy mistress of Nucingen, the banker, in *A Harlot High and Low*. Rastignac lives among the impoverished but genteel boarders and students in *Old Goriot* but circulates among the nobility (borrowing from his family to get the costume to do it). "Each social sphere projects its spawn into the sphere immediately above it," so that "the rich grocer's son becomes a notary, the timber merchant's son becomes a magistrate."[33] And, as we have seen, by adopting all the trappings of outward appearances of wealth, it is sometimes possible to actually realize that wealth through speculative action and the fraudulent management of social relations. Yet there are innumerable traps and limits to this process, as identifications and identities become glued together in the complex spaces of the Parisian social order.

ON SPATIAL PATTERN AND MORAL ORDER

In every zone of Paris "there is a mode of being which reveals what you are, what you do, where you come from, and what you are after." The physical distances that separate classes are understood as "a material consecration of the moral distance which ought to separate them." The separation of social classes exists as both spatial ecologies and vertical segregations. Paris has "its head in the garrets, inhabited by men of science and genius; the first floors house the well-filled stomachs; on the ground floor are the shops, the legs and feet, since the busy trot of trade goes in and out of them." Balzac toys with our curiosity about the hidden spaces in the city, turns them into mysteries that pique our interest. "One is loath to tell a story to a public for whom local colour is a closed book," he coyly states.[34] But he immediately opens the book to reveal a whole world of spatiality and its representations. The spatial pattern anchors a moral order.

The sociologist Robert Park once wrote a suggestive essay on the city as a spatial pattern and a moral order; social relations were inscribed in the spaces of the city in such a way as to make the spatial pattern both a reflection of and an active moment in the reproduction of the moral order. This idea plays directly throughout Balzac's fiction: "In every phase of history the Paris of the upper classes and the nobility has its own center, just as the plebeian Paris will always have its own special quarter."[35] Fine-grained variations are built into the sociospatial form of the city:

> In Paris the different types contributing to the physiognomy of any portion of that monstrous city harmonize admirably with the character of the ensemble. Thus the concierge, door-keeper or hall porter, whatever the name given to this essential nerve system within the Parisian monster, always conforms to the quarter in which he functions, and often sums it up. The concierge of the Faubourg St. Germain, wearing braid on every seam, a man of leisure, speculates in government stocks; the porter of the Chaussée d'Antin enjoys his creature comforts; he of the Stock Exchange quarter reads his newspapers; porters in the Faubourg Montmartre work at a trade; in the quarter given over to prostitution the portress herself is a retired prostitute; in the Marais quarter she is respectable, cross-grained, and crotchety.[36]

This spatial pattern enforces a moral order (even beyond that ensured by the concierges and porters). In "Ferragus," the first of three stories that constitute the *History of the Thirteen*, almost everyone who transgresses the spatial pattern, who moves into the wrong space at the wrong time, dies. Characters out of place disturb the ecological harmonies, pollute the moral order, and must pay the price. This makes the city a dangerous place, for it is far too easy to get lost in it, be swept away in its rushing stream, and end up in the wrong place. "I am convinced," says Madame Jules in "Ferragus," that "if I take one step into this labyrinth I shall fall into an abyss in which I shall perish."[37] A pure and perfect creature, Madame Jules ventures, out of filial devotion for Ferragus, her father, into a part of Paris inconsistent with her social status. "This woman is lost," declares Balzac, because she has strayed into the wrong space. Contaminated, she finally dies of "some moral complication which has gone very far and which makes the physical condition more complex." Auguste, Madame Jules's admirer, is likewise ordained to die because "for his future misfortune, he scrutinized every storey of the building" that is Madame Jules's secret destination. Ida Gudget, who looks after Ferragus and who dares to visit Jules in his bourgeois residence also dies.

Ferragus, Madame Jules's father, is, however, a member of a secret society of men—known as the Thirteen—sworn to support each other in any and all of their endeavors. They are, says Balzac, equipped with wings. They "soar[ed] over society in its heights and depths, and disdained to occupy any place in it because they had unlimited power over it." They are outside of and above the moral order because they cannot be located or placed. Sought by both Auguste and Jules (as well as by the police), Ferragus is never found. He appears only when and where he wants. He commands space while everyone else is trapped in it. This is a key source of his secret power.[38]

There is, however, an evolution in this perspective in Balzac's work. The spatial rigidities that play a deterministic role in *The History of the Thirteen* become malleable in later works. As Sharon Marcus observes, *Cousin Pons* in the novel of that name (and one of the last that Balzac completed) is brought down by the concierge because she not only commands the place where Pons resides (she supplies him with his meals) but she also can construct a web of intrigue (using the "nerve system" of the concierge system) and forge a coalition of conspirators networked across the city to gain access to his apartment with its art collection.[39] The capacity to command and produce space in this way is a power through which even the lowliest of people in society can subvert the spatial pattern and the moral order. Vautrin, the archcriminal-turned-police chief, thus uses his knowledge of the spatial ecology of the city and his capacity to command and control it to his own ends. The spatiality of the city is increasingly appreciated as dialectical, constructed, and consequential rather than passive or merely reflective.

STREETS, BOULEVARDS, AND PUBLIC SPACES OF SPECTACLE

In Paris there are certain streets which are in as much disrepute as any man branded with infamy can be. There are also noble streets; then there are streets which are just simply decent, and, so to speak, adolescent streets about whose morality the public has not yet formed an opinion. There are murderous streets; streets which are more aged than aged dowagers; respectable streets; streets which are always clean, streets which are always dirty; working class, industrious mercantile streets. In short, the streets of Paris have human qualities and such a physiognomy as leaves us with the impressions against which we can put up no resistance.[40]

These are hardly objective descriptions of individual streets. The hopes, desires, and fears of Balzac's characters give meaning and character to the streets and to the neighborhoods they traverse. They may tarry at their leisure or feel the stress of incompatibility, but in no case can they ignore their situatedness. Balzac provides us with what the situationists later called a "psychogeography" of the streets and neighborhoods of the city. But he does so more from the perspective of his multiple characters than of himself.[41] His characters even change their personas as they move from one locale to another. To enter into the Faubourg St. Germain (with all its aristocratic privilege) or merge with the chaos of the Palais Royale (with its motif of prostitution not only of women but also of literary talent to the seedy commercialism of journalism) places irresistible demands upon the participants. The only form of resistance is to move. Lucien, in *Lost Illusions*, fails to impress in the fashionable world of the Rue St Honoré (particularly after his disastrous showing at the Opera House), fails to master the sleazy world of publishing in the Palais Royale, and flees to the ascetic world of the Left Bank, close to the Sorbonne, where he adopts the persona of a penniless but ruthlessly honest student. There a tight circle of friends supports him in his worst moments. But when he moves in across town with the actress Coralie, who is infatuated with his good looks, Lucien accepts her judgment of his old habitat not only as a ghastly place of impoverishment but also as a denizen of simpletons. From his new perspective he even switches political positions and attacks the writings of his old friends.

FIGURE 18 *Balzac was fascinated by the personalities and moods of Paris streets. This Marville photo from the 1850s captures some of the moodiness. It depicts the Street of Virtues which at the time was a center of prostitution. It ran into the Rue des Gravilliers, where the International Working Men's Association was to set up its Paris headquarters in the 1860s.*

We learn to understand the city from multiple perspectives. It is on the one hand an incomprehensible labyrinth of kaleidoscopic qualities: twirl the kaleidoscope around, and we see innumerable compositions and colorations of the urban scene. Yet there are persistent nodal points around which the image of the city coalesces into something more permanent and solid. The Faubourg St. Germain, the commercial world of the Right Bank boulevards, the stock exchange ("all rattle, bustle and harlotry") and the Palais Royale, the rue St. Honoré, the student quarter around the Sorbonne, and the perpetual shadowy presence of working-class Paris (rarely invoked explicitly except in *Cousin Bette*, where both the infamous Petite Pologne and the Faubourg Sainte-Antoine are described in general terms, though one looks in vain throughout Balzac's work for the depiction of any character who suffers all the indignities and insecurities of industrial employment). The legibility of the city is, furthermore, lit up by spectacles; the Opera, the theaters, the boulevards, the cafés, the monuments, and the parks and gardens again and again appearing as luminous points and lines within the fabric of the city, casting a net of meanings over urban life that would otherwise appear totally opaque. The boulevards in particular are the poetry through which the city primarily gets represented.

Armed with such pointers at street level, we can picture the totality from on high and learn to situate events and people within the labyrinthine and kaleidoscopic world of Parisian daily life. Consider, for example, how Balzac does this in the extraordinary opening passages of *Old Goriot*. "Only between the heights of Montmartre and Montrouge are there people who can appreciate" the scenes to follow. We look down first of all into "a valley of crumbling stucco and gutters black with mud, a valley full of real suffering and often deceptive joys." Madame Vauquer's lodging house stands on a street between the Val-de-Grace and the Pantheon, where

> The absence of wheeled traffic deepens the stillness which prevails in these streets cramped between the domes of the Val-de-Grace and the Pantheon, two buildings that overshadow them and darken the air with the leaden hut of their dull cupolas. . . . The most carefree passer-by feels depressed, where even the sound of wheels is unusual, the houses gloomy, the walls like a prison. A Parisian straying here would see nothing around him but lodging houses or institutions, misery or lassitude, the old sinking into the grave or the cheerful young doomed to the treadmill. It is the grimmest quarter of Paris and, it may be said, the least known.

Likening this whole exercise to a descent into the catacombs, Balzac penetrates first into the neighborhood and then into house and garden, into rooms and people, with laserlike precision. A wicket gate by day and a solid door by night separate an enclosed garden from the street. The walls covered with ivy are also lined with espalier fruit trees and vines "whose pitted and dusted fruit is watched over anxiously by Madame Vauquer every year." Along each wall "runs a narrow path leading to a clump of lime trees" under which there is "a round, green-painted table with some seats where lodgers who can afford coffee come to enjoy it in the dog days, even though it is hot enough to hatch eggs out there." The three-story house "is built of hewn stone and washed with that yellow shade which gives a mean look to almost every house in Paris." Within the house we encounter a depressing sitting room with its "boarding house smell" and an even more dismal dining room (the furniture is minutely and horribly described) where "everything is dirty and stained; there are no rags and tatters but everything is falling to pieces in decay." And at the end of this depiction, we encounter the figure of Madame Vauquer herself, who makes her appearance, adorned with her tulle cap, and shuffles about in creased slippers. Her ageing puffy face dominated by a nose like a parrot's beak, her dimpled little hands, her body as plump as a church rat's, her bunchy shapeless dress are in their proper setting in this room where misery oozes from the walls and hope, trodden down and stifled, has yielded to despair. Madame Vauquer is at home in its stuffy air, she can breathe without being sickened by it. Her face, fresh with the chill freshness of the first frosty autumn day, her wrinkled eyes, her expression, varying from the conventional set smile of the ballet-dancer to the sour frown of the discounter of bills, her whole person, in short, provides a clue to the boarding-house, just as the boarding-house implies the existence of such a person as she is.[42]

The consistency between environment and personality is striking. Viewed from on high, we can see Madame Vauquer and all the other inhabitants of the house not only in relation to Paris as a whole but also in terms of their distinctive ecological niches within the urban fabric. The ecology of the city and the personalities of its inhabitants are mirror images of each other.

INTERIORITY AND THE FEAR OF INTIMACY

Interiors play a distinctive role in Balzac's work. The porosity of boundaries and the traffic that necessarily flows across them to sustain life in the city, in no way diminish the fierce struggle to limit access and to protect interiors from the penetration (the sexual connotations of that word are apt) by unwanted others into interior spaces. The vulnerability of apartment dwelling in this regard, as Marcus shows, provides a material terrain upon which such relations can most easily be depicted.[43] Much of the action in Balzac's novels is powered by attempts to protect oneself physically and emotionally against the threat of intimacy in a world where others are perpetually striving to penetrate, colonize, and overwhelm one's interior life. Successful penetration invariably results in death of the victim, a final resting place in the cemetery, where all threat of intimacy is eliminated. Those (mainly women) who willingly give in to real love and intimacy suffer mortal consequences (sometimes sacrificially and even beatifically, like the reformed harlot, Lucien's lover, in *A Harlot High and Low*). The desire for intimacy and the search for the sublime perpetually confront the mortal fear of its deadly consequences.

Balzac's central criticism of the bourgeoisie, however, is that it is incapable of intimacy or inner feelings because it has reduced everything to the cold calculus and egoism of money valuations, fictitious capital, and the search for profit. Crevel, the crassest of Balzac's bourgeois figures, seeks to procure the affections of his son's mother-in-law at the beginning of *Cousin Bette*. But when Adeline finally gives in because she has been reduced to chronic indebtedness by her husband's licentious profligacy, Crevel callously refuses, after elaborately and to Adeline's face adding up the loss of rents on his capital that such a gesture would demand. The theme of intimacy and its dangers is pervasive. In *The Girl with the Golden Eyes*, Henri de Marsay is struck by the beauty of a woman he sees in the Tuileries. He pursues her ardently through protective walls and overcomes all manner of social and human barriers to gain access to her. Led blindfolded through mysterious corridors, he gains Paquita's love in her hidden boudoir, which (like Madame Vauquer's lodging house) tells us everything we need to know about her:

> This boudoir was hung with red fabric overlaid with Indian muslin, its in-and-out folds fluted like a Corinthian column, and bound at top and bottom with bands of poppy-red material on which arabesque designs in black were worked. Under this muslin the poppy-red showed up as pink, the colour of love, repeated from the window curtains, also of Indian muslin, lined with pink taffeta and bordered with poppy-red fringes alternating with black. Six silver-gilt sconces, each of them bearing two candles, stood out from the tapestried wall at equal distances to light up the divan. The ceiling, from the centre of which hung a chandelier of dull silver-gilt, was dazzling white, and the cornice was gilded. The carpet was reminiscent of an Oriental shawl, reproducing as it did the designs and recalling the poetry of Persia, where the hands of slaves had worked to make it. The furniture was covered in white cashmere, set off by black and poppy-red trimmings. The clock and candelabra were of white marble and gold. There were elegant flower-stands full of all sorts of roses and white or red flowers."[44]

In this intimate space De Marsay experiences "indescribable transports of delight," and even becomes "tender, kind, communicative" as "he lost himself in those limbos of delight which common people so stupidly call 'imaginary space'." But Paquita knows she is doomed. "There was the terror of death in the frenzy with which she strained him to her bosom." She tells him, "I am sure now that you will be the cause of my death." When Henri, angered at the discovery of her involvement with another, returns with the idea of extracting her from that interior space in order to exact revenge, he finds her stabbed to death in a violent struggle with her woman lover, who turns out to be Henri's long-lost half sister. Paquita's "whole body, slashed by the dagger thrusts of her executioner, showed how fiercely she had fought to save the life which Henri had made so dear to her." The physical space of the boudoir is destroyed and "Paquita's blood-stained hands were imprinted on the cushions."

In *The Duchesse de Langeais* the plot moves in the opposite direction but with similar results. Women protect themselves from intimacy by resorting to evasions, flirtations, calculated relationships, strategic marriages, and the like. General Montriveau is outraged at the way the Duchesse (who is married) trifles with his passions. He abducts her from a public space (a ball in progress) and conveys her to his inner sanctum, which has all the Gothic aura of a monk's cell. There, in his own intimate space, he threatens to brand the Duchesse, to place the sign of the convict on her forehead (a fire flickers in the background and bellows sound ominously from an adjacent cell). The abducted Duchesse succumbs and declares her love as a soul in bondage—"a woman who loves always brands herself," she says. Returned to the ball, the emotionally branded Duchesse ends up fleeing, after some unfortunate missed connections, to a remote chapel on a Mediterranean island, giving herself to God as Sister Thérèse. Montriveau finally tracks down his lost love many years later. His plan to abduct the nun succeeds exquisitely, but it is only her dead body that is retrieved, leaving him to contemplate a corpse "resplendent with the sublime beauty which the calm of death sometimes bestows on mortal remains."[45]

Balzac extends this theme beyond relations between men and women. In *The Unknown Masterpiece* (which both Marx and Picasso intensely admired, though for quite different reasons) a talented apprentice is introduced to a celebrated painter but refused access to the inner studio where the masterwork is in progress. The painter wishes to compare the masterwork, a portrait, with a beautiful woman in order to satisfy himself that his painting is more lifelike than life itself. The apprentice sacrifices (and destroys the love of) his young lover by insisting (against her will) that she pose nude for the artist for purposes of comparison. In return, he is allowed inside the studio, full of wonderful paintings to see the masterpiece. But he finds the canvas almost blank. When he has the temerity to point this out, the old artist flies into a rage. That night the old artist kills himself, having first burned all his paintings.[46]

In *Cousin Bette*, a scheming relative of provincial and peasant origins inserts herself as intimate and angelic companion to the women of an aristocratic household only to destroy them. In *Cousin Pons*, the theme is repeated in reverse. Pons is a man whose sole identity in life is that of a collector of bric-a-brac. His collection is all that matters to him, but he has no idea how financially valuable it is. He protects it in the interior of his apartment. Penetration into this inner sanctum by a coalition of forces (led by the woman concierge who purports to look after him) brings about his death. Gaining illegal entry into Pons's apartment, Balzac writes, "was tantamount to introducing the enemy into the heart of the citadel and plunging a dagger into Pons's heart."[47] Pons does indeed die from consequences that flow from this incursion. But what, exactly, does he die of? In this case it is the penetration of commodity values into his private space; a space where the purity of values that animate Pons as a collector hitherto held sway. Benjamin surely had, or should have had, Pons in mind when he wrote:

> The interior is the asylum where art takes refuge. The collector proves to be the true resident of the interior. He makes his concern the idealization of objects. To him falls the Sisyphean task of divesting things of their commodity character by taking possession of them. But he can bestow on them only connoisseur value, rather than use value. The collector delights in evoking a world that is not just distant and long gone but also better—a world in which, to be sure, human beings are no better provided with what they need than in the real world, but in which things are freed from the drudgery of being useful.[48]

So why value or desire intimacy in the face of such dangers? Why castigate women for their preference for the superficial and the social when to risk intimacy is to be branded with love or to embrace death? Why mock the bourgeoisie so mercilessly for its avoidance of intimacy at any cost? Intimacy is a human quality we can never do without, but is perpetually threatened by the relentless pursuit of exchange values. Balzac's utopianism postulates a secure and pastoral place with a settled life of intimacy and valued possessions, secluded from the rough and tumble of the world and protected from commodification. But Balzac's dream seems always destined, like Montriveau's and the Duchesse's love, to remain at best frustrated or, as in the case of Paquita and De Marsay, highly destructive.

This proposition is voiced directly in *Cousin Pons*. Madame Cibot, the concierge who leads the way into Pons's apartment with such fatal consequences, dreams of using her ill-gotten wealth to retire to the country. But this she dare not do because the fortune-teller she consults warns her that she will suffer a violent death there. She lives out her days in Paris, deprived of the pastoral existence that she most desires. The bourgeoisie likewise stand condemned not because they avoid intimacy but because, given their pre-occupation with money values, they are incapable of it. But there is also something else at work here:

> Paquita responded to the craving which all truly great men feel for the infinite, that mysteri-ous passion so dramatically expressed in Faust, so poetically translated in Manfred, which urged Don Juan to probe deep into the heart of women, hoping to find in them that infinite ideal for which so many pursuers of phantoms have searched; scientists believe they can find it in science, mystics find it in God alone.[49]

Where does Balzac find it? By fleeing the intimacy of interior spaces into some wider exterior world or by experiencing through intimacy some kind of sublime moment of ecstasy that common people stupidly call "imaginary space"? Balzac oscillates between the two possibilities.

THE ANNIHILATION OF SPACE AND TIME

"In the whole work of Balzac," remarks Poulet "nothing recurs so frequently as the proc-lamation of the annihilation of space-time by the act of mind."[50] Balzac writes: "I already had in my power the most immense faith, that faith of which Christ spoke, that boundless will with which one moves mountains, that great might by the help of which we can abol-ish the laws of space and time." Balzac believed he could internalize everything within himself and express it through a supreme act of mind. He lived "only by the strength of those interior senses that constitute a double being within man." Even though "exhausted by this profound intuition of things," the soul could nevertheless aspire to be "in Leibniz's magnificent phrase, a concentric mirror of the universe."[51] And this is precisely how Balzac constitutes his interiors. Pons's interior is precious in the double sense that it is not only his but also a concentric mirror of a European universe of artistic production. Paquita's boudoir exerts its fascination because it is redolent of the exoticism associated with the Orient, the Indies, the slave girl, and the colonized woman. Montriveau's room to which the Duchesse de Langeais is forcibly abducted internalizes the ascetic sense of

Gothic purity associated with a medieval monk's cell. The interior spaces all mirror some aspect of the external world.

The annihilation of space and time was a familiar enough theme in Balzac's day. The phrase may have derived from a couplet of Alexander Pope's: "Ye Gods! annihilate but space and time / And make two lovers happy."[52] Goethe deployed the metaphor to great effect in *Faust*, and by the 1830s and 1840s the idea was more broadly associated with the coming of the railroads. The phrase then had widespread currency in both the United States and Europe among a wide range of thinkers contemplating the consequences and possibilities of a world reconstructed by new transport and communication technologies (everything from the canals and railroads to the daily newspaper, which Hegel had already characterized as a substitute for morning prayer). Interestingly, the same concept can be found in Marx (latently in the *Communist Manifesto* and explicitly in the *Grundrisse*). Marx uses it to signify the revolutionary qualities of capitalism's penchant for geographical expansion and acceleration in the circulation of capital. It refers directly to capitalism's penchant for periodic bouts of "time-space compression."[53]

In Balzac, however, the idea usually depicts a sublime moment outside of time and space in which all the forces of the world become internalized within the mind and being of a monadic individual. It "flashes up" as a moment of intense revelation, the religious overtones of which are hard to miss (and Balzac's dalliance with religion, mysticism, and the powers of the occult is frequently in evidence). It is the moment of the sublime (a favored word of Balzac's). But it is not a passive moment. The blinding insight that comes with the annihilation of space and time allows for a certain kind of action in the world. In *The Quest of the Absolute*, Marguerite, after a furious argument with her father, reacts as follows:

> When he had gone, Marguerite stood for a while in dull bewilderment; it seemed as if her whole world had slipped from her. She was no longer in the familiar parlour; she was no longer conscious of her physical existence; her soul had taken wings and soared to a world where thought annihilates time and space, where the veil drawn across the future is lifted by some divine power. It seemed to her she lived through whole days between each sound of her father's footsteps on the staircase; and when she heard him moving above in his room, a cold shudder went through her. A sudden warning vision flashed like lightening through her brain; she fled noiselessly up the dark staircase with the speed of an arrow, and saw her father pointing a pistol at his head.[54]

A sublime moment of revelation outside of space and time allows one both to grasp the world as a totality and to act decisively in it. Its connection to sexual passion and possession of "the other" (a lover, the city, nature, God) is unmistakable (as indicated in the original Pope couplet). But it allows Balzac a certain conceptual power, without which his synoptic vision of the city and of the world would be impossible. The dealer who yields the wild ass's skin to Raphael asks "how could one prefer all the disasters of frustrated

FIGURE 19 *Balzac's emphasis upon the annihilation of space and time was very much associated, in the 1830s and 1840s, with the coming of the railways. The punch line of this Daumier cartoon from 1843–1844 on "impressions and compressions," is that it is obvious that when the train moves forward, the passengers must go backward.*

desires to the superb faculty of summoning the whole universe to the bar of one's mind, to the thrill of being able to move without being throttled by the thongs of time or the fetters of space, to the pleasure of embracing and seeing everything, of leaning over the edge of the world in order to interrogate the other spheres and listen to the voice of God?"[55] Raphael, it transpires, was raised in a household where "the rules of time and space were so rigorously applied" as to be totally oppressive. He is therefore deeply attracted to that "privilege accorded the passions which gives them the power to annihilate space and time." The trouble is that every expression of desire shrinks the skin and brings Raphael closer to death. His only possible response is to adopt a time-space discipline that is far more rigorous than anything his father imposed. Since movement is a function of desire, Raphael has to seal himself up in space and impose a strict temporal order upon himself and those around him in order to avoid any expression of desire.[56]

The perpetual bourgeois desire to reduce and eliminate all spatial and temporal barriers would then appear as a secular version of this revolutionary desire. Balzac elaborates upon these mundane aspects of bourgeois business practices. "The crowd of lawyers, doctors, barristers, business men, bankers, traders on the grand scale," he says, must "devour time, squeeze time" because "time is their tyrant; they need more, it slips away from them, they can neither stretch nor shrink it." The drive to annihilate space and time is everywhere apparent:

> Man possesses the exorbitant faculty of annihilating, in relation to himself, space which exists only in relation to himself; of utterly isolating himself from the milieu in which he resides, and of crossing, by virtue of an almost infinite locomotive power, the enormous distances of physical nature. I am here and I have the power to be elsewhere! I am dependent upon neither time, nor space, nor distance. The world is my servant.[57]

The ideal of annihilation of space and time suggests how a distinctively capitalistic and bourgeois version of the sublime is being constituted. The conquest of space and time and the mastery of the world (of Mother Earth) appear, then, as the displaced but sublime expression of sexual desire in innumerable capitalistic fantasies. Something vital is here revealed about the bourgeois myth of modernity. For Balzac, however, the collapse of time future and time past into time present is precisely the moment at which hope, memory, and desire converge. "One triples present felicity with aspiration for the future and recollections of the past," he wrote. This is the supreme moment of personal revelation and social revolution, a sublime moment that Balzac loves and fears.

BALZAC'S SYNOPTIC VISION

The fantasy of a momentary annihilation of space and time allows Balzac to construct an Archimedean position from which to survey and understand the world, if not change it. He imagines himself "riding across the world, disposing all in it to my liking. . . . I possess the world effortlessly, and the world hasn't the slightest hold upon me." The imperial gaze is overt: "I was measuring how long a thought needs in order to develop itself; and compass in hand, standing upon a high crag, a hundred fathoms above the ocean, whose billows were sporting among the breakers, I was surveying my future, furnishing it with works of art, just as an engineer, upon an empty terrain, lays out fortresses and palaces."[58] The echo from Descartes's engineer as well as from Goethe's Faust is unmistakable. The dialectical relations between motion and stasis, between flows and movements, between interiors and exteriors, between space and place, between town and country, can all be investigated and represented.

Balzac is out to possess Paris. But he respects and loves it too much as a "moral entity," as a "sentient being," to want merely to dominate it. His desire to possess is not a desire to destroy or diminish. He needs the city to feed him images, thoughts, and feelings. He cannot treat of it as a dead object (as Haussmann and Flaubert, each in his own way, later did). Paris has a personality and a body. Paris, "the most delightful of monsters," is often depicted as a woman (playing opposite Balzac's male fantasies): "Here a pretty woman, farther off a poverty-stricken hag; here as freshly minted as the coin of a new reign, and in another corner of the town as elegant as a lady of fashion." Paris is "sad or gay, ugly or beautiful, living or dead; for [devotees] Paris is a sentient being; every individual, every bit of a house is a lobe in the cellular tissue of that great harlot whose head, heart and unpredictable behaviour are perfectly familiar to them." But in its cerebral functions, Paris takes on a masculine personality as the intellectual centre of the globe, "a brain teeming with genius which marches in the van of civilization; a great man, a ceaseless creative artist, a political thinker with second sight."[59]

The end product is a synoptic vision, encapsulated in extraordinary descriptions of the physiognomy and personality of the city (such as those that open *The Girl with the Golden Eyes*). Again and again we are urged to see the city as a totality, and graspable as such. Consider this passage from "Ferragus":

> Paris again with its streets, shop signs, industries and mansions as seen through diminishing spectacles: a microscopic Paris reduced to the tiny dimensions of shades, ghosts, dead people. . . . Jules perceived at his feet, in the long valley of the Seine, between the slopes of Vaugirard and Meudon, those of Belleville and Montmartre, the real Paris, wrapped in the dirty blue veil engendered by its smoke, at that moment diaphanous in the sunlight. He threw a furtive glance over its forty thousand habitations and said, sweeping his arm over the space between the column of the Place Vendôme and the gilded cupola of the Invalides: "there it is that she was stolen from me, thanks to the baneful inquisitiveness of this crowd of people which mills and mulls about for the mere pleasure of milling and mulling about.[60]

Rastignac, at the end of *Old Goriot*, standing in that same cemetery:

> saw Paris spread out below on both banks of the winding Seine. Lights were beginning to twinkle here and there. His gaze fixed almost avidly upon the space that lay between the Column of the Place Vendôme and the Dome of the Invalides; there lay the splendid world that he wished to conquer. He eyed that humming hive with a look that foretold of its despoliation, as if he already felt on his lips the sweetness of the honey, and said with superb defiance: "it's war, between us two."[61]

This synoptic vision echoes through the century. Haussmann, armed with balloons and triangulation towers, likewise appropriated Paris in his imagination as he set out to reshape it on the ground. But there is an important difference. Whereas Balzac obsessively seeks to command, penetrate, dissect, and then internalize everything about the city as a sentient being within himself, Haussmann converts that fantastic urge into a distinctive class project in which the state and the financiers take the lead in techniques of representation and of action. Intriguingly, Zola in *La Curée* replicates the perspective of Jules and Rastignac, but now it is the speculator, Saccard, who plans to profit from slashing through the veins of the city in an orgy of speculation (see pp. 116, 122).

"HOPE IS A MEMORY THAT DESIRES"

"Hope," wrote Balzac, "is a memory that desires."[62] This twinning of memory and desire helps clarify how the myths of modernity circulate with such powerful force. Most of Balzac's novels are, of course, historically situated. They often focus on processes of social change after the restoration of monarchy in 1814 and frequently lament the failure to accomplish a "real" restoration of progressive aristocratic, Catholic, and monarchical power in the wake of the catastrophic end of Empire. The legacy of that past weighs heavily. Many of his characters do not belong to any precise historical period: they are "divided between memories of the Empire and memories of the Emigration." Memory is therefore colored, and in some instances confronted, by historicism.

This is the theme of *Colonel Chabert*.[63] A famous military figure much favored by the Emperor, he is left for dead on the battlefield of Eylau in Germany. Stripped naked, he is thrown into a common grave but miraculously works his way up from under the bodies, and is rescued and cared for in the village nearby. It is many months before he remembers who he is but, since he is horribly disfigured, no one believes his identity. He wanders toward Paris, but en route is thrown in jail for two years as deranged. He is released only when he stops calling himself Colonel Chabert. We encounter him in Paris after the restoration, totally impoverished, seeking legal help to regain his identity and his rights. The Emperor, his protector, is gone. He has been taken for dead, so Chabert's personal assets have been distributed; his wife has remarried a Count and has two children. A lawyer who happens to represent the Countess is persuaded to take his case, but urges him to compromise rather than try to assert all of his former rights through a lengthy and costly court battle. His wife refuses to acknowledge him. In one excruciating moment of confrontation between them he reminds her, however, that he originally took her from the Palais Royale (the haunt of prostitutes). She whisks him away to her country estate and uses her wiles as woman and mother to try to persuade him to abandon his case (for the sake of the children), all the while plotting to get him committed to the madhouse as deranged. Learning of the plot, Chabert flees and disappears, only to be identified many years later by the lawyer as a vagabond case before the courts and then ultimately in 1840 as someone called Hyacinthe (denying the name Chabert) in the old people's asylum at Bicêtre. He has erased all memory of his wife but still proudly proclaims his military accomplishments to achieve another identity. He has lost all desire because historical forces and social institutions have failed him. Even the lawyer is disillusioned. Priests, doctors, and lawyers, he notes, all wear black robes "because they are in mourning for all virtue and hope." Declaring himself "sick of Paris," the lawyer resolves to retire to the country with his wife.

The reassertion of pastoral utopianism at the end of *Colonel Chabert* suggests that it is on this terrain that Balzac is perpetually in danger of losing his battle with nostalgia. Escaping what Christine Boyer calls "the stench of nostalgia" turns out to be one of the most troubling of all problems for conceptualizing and representing the city.[64] Balzac's failings here are generic, however, rather than unique. Marx saw the problem clearly. He objected to utopianism because it too often looked backward rather than forward, with deleterious consequences at revolutionary conjunctures:

> The tradition of all the dead generations weighs like a nightmare on the brain of the living. And just when they seem engaged in revolutionizing themselves and things, in creating something that never existed, precisely in such periods of revolutionary crisis they anxiously conjure up the spirits of the past to their service and borrow from them names, battle cries and costumes in order to present the new scene of world history in this time-honoured disguise and this borrowed language. . . . The social revolution of the nineteenth century cannot draw its poetry from the past, but only from the future. It cannot begin with itself before it has stripped off all superstition in regard to the past.[65]

This, however, is easier said than done. How could Marx reconcile the idea that revolutionaries must freely create some poetry of the future, let loose their imaginations upon the construction of the world, when he also held that the real foundations of consciousness lay in the material conditions of actually existing daily life?

Balzac has his own distinctive answer to this question. He distinguishes between history (that which is ordered and laid out) and memory (that which lies latent and unstructured but which can erupt in unexpected ways).[66] Chabert is supposed to bow down before the official history of his death and erase all memory, but in so doing goes mad. Montriveau in *The Duchesse de Langeais* has to face the same lesson: that the reduction of life to death can be "resisted only by remembering fully who we are." Benjamin here provides a critical standpoint. He attacks the historicism that culminates in universal history progressing "through homogeneous empty time." We should always be aware, writes Christine Boyer in her gloss on Benjamin, that history "is in need of redemption from a conformism that is about to overpower it in order to erase its differences and turn it into an accepted narration." Benjamin writes: "To articulate the past historically does not mean to recognize it 'the way it really was' (Ranke). It means to seize hold of a moment in history." The implication is that "memory, as opposed to history, responds more than it records, it bursts upon the scene in an unexpected manner," like the decisive moment when Colonel Chabert reminds his wife of her origins around the Palais Royale. In Benjamin's world, writes Boyer, "Memory springing from the natural chains of tradition should be like an epiphany, flashing up in ephemeral moments of crisis, searching to exhibit at that particular time the way of the world in order to direct one's pathway toward the future." Memory is, in Balzac's judgement, "the only faculty that keeps us alive."[67] It is active and energetic, voluntary and imaginative, rather than contemplative and passive. It permits a unity of time past and time future through action in the here and now, and therefore can erupt, in exactly the ways that Benjamin suggests, at moments of danger. It brings into the present a whole host of powers latent in the past that might otherwise lie dormant within us.

But memory also works in collective ways. Aldo Rossi once wrote:

One can say that the city itself is the collective memory of its people, and like memory it is associated with objects and places. The city is the locus of the collective memory. This relationship between the locus and the citizenry then becomes the city's predominant image, both of architecture and of landscape, and as certain artifacts become part of its memory, new ones emerge. In this entirely positive sense great ideas flow through the history of the city and give shape to it.[68]

Balzac assiduously works this connection throughout "The Human Comedy." He adds to and augments the flow of great ideas through the history of the city. He makes the city memorable and thereby constructs a distinctive locus in the imagination for a collective memory. This grounds a certain political sensibility that can "flash up" at moments of revolution. This is the myth of modernity as revolutionary transformation grounded in the city at work. Memory "flashed up" in 1830, as it did in 1848 and 1871, to play a key role in the articulation of revolutionary sentiments.[69] While these revolutionary moments were undoubtedly burdened by appeals to tradition, there was also an aspect to them that was intensely modernist, seeking that radical break through which a completely different path to the future might be opened up. It is not hope, therefore, that guides memory but memory that generates hope when it connects to desire. It was perhaps for this reason that Hugo and Baudelaire both thought Balzac a revolutionary thinker in spite of his reactionary politics.

THE FETISH AND THE FLANEUR

To represent the city as a sentient being runs the risk not only of anthropomorphizing it (a trope that Balzac shamelessly practices), but also of turning the city into a fetish object. By *fetish* I mean, in the first instance, the human habit of attributing to mere things (in this case the city) magical, mysterious, and usually hidden powers to shape and transform the world around us, and thereby to intervene directly in or even determine our lives. The qualities of urban environments in many of Balzac's novels appear on the surface to function in exactly such a way (as the example of Madame Vauquer in *Old Goriot* attests). But there is a deeper meaning of fetishism that Marx unravels through an analysis of the commodity. The fetish in this instance has a real basis; it is not merely imagined. We establish social relationships with one another by way of the objects and things we produce and circulate (social relations between people are mediated by material things). By the same token the objects and things are redolent with social meanings because they are embodiments of social labor and purposive human action (material things embody and represent social relations). To Marx, it was impossible to escape the fetishism of commodities under capitalism because this is precisely how the market works. Money (a thing) confers, for example, a social power upon its holder, and everyone is therefore to some degree captive to its fetish powers (the pursuit of it and acknowledgment of the kind of value that money imposes become central to understanding our behaviors in relation to each other). The task of the analyst, Marx therefore held, was to go beyond the fetish, to get beneath the surface appearance in order to provide a deeper understanding of the occult forces that govern the evolution of our social relations and our material prospects. "If everything were as it appears on the surface," he once remarked, "there would be no need for science." The fetish cannot be erased (except by revolution), but it can be confronted and understood. The danger always exists, however, that we will interpret the world solely through surface appearances and thereby replicate the fetish in thought.[70]

The capitalist city is necessarily a fetish object in exactly this latter sense. This is so not only because it is built upon the circulation of commodities, or because, as Balzac so frequently avers, everyone in it runs, leaps, and capers "under the whip of the pitiless goddess . . . the necessity for money," or is devoured by "the monster we call speculation." The streets, neighborhoods, apartments, stairways, and doorways are redolent with social meaning. Balzac gives human character to his streets in order to highlight that fact. Interiors internalize and mirror wider social forces. Human beings experience the chaos, the rushing stream of others, the multiple social interactions and accidental encounters as something outside of themselves to which they must adapt their actions and their mentalities (cultivating a blasé attitude, for example). Material relations between people are everywhere in evidence, as are the innumerable ways in which social relations are embodied within things. Any reconstruction of things therefore entails a reconfiguration of social relations: in making and remaking the city we make and remake ourselves, both individually and collectively. To construe the city as a sentient being is to acknowledge its potential as a body politic.

To live in the city is, however, always to be subject to its fetish powers. Lucien (in *Lost Illusions* and *A Harlot High and Low*), Madame Vauquer and Old Goriot (*Old Goriot*), Adèle (*Cousin Bette*), Pons (*Cousin Pons*), and César Birotteau, as well as many more, fall victim to these powers. But Balzac, along with many of his other characters, such as Rastignac, De Marsay, and the other members of "the Thirteen," seeks to soar above it—to understand, confront, and even master the fetish. Balzac's obsession with the annihilation of space and time reflects his drive to find an Archimedean point from which to escape the fetish, to command and transform the urban world. To be outside of space and time is, for Balzac, preparatory to dramatic and clairvoyant intervention in the world, not a preparation for contemplative withdrawal. The clarity achieved at moments of sublime insight must necessarily connect—lest it remain purely mystical—to some other way to penetrate the fetishism of the city.

That other way is given through the practices of the flaneur. Balzac is sometimes credited with the creation of that literary figure (though there is evidence that it goes back at least to the Empire, if not before).[71] In one of his very first works, *The Physiology of Marriage* (a work that many regard as the beginning of "The Human Comedy"), Balzac presents the figure as follows:

In the year 1822, on a fine morning in January, I was walking along the Boulevards of Paris from the peaceful district of the Marais to the fashionable Chaussée d'Antin, and observing for the first time, not without a certain philosophic enjoyment, those strange alterations of face and varieties of dress which, from the Rue du Pas-de-la-Mule to the Madeleine, make a different little world of each portion of the boulevard, and afford an instructive sample of the manners of that region of Paris. Having as yet no conception of the things life might have in store for me, and hardly doubting that one day I should have the audacity to enter the estate of matrimony, I was on my way to lunch with one of my college friends, who was saddled (perhaps rather too early in life) with a wife and two children. My old professor of mathematics lived but a short distance from my friend's house, and I had promised myself a visit to the worthy mathematician before feasting on the more delicate morsel of friendship. I easily found my way into a large sanctum where everything was covered with dust and gave evidence of the serious pursuits of the scholar. A surprise awaited me. [72]

Balzac's flaneur is more than an aesthete, a wandering observer, he is also purposive, seeking to unravel the mysteries of social relations and of the city, seeking to penetrate the fetish. Balzac depicts himself as one of those "few devotees, people who never walk along in heedless inattention," who "sip and savour their Paris and are so familiar with its physiognomy that they know its every wart, every spot or blotch on its face." There is something very democratic and anti-elitist in this conception. We are all in a position to play the flaneur, and therefore all in a position to rise above and escape the fetishism. This is where Balzac's perpetual urging to check the city out and figure things out for oneself becomes so important. His comments are worth repeating. "Could you really grudge spending a few minutes watching the dramas, disasters, tableaux, picturesque incidents which arrest your attention in the heart of this restless queen of cities?" "Look around you" as you "make your way through that huge stucco cage, that human beehive with black runnels marking its sections, and follow the ramifications of the idea which moves, stirs and ferments inside it." And it is not only men who are in a position to do this. Consider, for example, the way in which Madame Cibot purposefully explores the city's spaces and its social relations (roving among the art collectors, the concierges, the aristocratic households, the lawyers . . .) to construct the web of intrigue that brings Pons down and lays his art collection bare for all to see. The flaneur in Balzac is purposeful and active rather than motiveless and merely drifting.

Balzac's flaneur (or flaneuse) maps the city's terrain and evokes its living qualities. The city is thereby rendered legible for us in a very distinctive way. He evokes "the thousand uprooted lives," and in the most panoramic of his novels, such as *Cousin Bette*, he fuses them into a compelling evocation of the city as a sentient being. "The Human Comedy" approaches this totality, however, via the fragments of innumerable intersecting lives—Rastignac, Bette, De Marsay, Nucingen, Madame Cibot, Vautrin. "The overall system," Jameson writes, "posits the interrelationship of society as a certainty that we can, however, never see face to face. . . . there are hosts of interrelationships between the various characters, coincidences, meetings, passions, between the characters that exist but that never are and never will be present to our consciousness." The technique is kaleidoscopic. "In this," Jameson continues, "Balzac is somehow truer to individual experience, in which we never see anything but our own world, but in which we are absolutely convinced that that there is an outer surface, a coexistence with a host of other private worlds." This is how Balzac simultaneously confronts and represents the city as a fetish object.[73]

Balzac, as Baudelaire insisted, was just as much a visionary writer as a realist. That his social vision of the city became (or already was) increasingly circumscribed by the exclusive powers of the bourgeoisie, of the capitalist class of financiers in alliance with the state, was a condition that Balzac fought resolutely, though hopelessly. Sadly, as Balzac himself presciently observed, "When a literature has no general system to support it, it lacks solidity and fades out with the age to which it belongs."[74] If capital did not want the city to have an image, then Balzacian fantasy and democratizing cartographic power had also to be effaced and erased (as it all too frequently was in the years to come). But it is always open to us to exhume his vision. And it may be of more than passing interest to do so, for there is something subversive about Balzac's technique. It runs against the grain of ordinary and more passive forms of representation. Balzac exposes many of the myths of capitalist modernity by penetrating into the inner sanctums of bourgeois values. He scrutinizes the ways in which social relations are expressed through even the minutiae of built environments and how the visceral physical qualities of the city intervene in social relations. He exposes the denials (of rural origins and of memories). He demonstrates the utter emptiness of values based on the monetary calculus, the fictions of the fictitious forms of capital such as credit and interest that drive the realities of social relations and urban processes, the constant speculation on the desires of others that wreaks such destructive consequences. But he also has much to say about ruling thoughts and fears. He may unwittingly have written an appropriate epitaph for that day when the bourgeois era of seemingly endless capital accumulation and the fictional magic of interest and credit come to a crashing halt: "Thus I envelop the world with my thought, I mold it, I fashion it, I penetrate it, I comprehend it or think I comprehend it; but suddenly I wake up alone and find myself in the midst of the depths of a dark light."[75]

Appropriately rephrased and using Balzac's capacity to project his monadic thought as a concentric mirror of the bourgeois universe, we might one day say of the whole history of the bourgeoisie: *They enveloped the world with their thoughts, molded it, fashioned it, penetrated it, comprehended it—or thought they comprehended it; but suddenly they woke up alone and found themselves in the midst of the depths of a dark light.*

CHAPTER TWO

DREAMING THE BODY POLITIC

REVOLUTIONARY POLITICS AND
UTOPIAN SCHEMES, 1830–1848

Yesterday's beautiful utopia will be the morning's refreshing truth
—CLOSING SPEECH TO THE FIRST COMMUNIST BANQUET,
BELLEVILLE, JULY 1, 1840

In *The Painting of Modern Life*, the art historian T. J. Clark suggests that Haussmann's reshaping of Second Empire Paris depended critically upon a capitalistic reimagining of what the city both was and could be about. Capital, he argues: "did not need to have a representation of itself laid out upon the ground in bricks and mortar, or inscribed as a map in the minds of its city-dwellers. One might even say that capital preferred the city not to be an image—not to have form, not to be accessible to the imagination, to readings and misreadings, to a conflict of claims on its space—in order that it might mass-produce an image of its own to put in place of those it destroyed."[1] The argument is intriguing, but while Clark makes much of the mechanisms of commodification and spectacle that replaced what went before, he tells us very little about the image or images of the city that got displaced.

Clearly, the romanticism and socialist utopianism that flourished so wildly in the 1830s and 1840s in France were solidly repressed in the counterrevolution of 1848–1851. Many of those active in the swirling social movements that produced the revolution of 1848 were lost to the cause through death, exile, or discouragement. It is undeniable that some sort of shift in sensibility occurred after 1848 in France that redefined what political struggle was about on both the left and the right. Socialism, for example, became much more "scientific" (as Marx insisted), though it was to take a generation before that idea could bear much fruit, while bourgeois thought became much more positivist,

FIGURE 20 *Daumier's remarkable* Bourgeois and Proletarian *(1848) captures the distinction that many felt at the time was fundamental. The bourgeois, static and fat, avariciously eyes commodities in the shop window, while the worker, thin and in motion, determinedly scans a newspaper (the workers' press?) for inspiration.*

managerial, and tough-minded. And for some commentators this is very much what the transition to modernity and modernism was all about. Some markers are needed, however, because the story of what happened in Second Empire Paris is also a more complicated story of exactly what was repressed, destroyed, or co-opted in the counter-revolution of 1848–1851. How, then, did people in general and progressives in particular see and imagine the city and society before 1848? And what possibilities did they foresee for the future? What was it in all of this that the Empire had to work against?

THE REPUBLIC AND THE CITY AS A BODY POLITIC

On October 22, 1848, some eight thousand workers gathered in a Bordeaux cemetery to dedicate a monument, erected by public subscription, to Flora Tristan, who had died in that city in 1844, shortly after publishing her most famous work, *L'Union Ouvrière*, a vigorous plea for a general union of workers coupled with the emancipation of women. That a pioneering figure in socialist feminism should be the object of such reverence in 1848 might seem surprising. But there is another way to explain its significance. Ever since 1789, the Republic, the Revolution, and most particularly Liberty had been depicted as a woman. This countered a political theory of monarchical governance that, from the late Middle Ages onward, had appealed to the idea of the state and the nation as being constituted out of what Kantorowicz calls "the King's Two Bodies"—the king as a person and the king as an embodiment of the state and nation.[2] During the French Revolution this depiction of the King and the idea "l'état, c'est moi" came in for some radical satirical treatment. Placing the cap of liberty—a Phrygian cap—on the King's head was a way of signaling his impotence (the droop of the cap bore a resemblance to a nonerect penis). Daumier, a resolute republican, went to prison in 1834 for his savage depiction of Louis

FIGURE 21 *Daumier's* Gargantua *(1834) takes the idea of the body politic quite literally, and has a bloated Louis Philippe being fed by an army of retainers while protecting some bourgeois hangers-on beneath his chair. This cartoon earned Daumier six months in prison.*

FIGURE 22 *Delacroix's* Liberty Leading the People *is one of the most celebrated of the depictions of Liberty as a woman on the barricades. While it was meant as a celebration of the "July Days" that brought Louis Philippe to power, it was considered too incendiary for public exhibition, so the King bought it and stored it away.*

Philippe as Gargantua, a bloated figure being fed by impoverished masses of workers and peasants while he shelters a few affluent bourgeois under his throne.

Agulhon provides a fascinating account of this iconographic struggle throughout the nineteenth century.[3] The motif of Liberty and Revolution as woman reappeared very strongly in the revolution of 1830, most effectively symbolized by Delacroix's painting *Liberty Leading the People*. A veritable flood of parallel images arose throughout all France in the aftermath of 1848. How the woman was represented was, however, significant. Opponents of republicanism often went along with the representation but portrayed the woman as a simpleton (a "Marianne" from the country) or as an uncontrolled, lascivious woman no better than a common prostitute. Respectable bourgeois republicans preferred stately figures in classical dress and demeanor, surrounded with the requisite symbols of justice, equality, and liberty (an iconographic form that ended up as a French donation to adorn New York City's harbor (see figure 117). Revolutionaries expected a bit more fire in the figure. Balzac captured this in *The Peasantry* in the figure of Catherine, who(:)

> recalled the models selected by painters and sculptors for figures of Liberty and the ideal Republic. Her beauty, which found favor in the eyes of the youth of the valley, was of the same full-blossomed type, she had the same strong pliant figure, the same muscular lower limbs, the plump arms, the eyes that gleamed with a spark of fire, the proud expression, the hair grasped and twisted in thick handfuls, the masculine forehead, the red mouth, the lips that curled back with a smile that had something almost ferocious in it—such a smile as Delacroix and David (of Angers) caught and rendered to admiration. A glowing brunette, the image of the people, the flames of insurrection seemed to leap forth from her clear tawny eyes.[4]

FIGURE 23 *Daumier's* Republic *was created in response to the Revolutionary government's request for new art to celebrate Republican virtues. With two lusty infants suckling at her breasts and another with a book at her feet, Daumier suggests a body politic that nurtures and that takes seriously Danton's famous saying that "After bread, education is the primary need of the people."*

Flaubert took the negative view. In *Sentimental Education* he describes a scene witnessed during the invasion of the Tuileries Palace in 1848: "In the entrance-hall, standing on a pile of clothes, a prostitute was posing as a statue of Liberty, motionless and terrifying, with her eyes wide open."[5]

It is on this contested terrain that Daumier's version, painted in response to the Republican government's invitation in 1848 to compete for a prize representation of the republic, is doubly interesting. For not only is the body politic of the Republic represented as a woman—indeed, it would have been surprising, under the circumstances, if it had not been—but it is also given a powerful maternal rendering. It is a nurturing social republic that Daumier depicts, as opposed to the political symbolism of bourgeois rights or the revolutionary symbolism of woman on the barricades. Daumier echoes Danton's revolutionary declaration: "After bread, education is the primary need of a people." This nurturing version of the body politic had become deeply embedded in left socialism and utopian programs during the 1840s.

This imagery of the ideal republic was indissolubly linked with that of the ideal city. "There is," wrote Foucault, "an entire series of utopias or projects that developed on the premise that a state is like a large city." Indeed, "the government of a large state like France should ultimately think of its territory on the model of the city."[6] Historically this connection had always been strong, and for many radicals and socialists of the time, the identity was clear. The Saint-Simonians, for example, with their obvious interest in material and social engineering were totally dedicated to the production of new social and spatial forms such as railways, canals, and public works of all kinds. And they did not neglect the symbolic dimension of urban development. Duveyrier's description of "The New Town or the Paris of the Saint-Simonians" in 1833 "was to have as its central edifice a colossal temple in the shape of a female statue (the Female Messiah, the Mother); it was to be a gigantic monument where the garlands on the robe were to act as so many promenade galleries, while the folds in the train of the gown were to be the walls of an amphitheatre for games and roundabouts, and the globe on which her right hand rested was to be a theatre."[7] Fourier, though primarily interested in agrarian preindustrial communities, had plenty to say about urban design and planning, and constantly complained about the appalling state of the cities and the degrading forms of urban life. With few exceptions, socialists, communists, feminists, and reformers of the 1840s paid attention to the city as a form of political, social, and material organization—as a body politic—that was fundamental to what the future good society was to be about. Hardly surprisingly, this broad impetus carried over into architecture and urban administration, where the imposing figure of César Daly set out to translate ideas into architectural forms and practical projects (some of which were set in motion in the 1840s).[8]

While the general connection between thinking about the republic and about the city may have been clear, the details were lost in a mess of confusions as to how, exactly, the body politic was to be constituted and governed. From the 1820s onward, groups of thinkers formed, bonded, imploded, or fractured, leaving behind shards of ideas that were picked up and recombined into entirely different modes of thought. Factions and fragmentations, schisms and reconfigurations flourished. Rational Enlightenment principles were combined with romanticism and Christian mysticism, science was applauded but then given a visionary, almost mystical, status. Hard-nosed materialism and empiricism intermingled with visionary utopianism. Thinkers who aspired to a grand unity of thought (like Saint-Simon and Fourier) left behind such a chaos of writings that almost anything could be deduced therefrom. Political leaders and thinkers jostled for power and influence, and personal rivalries and not a little vanity took their toll. And as political-economic conditions shifted, so innumerable adaptations of thinking occurred, making the ideas of 1848 radically different from those of 1830. How, then, are we to understand these turbulent currents of thought?

TURNING THE WORLD RIGHT SIDE UP

"Society as it exists now," wrote Claude-Henri de Saint-Simon sometime in 1819–1820, "is indeed an upside-down world."[9] And, of course, the only way to improve upon things was to set it right side up, which implied making some sort of revolution. Saint-Simon, however, abhorred the violence of the Revolution (he narrowly escaped the guillotine) and preferred to seek pacific, progressive, and rational change. The body politic was sick, he said, and needed resuscitation. But the end result was to be the same: the world must be turned right side up.

This sense of a world turned upside down had, as Christopher Hill (1975) so brilliantly documents, already had its day across the English Channel in the turbulent years 1640–1688 that followed upon Cromwell's seizure of power and the execution of King Charles.[10] Much the same phenomena are to be observed in France between 1830 and 1848, when speculation and experimentation were rife. But how can this efflorescence of utopian, revolutionary, and reformist ideas in the period 1830–1848 be explained? The French Revolution left a double legacy. There was, on the one hand, an overwhelming sense that something rational, right, and enlightened had gone very wrong, as well as a desperate need to come to terms with what (or whom) to blame. In this the historians of the 1840s played a crucial role by building a potent historical analysis and memory of much that had been lost. But the Revolution also left behind the sense that it was possible for "the people" (however construed) to right things by the mobilization of a collective will, most particularly within the body politic of Paris. The revolution of 1830 demonstrated this capacity, and for a short time it seemed as if constitutional monarchy and bourgeois right could march hand in hand, much as they had in Britain after the settlement of 1688, so as to make republicanism irrelevant. But the disillusionment that followed, as the aristocracy of money took over from the aristocracy of position (with a concomitant repression of many constitutional freedoms, such as those of speeech and the press) sparked an eruption in oppositional thinking (symbolized by Daumier's savage depiction of Louis Philippe as Gargantua). The effect was to revive interest in republican alternatives. But behind this loomed another set of pressing problems—the grinding poverty and insecurity, the cancerous social inequality, and how work and labor might best be organized to alleviate the lot of an oppressed peasantry and a nascent industrial working class more and more concentrated in large urban centers such as Paris and Lyon. And this provoked thought of a socialist alternative, both among the workers themselves and among the progressive intelligentsia.

The legacy of Revolutionary-period thinkers was important. François Babeuf's "conspiracy of the equals," for example, had proclaimed economic and political socialism as the inevitable next step in a French Revolution deemed to be "only the forerunner of another revolution, far greater, far more solemn, which will be the last." Babeuf sought to overthrow the existing social and political order by force (only to be guillotined, on the orders of the Directory, as a martyr to this cause in 1797). Buonarotti, a coconspirator with Babeuf, escaped the guillotine because of his Italian nationality and lived to publish a full (and possibly much embellished) account of the work of the conspiracy in 1828 (leading Babeuf thereafter to be considered, erroneously in Rose's view, by Marx and Lenin as a pioneering figure in revolutionary communism).[11] This was the tradition that August Blanqui resurrected in several conspiratorial schemes, such as the Société des Saisons that sought unsuccessfully to overthrow the July Monarchy in 1839. The oath of this secret society proclaimed that the aristocracy is "to the social body what a cancer is to the human body," and that "the first condition of the social body's return to justice is the annihilation of aristocracy." Revolutionary action, the extermination of all monarchy and aristocrats, and the establishment of a republican government based on equality was the only way to rescue the social body from "its gangrenous state."[12]

Blanqui added two specific twists to this argument. When arrested and charged with conspiracy in 1832, he declared his profession before an incredulous President of the Court as "proletarian"—the profession of "thirty million Frenchmen who live by their work and who are deprived of political rights." In his defense he evoked the "war between rich and poor" and denounced "the pitiless machine that pulverises, one by one, twenty-five million peasants and five million workers to extract their purest blood and transfuse it into the veins of the privileged. The cogs of this machine, assembled with an astonishing art, touch the poor man at every instant of the day, hounding him in the least necessity of his humble life, and the most miserable of his pleasures, taking away half of his smallest gain." But Blanqui detested utopian blueprints. "No one has access to the secrets of the future," he wrote. "The Revolution alone, as it clears the terrain, will reveal the horizon, will gradually remove the veils and open up the roads, or rather multiple paths, that lead to the new social order. Those who pretend to have in their pocket a complete map of this unknown land—they truly are madmen."[13] Blanqui did have a transition program. Those who mounted the revolution—for the most part déclassé radicals—would have to assume state power and construct a dictatorship in the name of the proletariat in order to educate the masses and inculcate capacities for self-governance. Blanqui, when not in prison, mounted one revolutionary conspiracy after another, instilling fear into the bourgeoisie, most particularly the republicans. Only after the failure of the 1871 Commune did he finally give in, as Benjamin notes, "to resignation without hope." He tacitly recognized that the social revolution had not, and perhaps could not, keep pace with the material, scientific, and technical changes that the nineteenth century was experiencing.[14]

Saint-Simon (who died in 1825) and Fourier (who died in 1837) provided quite different grist to the socialist/reformist mill of oppositional and utopian thought. They were key link figures who reflected on the errors of the Revolution while pursuing alternatives. Both of them left behind legacies that aspired to universality (they both compared themselves to Newton) but which were incomplete, often confusing, and therefore open to multiple interpretations.

Saint-Simon is generally credited with being the founder of positivist social science.[15] The task of the analyst, he argued, was to study the actual condition of society and, on that basis, recognize what needs to be done to bring the body politic into some more harmonious and productive state. Many of his works were therefore written as open letters, tracts, or memoranda to influential people (the King, diplomats, etc.). It is hard to extract general principles from such sources. His thinking also evolved in a variety of ways from 1802 until his final, unfinished work on the new Christianity (published posthumously in 1826–1827).

The body politic had, Saint-Simon held, assumed harmonious forms in the past (such as feudalism in the twelfth and thirteenth centuries), only to dissolve in contradictions out of which a new body politic should emerge. The seeds of the new were contained within the womb of the old. This historicist view of human evolution influenced many subsequent thinkers (including Marx). The crisis in the body politic in Saint-Simon's own time derived from an incomplete transition from "a feudal ecclesiastical system to an industrial and scientific one."[16] The French Revolution had addressed the problem of hereditary privileges, but the Jacobins had failed because they sought to impose constitutional and juridical rights by centralized state power. They had resorted to terror and violence to impose their will. "The eighteenth century has been critical and revolutionary," he wrote, but the nineteenth has to be "inventive and constructive." The central problem was that the industrial—by whom Saint-Simon meant everyone who engaged in useful productive activity, including workers and peasants, as well as owners of enterprises, bankers, merchants, scientists, thinkers, and educators—were governed by an idle and parasitic class of aristocrats and priests whose mentality derived from the military and theocratic powers of feudalism.

Spiritual power must therefore pass from the hands of priests to those of savants—the scientists and artists—and temporal power to the leading figures among the industrials themselves. The latter's interest would be to minimize the interventions of government and to devise a least-cost and efficient form of administration to facilitate the activities of the direct producers. The function of government would be to ensure that "useful work is not hindered." Government by command should give way to effective administration.

This system would, furthermore, have to be Europe-wide rather than national in scope (part of Saint-Simon's current reputation lies in his prescient view of the necessity for a European Union for a peaceful and progressive organization of economic development). "All men will work," Saint-Simon declared as early as 1803, and it is to the proper organization of production and useful work that we must appeal if the ills of the social body are to be cured. He emphasized individual initiative and liberty, and sometimes appears to echo the laissez-faire ideals of many political economists (such as Adam Smith).

But Saint-Simon is concerned with the exact nature of the political institutions that could maximize individual liberty and promote useful work through collective projects. The principle of association reflective of divisions of labor plays a vital role, though the ideal of a grand association among all industrials (including workers and peasants as well as employers, financiers, and scientists) is frequently invoked. At one point he proposed the formation of three chambers of governance, elected by the industrials—a Chamber of Invention (made up of scientists, artists, and engineers who would plan systems of public works such canals, railroads, and irrigation "for the enrichment of France and the improvement of the lot of its inhabitants, to cover every aspect of usefulness and amenity"); a Chamber of Execution (made up of scientists who would examine the feasibility of projects and organize education); and a Chamber of Examination (made up of industrials who would decide on the budget and carry out large-scale projects of social and economic development).[17]

The industrials were not construed by Saint-Simon as homogeneous. But he did not accept that the divisions among them would blind them to their common interests or lead them to object to the hierarchy of powers in which educated elites of producers, bankers, merchants, scientists, and artists would take decisions in the name of the ignorant masses (whose education was a primary goal). "Natural leaders" were defined according to technical ability and merit. "Each man will be placed according to his capacity and rewarded according to his work." Popular sovereignty was not a useful principle of governance because "the people know very well that, except for a few moments of very brief delirium, the people have no time to be sovereign." But he became deeply concerned with the question of moral incentives. Naked egotism and self-interest were important, but they had to be ameliorated by other motivations if the economy was to realize collective goals. This was the power that Christianity had always promised but never delivered. A new form of Christianity, founded on moral principles, was required to ensure universal well-being as the aim of political-economic projects. "All men should treat each other as brothers," he argued, and "the whole of society should work to improve the moral and physical existence of the poorest class."[18] With this, Saint-Simon opened the floodgates to millennarian thinking and religious mysticism as a basis for radical change.

How his ideas spread is a complicated story. His immediate followers published a selective (some would say bowdlerized) account of his ideas after his death, and interest flourished after the July Revolution (in which the Saint-Simonians played no active role). There were many well-attended meetings during the early 1830s that garnered support from reform-minded bourgeois and workers, and a movement was launched to educate workers, though, as Rancière shows, many workers had trouble appreciating the motivations and the paternalism involved.[19] Almost anyone exercised about the right to work and its proper organization to relieve poverty and insecurity among peasants and workers during the early 1830s was likely to have had some contact with Saint-Simonian ideas. Much of the thinking about alternative urban forms was deeply influenced by this mode of thought (see below). The role of women and religion became controversial issues, however, and the movement soon imploded in a conflict between factions led by a charismatic (and some said hypnotic) Barthélemy Enfantin (with Godlike pretensions) and a less fanatical Saint-Amand Bazard. Thereafter the legacy of influence dispersed in all manner of directions, and much of the movement's energy dissipated in religious cult activities. Saint-Simonian feminists, however, evolved their ideas (sometimes in contact with Fourierism) on topics such as divorce and the organization of women's work. They became vocal and strong enough to come in for satirical commentary from Daumier, and they played an important role in 1848.

Some Saint-Simonians took the Christian path, and Pierre Leroux turned to an associationist kind of Christian socialism. Leroux identified individualism as the primary moral disease within the body politic; socialism—and he is generally credited with being the first to coin the term in 1833—would restore the unity of reciprocal relations between the parts and revive the body politic, he argued. But the role of the body politic was not to impress conformity upon everyone; it should, rather, service "autonomously developing individuals who were realizing their felt needs."[20] Others shifted their allegiance to Fourier. Marx absorbed ideas of social scientific inquiry, productivism, historicism, contradiction, and the inevitability of social change from Saint-Simon but turned to class struggle as the motor of historical change. Still others, like the Pereires, Enfantin, and Michel Chevalier, pursued the idea of association of capital and leadership by a scientific-engineering and financial elite. They became major figures within the Second Empire structures of governance, administration, and capital accumulation through large-scale public works (such as the Suez Canal and the railroads).

That this last group were able to evolve in this way in part reflected Louis Napoleon's engagement with Saint-Simonian ideas.[21] Large-scale public works fascinated the Emperor-to-be. As early as the 1840s, while imprisoned at Ham (after an ill-fated attempt to invade and launch a revolution in Boulogne), he studied a proposal by the newly independent Nicaraguan government to build a canal between the Atlantic and Pacific oceans (to bear Napoleon's name). He also published a pamphlet titled *The Extinction of Pauperism*. In this he championed the right to work as a basic principle and proposed state legislation to set up associations of workingmen empowered to engage in the compulsory purchase (with state loans) of wastelands. Put under cultivation, he argued, these would provide employment as well as profitable and healthy activity in the production and sale of agricultural products. A rotating fund for repayment of the state loans and the indemnification of landholders would finance the project. Socialist leaders and reformers rallied to his cause and some, like Louis Blanc and George Sand, even visited him at Ham. Employers and economists mocked the proposal and depicted him as an idle and (based on his failed revolution) incompetent utopian dreamer (an image that led many to underestimate his potential when elected President of the Republic in 1848). While his proposals owed something to Saint-Simon, they also smacked of Fourierist influence (as late as 1848 Louis Napoleon was said to be in touch with Fourierist groups and early in the Empire he showed considerable interest in building *cités ouvrières* on the model of Fourier's Phalanstères as a solution to the working-class housing problem).

FIGURE 24 *The feminist movement became strong enough in the 1830s and 1840s for Daumier to devote a series to "bluestockings" (women with artistic and literary pretensions), divorcees, and socialist women. In this cartoon the man is accused of trying to prevent the women from going to a public meeting. Rather than punish him, they leave him to wrestle with his guilty conscience.*

So what, then, can we say of Fourier himself? An autodidact, he published his foundational work, *The Theory of the Four Movements*, in 1808. In it, he sought a transition from "social chaos to universal harmony" by appeal to two basic principles: agricultural association and passionate attraction. Even Fourier's admirers admit that the work is "diffuse and enigmatic" and "a veritable crazy quilt of 'glimpses' into the more arcane aspects of the theory, 'tableaux' of the sexual and gastronomic delights of Harmony, and critical 'demonstrations' of the 'methodological mindlessness' of contemporary philosophy and political economy." Some of Fourier's arguments (concerning, for example, the copulation of planets) are bizarre, and others so outlandish that it is easy to dismiss him as a crank. A lonely and often beleaguered figure, he produced a mass of writings that did little to clear up the confusions even as they elaborated and deepened his critical understanding of the defects of the existing order. He sought to conceal some of his more outrageous ideas about passionate attraction and sexuality (his defense of what many regarded then, as now, as sexual perversions, for example). After his death this concealment was even more vigorously pursued by the Fourierists, who, under the authoritarian leadership of Victor Considérant, carefully controlled expurgated versions of his writings to shape what became an important wing of the pacific social democratic movement (with an influential newspaper, the *Phalanstère*). This "became an intellectual and even political force of some significance during the last years of the July Monarchy and the early phases of the 1848 revolution." But with the crushing of the revolution, many of the leaders, like Considerant, had to go into exile and the movement lost direct influence.[22]

Fourier mounted a generic attack upon "civilization" as a system of organized repression of healthy passionate instincts (in this he anticipated some of Freud's arguments in *Civilization and Its Discontents*). The insidious problem of poverty derived from the inefficient organization of production, distribution, and consumption. The main enemy was commerce, which was parasitic upon and destructive to human well-being. While we may be destined to work, we need to organize it to guarantee libidinal satisfactions, happiness, comfort, and passionate fulfillments. There was nothing noble or fulfilling about grinding away at awful and monotonous tasks, hour after hour. Civilization not only starved millions a year but it also "subjected all men to a life of emotional deprivation which reduced them to a state below that of animals, who at least were free to obey their own instinctual promptings."[23] So what was the alternative? Production and consumption had to be collectively organized in communities called "Phalanstères." These would offer variety of work and variety of social and sexual engagements to guarantee happiness and fulfillment of wants, needs, and desires. Fourier took immense pains to specify how Phalanstères should be organized and around what principles (he had a very complicated, mathematically ordered description of passionate attractions, for example, which needed to be matched up between individuals to guarantee harmony and happiness).

1840 AND ALL THAT

If Saint-Simon, Blanqui, and Fourier provided the initial sparks, then a host of other writers spread the flames of alternative thought in all manner of directions. The year 1840, for example, saw the publication of Proudhon's *What Is Property*; Etienne Cabet's influential utopian tale, *Voyage in Icaria* (shortly after his lengthy study of the French Revolution that depicted Robespierre as a communist hero); Flora Tristan's expose of misery and degradation among the working classes of London in *Promenades in London*; Louis Blanc's social democratic text, *The Organization of Work*; Pierre Leroux's two-volume study, *On Humanity* (which explored the Christian roots of socialism); Agricol Perdiguier's *Book of Compagnonnage* (which sought reforms within the system of migratory labor); and a host of other books and pamphlets that offered critical commentary on social conditions while exploring alternatives.[24] Villermé's study of the conditions of labor in the French textile industry was being widely read, and Frègier's dissection of the problem of the Parisian underclass struck fear into the hearts of many bourgeois readers. Romantic writers (Hugo, Lamartine, Musset, Sand) were throwing their support to radical reform and fraternizing with worker-poets, the first organized communist banquet took place in Belleville, a general strike occurred in Paris, and a communist worker tried to assassinate the King. The floodgates were open, and in spite of attempts at repression and police control, there seemed to be no way, short of revolution and counterrevolution, to stem the turbulence.

It is hard to capture the intensity, the creativity and the commonalities within the diversity of radical arguments articulated during these years. But there was widespread agreement on the nature of the problem. A frustrated Flora Tristan in her influential book *l'Union Ouvrière* (published in 1843) invoked the innumerable commentators who had preceded her:

> In their writings, speeches, reports, memoirs, investigations and statistics, they have pointed out, affirmed and demonstrated to the Government and the wealthy, that the working class is, in the present state of things, materially and morally placed in an intolerable condition of poverty and suffering. They have shown that, from this state of abandonment and neglect, it necessarily follows that the greater part of workers, embittered by misfortune, brutalised by ignorance and exhausting work, were becoming dangerous to society. They have proved to the Government and to the wealthy that not only justice and humanity imposed the duty of coming to the aid of the working classes by a law permitting the organisation of labour, but that even general interest and security imperiously recommended this measure. But even so, for nearly twenty-five years, many eloquent voices have been unable to awaken the solicitude of the Government concerning the dangers courted by society in the face of seven to eight million workers exasperated by neglect and despair, among whom a great number find themselves torn between suicide . . . or theft![25]

While Tristan shaped her account to suit her cause, none of her contemporaries would, I think, dispute the general situation she portrayed, even down to the problem of worker suicides, which were by no means uncommon.

The diagnostic, however, varied greatly: civilization and commerce (Fourier), the anachronistic power of aristocrats and priests (Saint-Simon, Blanqui), individualism (Leroux), indifference to inequality, particularly of women (Tristan), patriarchy (Saint-Simonian feminists), property and credit (Proudhon), capitalism and unregulated industrialism (Considérant, Blanc), corruption of the state apparatus (romantics, republicans, and even Jacobins), failure of workers to organize and associate around their common interests (Cabet and the communists). The list goes on and on. And what to do about it, what the aims and goals of transformative social movements should be, was even more confused. The problem of diagnosis and remedy of the ills of the body politic was made more difficult by a common language undergoing rapid and treacherous shifts in meanings. Among the workers, Sewell shows, linguistic shifts played a crucial role in changing political interpretations and actions between 1793 and 1848.[26] But there were some common themes. The differences often reflected the specific ways in which ideas about equality, liberty, republicanism, communism, and association got blended together programmatically. The principles laid out by Leroux in 1833 for the Society of the Rights of Man, shortly after his break with the Saint-Simonians, were typical of this genre:

> This party unanimously conceives of equality as its goal, of assistance to proletarians as its first duty, of republican institutions as its means, of the sovereignty of the people as its principle; finally it considers the right of association to be the final consequence of this principle and the means of implementing it.[27]

But what might these individual terms mean?

Equality

Everyone agreed inequality was a problem. But if the aim was improvement, then what kind of equality should be striven for, and by what means and for whom? This had, of course, been a contentious issue ever since the Revolution inscribed the word *égalité* upon its banner. But by 1840, consensus was submerged beneath a welter of different interpretations. Blanqui persisted with a radical Jacobin idea of secular egalitarianism—to be achieved, however, by means of a dictatorship of the proletariat. Again and again speakers at the 1840 communist banquet (with more than a thousand in attendance) asserted that political equality was meaningless in the absence of social equality. Equality of wellbeing was important to the Saint-Simonians, but the working classes were to be raised up by education, proper governance, and resources assembled thanks to the initiative of a meritorious and technically superior elite of industrials. The health and well-being of the body politic as a whole was more important than the well-being of individuals (a point upon which Leroux broke with the Saint-Simonians and which has sometimes led them to be portrayed as protofascists). The communists and Jacobins wanted equality of empowerment as well as of life chances. But there was very little support among the workers themselves for revolutionary action to overthrow the whole system and put an egalitarian communism in its place; it was more a matter of wanting to be treated as human beings, placed on the same footing as the bourgeoisie, while being accorded a modicum of security and fair remuneration for employment.[28] Workers objected, for example, to the patronizing attitude of the petit bourgeois radicals (particularly the Saint-Simonians) who sought to educate them (rather than give them secure jobs), and found this arrogance almost as hard to bear as the indifference of their employers. Agricol Perdiguier, a worker, insisted on exactly this kind of equality: "You should understand that we are not made of any substance less delicate or less pure than the rich, that our blood and our constitutions are in no way different from what we see in them. We are children of the same father and we must live together as brothers. Liberty and equality must be brought together and reign in concert within the great family of humanity."[29]

Inequality was also manifested through the subordination of women. In 1808, Fourier argued that "social progress and changes from one era to the next are brought about in proportion to the progress of women towards freedom, and social decline is brought about in proportion to the decrease in women's freedom."[30] The emancipation of women was a necessary condition for the emancipation of humanity and the liberation of passionate attractions. Enfantin also promoted the emancipation of women (though from a different male perspective), and several women within the Saint-Simonian movement struggled to connect these ideas with actual practices, launching their own journal, *La Tribune des Femmes*, to debate issues of sexual liberation and women's equality. While the Fourierists downplayed questions of sexuality and gender, most feminists were soon drawn to Fourier's ideas. Flora Tristan, for example, considered the right to work for a remunerative wage equal to that of men and the legal right to divorce as by far the most important reforms needed to liberate women from a form of marital bondage that was nothing less than enslaved prostitution. Questions of sexual liberation gradually gave way, however, to arguments about women's autonomy and right to work as a condition of freedom from male domination. "What we mean when we speak of liberty, or equality," wrote a contributor to the *Tribune des Femmes*, "is to be able to own possessions; for as long as we cannot, we shall always be slaves of men. He who provides us our material needs can always require, in exchange, that we submit to his wishes."

But on this point there arose another barrier (with which we continue to be dismally familiar). "In industry, very few careers are offered to us. Agreeable work is all done by men; we are left only the jobs that hardly pay enough for survival. And as soon as it is noticed that we can do a job, the wages there are lowered because we must not earn as much as men"[31] Tristan in no way romanticized (as Sand did) the working-class or peasant woman. Ill-educated, legally deprived, forced into marriage and dependency at an early age, deprived of rights, she learned to become a sharp-tongued harridan, more likely to drive her husband to the cabaret and her children to theft and violence than to establish a domestic hearth capable of giving succor to all (including herself). Tristan appealed to male self-interest: the education and emancipation of women was a necessary condition for the emancipation of the male working class. Proudhon, however, would have no truck with this; the family was sacrosanct, women belonged in the home under the control of men, and that was that.

The dialogue between material and moral egalitarianism, between the right to gain a living wage under conditions of security and to be treated with dignity and respect, no matter one's position in terms of class or gender, was a complex one. But it is then not hard to see how conceptions of individual dignity and self-worth, deeply embedded in Christian teachings though not in priestly practices, could also be evoked among authors as diverse as Proudhon (in his early years), Tristan, Saint-Simon, Cabet, and many other reformers. To be anticlerical was one thing, but a radicalized Christianity (of the sort that Saint-Simon and Leroux proposed) seemed to many to be part of the answer. Theologies of liberation abounded, as did millenarian thinking and even mystical musings. Not a few leaders either adopted (like Enfantin or even Fourier, who liked to call himself "the messiah of reason"), or had forced upon them (like Cabet), the status of a "new messiah" ready to announce "the good news" and offer a path to social redemption of society's ills. It was not clear whether equality was to be regarded as a divine gift or as a triumph of secular reason. The romantic poet Lamartine looked to "an industrial Christ" to guarantee the right to work.

Association

One cannot probe far into the literature of the time without encountering the principle of association either as means or as an end of political institutions and actions. But, again, association encompassed a variety of meanings, and it was sometimes defined so narrowly that others downplayed it in favor of some other principle, such as union (Tristan) or community (Leroux). What was at stake here was how the collectivity might be better organized to take care of material wants while creating a milieu suitable for education and personal fulfillment. Fourier certainly saw it this way in his tract *Agricultural and Domestic Association*, published in 1822, and it was fundamental to his proposal to construct Phalanstères. But Fourier confined his vision to agricultural production (and even then of a horticultural variety), and never adapted his theory of association to industrial settings. Furthermore, for him, the establishment of associations depended either on philanthropic finance or on private investments in stock, the self-organization of the laborers played no part.

For the Saint Simonians the idea of association among the industrials was fundamental, but it operated at two distinct levels. Differentiated interests (particularly those resulting from divisions of labor or of function) within the body politic were to be organized as associations expressive of those interests. Scientists and artists, for example, would have their own deliberative organizations. But these associations had to be embedded in a "universal association" that depended on a class alliance among all the industrials working for the common good, pooling resources, and contributing and receiving according to productivity and talents. It is not hard to see how such ideas could reappear during the Second Empire as principles of organization, administration, credit, and finance with even a limited role for worker associations under the umbrella of imperial power. This ideal of some grand association of interests and of a class alliance that could bridge bourgeois and worker interests retained considerable importance because many radicals (true to their own class origins and perspectives) felt that the workers and peasants themselves were not strong enough or educated enough to initiate action. Cabet in the early 1840s looked for bourgeois support, and only after repeated rejections did he take a separatist road and define a communistic communitarianism as his goal. Leroux likewise looked for bourgeois support (based on Christian values), and received enough of it (primarily from George Sand) to finance his ultimately unsuccessful agrarian commune and printing works in Lussac.

The idea of independent associations formed by the workers themselves had a long history. Repressed after the Revolution, it reemerged strongly in the revolutionary days of 1830 and found immediate support in the work of Buchez, a dissident Saint-Simonian. Buchez objected to the top-down perspective given by principles of universal association, and argued for bottom-up associations of producers with the aim of freeing workers from the wage system and shielding them from the unjust results of competition. From this perspective, factory owners and employers were just as parasitic as the aristocracy and landowners. This idea was later taken up forcefully by Louis Blanc in his influential *The Organization of Work*, as well as by Proudhon. Blanc, however, saw it as a duty of state power and political legislation to establish and finance the associations and to supervise their management (much as he later insisted upon the state financing of the national workshops in 1848). Proudhon, for his part, wanted the state kept entirely out of it and looked toward a model of self-governance that would turn the workshop into the social space of reform. But his thinking kept shifting, in part because he did not trust associations to solve the problem or workers necessarily to do the right thing. At some points he invokes a strong disciplinary role for competition between workshops, and at others says that not all workshops needed to be organized on associationist lines. Vincent reconstructs his views as follows:

> Basically, what Proudhon desired was to organize an interconnected group of mutual associations which would overcome the contradictions of existing society and thereby transform it. This projected social transformation would commence with the organization of small companies of around one hundred workers which would form fraternal ties with one another. These associations would be primarily economic . . . but also (functioning) as the focuses of education and social interaction. They would, he claimed, set examples for the establishment of similar associations because of their superior moral and economic qualities. . . . [and] . . . resolve "the antinomy of liberty and regulation" and provide the synthesis of "liberty and order." . . . The decisive function of the association was to introduce an egalitarian society of men producing and consuming in harmony; they would thereby uproot the opposition between capitalist and worker, between idler and laborer.[32]

This was very different from Fourier's or Louis Blanc's vision, though it did have some commonalities with Cabet. But Proudhon worried that associations might stifle individual liberty and initiative, and he never sought to abolish the distinction between capital and labor; he merely wanted to make relations more harmonious and just. Proudhon also recognized that the mutual associations needed money and credit to function. Anxious to turn his ideas into practice, he launched a People's Bank in the revolutionary days of 1848, only to have it fail almost immediately.

The idea that workers could form their own associations was, however, fundamental and increasingly popular within the various trades. It became a major topic of discussion in republican and worker-based publications. The main difference was between those who wished to keep competition between associations in order to ensure labor discipline and technological innovation and those who looked for eventual monopolistic control of a whole trade. The movement was to culminate in statutes for a Union of Associations in 1849 (largely passed through the efforts of the socialist feminist Jeanne Deroin), which were just about to be put into practice when the leaders were arrested and the movement suppressed. There were, at that time, nearly three hundred socialist associations in Paris in 120 trades with as many as fifty thousand members. More than half of these survived until the coup d'état of 1851 led to their suppression.[33]

Community/Communism

Proudhon was vigorously opposed to community. If "property was theft," then "community is death," he argued.[34] Many speakers at the 1840 communist banquet viewed *communism* and *community* as interchangeable terms, and Proudhon abhorred centralized political power and decision-making. Dézamy, one of the chief organizers of the banquet, wrote out an elaborate Code of Community in 1842, complete with a plan of the communal palace. Industrial parks and noxious facilities were dispersed into the countryside, and gardens and orchards were closer in. The code constituted a whole legal system governing relations within and between communities. Distributive and economic laws, industrial and rural laws, hygienic laws, educational laws, public order, and political laws and laws on the union of the sexes, absent the family, "with a view to preventing all discord and debauchery," were all specified. These laws were subsumed within a concept of community construed as "nothing other than the realization of unity and fraternity" as "the most real and fully complete unity, a unity in everything; in education, language, work, property, housing, in life, legislation and political activity, etc."[35] To many, like Proudhon, this seemed horribly oppressive.

Dézamy had been a close collaborator of Cabet but broke with him in part over the level of militancy, as well as over the details of how the ideal community might be organized. By the late 1840s, however, Cabet was by far the more influential communist, espousing pacific methods and rather more acceptable forms of community organization in Icaria: "The community suppresses egoism, individualism, privilege, domination, opulence, idleness and domesticity, transforming divided personal property into indivisible and social or common property. It modifies all commerce and industry. Therefore the establishment of the community is the greatest reform or revolution that humanity has ever attempted."[36] Both Proudhon and Cabet, as opposed to Fourier, Enfantin, and Dézamy, advocated traditional family life, arguing that the negative aspects of women's lives (which Cabet in particular recognized) would largely disappear with the reorganization of production and consumption along communal lines.

Cabet and Proudhon were indefatigable polemicists and organizers, and by the late 1840s the former's Icarian communist movement had become substantial, drawing support mainly from the working classes as then defined rather than from educated professionals (who tended to be Fourierist or Saint-Simonian in orientation), or from the déclassé radicals who supported Blanqui or the more radical wing of communism. As early as 1842, over a thousand Parisian workers signed the following declaration in Cabet's newspaper, *Le Populaire* (whose circulation rose to more than five thousand by 1848):

> It is said we want to live in idleness. . . . That is not true! We want to work in order to
> live; and we are more laborious than those who slander us. But sometimes work is lacking,
> sometimes it is too long, and kills us or ruins our health. Wages are insufficient for our most
> indispensable needs. These inadequate wages, unemployment, illness, taxes, old age—which
> comes so early to us—throw us into misery. It is horrible for a great number of us. There
> is no future, either for us or our children. This is not living! And yet we are the producers
> of all. Without us the rich would have nothing or would be forced to work to have bread,

clothes, furniture, and lodging. It is unjust! We want a different organization of labor; that is why we are communists.[37]

Cabet's efforts at class collaboration with reform-minded republicans were, however, rebuffed, forcing him to recognize by the late 1840s that his was a workers'-only movement. In 1847 his thinking turned to Christianity, and he suddenly decided that emigration to the United States and the founding of Icaria there was the answer. Johnston surmises that Cabet was not temperamentally able to confront the possibility, as Marx and Engels subsequently did, that class struggle (perhaps even violent forms of it) against the bourgeoisie was the only path to radical progress. In this, Cabet may well have been in tune with much worker sentiment; as Rancière repeatedly shows, the workers writing in their own journals "demanded dignity, autonomy, and treatment as equals with masters without having to resort to undignified street demonstrations."[38] Cabet carried many of his followers with him and thereby, as Marx complained, diverted many a good communist from the revolutionary tasks in Europe. But what also clearly separated Marx from Cabet was the geographical scale on which they envisaged solutions. Cabot could never think much beyond the small-scale integrated community characterized by face-to-face contact and intimacy as the framework within which communist alternatives must be cast.

THE ORGANIZATION OF WORK AND LABOR

While the writers of the time criticized many aspects of their contemporary social order, everyone acknowledged that the question of work and of labor was fundamental both to the critique of existing social arrangements and to proposed solutions. Again and again, the degrading conditions that did exist were contrasted with a world that might be. And the belief that labor produced the value which the bourgeoisie appropriated and consumed was widespread. But alternative visions varied widely.

Fourier, for example, saw the solution as a matter of matching variety of work with his elaborate understandings of passionate attractions. The social division of labor would disappear entirely, and work would be equivalent to play. This was probably the least practicable aspect of Fourier's system, since it probably could happen only in a world devoid of significant industry and then at only the smallest of scales. When something akin to his Phalanstères did come into being, they functioned more as pioneer forms of localized consumer and living cooperatives than as vigorous production enterprises. Nevertheless, Fourier's insistence that the activity of laboring defines our relation to nature and the inherent qualities of human nature has been a recurrent locus of critique of the labor process under both capitalism and socialism/communism. It continues to echo down to this day. The Saint-Simonians, on the other hand, were prepared to reorganize the division of labor on much larger scales and with an eye to greater efficiency. But this depended upon the administrative and technical skills of an industrial elite who would designate tasks and positions for workers who would be expected to submit willingly to their dictates. The benefit to the workers depended on the moral presumption that everything would be organized to be of greatest benefit to the poorest classes (the parallel with John Rawls's contemporary theory of justice is interesting).

There was little in Saint-Simonian doctrine to suggest that quality of work experience was important. Almost any kind of labor system, such as those later called Taylorism and Fordism, would be entirely compatible (as Lenin believed) with socialism/communism as well as with capitalism. The Saint-Simonians who became influential during the Second Empire adopted an eclectic stance to the labor question, conveniently forgetting the moral imperative to render justice. Proudhon's sterling defense of principles of justice in 1858 was designed to highlight this omission. But the "Saint-Simonian vision as well as the subsequent Marxist dream of mechanized socialist mankind wresting a bountiful living from a stingy and hostile environment would have seemed a horrible nightmare of rapine to Fourier, for he knew that the natural destiny of the globe was to become a horticultural paradise, an ever-varying English garden."[39]

Models of what much later came to be called worker self-management or *autogestion* also abounded in the 1840s with Proudhon's mutualism, Cabet's communism, and even Leroux's Christian communitarianism emerging as competing variants. But Proudhon got into all manner of tangles as he sought to come up with a labor *numéraire* (money notes) to reflect the fact that laborers produced the value and needed to be remunerated according to the value they produced. Proudhon mainly oriented his thinking to the small-scale workshop or enterprise, and was far less comfortable with any attempt to consciously organize large-scale projects that might involve what he considered degrading conditions of detailed divisions of labor. This led him back to accept the necessary evil of competition as a coordinating device, and he tried to put a positive gloss on the anarchy of the market by praising what he at one point called "anarchistic mutualism" as the most adequate social form to allocate labor to tasks in a socially beneficial manner. All of this was to bring a series of scathing responses from Marx after 1848.[40]

These arguments have, interestingly, been revived in recent years, particularly since the publication of Piore and Sable's *The Second Industrial Divide*. They argue that a magnificent opportunity to organize labor according to radically different principles, in small-scale firms under worker control, was lost around 1848, only to appear again with the new technologies that allowed flexible specialization, self-management at a small scale, and the dispersal of production to new industrial districts (such as "the third Italy") from the 1970s onward. The organizational form that got lost in 1848 was, according to them, largely that proposed by Proudhon (minus his misogyny) rather than those of Fourier, Cabet, Louis Blanc, Saint-Simon, or the communists. Competition was beneficial, and there was nothing inherently wrong with capital ownership and dependency on institutions of credit, provided these could be organized along "mutualist" lines. Had this transpired in the mid-nineteenth century, we would, they argue, have been spared the disasters that flowed from the factory system organized by large-scale (often monopoly) capital and the equally miserable factory systems of communism.

This has been a controversial argument, of course, both historically and today. Piore and Sable shunted aside the problem that what might be attractive to labor about flexible specialization might also provide abundant opportunities for irresponsible and decentralized forms of subcontracting and flexible accumulation on the part of capital. That the latter is the dominant story in the recent history of capitalism seems to me undeniable and, as we shall see, industrial organization in Second Empire Paris avidly exploited small-scale structures of subcontracting more than large-scale factories (see chapter 8).[41] But by the same token, it also has to be admitted that the Saint-Simonian and Marxist solutions have been found wanting. The labor question, as debated in France in the 1840s, placed a whole range of issues on the table that still need to be addressed. And if we can hear echoes in today's anti-globalization movements of Proudhon's mutualism, Leroux's Christian communitarianism, Fourier's theories of passionate attraction and emancipation, Cabet's version of community/communism, and Buchez's theories of associationism, then we can derive some historical lessons from France in the 1840s at the same time that we can deepen our grasp of the key issues involved.

THE URBAN QUESTION:
MODERNITY BEFORE HAUSSMANN?

It was in the banner year of 1840 that the twenty-nine-year-old engineer/architect César Daly launched his *Revue Générale de l'Architecture et des Travaux Publics*, a journal that was to be a central vehicle for discussion of architectural, urban design, and urbanization questions for the next fifty years or more.[42] In introducing the first issue, Daly wrote:

> When one recalls that it is engineers and architects who are charged to preside over the constructions that shelter human beings, livestock and the products of the earth; that it is they who erect thousands of factories and manufacturing establishments to house prodigious industrial activity; who build immense cities furnished with splendid monuments, traversed by straightened rivers encased in cyclopean walls, basins carved out of rock, and docks which harbor entire fleets of ships; that it is they who facilitate communications between peoples by the creation of roads and canals, who throw bridges over rivers, viaducts across deep valleys, pierce tunnels through mountains; that it is they who take the surplus waters from low and humid places to spread them over arid and sterile lands, thereby allowing of an immense expansion of agricultural lands, modifying and improving the soil itself; it is they who, undeterred by any difficulty, inscribe everywhere in the land through durable and well-made monuments testimonials to the power of genius and the works of man; when one reflects on the immense utility and the absolute necessity of these works and the thousands to whom they give employment, one is naturally led to appreciate the importance of the science to which we owe these marvelous creations and to feel that the slightest progress in these matters is of interest to all the countries of the globe.[43]

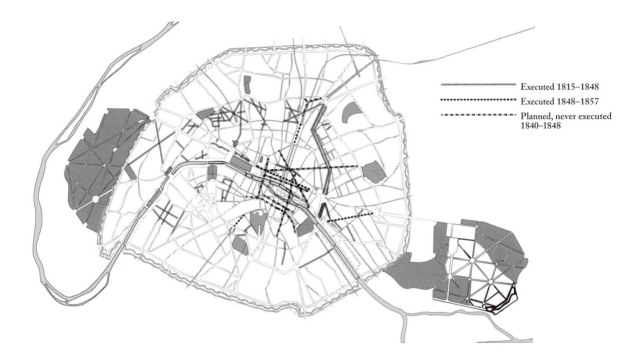

Executed 1815–1848

Executed 1848–1857

Planned, never executed
1840–1848

The tone is Saint-Simonian, which is, on the surface, somewhat odd, given that Daly had been very much influenced by Fourier. The *Revue* often merged the Saint-Simonian penchant for large-scale public projects and the Fourierist insistence that they be articulated according to well-reasoned, "scientific," and harmonic (i.e., Fourierist) principles. Considérant, the leading Fourierist of the time, contributed to the *Revue*, and his occasional collaborator Perreymond (whose actual identity is not known) wrote an extraordinary series of articles on the need to reorganize the interior space of Paris.

Most of the administrators, thinkers, and writers of the period had something to say, either directly or indirectly, about the urban question. They had to, because it was too obvious and too pressing an issue to be avoided. The up and coming Adolphe Thiers took on the Ministry of Commerce and Public Works in 1833, and spent a good deal of time and money on monumental projects and getting bills passed to finance canals, roadworks, and railways. His main contribution, for which he was roundly criticized, was to spend vast sums on the new system of fortifications to protect Paris from invasion. Thirty-five years later, in an odd twist of fate, he had to break through those same fortifications in order to crush the Paris Commune. The prefect of Paris, Rambuteau, set about devising and implementing plans to improve communications (including the street that still bears his name). Urban health and hygiene became a big issues after the devastating cholera epidemic of 1832. And the architect Jacques Hittorff was busy designing the Place de la

FIGURE 25 *The new road systems realized and proposed during the 1840s.*

Concorde and several other projects that animated the drift of the center of Paris toward the north and west. This drift, largely impelled by speculative building (of the sort that Balzac describes around the Madeleine in *César Birroteau*) was creating a new Paris to the north and west of the overcrowded and congested center. Lanquetin, an ambitious businessman who headed up the City Council in the late 1830s, commissioned a plan for the revitalization of Paris that was far-reaching as well as fiscally ambitious. This was not, therefore, a period of inaction. What Pinon somewhat inaccurately calls "the utopians of 1840" pressed a number of concrete plans for reordering the city streets, some of which were actually realized (see figure 28).[44] The difference between this activity and Haussmann's was twofold. First, there was little in the way of grand vision at the metropolitan scale incorporated into practices (as opposed to ideas). The clearances were piecemeal and the scale of action cautious. Second, Rambuteau was reluctant to exceed the city's budget; fiscal conservativism was the rule, and Rambuteau was proud of it.

There was, however, no shortage of ideas. Most of the grand thinkers of the period had something to say about the urban question. Fourier's first encounter with Paris in the 1790s, with "its spacious boulevards, its handsome town houses and its Palais Royal had inspired him to devise the 'rules' of a new type of 'unitary architecture' which was later to become the basis for the blueprints of his ideal city." As early as 1796 he had been "so struck by the monotony and ugliness of our modern cities" that he had conceived of "the model of a new type of city," designed in such a way as to "prevent the spread of fires and banish the mephitism which, in cities of all sizes, literally wages war against the human race."[45] And by 1808 he clearly saw "the problems of urban squalor and cut-throat economic competition as symptoms of a deeper social sickness." But his alternative designs for urban living, elaborated over the years, were far more suited to an agrarian horticultural society with internalized production and consumption, and harmonized sexual relations, than they were to industrial activities and the extensive networks of trading relations arising out of improved communications in the Paris of the time. Benjamin suggests that "Fourier recognized the architectural canon of the phalanstère" in the arcades. But there are, Marrey notes, reasons to doubt this.[46] The arcades were mostly built before the 1830s as ground-level commercial spaces; Fourier's analogous spaces were residential and on the second floor, and more likely modeled on the long galleries in the Louvre and at Versailles. Fourier made no explicit mention of the arcades until the 1830s. The Phalanstère did, however, prove influential within the history of urban design, though not necessarily in the way that Fourier thought of it. It provided an architectural prototype (once modified and stripped of many of its social features, particularly those pertaining to sexual and social relations) for various experiments by industrialists with collective and cooperative living arrangements, such as the *cités ouvrières* tried out in the early years of the Second Empire. But the Phalanstère did not offer an alternative urban plan for restructuring the urban body politic as a whole. Fourier's schemas were too freighted with nostalgia for some lost past and too small-scale to offer tangible help for reconstruction of a city like Paris.

The same difficulty arose with many of the other thinkers of the time. While

Proudhon showed occasional glimpses of being able to think bigger (witness his intuition that much depended upon the restructuring of credit institutions), he never really escaped the scale of the artisan workshops of Lyon that inspired much of his thinking. Leroux (expectedly) and Cabet (disappointingly) got no further than experiments with small-scale communities. Cabet's efforts turned out to be as disastrous in practice when founded in America as they were in theory. The communists showed some signs of being able to think bigger. Dézamy's urban code diverged from Fourier's in part because he emphasized collective property rights and radical egalitarianism, but also because he proposed the communal organization of both work and living within a system of territorially organized communes in fraternal communication and support of each other. Industrial armies would "carry out immense work projects of culture, afforestation, irrigation, canals, railroads, embankments of rivers and streams, etc." Careful attention would be paid to matters of health and hygiene, and the communes should be situated in locations most suited to health.[47] In addition to zoning codes to assure rational land uses in relation to human health and well-being, the communes should be administered and regulated in such a way as to provide equal education, sustenance, and nurture to everyone. Here, indeed, was a complete body politic on an extensive if not large scale, which incorporated the best of Cabet and Fourier in combination with the principles of Babeuf and Blanqui and the administrative ideals of Saint-Simon. But what rendered so much of this utopian and nostalgic was a fierce attachment to the ideal of small, face-to-face communities.

There was a disjunction, therefore, between the rapidly transforming realities of urban life and many of these utopian plans. There were exceptions, however. Saint-Simon had appealed to the leading industrialists and scientists to take matters in hand, and to the polytechnicians and engineers who had the know-how to rethink the city at the requisite scale. He also insisted that the seeds of any alternative must be found in the contradictions of the present. And although Saint-Simonians dispersed and dissipated their energies as a coherent movement in the early 1830s, their ideas had wide currency among a technical elite of financiers, scientists, engineers, and architects (as Daly's statement illustrates). The reforms envisaged by others were on such a small scale that they could never aspire to anything more than a localized radicalization of social relations, of working and living conditions in the city. Either that, or they were conceptualized as new communities to be constructed in "empty" spaces such as the Americas (Cabet) or the colonies (Algeria, then in course of occupation, frequently featured in discussions; Enfantin, still considering himself the father of the Saint-Simonian movement, wrote a detailed book on plans for the colonization of Algeria along Saint-Simonian lines in 1843).

The big exceptions were the Fourierists, Considérant and Perreymond, who in effect scaled up Fourier's ideas of harmony and passionate attraction to merge with Saint-Simonian thought. Both considered the railroads as they were then being built to be destructive of human interests and a primary agent in the degradation of the human relation to nature. They were not opposed to improvements in communications, but objected that they were being implemented in an irrational way; that they promoted increasing centralization of power and capital among a financial elite in the large cities; that they operated to stimulate industry and urban development rather than the all-important agriculture; and that the penchant for the "straight line" was being superimposed upon a sensually more satisfying relation to nature. They proposed the nationalization of the rail network and its construction according to rational harmonic (i.e., Fourierist) principles and without resort to private capital. The government was impressed, and produced a national charter for railroad construction, but centered it radially on Paris and inserted a clause that allowed of private exploitation. Interestingly, Benjamin cites Considerant's objections to the railways at some length but ignores his positive suggestions.[48]

Considérant and Perreymond likewise offered extensive arguments for the thorough amelioration of Paris's problems, and did so in a way that was practical and plausible enough to avoid the charge of vacuous utopianism. The most systematic consideration of this question was given by Perreymond in a series of articles beginning in 1842, titled "Studies on the City of Paris."[49] The chaos, disorder and congestion that beset the city center, the lack of harmonious relations between the parts, and the drift of activity toward the north and west was the main focus of concern. Perreymond produced a careful and empirically grounded diagnostic of the situation and then appealed to Fourier's scientific principles to come up with a solution. He argued that the city must return to its traditional center and then be linked outward to its many growing parts in a coherent and harmonious way. This entailed a radical restructuring of internal communications within the city (including a better positioning of rail access and the building of boulevards), but just as important was a complete reconstruction of the city center. He proposed that the left branch of the Seine be covered over from Austerlitz to the Pont-Neuf and the space used to bring together commercial, industrial, administrative, religious, and cultural functions in a rejuvenated city center that would also depend on the total clearance of properties from the Ile de la Cité.

Perreymond provided engineering specifications and financial calculations to prove the feasibility of his project. He was prepared for debt financing and was critical of Rambuteu's fiscal conservativism. Here was a plan every bit as daring and ambitious as anything that Haussmann was later to devise. When taken together with proposals on the railways, it effectively addressed the issue of the role and structure of the Parisian metropolitan space in relation to the national space. It was by almost any measure modernist in tone but the big difference from Haussmann is that Perreymond eschewed appeal to the circulation of capital and private speculation in land and property. He insisted that state interventions should work to the benefit of all rather than for a privileged elite of financiers. Probably for that very reason this grand but practical plan was never seriously discussed.

Similarly far-reaching proposals came from Meynadier, whose book *Paris Pittoresque et Monumentale* was published in 1843. Like Perreymond, Meynadier insisted on the revitalization of the city center by clearances and by the construction of a much more rational system of roads to integrate with the rail system. His detailed plans for new boulevards in many ways anticipated, as Marchand points out, Haussmann's proposals (particularly given his advocacy of the straight line).[50] The clearance and replacement of insalubrious dwellings was also considered a priority, particularly in the old city center. Meynadier was deeply concerned with questions of health and hygiene, and also pushed very hard on the idea of a park system for Paris to rival that of London. And if access to the rejuvenating powers of nature was not to be available within the city, then the suburbs and the countryside could provide a restful alternative if access was created. Balzac's pastoral fantasy could be realized in the form of the little house in the country. In many respects, Haussmann realized in practice in the 1850s much of what Meynadier had earlier proposed.

Considérant, Perreymond, Meynadier, and even Lanquentin, produced practical plans rather than utopian ideals, even though their thinking was animated by Saint-Simonian and Fourierist ideas. It is against the ferment of this kind of thinking that we have to read what Haussmann actually did. He did not begin from scratch, and owed an immense debt to these pioneering ways of thought (he surely read Daly's *Revue*). The problem for him was that these ideas arose out of political presuppositions and utopian dreams that were in many respects anathema to Bonapartism. Hence the myth that Haussmann propagated of a radical break. That much of what he did was already present in embryo in the 1830s and 1840s does not, however, detract from the fact that modernity, as argued in the introduction, entered a new and distinctive phase after 1848 and that Haussmann contributed immensely to how this new form of modernity was articulated.

WHAT GOT LOST IN 1848?

The world did not get turned right side up in 1848. The socialist revolution failed, and many of those who had been engaged in its production were sidelined, exiled, or simply repressed after the coup d'état of December 1851. The counterrevolution that set in after 1848 had the effect of turning upside down many of the hopes and desires, and reining in the proliferating sense of possibilities, that had been so fulsomely articulated in the 1830s and 1840s. For what really clashed on the boulevards in June of 1848 were two radically different conceptions of modernity. The first was thoroughly bourgeois. It was founded on the rock of private property and sought freedoms of speech and of action in the market, and the kind of liberty and equality that goes with money power. Its most articulate spokesman was Adolphe Thiers, who would have been perfectly content with a constitutional monarchy if the monarch had not perverted matters. Thiers, who had been a minister in the 1830s, was certainly willing to step in to try to save the monarchy in the February days of 1848. He then became the guiding light for the so-called "Party of Order" that emerged in the National Assembly after the elections of April 1848, and avidly sought to guide national policy toward the protection of bourgeois rights and privileges.

The second conception of modernity, far less coherent than the first, was founded on the idea of a social republic, capable of nurturing the population as a whole and dealing with the conditions of impoverishment and degradation in which the majority of the French people, both in the countryside and in the burgeoning cities, lived. It was ambivalent about private property and frequently confused over what might be meant by equality, liberty, and community, but it had a deep faith in the idea that associated forms of labor and of communal activities would provide an alternative basis for more adequate forms of social relations and standards of provision. This movement spoke with many voices—Louis Blanc, Lamartine, Blanqui, Proudhon, Jeanne Deroin, Cabet, Considérant, Leroux—and often pointed in multiple directions. But it had a sufficiently powerful following to constitute a serious threat to the bourgeois version—itself beset also by threats from the more traditional right with its largely conservative provincial base, which was thoroughly alarmed by any kind of modernity. This quest for the social republic was what was smashed on the barricades of June, just as the hopes for the bourgeois version were put on hold by the coup d'état of December 1851. The Second Empire, it turned out, sought a third kind of modernity, one which mixed authoritarianism with an uneasy respect for private property and the market punctuated with periodic attempts to cultivate its populist base.

But all kinds of consequences followed from the debacle of 1848. For if the conception of a social republic was repressed, then how could that powerful association between the city and the republic as a body politic be sustained? How, even, might the city be represented once its status as a sentient being and a body politic was denied? The result was a crisis of representation. The Revolution of 1848 was, therefore, the crucial factor separating radically different ways of representing the city. This was true not only for Haussmann's difference from his predecessors Berger and Rambuteau. The difference can also be traced in the way the city gets represented in the works of Balzac and Flaubert.[51]

Balzac wrote impressionistically and with broad brushstokes, producing a visionary psychogeography of an urban world in perpetual flux. In Balzac's world, the flaneur had the possibility of absolute knowledge and could aspire to mastery of the city and its secrets. Flaubert wrote with an analytical scalpel, dissecting things, sentence by sentence, to produce a positivist aesthetic in which the city is presented as a static work of art. Reduced to an aesthetic object, however, the city loses the social and political, as well as personal, meanings that Balzac communicated so well. The flaneur in Flaubert's world stands for anomie and alienation rather than for discovery. Frédéric in *Sentimental Education* is a flaneur who wanders the city without ever clearly knowing where he is or registering the significance of what he is doing. "Frédéric never perceives [the city] clearly"; the "line between reality and reverie" remains perpetually blurred.[52]

Recall, for example, how Balzac puts together environments, including the minutest details of furnishings of rooms and the personalities of the people who inhabit them (the vivid description of Paquita's boudoir in *The Girl with the Golden Eyes*, or the way Madame Vauquer's character is established in *Old Goriot*). Flaubert gets the idea. In *Sentimental Education*, the first sight Frédéric has of Madame Arnoux (with whom he falls madly in love) has him wondering "What was her name, her home, her life, her past?

He longed to know the furniture in her room. . . ." But when Flaubert does offer actual descriptions of furniture, rooms and even whole neighborhoods (as minute and careful as anything Balzac delivers), any relation to their human occupants is entirely coincidental. Consider the following passage:

> Finally he entered a sort of boudoir which was unevenly lit by stained-glass windows. The wood above the doors had been carved in a clover design; behind a balustrade, three purple mattresses formed a divan, on which there lay the tube of a platinum hookah. Instead of a mirror there was a pyramid of little shelves over the mantelpiece, bearing a whole collection of curios: old silver watches, Bohemian vases, jewelled brooches, jade buttons, enamels, Chinese porcelain figures and a little Byzantine Virgin with a silver-gilt cope. All of this merged together in a kind of golden twilight, with the bluish colour of the carpet, the mother of pearl gleam of the stools, and the fawned tint of the wall lined with brown leather. On pedestals in the corners of the room there were bronze vases containing bunches of flowers whose scent hung heavy in the air.
>
> Rosanette appeared, dressed in a pink satin jacket, white cashmere trousers, a necklace of piastres, and a red skull-cap with a spray of jasmine twined around it."[53]

No wonder Frédéric (like the reader) "gave a start of surprise" at the incongruity of it all. The difference between this description and Balzac's handling of Paquita's boudoir in *The Girl with the Golden Eyes* (see above, p. 45) is striking. Concludes Ferguson:

> Ultimately Paris, like Mme Arnoux, is not so much unconquerable as evanescent. Flaubert takes such care to join the two because Frederic views each in much the same light. Everything about Paris "related to her" and Frederic's conviction that "any attempt to make her his mistress would be in vain" applies equally to his perception of Paris. The city, too, is a sphinx whose enigma Frederic never solves. His halfhearted attempts to conquer the one and the other, the woman and the city, succumb to the inertia induced by reverie. It is not by accident that here as elsewhere Flaubert takes the Balzacian model only to reverse it. Both writers associate Paris with a woman and flaneur with male desire. But the correspondence of the trope only highlights the difference between these worlds. The metaphor that Balzac uses to imply possession is used by Flaubert to signify precisely the opposite. In *l'Education Sentimentale* desire is dreamed, never realized.[54]

Rightly or wrongly, Balzac, along with many others of his time (such as the utopian thinkers and urban theorists who sought an adequate reconstruction of the city), believed they could possess their city and make it their own, and in remaking it, remake themselves if not the social order. But after 1848, it was Haussmann and the developers, the speculators, and the financiers, and the forces of the market that possessed the city and reshaped it to their own specific interests and ends, leaving the mass of the population with a sense of loss and dispossession. This is a condition that Flaubert for one passively accepts.

There is, therefore, no unitary definition of the city as a totality, let alone as a "sentient being" or a "body politic." Flaubert reduces the city to a stage set that, no matter how beautifully constructed and sublimely furnished, functions as a backdrop to the human action that proceeds in and upon it. The city becomes a dead object (as it largely does in Haussmann's planning). *Sentimental Education*, published in 1869, after Haussmann has done his work, is rife with elaborate (and quite brilliant) descriptions of the inanimate objects that make up the city. The city gains in our sense of it as an independent work of art (to be admired and criticized as such) but entirely loses its character as a "sentient being" or "body politic."

It was, we might infer, the idea of the city as a body politic that got smashed in 1848 and then interred in the commercial world of commodification and spectacle in Second Empire Paris. This, presumably, is what Clark had in mind. But he is not quite right, however, to imply that the idea of the city as a body politic got entirely lost through the advent of Empire and Haussmannization. Louis Napoleon evoked "the Emperor's two bodies" in a masculine and paternalistic (as opposed to feminine) form. The body politic of Empire functioned as a captivating ideology, and it was within that frame that certain Saint-Simonian principles and influences could play their role, albeit in bowdlerized form (Enfantin even opened his *Science of Man*, published in 1858, with an open letter of praise for Louis Napoleon). The history of the Second Empire can be read as an attempt to reconstitute a sense of the body politic around imperial power in the face of forces of capital accumulation that Clark is quite correct to see as antagonistic to such a political form. Economic liberalization (beginning with the former Saint-Simonian Michel Chevalier's free trade treaty with Britain in 1860) gradually undermined imperial power. The Empire was brought down just as much by capital as by republicanism (much of which was attached in any case to the liberties of private property and entrepreneurial freedoms) or worker opposition. What was clearly lost in 1848 was, however, any idea of the body politic as a nurturing state, as signified in Daumier's iconography.

The ferment of debate also got lost. The period between 1830 and 1848 in France was incredibly rich in ideas about alternatives. It was the period when both socialism and communism began to take shape intellectually as well as politically. There was a general unsettling of ways of thought. All manner of different visions and speculative possibilities were opened up. Some of the wilder and more bizarre suggestions have all the qualities of science fiction and real utopian writing, but much of it also had a strong practical bent, producing a plethora of political movements and not a few practical plans, some of which actually saw the light of day. Something plainly had to be done about the condition of the working classes, the degraded condition of the poor, the insalubrity and chaotic disorder of the cities, and the impoverished life imposed upon the masses (including the peasantry) by a rigidly class-bound society. As with any unduly rigid structure, the pressures that were building within it could in the end only crack it apart. And crack apart they finally did in the Revolution of 1848. How it all subsequently got put back together again in an equally rigid structure of Empire from which creative thinkers were banished and within which creative alternative thoughts were repressed is another story. The Empire flourished for a while, but then it in turn gradually weakened before the power of capital.

It finally also cracked apart in war and revolutionary violence in 1870–1871. But by then much had been changed in Paris as a distinctively capitalist form of modernity came to dominate and shape the capital city in very specific ways. Open questions of representation, made so much of before 1848, were, after 1851, rendered subservient to a remarkable program of materialist transformation. But if, as Marx has it, what separates the worst of architects from the best of bees is that the architect erects a structure in the imagination before making it real upon the ground, then the imaginative exercises undertaken during the period from 1830 to 1848 prepared the way for much that was to follow, even though those who carried out the practical work upon the ground saw fit to deny many of the sources of their own inspiration.

Part Two

Materializations:
Paris 1848–1870

FIGURE 26 *Gustave Doré (1860) uses all his allegorical power to evoke the radical transfor-mation of Paris—Haussmann pores over the map of Paris above, and below the carters take away the medieval structures, to the cheers of the workers.*

CHAPTER THREE

PROLOGUE

Paris is indeed an ocean. Sound it: you will never touch bottom. Survey it, report on it! However scrupulous your survey and reports, however numerous and persistent the explorers of this sea may be, there will always remain virgin places, undiscovered caverns, flowers, pearls, monsters—there will always be something extraordinary, missed by the literary diver.

—BALZAC

If everything were as it seems on the surface, there would be no need for science.

—MARX

Paris in 1850 was a city seething with social, economic, and political problems and possibilities. Some saw it as a sick city, wracked by political torments, torn apart by class struggles, sinking beneath its own weight of decadence, corruption, crime, and cholera. Others saw it as a city of opportunity for private ambition or social progress; if the right keys to the mystery of the city's possibilities were found, the whole of Western civilization stood to be transformed. The city had, after all, grown rapidly in population, from 786,000 in 1831 to more than 1,000,000 in 1846 (table 1). Its industry had undergone a remarkable growth, and it had even enhanced its traditional centralized role as the national hub of communications, finance, commerce, culture, and, of course, state administration. With such a dynamic past, how could it not have a dynamic future?

But in 1850 the city seemed to be trapped within a double straitjacket, each of which appeared to reinforce the other. It was, first of all, caught in the aftermath of the deepest and most widespread crisis of capital yet experienced. The city had seen many an economic crisis before, usually triggered by natural calamity or war. But this one was different. It could

FIGURE 27 *Daumier's Nouveau Paris (1862) captures many facets of the changes that Haussmannization brought about. It reads: "How happy it is for people in a hurry that they have enlarged the means of communication." The bourgeois studies his watch, the wife and child hesitate, the traffic is intense.*

not easily be attributed solely to God or nature. To be sure, there had been harvest failures in 1846–1847 that brought misery to the countryside and a flood of distressed people to the city, seeking employment or assistance. But capitalism had matured by 1848 to a sufficient degree that even the blindest bourgeois apologist could see that financial conditions, reckless speculation (particularly with respect to the railways), and overproduction had something to do with the human tragedy that swept out of Britain in 1847 and quickly engulfed the whole of what was then the capitalist world. Most of Europe experienced the same crisis simultaneously, making it difficult to confine its interpretation solely within national narratives of government failure of this or that sort. This was a full-fledged crisis of capitalist overaccumulation, in which massive surpluses of capital and labor power lay side by side with apparently no way open to reunite them in profitable union. In 1848, reform of capitalism or its revolutionary overthrow stared everyone starkly in the face.

TABLE 1 *The Population of Paris, 1831–1876*

Year	Old Paris	Communes Annexed in 1860	Paris after 1860	% Change
1831	785,866	75,574	861,436	
1836	899,313	103,320	1,002,633	16.39
1841	936,261	124,564	1,059,825	5.70
1846	1,053,897	173,083	1,226,980	15.77
1851	1,053,261	223,802	1,277,064	4.08
1856	1,174,346	364,257	1,538,613	20.48
1861			1,696,141	10.24
1866			1,825,274	7.61
1872			1,851,792	1.45
1876			1,988,800	7.45

Source: Chevalier (1950).

That Paris led the way and took the revolutionary path was not entirely fortuitous. And it was more than just that famed revolutionary tradition, which had the citizens of Paris put political interpretations on the least sign of economic difficulty, take to the streets, erect barricades, and proclaim their rights as the rights of man.[1] For the other straitjacket that held the city down was a veritable eighteenth-century structure of social practices and infrastructures dominating manufacturing, finance, commerce, government, and labor relations, to say nothing of the still mainly medieval frame of physical infrastructures within which these activities and practices were confined. Despite all of the talk of urban renewal and occasional practical stabs at it during the July Monarchy, Paris had been overwhelmed. Chevalier writes:

> In these years Paris looked around and was unable to recognize itself. Another, larger city had overflowed into the unaltered framework of streets, mansions, houses and passageways, piling man on man and trade on trade, filling every nook and corner, making over the older dwellings of the nobility and gentry into workshops and lodging houses, erecting factories and stockpiles in gardens and courts where carriages had been moldering quietly away, packing the suddenly shrunken streets and the now overpopulated gothic graveyards, resurrecting and overloading the forgotten sewers, spreading litter and stench into the adjacent countryside.[2]

While there was nothing unique about the accompanying human misery, degradation, disease, crime, and prostitution—common enough features within the industrial capitalism of the time—this ancient urban infrastructure was incompatible with the

FIGURE 28 *The streets of the old Paris, here represented by two Marville photos of the early 1850s, were narrow and inhospitable to movement, insalubrious (note the sewage perpetually draining on the streets) and lined with often crumbling buildings. Note how on the right, the advertisements for omnibus and railway travel promise another world of space relations to that with which the old Paris is encrusted.*

increasingly sophisticated and efficient capitalist organization of production and consumption emerging in the new manufacturing towns not only in Britain—France's main commercial rival—but also in Belgium, Germany, Austria, and even certain other regions of France. For though Paris had enhanced its position in the international division of labor after the revolution of 1830, it had done so less through transformations in its systems of production than through piecemeal adaptation of old methods. A growing detail and social division of labor, backed by the special qualities of its output and the volume of its internal market, had been the basis of its manufacturing dynamism. Even its commerce—long far more important to its economic health than its manufacturing—was bottled up in congested streets, hindered by tolls and barriers of all kinds, and chronically inefficient in its mode of handling and distributing goods. To the degree that Paris had not moved effectively to meet the new and rather exacting requirements of capital accumulation, its agony during the crisis of 1847–1848 was double and more prolonged, its path to recovery strewn with all manner of particular obstacles, compounded by a political and cultural evolution that created nothing but doubt, confusion, and fear.

Different segments of society saw the crisis quite differently. The craft workers, for example, armed with corporatist traditions, saw deskilling, loss of independence, dignity, and respect, fragmentation of tasks—and chronic insecurity of employment—all increasingly imposed by capitalist control of production and distribution, as the core of the problem. The February Revolution allowed them to put the question of labor and the right to work on the political agenda and to assert their right to be treated with dignity and respect, as equals in the body politic. The social republic, as we have seen, was as important to them as the political republic. In this they had a strange assortment of bourgeois allies, running all the way from small masters and shopkeepers, who felt equally threatened by the new systems of production and distribution, to déclassé radicals (journalists, artists, and writers, as well as die-hard Jacobin revolutionaries like Blanqui) and Romantic poets and writers (like Lamartine, Hugo, and George Sand), who believed in the nobility of work and labor within the relatively safe confines of a romanticized artisan tradition. Though the Romantics were quickly undeceived when they encountered real workers on the barricades, the social movements of the 1840s intersected with craft workers' consciousness to generate, as we saw in chapter 2, a host of expectations as to how a nurturing social republic would work.

Such socialist sentiment plainly alarmed the bourgeoisie. Fear of the "reds" compounded their confusion as to how to represent, explain, and react to a political-economic crisis that demanded remedial action. Some saw archaic structures and practices of government and finance as the root of the problem, and sought to modernize the French state, liberate the flows of capital, and give greater impetus to the economy. Progressive elements in Paris had also long sought strong state interventions to rationalize and renew plainly failing physical infrastructures. But their efforts were stymied by other factions of the bourgeoisie, trapped either in a fiscal conservatism that guaranteed total paralysis at a time of severe economic depression, or by traditional rights to property ownership (largely absentee and rural) that seemed to offer hope of personal salvation in the midst of national ruin. Many of the landowners fled the city in 1848 and took their purchasing power with them. This helped plunge Parisian industry, commerce, and property markets even deeper into the mire of depression.

The confused series of events that brought "that cretin" (the phrase is due to that impeccable bourgeois, Adolphe Thiers, rather than to Marx) Louis-Napoleon Bonaparte to power, first as President of the Republic (elected by universal suffrage) in December 1848 and four years later as emperor, need not detain us unduly, since there are abundant and quite brilliant accounts elsewhere, beginning, of course, with Marx's *Class Struggles in France, 1848–1850* and the *Eighteenth Brumaire*.[3] Suffice it to remark that the questions of work and of a socialist response to the crisis were swept off the immediate political agenda in the savage repression of the June Days of 1848, when Parisian workers took to the streets to protest the closure of the National Workshops (the Second Republic's response to the demand for the right to work). But subsequent elections indicated that democratic socialist sentiment was alive and well. Worse still, it appeared not only in Paris and Lyon (where it was to be expected) but also in some rural areas, reminding France that the roots of its revolutionary as well as its reactionary tradition lay very much in the countryside. In the face of this threat, the bourgeoisie broadly welcomed the hitherto exiled but populist Louis Napoleon's election as President of the Republic in December 1848 and then submitted rather easily to the coup d'état of December 1851 and the declaration of Empire in December 1852.

FIGURE 29 *A photo portrait, by Riffaut, Mayer, and Saint-Victor, of Louis Napoleon Bonaparte.*

The other threat to the social order derived from the destruction and devaluation of assets attendant upon the general economic crisis. Caught up in internecine struggles, no single faction of the bourgeoisie had the authority or legitimacy to impose its will. To the degree that Louis Napoleon appeared to be a compromise whom each faction thought could be controlled, he was put in a position where he could play off popular will, factionalism, and traditional loyalties to the Napoleonic legend (particularly in the army), and thus consolidate a very personal power. This left him to face up to the whole complex of problems of reform and modernization, control of the labor movement and its pretensions, revival of the economy, and how to exit from the profound economic, political, and cultural malaise in which France languished between 1848 and 1851.

The eighteen years of the Second Empire were nowhere near as "cretinous" or "farcical" as Thiers and Marx (from opposite ends of the political spectrum) had predicted. They were a deadly serious experiment with a form of national socialism—an authoritarian state with police powers and a populist base. It collapsed, like most other experiments of its ilk, in the midst of dissension and war, but its tenure was marked by the imposition of intense labor discipline and the liberation of capital circulation from its preceding constraints. But it was not evident then (any more than now) exactly which new social practices, institutional frames and structures, or social investments would work. The Second Empire was, then, a phase of striving for adjustment to a burgeoning and demanding capitalism in which diverse economic and political interests consciously sought this or that advantage or this or that solution, only to find themselves all too frequently caught in the unintended consequences of their own actions.

It was in such a context that the Emperor and his advisers sought to liberate Paris—its life, culture, and economy—from constraints that bound it so tightly to an ancient past. While certain immediate needs were clear, such as improved access to the central market of Les Halles, slum clearance around the city center, and improved traffic circulation between the rail stations and into the civic center—there were a host of other questions that were much more problematical. There were problems of ends and means; the proper role of the state in relation to private interests and the circulation of capital; the degree of state intervention in labor markets, in industrial and commercial activity, in housing and social welfare provision; and the like. There was, above all, the political problem of how to get the Parisian economy back on its feet without sparking the solid resistance of a still powerful haute bourgeoisie, feeding the insecurities of a middle class always under threat of marginalization in spite of its seemingly solid implantation, and pushing the workers to outright revolt. From this standpoint we have to see the Emperor as ultimately the prisoner of the class forces he began by seeming to outwit with such abandon and disdain. That he was able to get so far and do so much merely testifies to the tremendous upset generated out of the heat of 1848, an upset that affected not only economy and polity but also traditional ways of representing the world and acting upon those representations. Here, too, Parisian life in the period 1848–1851 was in total turmoil, a turmoil that affected painting (this was, after all, the period of Courbet's breakthrough into an art world that could not comprehend what he was about), letters, science, and management, as well as industry, commerce, and labor relations. Only after all the tumult had quieted could the solid resistance to the authoritarianism of Empire begin.

Paris in 1870 was fundamentally changed from its condition in 1850. And the changes were far-reaching and deeply rooted, though not enough to prevent that other great event in Parisian history, the uprising that gave birth to the Paris Commune of 1871. But while there were continuities between the revolutions of 1848 and 1871, there was much that separated them. The eighteen years of Empire had bitten as deep into the consciousness of Parisians as Haussmann's works had cut open and reconstructed the physical fabric of the city.

As concerns the fate of the city, its delivery into Haussmann's hands in June 1853, seven months after the declaration of Empire, was undoubtedly significant.[4] Haussmann, as we have seen above (pp. 8–10), built a certain mythical account of its importance and fostered the perception of a total break with the past, with himself innocently implementing the Emperor's will. There may not have been a total break, but there certainly was a turning point. Haussmann was a far more Machiavellian figure than he revealed in his *Mémoires*. He was ambitious, fascinated by power, had his own passionate commitments (including a very particular view of public service), and was prepared to go to great lengths to realize his goals. He derived an extraordinary level of personal power directly from the authority of Louis Napoleon, and he was prepared to use it to its utmost. He was incredibly energetic and well-organized, had a great eye for details, and was prepared to flout opinion and subvert authority (even that of the Emperor), skate close to the limits of legality, finesse finances by what we now call "creative accounting," ride roughshod over the opinions of others, and make absolutely no concessions to democracy. He had long exhibited these traits, and almost certainly this is what made him so attractive to Louis Napoleon, compared to the fiscally conservative and democratically constrained prefect,

Berger, who Haussmann replaced. Haussmann reckoned, correctly up until at least the early 1860s, that the Emperor would always back him up. He immediately sidelined the municipal council (that had so constrained the cautious Berger) and ignored the planning commission (he claimed he did this with the Emperor's connivance but on this point, too, he plainly invented). He was, in short, an authoritarian Bonapartist, and he survived and thrived all the time Bonapartism remained intact. But as Bonapartism weakened and gradually gave way to liberalism in the 1860s, so Haussmann's position also weakened, culminating in his sacrificial dismissal in January 1870, when a liberal democrat, Emile Ollivier, became Prime Minister.

What is so intriguing about Haussmann is that while he understood only too well the seriousness of the macroeconomic problem he faced in the context of the specific crisis of Paris as an urban economy, his response included intense and often excruciating attention to details. He closely monitored the design of street furnishings (such as gas lamps, kiosks, and even the design of those street urinals known as *vespasiennes*). He was obsessed with details of alignments. He angled the Sully Bridge across the Seine so that it brought the Parthenon into a direct line with the Bastille column, and in an extraordinary feat of engineering he moved the Victory Column so that it was centered in the newly created Place Châtelet. Even more bizarre was his insistence that the architect Bailly displace the dome on his Tribunal de Commerce so that it was in the line of sight of those moving down the newly constructed Boulevard de Sebastopol. A local asymmetry was created to produce a symmetrical effect at a grander urban scale.

By the time Haussmann was dismissed, the processes of urban transformation he had set in motion had assumed such momentum that they were almost impossible to stop. Haussmannization—as represented, for example, by the completion of the Avenue de l'Opéra—continued for many years after his dismissal. The continuity in part depended upon the strong and loyal team of talented administrators and technocrats he assembled around him—Alphand to do the parks, Belgrand to engineer the water and sewers, Baltard to redo Les Halles, architects like Hittorff to build monumental works, Davioud to create fountains. They all had strong personalities and talents, and after their initial (and sometimes continuing) conflicts with Haussmann, they came to recognize that they, too, could give free reign to their talents with Haussmann's personal backing in the same way that Haussmann could give free reign to his with the backing of the Emperor. The fruits of the collaborations of these men are to be seen to this day. The park that centers the Square de Temple is by Alphand, the Mairie of the Third Arrondissement that faces onto it is by Hittorff, and the covered market alongside is by Baltard. The worth of these works had been so well proven, the reputations of the architects and administrators so well established, the logic of the unfolding of the urban plan so well entrenched, and the overall conception so well accepted that Paris developed largely along the lines Haussmann defined for the next thirty years or more.

By then, a new scale of action and thinking had also been defined that was difficult to reverse. This was nowhere better represented than in the transformation of Les Halles,

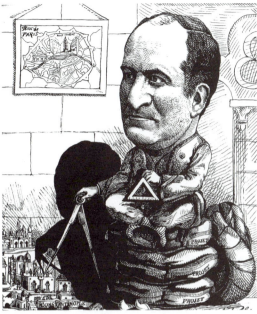

Figure 30 *Portrait of Haussmann by Petit, and a cartoon representation of him, as "Attila of the Straight line," armed with compass and set square, dominating the plan of Paris.*

because it was not simply a matter of the scale of individual buildings and of architectural style, but of a "new concept of commercial urbanism" that amounted to the production and engineering of a whole quarter of the city given over to a single function. The effect was to produce a whole new city texture. But then, Van Zanten argues, Haussmann seems to have lost his way: "In the early 1860s, when the initial projects of 1853 were finished or well underway, something happened—scale changed, focus was lost, coordination lapsed—as new projects were undertaken that were inflections, elaborations, and extensions of the original project. . . . which the amazing success of the first decade of work made seem possible, but that now got out of control and led to the financial crisis of 1867–1869 and thence to Haussmann's ouster."[5] Haussmann may have aspired to and briefly achieved total mastery, but he failed to sustain it.

How is the story of this massive transformation of Second Empire Paris to be told? A simple and direct narrative of historico-geographical change might suffice. There are, in fact, several excellent extant accounts that do just that.[6] But how are we to build that narrative without a proper understanding of the inner workings and relations of urban economy, polity, society, and culture? How can some vision of Paris as a whole be preserved while recognizing, as Haussmann himself so clearly did, that the details matter? Dissecting the totality into component parts runs the risk of losing track of the complex interrelations that intertwine. Yet we cannot understand the whole without grasping the details, without appreciating how the component parts, the fragments, worked. I shall take a middle course and try to understand the historico-geographical transformation of Paris during the Second Empire in terms of a series of intersecting and interlocking themes, none of which can properly be understood without the others. The problem is to present the interrelations without lapsing into tedious repetitions. I must here put a burden upon the reader, to try to keep the themes in perspective as part of a totality of interrelations that constitutes the driving force of social transformation in a given place and time.

FIGURE 31 *Paris, decked out as a beautifully garbed, imperious-looking woman, ungratefully spurns Haussmann in 1870, according to this rendition, in spite of all his magnificent gifts to her.*

The themes collect together under certain headings. I begin with space relations, in part because I think it important to put the question of the materiality of space relations and their social consequences in the very forefront of analysis, if only because it is so often relegated to the position of afterthought. I do not mean by so positioning it to privilege it in the overall analysis, but if some privilege attaches to position in an argument (which is invariably the case), then why not accord the production of space relations that privilege, if only for a change? The following three themes—finance capital, the propertied interest, and the state—link together as part of a theory of distribution of the social product into interest, rent, and taxes. Putting considerations of distribution before those of production might appear a little odd, but there is, as Marx commented, "an initial production-determining distribution," which has great significance for understanding how capitalism works. In this case, the positioning largely follows from the facts that the new space relations (both external and internal) were created out of a coalition of the state, finance capital, and the landed interest, and that each had to go through a painful adjustment to the other to do what had to be done in the way of urban transformation. The state is, of course, more than just a facet of distribution (though without taxes it would not get very far), so other aspects of state action, legitimacy, and authority are taken up here as well as in later sections where appropriate.

Production and labor processes are then examined. Shifts in technique, organization, and location were tied to changing space relations (the rise of a new international division of labor and the interior reorganization of Paris) as well as to credit, rent costs, and state policies (thus illustrating how distribution and production interlock within an urban context). But producers also need labor as a prime productive force. This brings us to consider the Parisian labor market, with its multiple facets of population growth, immigration, wage rate determination, mobilization of an industrial reserve army of unemployed, levels of skill, and attitudes toward work and labor organization.

The participation of women in the labor force was important and controversial. To the degree that they occupied a bridge position between the labor market and the reproduction of labor power in the home, their position in Parisian society as a whole deserves explicit consideration. This provides a sociological context for considering the reproduction of labor power in its long-term aspects. That process occurred largely outside of Paris

FIGURE 32 *Haussmann's attention to detail was extraordinary. Here, on the left, he combines new gas lighting with a vespasienne (a street toilet for men). The photo on the right captures the mix of street detail (the gas lighting) and the passion for both the straight line and uniformity of construction style (in this case on the Boulevard de Sebastopol). Marville's hundreds of street photos of the period are a wonderful source of detailed information.*

FIGURE 33 *Haussmann's passion for alignment made him insist that Bailly change his design for the new Tribunal of Commerce. The cupola was displaced toward the side of the building to create a symmetrical effect with the tower of the Conciergerie when viewed from the Boulevard Sebastapol. Symmetry of the building is sacrificed for symmetry of the city as a whole. The photo is by Marville.*

because the provinces fed the Parisian labor market with immigrants during the 1850s and 1860s. This leads us to consider how class relations were reproduced and subjected to social control within Paris through structures of consumption and of spectacle. From this perspective it becomes easier to reflect upon the mutually reinforcing realities and conceptions of community and class in a society where both were undergoing radical transformation.

While cities have often been regarded as artificial constructs engineered according to human wants, needs, desires, capacities, and powers, it is impossible to ignore their implantation in an ecological and "natural environment" in which questions of metabolism and of a "proper" relation to nature are clearly posed. The cholera epidemics of 1832 and 1849 had, for example, sharply highlighted the problem of urban health and hygiene. These

issues were seriously addressed in Second Empire Paris. Questions of science and sentiment, and of rhetoric and representation, are then taken up to try to uncover what people
knew, how they knew it, and how they put their ideas to work socially, economically, and
politically. I am here looking to reconstruct ideologies and states of consciousness, at least
as far as these were articulated and are recoverable for present consideration. This puts us
in a better position to understand what I call, in the final section, the "geopolitics of an
urban historical geography." I envisage, then, a spiral of themes that, starting with spatial
relations, moves through distribution (credit, rent, taxes), production and labor markets,
reproduction (of labor power, class and community relations), and consciousness formation to set the space in motion as a real historical geography of a living city.

CHAPTER FOUR

THE ORGANIZATION
OF SPACE RELATIONS

*The more production comes to rest on exchange value, hence on exchange, the more important
do the physical conditions of exchange—the means of communication and transport—become
for the costs of circulation. . . . While capital must on one side strive to tear down every
spatial barrier. . . . and conquer the whole earth for its market, it strives on the other side to
annihilate this space with time.*

—MARX

The integration of the national space of France had long been on the agenda. But by
1850, "the implantation of the structures and methods of modern large scale capitalism rendered the conquest and rational organization of space, its better adaptation to
new needs, imperative."[1] The amelioration of the interior space of Paris had, as we have
seen (chapter 2), been sporadically debated and partially acted upon throughout the July
Monarchy. By 1850, it had become imperative. Louis Napoleon was prepared to act on
both counts. As early as December 1850, he spoke directly of the need to make every
effort to embellish the city and ameliorate the living conditions of its inhabitants. We
will, he said, "open new roads, open up popular quarters which lack air and light so that
sunlight may penetrate everywhere among the walls of the city just as the light of truth
illuminates our hearts." On October 9, 1852, he signaled the forthcoming declaration of
an Empire dedicated to peaceful works. "We have," he declared, "immense uncultivated
lands to clear, roads to open, harbors to excavate, rivers to make navigable, canals to finish,
our railway network to complete."[2] The echoes of Saint-Simonian doctrine were unmistakable. On June 23, 1853, Haussmann took office as Prefect of the Department of the
Seine with a mandate to remake the city according to plan.

FIGURE 34 *As Daumier represents matters, the railroads contributed to the sense of chaotic rush and confusion in the city at the same time they integrated the countryside around Paris into the urban network. But timing was everything!*

Table 2 *Internal Transport by Mode and Volume, 1852–1869*

		Commodities (thousands of km/tons)				Passengers (thousands of passenger kms)		
Year	Road	Canal & Navigable Waterway	Coatal Shipping	Rail	Total	Road	Rail	Total
1852	2.6	1.7	1.3	0.6	6.2	1.36	0.99	2.35
1869	2.8	2.1	0.8	6.2	11.8	1.46	4.10	5.56

Source: Plessis (1973), 116.

Power was now highly concentrated at the very moment when there was a nascent social and political system bursting to undertake the work and turn long-held hopes and visions into living reality. The surpluses of capital and labor power, so crushingly evident in 1848, were to be absorbed through a program of massive long-term investment in the built environment that focused on the amelioration of space relations. Within a year of the declaration of Empire, more than a thousand were at work on the construction site of the Tuileries; untold thousands were back at work building the railroads; and the mines and forges, desolate as late as 1851, were racing to meet the burgeoning demand. What was perhaps the first great crisis of capitalism was overcome, it seemed, through the long-term application of surpluses of capital and labor to the reorganization of the transport and communications system.

The achievements appeared remarkable, and the effects even more so. The railway network expanded from a few strands here and there (1931 kilometers, to be exact) in 1850 to an intricate web of some 17,400 kilometers in 1870 (figure 35). The volume of traffic expanded twice as fast as industrial output at the same time as it shifted to the rail system and away from other modes of transport (table 2). Although the imperial roads languished, the feeder roads to the rail system were increasingly used and improved. The telegraph system went from nothing in 1856 to 23,000 kilometers ten years later when it could be used not only for governmental purposes. "The supreme glory of Napoleon III," wrote Baudelaire, "will have been to prove that anybody can govern a great nation as soon as they have got control of the telegraph and the national press."[3] But the telegraph also facilitated the coordination of markets and financial decisions. Prices of commodities in Paris, Lyon, Marseille, and Bordeaux were instantly available, and shortly thereafter the same information could be had for London, Berlin, Madrid, and Vienna. Only with respect to ports and maritime trade did the emperor not live up to his promises, but this was more than offset by the surge of surplus French capital abroad. About a third of the disposable capital went to open up space in other lands.[4] French-financed railroads and telegraph systems spread their tentacles down into the Iberian and Italian peninsulas and across central Europe into Russia and the Ottoman Empire. French finance built the Suez Canal, opened in 1869. The transport and communications system that was to be the foundation of a new world market and a new international division of labor was broadly laid out between 1850 and 1870.

Whether or not all this would have happened, no matter what the regime, is debatable. This was, after all, the era of massive investment in transport and communications throughout the whole of what was then the advanced capitalist world, and France's performance, following the initial burst of energy after 1852, barely kept pace with, and in some cases lagged behind, that of the other major powers. In a few instances, such as the Suez Canal, France could reasonably claim that its guiding vision and material help were essential to the projects' completion. And there is general agreement that the particular mix of financial reforms and governmental policies, largely derived from the Saint-Simonian orientation of the Emperor and some of his close advisers (with Persigny at the Ministry of Finance in the lead), had a great deal to do with the spectacular boom of the period immediately after 1852. That there were limits to such a process of absorbing surpluses of capital and labor soon became apparent. The problem, of course, was that "productive" employment under capitalism has always meant profitable employment. Once the choicer and more lucrative segments of the railroad network were completed by 1855, followed by Haussmann's first network of roads in 1856, the state had to find increasingly sophisticated ways to keep the work in progress. And by the mid-1860s, the whole process ran up against the realities of capitalist finance. For this was, make no mistake, a project undertaken not simply at the behest of an all-powerful Emperor and his key advisers (including Haussmann) but organized through and for the association of capitals. As such, it was subject to the powerful but contradictory logic of profit-taking through capital accumulation.

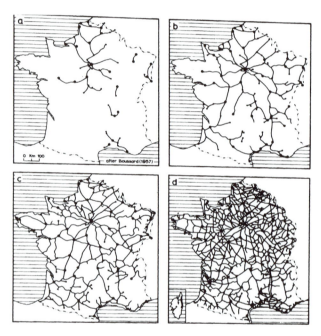

FIGURE 35 *The changing rail network in France: (a) 1850, (b) 1860, (c) 1870, (d) 1890.*

For example, the decision to put Paris at the hub of the new rail network, ostensibly for political and strategic reasons, made perfect economic sense to the degree that Paris was both the principal market and the principal manufacturing center in the nation. Agglomeration economies naturally drew new transport investments and new forms of economic activity toward Paris because this was where the rail links were most profitable. The effect was to open up Parisian industry and commerce to interregional and international competition. But they in turn also gained easier access to export markets. The position of Parisian industry and commerce therefore changed appreciably in relation to a shifting international division of labor. The costs of assembly of raw materials in Paris declined (the price of coal in Paris fell while the pithead price in Pas-de-Calais was rising); the effect was to make many of the inputs upon which Parisian industry relied correspondingly cheaper. The increased regularity, volume, and speed of flow of goods into the factories and out into the city markets reduced the turnover time of capital and opened up the possibility for big business operations in both production and distribution.

The revolution in retailing—the rise of the big department stores pioneered in the 1840s—and the shifting power relations between merchants and producers was in part a product of the new space relations.[5] The Parisian food market was likewise relieved of close dependency upon local and often hazardous supplies, and increasingly drew upon provincial and foreign sources, provoking "a veritable revolution in consumption."[6] The vegetable gardens, orchards, and animal husbandry that had once flourished in the city had largely disappeared by 1870.[7] The bourgeoisie could then look forward to fresh vegetables from Algeria and the Midi, and the poor could supplement their diets with potatoes from the west and turnips from the east. And it was not only goods that moved. Tourists flooded in from all over the world (adding to the effective demand), shoppers poured in from the suburbs, and the Parisian labor market spread its tentacles into ever remoter regions in order to satisfy a burgeoning demand for labor power.

The transformation of external space relations put intense pressure on the thrust to rationalize the interior space of Paris itself. Haussmann's exploits in this regard have, of course, become one of the great legends of modernist urban planning.[8] Backed by the Emperor and armed with the means to absorb surpluses of capital and labor in a vast program of public works, he devised a coherent plan to reorganize the spatial frame of social and economic life in the capital. The investments covered not only a new network of roads but also sewers, parks, monuments and symbolic spaces, schools, churches, administrative buildings, housing, hotels, commercial premises, and the like.

The conception of urban space that Haussmann deployed was undoubtedly new. Instead of "collections of partial plans of public thoroughfares considered without ties or connections," Haussmann sought a "general plan which was nevertheless detailed enough to properly coordinate diverse local circumstances."[9] Urban space was seen and treated as a totality in which different quarters of the city and different functions were brought into relation to each other to form a working whole. This abiding concern for the totality of the urban space led to Haussmann's fierce struggle, by no means fully supported by the Emperor, to annex the suburbs where unruly development threatened the rational evolution of a spatial order within the metropolitan region. He finally succeeded in 1860. Within this new and larger space he created a sophisticated hierarchical form of territorial administration—with himself, naturally, positioned at the top—through which the

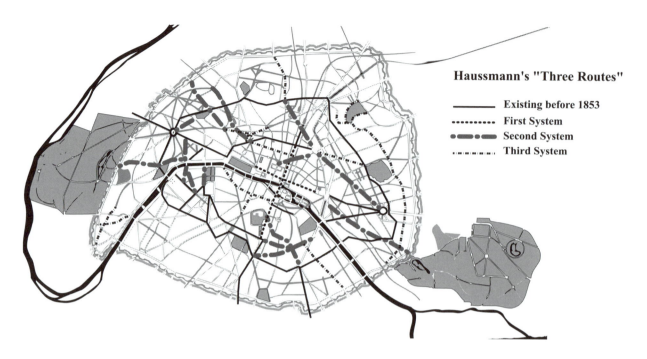

Haussmann's "Three Routes"

———	**Existing before 1853**
- - - - - - -	**First System**
●–●–●–●	**Second System**
·–··–··–·	**Third System**

complex totality of Paris could be better controlled by an organized decentralization and delegation of power and responsibility to the twenty *arrondissements*. He built a *mairie* (city hall) in each to symbolize such an administrative presence to the populace. And he fought throughout, in the end not so successfully, to counter the privatism and parochialism of individual and local interests through legislation and rhetoric focused on the public interest for a rational and orderly evolution of space relations in the city.

Haussmann's passion for exact spatial coordination was symbolized by the triangulation that produced the first accurate cadastral and topographical map of the city in 1853. And there is no question that it was Haussmann, and not the Emperor, who imposed the logic of the straight line, who insisted upon the symmetry, who saw the logic of the whole, and who set the tone for both the scale and style as well as the details of spatial design. But it was the largeness of scale and the comprehensiveness of plan and conception that were to assure Haussmann's place as one of the founding figures of modernist urban planning. "Make no little plans," urged Daniel Burnham many years later, and this was certainly Haussmann's way.

But whatever else he and the Emperor may have had in mind—the creation of a Western capital to rival imperial Rome and celebrate a new form of Empire, the expulsion of "dangerous classes" and insalubrious housing and industry from the city center—one of the clearest effects of their efforts was to improve the capacity for the circulation of goods and people within the city's confines. The flows between the newly established rail stations, between center and periphery, between Left Bank and Right Bank, into and out of central markets like Les Halles, to and from places of recreation (Bois de Boulogne by day, the grand boulevards by night), between industry and commerce (to the new department stores) were all facilitated by the construction of some ninety miles of spacious boulevards that reduced the cost, time, and (usually) aggravation of movement remarkably. Along with the Pereire brothers, Haussmann engineered the consolidation by merger of all the omnibus companies in 1855 into one private monopoly—the Compagnie des Omnibus de Paris—thereby increasing the number of passengers moved from 36 million in 1855 to 110 million by 1860. The new road system had the added advantage that it neatly surrounded some of the traditional hearths of revolutionary ferment and would permit the free circulation of forces of order if needed. It also contributed to the free circulation of air into insalubrious neighborhoods, while the free play of sunlight by day and of newly installed gas lighting by night underscored the transition to a more extroverted form of urbanism in which the public life of the boulevard became a highlight of what the city was about. And, in an extraordinary engineering achievement, a marvel to this day, the flows of water and sewage were revolutionized.

It was ruthlessly done and took time, money, technical skill, and Haussmann's incredible drive and administrative ability to do it. No one can doubt Haussmann's passionate and long-standing committment to improving the means of transport. Had he not, after all, in his very first appointment as subprefect of the remote rural commune of Nerac in 1832, bypassed the authority of the prefect and resorted to creative financing of dubious legality to leave the commune, some five years later, with several kilometers of paved local roads, new bridges, and a properly surfaced highway connecting to the main town?

Yet the dramatic transformation of the interior space of Paris was by no means all due to Haussmann. The realignment of traffic movement from the principal axis of the Seine to multiple railheads, long debated during the July Monarchy (see figure 25), was less a consequence than a compelling condition for that work. Haussmann immediately recognized that it was a "necessity of the first order" to put the rail stations, now the principal points of entry into Paris, "into a direct relation with the heart of the city by way of large thoroughfares."[10] The Petite Ceinture railroad, which ringed Paris and gave such dynamism to suburban growth, also owed little to Haussmann. And, as we shall see, there were all manner of shifts in the operation of land and property markets, in industrial location and labor processes, in marketing and distribution systems, in population distribution and family formation, to which Haussmann was adjusting rather than leading. The reshaping of the interior space of Paris was, therefore, a response to processes already in motion. But it also became a spatial framework around which those very same processes—of industrial and commercial development, of housing investment and residential segregation, and so on—could cluster and play out their own trajectories, and thus define the new historical geography of the city's evolution.

To his credit, Haussmann well understood his limited role. For though he had authoritarian powers and frequent delusions of grandeur, he also recognized that he had to liberate more than just the flows of goods and people from their medieval constraints if Paris was to be transformed. The force he had to mobilize—and it was in the end the force that mastered him—was the circulation of capital. But this, too, was a compelling condition present at the very birth of Empire. The surpluses of capital and labor power absolutely had to be absorbed if the Empire was to survive. The absorption of such surpluses via the public works that so transformed the interior space of Paris entailed the free circulation of capital through the construction of a particular spatial configuration of the built environment. Freed from its feudal straitjacket, capital reorganized the interior space of Paris according to principles that were uniquely its own. Haussmann wanted to make Paris a modern capital worthy of France, if not of Western civilization. In the end he simply helped make it a city in which the circulation of capital became the real imperial power.

The new space relations had powerful effects on Parisian economy, politics, and culture, and the effects on the sensibilities of Parisians were legion. It was as if they were instantly plunged into a bewildering world of speedup and rapid compression of space relations. The Second Empire experienced a fierce bout of space-time compression, and the contradictory effects of this (particularly with respect to space and place) were everywhere in evidence. The orientation of the new transport investments reemphasized, for example, the tendency toward centralization of administration, finance, economy, and population in Paris. It re-posed the thorny issue of the proper balance between geographical centralization and decentralization of political power within the nation, and it did it in such a way as to make the role of the commune in the construction of citizenship and political identities a vigorous topic of debate.[11] Centralization was seen as a virtue by many. "Paris is centralization itself," proclaimed the Emperor with pride; "it is the head and heart of France," elaborated Haussmann.[12] But this challenged the viability and meaning of local community even within Paris itself; political interests seemed to have less and less clear-cut geographical boundaries, and political identities based on territory had more and more to be asserted rather than just lived.

The problem of scale was not an issue only for Haussmann, the financiers and the bourgeoisie. The new internationalism of the workers' movement sat uneasily with that desire and struggle for local autonomy which had so animated workers during the 1840s and which later on was to give the Paris Commune (with its absolute insistence on the right to local self-governance) so much of its specific political coloration. The coming unification of the world through monetization and commodity exchange was likewise celebrated in the Universal Expositions held in Paris in 1855 and 1867. In both cases the focus was not only on technological progress but also on the new world of spatial interconnections facilitated by modern networks of communication and materialized through commodity exchange. Hugo, in his essay in the *Paris Guide* of 1867, largely written for the Universal Exposition of that year, produced a simplistic panegyric to a unified Europe (of the sort that Saint-Simon had articulated in the 1820s), one free of national boundaries and expressive of a common culture, at the very moment when geopolitical tensions were on the rise and three years before the Franco-Prussian War wracked European unity and brought an end to Empire. The phantasmagoria of universal capitalist culture and its space relations incorporated in the Universal Exposition blinded even him to the significance and power of loyalties to and identifications with place.

And, as so often happens with improvements in transport and communications, the effect was not so much to relieve congestion as to re-create it at a different speed and scale. The threefold increase in the number of omnibus passengers carried between 1855 and 1860 tells much of the story. Many of Daumier's cartoons drawn in response the new forms of transport emphasize the rush and speedup on the railroads, in the stations, and along the boulevards; the intense pressure of overcrowding; and a shifting balance between private intimacies and public presences (see figures 19, 34, 37, and 38). Segregation by classes in the railway carriages and by "on top or inside" in the omnibuses allowed some separation, but it was hard to maintain any sense of privacy or intimacy in crowded railway carriages, no matter what the class of compartment. The railways revolutionized not only the materialities of space relations but also social relations, intimacies, and sensibilities.[13] The incorporation of the suburbs and the remoter rural fringes into the maelstrom of Parisian life also meant that there was no place to hide from the process of urbanization, while the compulsion of the middle and affluent classes to seek leisure and pleasure in the now more easily accessible countryside was soon to become one of the great subjects of impressionist painting.

Speedup also expanded the spaces within which people, commodities, and ideas could move. This made it imperative to rethink and reengineer the urban process at a quite different scale. Not only did Haussmann and his aides have to adapt (and there is no question that in this they led the way). The financiers, commercial interests, and industrialists also had to adapt their thinking and find organizational means to work at grander geographical scales. Haussmann's drive to annex the suburbs into his urban administration was symbolic of this shifting scale. Urbanists like Perreymond and Meynadier had, of course, pioneered this way of thinking in the 1840s, and had simultaneously managed to adapt a tradition of rationalizing urban space that went back at least to Voltaire and Diderot, to Paris's chaotic and ever accelerating urban growth. Balzac, recall, had also set out to see the city as a whole, and in his celebrated ending to *Old Goriot* has Rastignac prepare to seize the city for himself as he contemplates it from the heights of Père Lachaise Cemetary. But Rastignac's project is one of personal advancement.

FIGURE 37 *The increase in omnibus traffic along the boulevards did not diminish overcrowding and the inconvenience of travel within the city, at least according to this rendition by Daumier from 1856.*

Zola, many years later, reruns Balzac's scene in *La Curée* (*The Kill*). Saccard, the great Second Empire speculator, dines one evening with Angèle on the heights of the Butte Montmartre. Looking down on Paris and imagining "it is raining twenty franc pieces" there, he gleefully observes how "more than one district will be melted down, and gold will stick to the fingers of those who heat and stir the mortar." Angèle stares "with a vague terror, at the sight of this little man standing erect over the recumbent giant at his feet, and shaking his fist at it while ironically pursing his lips." Saccard describes how Paris has already been cut into four by the Grand Croisée, and will be further slashed by "Navvie cuts" of the second and third networks, "its veins opened, giving sustenance to a hundred thousand navvies and bricklayers." Saccard's "dry nervous hand kept cutting through space," and Angèle "shivered slightly before this living knife, those iron fingers mercilessly slicing the boundless mass of dusky roofs . . . the smallness of this hand, hovering pitilessly over a gigantic prey, ended by becoming disquieting; and as, without effort, it tore asunder the entrails of the enormous city, it seemed to assume the strange reflex of steel in the blue of the twilight."[14] Thus does Zola re-create the creative destruction of Paris as seen from on high and at the scale of the city as a whole. But now it is the speculator who grasps the totality with the ambition to carve it up and feed off the entrails.

FIGURE 38 *Railway travel had dramatic implications for the manner in which people could experience the public spaces of travel. It was particularly difficult to preserve any sense of intimacy, and many Daumier cartoons address that problem. An early attempt to protect upper-class passengers from contact with the mob by building isolated compartments was quickly abandoned when a traveler was found murdered in one. In this cartoon Daumier (1864) celebrates third-class travel because, though one might be asphyxiated, one would never be assassinated.*

The reshaping of space relations and the transformations in spatial scale that occurred were active rather than passive moments in the urban process. The actual organization of space through transport and communications is a first-order material fact with which all historical and geographical analysis must come to grips. The Second Empire revolution in space relations, both within Paris and beyond, may have had its roots in earlier phases, but there is no question that there was an order of difference between the pace of change, spatial scale, and geographical extension after 1852 compared to that which had prevailed before. How this revolution was accomplished remains to be explored.

CHAPTER FIVE

MONEY, CREDIT, AND FINANCE

The credit system accelerates the material development of the productive forces and the establishment of the world market.

—MARX

On the morning of December 2, 1851, Emile Pereire hurried to the house of James Rothschild to reassure the bedridden banker that all had gone smoothly with the coup d'état. The story of their subsequent break and awesome struggle, which lasted until the Pereire brothers' downfall a year before James died in 1868, is one of the legendary battles of high finance. It became the subject much later of Zola's novel *L'Argent* (*Money*).[1] Behind it lay two quite different conceptions of the role of money and finance in economic development. The *haute banque* of the Rothschilds was a family affair—private and confidential, working with opulent friends without publicity, and deeply conservative in its approach to money, a conservatism expressed through attachment to gold as the real money form, the true measure of value. And that attachment had served Rothschild well. He remained, as a worker publication of 1848 complained, "strong in the face of young republics" and a "power independent of old dynasties." "You are more than a man of state. You are the symbol of credit." The Pereires, for their part, schooled in Saint-Simonian ways of thought from the early 1830s on, tried to change the meaning of that symbol. They had long seen the credit system as the nerve center of economic development and social change. Amid a welter of publicity, they sought to democratize savings by mobilizing them into an elaborate hierarchy of credit institutions capable of undertaking projects of long duration. The "association of capital" was their theme, and grand, unashamed speculation in future development was their practice. The conflict between the Rothschilds and the Pereires was, in the final analysis, a personalized version of a deep

FIGURE 39 *The stock exchange "is other people's money," said Dumas and Chargot's cartoon depicts the Bourse as a haunt of vampires.*

tension within capitalism between the financial superstructure and its monetary base.[2] And if, in 1867, those who controlled hard money (like Rothschild) managed to bring down the credit empire of the Pereires, it was, as we shall shortly see, a Pyrrhic victory.

The problem in 1851 was to absorb the surpluses of capital and labor power. The Parisian bourgeoisie universally recognized the economic roots of the crisis through which they had just passed but were deeply divided as to what to do about it.[3] The government took the Saint-Simonian path and sought by a mix of direct governmental interventions, credit creation, and reform of financial structures to facilitate the conversion of surplus capital and labor into new physical infrastructures as the basis for economic revival. It was a politics of mild inflation and stimulated expansion (a sort of primitive Keynesianism) lubricated by the strong inflow of gold from California and Australia. The *hautes banques* and their clients were deeply suspicious. Rothschild wrote to the Emperor, vigorously condemning the new initiatives. The government, distrustful of the bankers' Orléanist political sympathies, turned to administrators like Persigny, the Pereires, and Haussmann, who accepted the idea that universal credit was the way to economic progress and social reconciliation. In so doing, they abandoned what Marx called the "Catholicism" of the monetary base, turned their banking system into "the papacy of production," and embraced what Marx called the "protestantism of faith and credit."[4] The religious imagery at work here has, however, more than casual significance. The Catholic Church formally equated interest with usury well into the 1840s, and sought to outlaw it. For many devout Catholics, the immorality of the new system of finance was therefore a serious issue. The fact that Rothschild and the Pereires were Jewish, and Haussmann was Protestant, did not help matters in their eyes. Many of them equated capitalism with prostitution, as Gavarni's cartoon wittily confirms. The moral condemnation of Empire that resurfaced so strongly after its collapse frequently harked back to its financial dealings as irregular and sinful. There were, evidently, moral as well as political, technical, and philosophical barriers to be overcome if a new financial system was to be created.

The story of financial reform under the Second Empire is complicated in its details.[5] But the Pereires' Crédit Mobilier was undoubtedly the controversial centerpiece. Initially formed to get railroad construction and all ancillary industries back in business, it was an investment bank that held shares in companies and helped them assemble the necessary finance for large-scale undertakings. It could also sell debt to the general public at a rate of return guaranteed by the earnings of the companies controlled. It thus acted as an intermediary between innumerable small savers hitherto denied such opportunities for placement (the Pereires made much of the supposed "democratization" of credit) and a wide range of industrial enterprises. They even hoped to turn it into a universal holding company that, through assembly of funds and mergers, would bring all economic activity (including that of the government) under common control. There were many, including those in government, who were suspicious of what amounted to a planned evolution of what we now know as "state monopoly capitalism." And although Pereires were ultimately to fall, the victim of an aroused conservative opposition and their own overextended speculation (a fate that Rothschild had predicted in his letter to the Emperor and had helped seal), their opponents were forced to adopt the new methods. Rothschild hit back with the same form of organization as early as 1856, and by the end of the Second Empire a host of new financial intermediaries (such as the Crédit Lyonnais, founded in 1863) had emerged and were to dominate French financial life from then until today.

FIGURE 40 *Many conservative Catholics regarded the charging of interest as akin to prostitution. In this cartoon by Gavarni, a prettily dressed young woman tries to lure a reluctant customer into an investment house (a house of ill repute) by promising him that she will be kind and gentle with him, that she will give him a good percentage return on whatever he cares to lay out!*

In itself, as the Pereires recognized, the Crédit Mobilier would not be effective without a wide range of other institutions integrated into or subordinated to it. The Bank of France (a private but state-regulated institution) increasingly took on the role of a national central bank. It was much too fiscally conservative for the Pereires' taste. It took the tasks of preserving the quality of money very seriously, even at the price of tightening credit and raising the discount rate to levels that the Pereires regarded as harmful to economic growth.[6] The Bank of France turned out to be the major center of financial opposition to the Pereires' ideas. It dealt almost exclusively in short-term commercial paper, discounting commercial bills of exchange. The Crédit Foncier, a new institution finally stitched together on December 10, 1852 (shortly after the Crédit Mobilier), was to bring rationality and order to the land and property mortgage market. Founded under the Pereires' influence, it was to be an important ally in their concerns. Other organizations, such as the Comptoir d'Escompte de Paris (founded in 1848) and the Crédit Industriel et Commercial (1859), dealt in special kinds of credit. And within their own empire, the Pereires, with government blessing, spawned a wide range of hierarchically ordered institutions, such as the Compagnie Immobilière, which concentrated on the finance of property development. At its height the Crédit Mobilier integrated twenty French-based and fourteen foreign-based companies into its extraordinarily powerful organization.

The effects of all this on the transformation of Paris were enormous. Indeed, without some reorganization of finance the transformation simply could not have progressed at the pace it did. It was not just that the city had to borrow (a topic I take up later), but that Haussmann's projects depended upon the existence of companies that had the financial power to develop, build, own, and manage the spaces he opened up. Thus did the Pereires become "in many respects and in many places the secular arm of the prefect."[7] The Compagnie Immobiliere de Paris emerged in 1858 out of the organization of the Pereires created in 1854 to take on the first of Haussmann's big projects, the completion of the Rue de Rivoli and the Hotel du Louvre. How the new system worked is well illustrated by what happened in this first case. The decision to raise the capital and build the shopping spaces and the hotel along the Rue de Rivoli was taken as a speculative venture in preparation for the Universal Exposition planned for 1855. The original plan for an arcade of individual shops failed to attract, and so the Pereires accepted a proposal to turn the whole shopping space into one large department store, a new and equally speculative venture. Opened in 1855, the store was badly run and financially unprofitable. The Pereires had to reorganize and recapitalize the whole venture, and it was not until 1861 that it finally made a profit.[8] Meanwhile, the Pereires in effect raised capital to lend to the department store to pay off the debt on the capital they had raised for the building venture. If, at any moment before 1861, anyone had questioned the creative accounting involved (or even refused to invest more money) the Pereires would have been in deep financial difficulty. But they finessed the short term and achieved over the long term.

The company went on to build along the Champs Elysées and the Boulevard Malesherbes, and around the Opéra and the Parc Monceau. It increasingly relied, however, on speculative operations as a source of profit. In 1856–1857, it drew three-quarters of its income from rents received on housing and industrial plants, and only a quarter from the buying and selling of land and property. By 1864 the proportions were exactly the reverse.[9] The company could easily augment its capital via the Crédit Mobilier (which held half its shares) and bolster its profits by a leveraging operation based on a cosy relationship with the Crédit Foncier (borrowing half of its capital from the latter at 5.75 percent on a project that returned 8.7 percent yielded the company 11.83 percent, Pereire explained to astonished shareholders). The company increasingly shifted to short-term financing, which made it vulnerable to movements in the interest rate dictated by the Bank of France (which explains the Pereires' impatience with the policies of that institution and their obsession with cheap credit). It also contracted building work out to enterprises financed by the Crédit Mobilier (thereby provoking considerable concentration and increase of employment in the building industry; see table 4), and it sold or rented the buildings to management companies or commercial groups in which the Crédit Mobilier often had a like stake.

The Pereires were masters at creating vertically integrated financial systems that could be put to work to build railroads; to launch all manner of transportation, industrial, and commercial enterprises; and to create massive investments in the built environment. "I want to write my ideas on the landscape itself," wrote Emile Pereire—and indeed he and his brother did. But they were not alone. Even Rothschild stooped so low as to parlay his property holdings around his Gare du Nord into a profitable real estate venture, and many a builder, contractor, architect, or owner sought profit by the same route. And while this was not, as we shall see, the only system of land development in Paris, it was the primary means for engineering the Haussmannization of Paris.

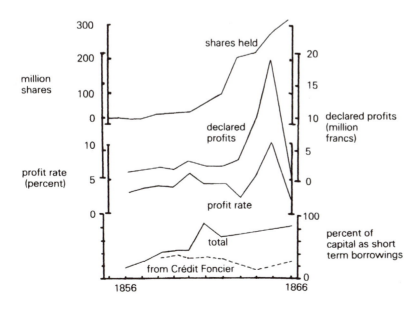

FIGURE 41 *The operations of the Compagnie Immobilière, 1856–1866 (after Lescure, 1980), distinguishing between total number of shares (rising rapidly after 1866, just before the crash of 1867), the declared profits and profit rates (which plunged after 1865), and the increasing reliance on short-term borrowings after 1860.*

But this was only the tip of a veritable iceberg of effects on the economy and life of Paris. Money, finance, and speculation became such a grand obsession with the Parisian bourgeoisie ("business is other people's money," cracked Alexandre Dumas the younger) that the bourse became a center of corruption as well as of reckless speculation that gobbled up many a landed fortune. Its nefarious influence over daily life was immortalized afterward in Zola's *La Curée* (*The Kill*) and *L'Argent* (*Money*) through the figure of Saccard (loosely based on the Pereires), who in the first of these novels is cast as the grand speculator engaging with the transformation of Paris, and in the second as the financier masterminding investment schemes in the Orient where, he says:

Fields will be cleared, roads and canals built, new cities will spring from the soil, life will return as it returns to a sick body, when we stimulate the system by injecting new blood into exhausted veins. Yes! money will work these miracles. . . . You must understand that speculation, gambling, is the central mechanism, the heart itself of a vast affair like ours. Yes, it attracts blood, takes it from every source in little streamlets, collects it, sends it back in rivers in all directions, and establishes an enormous circulation of money, which is the very life of great enterprises. . . . Speculation—why it is the one inducement that we have to live; it is the eternal desire that compels us to live and struggle. Without speculation, my dear friend, there would be no business of any kind. . . . It is the same as in love. In love as in speculation there is much filth; in love also, people think only of their own gratification; yet without love there would be no life and the world would come to an end."[10]

La Curée (*The Kill*) invokes exactly the same process, but this time within Paris itself. Saccard, having gotten wind of "the vast project for the transformation of Paris," sets out to profit from the insider knowledge he has (he had even "ventured to consult, in the prefet's room, that famous plan of Paris on which 'an august hand' had traced in red ink the principles of the second network"). Having "read the future in the Hôtel de Ville," knowing full well "what may be stolen in the buying and selling of houses and ground," and being "well up in every classical swindle," he

knew how you sell for a million what has cost you five hundred thousand francs; how you acquire the right of rifling the treasury of the State, which smiles and closes its eyes; how, when throwing a boulevard across a belly of an old quarter, you juggled six-storied houses amidst the unanimous applause of your dupes. And in those still clouded days, when the canker of speculation was but at its incubation, what made a formidable gambler of him was that he saw further than his chiefs themselves into the stone-and-plaster future reserved for Paris."[11]

The figure of the great speculator not only takes charge of shaping Paris and its urban form but also aspires to command the whole globe. And the tool is the association of capitals. That Zola should feel so comfortable invoking Saint-Simonian doctrine in its most hubristic form some seventy years after its initial formulation says much about the persistence of this mode of thought in France throughout the century. The formula "money, aiding science, yields progress," which Zola invoked, resonated at all levels. There could, evidently, be no modernity without assembling the speculative capital to do it. The key was to find a way to bring together the little streamlets of capital into a massive circulation that could undertake projects at the requisite scale. This was precisely what the Pereires were about and what the institutional shifts in finance were meant to accomplish.

It was, however, through the democratization of money at one end that immense centralization of financial power became possible at the other. The top six families held 158 out of 920 seats on company boards registered in Paris in the mid-1860s—the Pereires held forty-four and the Rothschilds thirty-two.[12] Complaints about the immense power of a new "feudality of finance" were widespread and exposed critically to the public in popular works such as that of Duchêne.[13] This power was felt internationally (the Pereires threatened, said their detractors, to substitute a new international paper money, under their control, for gold) as well as in all realms of urban organization—the Pereires merged the gas companies into a single regulated monopoly, bringing industrial and street lighting to much of Paris; founded (again by merger) the Compagnie des Omnibus de Paris; financed one of the first department stores (the Louvre); and tried to monopolize the dock and entrepôt trade.[14]

The reorganization of the credit system had far-reaching effects upon Parisian industry and commerce, the labor process, and the mode of consumption. Everyone, after all, depended on credit. The only question was who was to make it available to whom and on what terms. Workers bedeviled by seasonal unemployment lived by it; small masters and shopkeepers needed it to deal with the seasonality of demand—the chain was endless. Indebtedness was a chronic problem in all classes and arenas of activity. But the credit system of the 1840s was as arbitrary and capricious as it was insecure (only land and property gave true security). Proposals for reform of the credit system abounded in 1848. Artisans, small masters, and craft workers sought some kind of mutual credit system under local and democratic control. Proudhon's experiment with a People's Bank offering free credit under the banner "Merchants of money, your reign is over!" collapsed with his arrest in 1849.[15] But the idea never died. When workers began to organize in the 1860s, it was to questions of mutual credit that they increasingly turned. Their Crédit au Travail, started in 1863, foundered in 1868, hopelessly insolvent with "loans outstanding to forty-eight cooperatives, of which eighteen were bankrupt and only nine could pay."[16] Indifference on the part of government and, more surprisingly, on the part of fellow workers was blamed. Consumer cooperatives ran into similar problems, many families preferring the antagonistic relation and default on debts to local shopkeepers to the economic burden of cooperation in the face of periodic unemployment and lagging real incomes. The municipal pawnshop of Mont-de-Piété continued to be the last resort for the mass of the Parisian populace. The dream of free credit appeared more and more remote. "It entailed," said a member of the Workers' Commission of 1867, "the reversal of the entire system of private property on which merchants, landlords, government, etc. lived."[17]

The credit system was rationalized, expanded, and democratized through the association of capitals, but at the expense of often uncontrolled speculation and the growing absorption of all savings into a centralized and hierarchically organized system that left those at the bottom even more vulnerable to the arbitrary and capricious whims of those who had some money power. Yet it took a revolution in the credit system to produce the revolution in space relations. Within Paris that process depended, however, upon a much tighter integration of finance capital and landed property. To the manner of this integration we now turn.

CHAPTER SIX

RENT AND THE PROPERTIED INTEREST

It is the ground-rent, and not the house, which forms the actual object of building speculation in rapidly growing cities.

—MARX

Between 1848 and 1852, the Parisian property market underwent its severest and most prolonged depression of the century. In some bourgeois quarters, where the depression hit hardest, vacancy rates stood as high as one-sixth, rents fell by half, and property prices (if sales were possible at all) were severely depressed.[1] The Second Empire reversed all that. It proved to be the golden age in a century noted for relatively secure and high rates of return and appreciation on Parisian property. But it was also an era in which the social meaning and orientation of property ownership in the city changed radically. Parisian property was more and more appreciated as a pure financial asset, as a form of fictitious capital whose exchange value, integrated into the general circulation of capital, entirely dominated use value. There was a world of difference, as Zola himself recognized, between Saccard's massive speculations and the minor dabblings described in Balzac's *Cousin Bette* or even the more systematic exploitations set in motion in *César Birotteau* and *Old Goriot*.

Speculation on the Parisian property market had, of course, a long and not so respectable history. When Louis Philippe's prime minister, François Guizot, issued his famous invitation, "enrichissez-vous," the Parisian bourgeoisie responded with a speculative mania that lasted well into the 1840s. It was during this period that the speculative apartment house design that became such standard fare in the Second Empire was effectively pioneered as a solution to high-density urban living. The bourgeoisie turned

FIGURE 42 *Daumier frequently criticized landlords and the propertied interest. Here, landlords collude to raise rents at the next due date.*

FIGURE 43 *M. Vautour was the popular name for the grasping landlord. Daumier (1852) depicts him as delighted with the demolitions because, for every house demolished, he can raise his rents by 200 francs.*

126

in this direction in part because property was one of the few secure forms of investment open to them. It was remunerative simply because housing provision lagged behind growth of population, and they could exploit the scarcity (making the fictional figure of M. Vatour, the exploitative landlord, a standard focus of popular opprobrium in the 1840s and a major target in 1848). The number of houses in the city increased from 26,801 in 1817 to 30,770 in 1851, while population rose from 713,966 to 1,053,897. The rate of return on worker housing stood at 7 percent in the 1820s and probably continued at that level, at the cost of undermaintenance and overcrowding in those insalubrious quarters so graphically described in the novels of Eugène Sue as well as in Balzac's *Cousin Bette*. In bourgeois quarters the return was closer to 5 percent (rarely less), since tenants were harder to come by and more exacting.[2] This nevertheless compared very favorably with the 3 percent or so to be had on state debt.

Thanks to Daumard's meticulous studies, we can discern the main lines of change that followed. Parisian property, while a favored means of storing wealth within all segments of the bourgeoisie, was dominated in the 1840s by shopkeepers and artisans (half), with liberal professions and commercial interests holding another third. By 1880, the pattern had changed completely. Shopkeepers and artisans had dropped to 13.6 percent and liberal professions to 8.1 percent, being supplanted by a class of people who identified themselves solely as landowners (53.9 percent). Only commercial interests (particularly when joined with the new category of "companies") maintained their position (table 3). And only in the periphery did shopkeepers retain a significant presence, having a quarter of the sales there in 1870 but falling to 18.1 percent in 1880. Commerce, companies, and liberal profes-

FIGURE 44 *Marville's photos testify to the insalubrious and rickety state of much of Paris housing in the early 1850s.*

sions had a disproportionate share of center city property, though they were nowhere near as dominant as the property owners. The lower middle class and petite bourgeoisie, therefore, were steadily excluded from property ownership (particularly in central locations) and replaced by a haute bourgeoisie of landlords and commercial interests. Such a change is consistent with important shifts in commercial, financial, and manufacturing structure that saw the subordination of artisans and small-scale producers and shopkeepers to the

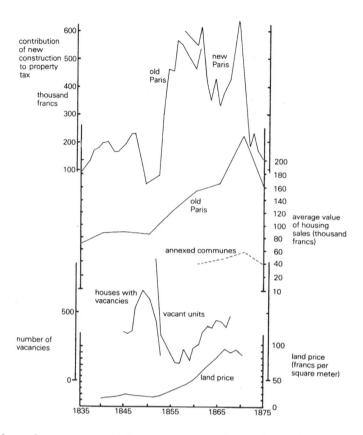

FIGURE 45 *Property price move-*
ments in Paris, distinguishing
between contribution of new con-
struction to property tax (note the
incredible jump after 1855 and
the collapse after 1866); the steady
increase in housing values after
1848 until 1866 (though note the
far lower values in the annexed
communes); the precipitous fall in
vacancy rates and rise in land prices
after 1852 (after Daumard, 1965;
Gaillard, 1977).

hegemony of grand commerce and finance. There is also evidence that all social groups were increasingly willing to engage in the buying and selling of property as a speculative activity.

Ownership began and remained highly dispersed. In 1846, Daumard calculates, the average owner controlled only two properties, and although some of these may have been individually large, the majority were not. There was, and continued to be, considerable variation from quarter to quarter. If there was any pattern to it all in 1850, Gaillard suggests, the "progressive" large-scale propertied interests were Right Bank rather than Left Bank, central rather than peripheral.[3] The tendency toward concentration of ownership, which Daumard detects in some central areas on the Right Bank, was merely a perpetuation of a pattern already evident in 1850 and earlier. Indeed, the prior manner of appropriation of space in Paris had a key role to play in the subsequent reorganization of that space. The form and style of landownership on the Left Bank (large-scale aristocratic owners intermingled with artisans and shopkeepers) kept it deeply resistant to Haussmann's works, with results that can still be discerned today. The large-scale commercial interests collected in the Right Bank's center not only were amenable to change but had actively promoted and planned for it under the July Monarchy.

Table 3 *Role of Property in Personal Wealth, 1840–1880*

Socioeconomic Category	% of Parisian Fortunes Held as Property, 1847			% of Parisian Property Held by Social Group			
				1840	1880		
	in Paris	ex-Paris	Total	%	Total %	Center %	Periphery %
Landowner[a]	39.8	21.3	61.1	8.9	53.9	49.1	59.3
Merchants[b]							
active	16.0	5.3	21.3	14.2	14.5	17.7	11.0
retired	23.5	20.5	43.7				
Company					3.5	5.9	0.9
Shopkeeper[c]							
active	18.0	7.0	25.0	48.8	13.6	9.6	18.1
retired	38.8	2.2	41.0				
Functionary	13.0	33.4	46.4	4.3	2.2	3.1	0.7
State employee	10.7	16.5	27.2	4.0	0.6	1.0	0.2
Diverse employees	14.0	10.2	24.2	2.3	2.7	2.8	2.6
Liberal professions[d]	37.5	7.3	44.8	17.2	8.1	10.1	6.0
Diverse[e]	8.7	0.9	9.6	0.3	0.8	0.5	1.1
Home worker	15.8	2.3	18.1				
Day worker	15.6	1.6	17.2				
Domestic	2.8	5.3	8.1				
Total	27.4	17.3	44.7				

Sources: Daumard (1965), 237, 241; Daumard (1973), 216.

[a] Included those who listed this as their position.

[b] Includes industriatlists as well as wholesakers and mechants.

[c] Includes artisans.

[d] Doctors, lawyers, teachers, etc.

[e] Probably includes the home workers, day workers, and domestics in property ownership columns.

FIGURE 46 *This
Marville photo
(probably from the
mid-1850s) captures
the conditions of liv-
ing in the numerous
shantytowns that
sprang up on the
periphery and in the
interstices of existing
developments as the
demolitions took hold
in the center.*

In Paris, the urban-based propertied interests constituted a powerful political force under the July Monarchy and were considered Orléanist in their political sympathies. Their social attitudes and power left an indelible mark upon the Parisian landscape of 1850. They typically undertook few improvements except those dictated by personal gain, whim, or the search for status. The capital they engaged was mainly seen as securing revenue or, in the case of shopkeepers, a use value, rather than as the productive circulation of capital via the construction of the built environment. Speculative as opposed to custom building was still relatively restricted, haphazard, and small in scale, and was largely peripheral (which, at that time, meant the urban expansion toward the northwest around the new quarters of the Chaussée d'Antin and beyond). Insufficient to meet popular needs, it was supplemented by the formation of shantytown slums such as the infamous Petite Pologne. The housing stock was expensive, and by and large in bad condition. The owners tended to resist public improvements, partly because of the myopic spatial perspective that typically attaches to small-scale ownership, partly because the uneven distribution of benefits among dispersed owners militated against any easy consensus for change, and partly out of their mortal fear of higher taxes and diminished revenues. That Parisian physical infrastructures were deteriorating in relation to burgeoning needs was evident enough. But little had been done, largely because of the attitudes and political power of the property owners. This was the condition that absolutely had to change if Paris was to be modernized.

The circumstances under which Haussmann came to Paris were propitious in a number of respects. The Emperor was not particularly indebted to a class openly Orléanist in its political sympathies. It was, moreover, a class that had been put very much on the political defensive. Years of accumulated hate for grasping and negligent landlords—popularly caricatured as M. Vautour—spilled out in the workers' movement of 1848. And even after the June Days and the remarkable electoral triumph of the "party of order" in 1849, a social democratic socialism deeply antagonistic to landlordism (occasionally waving Proudhon's slogan, "property is theft") was all too much in evidence, particularly in Paris. To these political troubles was added the chronic depression in the Parisian property market. Much weakened, therefore, the propertied interest was willing to accept almost anything that would guarantee the perpetuation of its rights and a resurgence of the market.

The Empire obliged on both counts. It suppressed the left without compunction and laid the foundation for a spectacular recovery in the Parisian property market. By 1855, the vacancy rate had fallen to an all-time low, property prices were rising rapidly, and Louis Lazare, who had his fingers on a great deal of detailed information, was complaining of rates of return of 12 percent or more. Daumard's carefully reconstructed figures for housing built along the new boulevards in selected central city locations indicate solid rates of return throughout the whole Second Empire period.[4]

Rate of Return (%)	>5	5–5.9	6–6.9	7–7.9	8–8.9	9<
Number of Cases (%)	4.6	6.8	32.7	36.7	13.8	5.2

There is little reason to suspect that rates of return on old housing were much less. The owners could simply dictate terms to tenants. Parisian property, in short, became a secure and high-yielding investment protected from the fluctuations that typified the stock market.

A material foundation was laid for a political rapprochement between Parisian property owners and Empire.[5] Unbeholden at the beginning, the Empire increasingly looked to them as a base of support in a capital where opposition sentiment dominated as early as 1857. Yet Haussmann's relations with the propertied interest were often troubled and at best ambivalent. This helps explain why the latter's support for Empire was less enthusiastic than might have been expected. To begin with, Haussmann's conception of urban space was radically different from that of typically myopic and dispersed owners. While very much in favor of private property in general, Haussmann was not solicitous of anyone's private property rights in particular. He was prepared to

FIGURE 47 *The demolitions affected everyone. In this Daumier rendition (1852), a workman is telling a bourgeois couple to hurry and get up, because they are next in line for the pickax.*

ride roughshod over particularist opposition, and that stirred resentment. Furthermore, it was hard to bring equal benefits to so many dispersed owners. Toward the end of the Empire, Gaillard notes, there were many complaints from property owners who felt left out of the grand speculative feast accompanying the public works.[6] Haussmann also had to battle the fiscal conservatism of owners that kept them from investing productively in the transformation of urban space or from approving of public action with such an aim. If Paris was to be transformed, then capital had to be mobilized, not only into buying and selling but also into demolition, reconstruction, and long-term management of the urban space according to collectivist principles that were quite alien to the privatism of traditional property owners.

It was, in short, the capitalist form of private property in land that Haussmann encouraged, and in so doing he collided head-on with more traditional and deeply entrenched attitudes and practices. Haussmann well anticipated the resistance he might encounter. He sidelined the two main channels of landowner influence over renewal decisions. The planning commission was in effect reduced to just him; and the municipal council, appointed rather than elected, was easily co-opted. He nevertheless found it prudent to still the property owners' fears of higher taxes by devising creative methods of debt financing that rested on expansion of the tax base rather than on any increase in the rate of taxation. He also came armed with strong powers of expropriation "for reasons of public interest" and of condemnation for "insalubrity" bequeathed to him out of the social legislation of the Second Republic. He was prepared to use both in ways their initiators had hardly envisaged. With the propertied interest in any case demoralized, Haussmann struck hard and fast at the core of the problem with scarcely any opposition.

The property owners subsequently staged a successful counterattack through the judiciary and the Council of State (both of which they came to dominate). In 1858, they regained the right to betterment values, which Haussmann had previously retained (with much financial benefit) for the city. They gained increasingly favorable compensation judgments for land taken and, via a maze of decrees and legal judgments, managed to turn the tables entirely on Haussmann by the early 1860s. Haussmann was later to claim that this "victory of privatism over public interests" and the rising costs of compensation, coupled with loss of revenues consequent upon these judgments, lay at the root of the fiscal problems that beset the city in the 1860s. Daumard's data certainly show that owners received compensation well above market value after 1858.[7] This was the trough at which Zola had Saccard feed in *La Curée*. If the property owners consolidated their alliance with the Empire, therefore, they did so partly at Haussmann's expense. And although it would be stretching matters somewhat to argue that they had a direct role in his downfall, enough of them were sufficiently discontented to raise no protest when he fell.

There were deeper processes at work, however, that deserve finer scrutiny. They illustrate the conflicts that arise not only when purely and partially capitalistic practices with respect to the use of property collide, but also when the tensions inherent in the capitalistic form of rationality rise to the surface. Haussmann set out to master such tensions. It was no reflection on his genius that they ended up mastering him. It was his genius to see with such clarity that new practices of property ownership had to be mobilized if Paris was to be transformed and modernized.

THE CIRCULATION OF CAPITAL IN THE BUILT ENVIRONMENT

The mobilization of capital flow to transform the built environment of Paris during the Second Empire was a spectacular affair. "Capital rushed like air into a vacuum," wrote Halbwachs, but it was mainly capital of a certain sort which rushed in, that of the associated capitalists mobilized via the new system of financing.[8] Haussmann's strategy was two-pronged. If he could not find development companies willing or resourceful enough to undertake the massive projects he had in mind, he used the power of the state to mobilize the financing and undertake the brunt of the work. The city could then recapture the betterment values derived from its own investments, thereby becoming, as critics complained, the biggest speculator of all. Private landowners stood by aghast as benefits

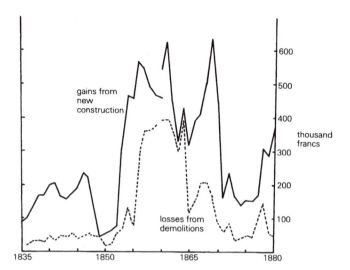

gains from
new
construction

thousand
francs

losses from
demolitions

1835   1850   1865   1880

FIGURE 48 *Increases in the property tax base from new construction (solid line) versus losses through demolitions (broken line) in Paris, 1835–1880 (after Daumard, 1965).*

they felt legitimately belonged to them poured into the city's coffers. It was on this basis that they mobilized their successful legal counterattack of 1858.

But Haussmann's second and preferred strategy was, in the end, even more powerful and compelling. It was, he argued, "best to leave to speculation stimulated by competition" the task of "recognizing the people's real needs and satisfying them."[9] To this end he forged an alliance between the city and a coterie of financial and real estate interests (builders, developers, architects, etc.) assembled under the umbrella power of "associated," or "finance," capital. It was, therefore, a well-organized form of monopolistic competition that he had in mind. And it had to be this way, because the city subsidized the works through donations of land rather than money. In this way, as Zola put it, "the new streets were speculated in as one speculates in stocks and shares."[10] The land itself, as well as the buildings upon it, became a form of fictitious capital. To draw the benefits, however, companies had to be large enough to orchestrate their own externality effects (by, for example, holding onto the prime real estate locations that rapidly improved in value as they developed the land around) and to be able to wait (sometimes several years) for the rise in land value to materialize.

The renewal put large concessions in the hands of a few capitalists who had privileged access to the state (including funds from the newly founded Crédit Foncier) and behind whom stood a phalanx of financiers (like the Pereires) who had a plethora of other interests, including insurance, construction, and building management companies. It was associated, or finance, capital applied to land development, an innovation born out of the particular structures of Empire and opposed to traditional forms of landownership and use. But the very nature of their operations restricted the financiers to meeting the demand for housing and commercial premises from the affluent classes or large-scale commerce. Largely active in the center and west, they played a crucial role in the formation of the predominantly bourgeois quarters that adorned Haussmann's new boulevards. But their permanent impact upon landownership (as opposed to short-term buying and selling, which, as we saw in the case of the Pereires, increasingly dominated their operations) was relatively weak, companies holding less than 6 percent of central city properties in 1880 (see table 3). This was, nevertheless, the system that aroused the jealousy, fear, and ire of the conventional propertied interests. And although some private owners, small-scale builders, architects, and the like evidently participated to some degree in the renewal, they found it increasingly difficult to do so.[11]

The provision of middle-and low-income housing lay entirely outside this system of development. A radically different system of land and housing development arose through the agency of "relatively impoverished" small-scale owners. "Tardily nourished by expropriation and modestly irrigated with credit from the Crédit Foncier," they nevertheless had considerable opportunity to speculate in housing construction, particularly on the northern and eastern peripheries, which formed a veritable urban frontier where low land prices allowed even those with modest savings (lawyers, merchants, shopkeepers, artisans, and even workers) to parlay processes of demographic growth and rising demand for low-income housing into a little personal gain. In the course

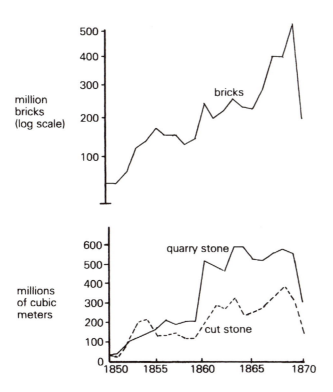

FIGURE 49 *Volume of construction materials entering Paris, 1850–1870. Note that quarry stone and cut stone leveled off after 1860 but that the volume of bricks (attached to lower-quality speculative housing construction) continued to rise in the 1860s.*

of the Second Empire, some of these developers built up a very substantial business, mainly in the peripheral *arrondissements* and entirely outside the system of land development that dominated in the center. They were doubtless stimulated by the example set by the central city renewal to accumulate capital through their own mode of investment in the built environment. Their generally favorable response to the annexation of the suburbs in 1860 rested on their hope—vain, as it turned out—that incorporation within the city would both enhance land values and bring them the rich benefits of expropriation and privileged access to credit. Their sense of having been deceived when such benefits did not materialize led them to become leading critics of Haussmann's politics toward the end of the 1860s.[12]

There was, however, a remarkable surge in housing construction that, after an initial phase when demolitions exceeded new units, added substantially to the city's housing stock, more than keeping pace with population growth for the first time in the century during the 1860s, when housing units expanded by 27 percent and population by only 11 percent. But within this remarkable overall performance there were some equally remarkable divergencies. Paris, Gaillard notes, was divided into two types of development and construction, "each with its own geographical domain, its own clientele, and its own rhythms." Small-scale, largely brick construction of low-income housing on the periphery (Belleville, Batignoles, and similar areas), active in the 1850s, exploded in the 1860s under the pressure of family formation out of the preceding immigration wave coupled with population displacement from the center.[13] The number of bricks entering the city (a good index of this sort of activity) rose continually until 1870. Speculative activity of this sort served the mass of the population and drew its profits out of already low worker incomes. In contrast, the flow of stone to adorn the facades of Haussmann's new boulevards fluctuated more closely with the number of expropriations and the supply of credit. After an initial surge up until 1854, competition for funds (mainly from railroad building) and high-interest rates checked growth until 1859, while the financial troubles of 1864 and 1867–1868 led to rapid contractions in this kind of construction.[14]

And it is also noticeable how the overall pace of growth in this sector slackened in the 1860s as the demand for high-income housing reached a saturation point. The mass of the Parisian housing market oriented to working-class needs marched to an entirely different drummer than that which Haussmann sponsored around the urban renewal. The glamour of the latter has led to undue emphasis upon it, although special attention is warranted to the degree that it represented a radical and innovative departure from traditional forms of land development. What is interesting, however, is the way in which the increasing liberty of circulation of capital in the production of built environments spilled over and outward to the small-scale urban developers of the periphery. From this standpoint Haussmann's integration of the suburbs into the urban frame had, both administratively and spatially, a crucial role to play in facilitating the growth of systems of land development that had languished in preceding periods. And to this system the working class appeared to have no effective answer. A few feeble attempts to mount cooperative endeavors collapsed ignominiously. In this sense the divergencies within the Parisian development process were held together by a common underpinning, that of the circulation of capital.

RENT AND THE SORTING OF LAND TO USES

Large- and small-scale developers also had this in common: they increasingly sought to profit from rising land and property values rather than investing in rents as a steady source of income. The separation between developer and ultimate owner had important impacts upon the level and pattern of land rents and property prices, which in turn generated a different land-use rationale within the city. We here encounter another major transformation worked through during the Second Empire: Land and property rents and prices increasingly functioned to allocate land to uses according to a distinctively capitalistic logic.

Parisian land and property values more than doubled during the Second Empire (see figure 43). The details are hard to reconstruct and indicate a geographical pattern and a rhythm of temporal change of such intricate complexity as to defy easy description.[15] Land prices on the inner streets could be half those along the new boulevards and could vary even more strongly from quarter to quarter. It was precisely across such steep land value gradients that the large-scale developers could operate so successfully, since the new road system created marvelous opportunities to capture rising location rents. The Pereires, for example, paid Fr 430 per square meter at the midpoint of Boulevard Malesherbes to help open the way to land they had purchased around the Parc Monceau (about a kilometer away) for Fr 50 and land a bit beyond that, which they had purchased earlier for less than Fr 10. As soon as the renewal passed, land prices shot up. Land along the Boulevard Sebastopol that went for Fr 25 in 1850 sold for Fr 1,000 per square meter in 1857, and land values increased tenfold in two years on certain areas of the Left Bank after the 1867 Exposition.[16] With geographical gradients and temporal shifts of this order, it is small wonder that speculation in the Parisian land market was an active business. But as the speculation proceeded, the intricate pattern of local peaks and troughs that had once characterized the Parisian rent surface began to be ironed out, leaving a more systematic map of land values in its place. In this way the systematization of space relations implicit in the new road system carried over into a more systematic organization of land values and uses. Uses that could not sustain the rents were gradually forced out and replaced by those that could.

The pattern that emerged showed, as might be expected, a marked gradation from center to periphery (where land could still be had for between Fr 15 and Fr 30 per square meter in 1870) and a tremendous distinction between the bourgeois west and the working-class east, separated by a high-rent commercial center that distinguished a dynamic Right Bank from a rather more lethargic Left Bank. Within this regional structure of land values some sharp gradients continued to exist, but they now tended to represent distinctions of use. For example, land prices fell from Fr 1,000 per square meter around Les Halles to Fr 600 at the Rue Saint-Denis to between Fr 150 and Fr 250 farther east in solidly working-class quarters. And then there were the usual (by modern standards) distinctions between prime sites at key intersections, along the new boulevards, or within the burgeoning commercial complexes, and the lower values on back streets and in residential areas.

This rental sorting of land to uses—a process pushed by land speculation—becomes even more evident when we consider geographical and temporal shifts in property values. The extent of the property boom is indicated by a rise in the total value of Parisian property from 2.5 billion to 6 billion francs between 1852 and 1870, with the increased value of already existing property accounting for 1.5 billion of the increase. The average sale price of houses in old Paris tripled during the same period (see figure 45). Again, there is much intricate variation to be considered. But we can also detect some generalizing processes at work behind the overall rise and increasing geographical segregation in property rents and values.

Haussmann treated it all as a matter of demand and supply, arguing that housing rents would have gone up much faster if he had not opened up access to fresh land at the periphery for development. His critics replied that the demolitions restricted supply and that the renewal sparked the immigration wave that so stimulated demand. While there is an element of truth to both positions, matters were somewhat more complicated. To begin with, construction costs were falling with improved efficiency in the building industry, while there was also, as discussed earlier, a strong surplus of housing construction relative to population, particularly in the 1860s. Rising land costs, though a vital source of gain to developers and builders, were not in themselves sufficient to account for rising rents and property values. A more cogent explanation lies in Gaillard's account of the "embourgeoisement" (or "gentrification," as we might now call it) of much of the Parisian housing market.[17]

Haussmann's policies and access to credit privileged high-value housing construction. Falling construction costs, coupled with interior designs that economized on use of space, put this kind of housing within reach of the segment of the middle class whose incomes were rising. The value of Parisian housing stock increased accordingly. There is also considerable evidence of overproduction of high-value housing, relative even to rising effective demand. The Pereires, for example, found it hard to dispose of all their properties on the Boulevard Malesherbes in the 1860s—a foretaste of their distress to come. But the logic of this kind of "growth machine," once set in motion, is hard to stop. And part of that logic is to seek protection for both the property values created and the clientele served through increasing spatial segregation.

The Second Empire witnessed, therefore, not only the progressive gentrification of the renewed city center but also the rapid creation of exclusive bourgeois quarters toward the west. Contrast this with that "relatively impoverished" system of housing provision for the lower classes, who lacked the privileges accorded high-value construction. Falling costs were more than offset by rising land prices, since it was hard for worker families already crowded into one room to economize much further on space. Furthermore, as we shall see, family formation in the 1860s out of the largely celibate immigration wave of the 1850s changed the nature of the housing demand. Demolition and gentrification in the center restricted low-income supply there and forced low-income demand into other spaces (such as the Left Bank boardinghouses, which saw a rapid increase in rents as a consequence) or into new zones of building on the periphery. And although there was a considerable building boom at the periphery, there is little evidence of overproduction. Rising property values in the working-class sector of the housing market are better explained by the nature of the speculative building process and the increasing proportion of disposable income that most workers were forced to spend on housing. There was also increasing spatial segregation, but largely by default, since it proved hard to attract bourgeois property owners or tenants into areas where the land development process was more and more oriented to low-income speculative housing. The east-west distinction (which had the average property values on the west side exceed that of any quarter on the east) consolidated out of this dual and class-oriented system of housing provision.

The speculative process also entailed heightened competition between different types of users. Financial and commercial uses raised rents between the Bourse and the Chaussée d'Antin to the point where all other uses were precluded, thus imparting a strong dynamic to the northwest center that was lacking elsewhere. Property development on the Left Bank, which lacked such a commercial center and which in any case absorbed a disproportionate number of educational and religious institutions, therefore had a very different dynamic. Though rents rose (from nearly Fr 500 per year in 1860 to over Fr 800 in 1864 for a furnished room near Odéon) under the pressure of demand from displaced central city workers and a rising student population, the pace of renewal was leisurely, and speculation was restrained by the peculiar qualities of landownership structure and the absence of strong competition for the use of land from finance, commerce, or industry.[18] Industry, for its part, also had to cope with the shifting surface of property values, holding on close to the high-rent center only at the price of a drastic reorganization of its labor process or out of access advantages, which made the payment of high rents feasible and desirable. Those industries closely tied to central city markets tended, therefore, to agglomerate toward the inner northeast in the midst of craft worker quarters where rents, though much higher than on the periphery, were much lower than in the commercial and financial inner northwest or the bourgeois residential west. Otherwise industry was forced to seek out cheaper land on the periphery or land of special qualities (nodal points within the communication system, for example) for which it was worth paying a premium rent.

The reorganization, stimulated by the rise of a new credit system, of land and property markets along more purely capitalistic lines (with, to be sure, some strong centers of traditionalist resistance, as on the Left Bank) had important effects. It increasingly bound the organization of the interior space of Paris to price competition between different users for control of space. Industrial, commercial, governmental, and residential uses competed with each other, as did industries of different sorts and housing of different qualities. That Paris was more spatially segregated in 1870 than in 1850 was only to be expected, given the manner in which flows of capital were unleashed to the tasks of restructuring the built environment and its spatial configuration. The new condition of land use competition organized through land and property speculation forced all manner of adaptations upon users. Much of the worker population was dispersed to the periphery (with longer journeys to work) or doubled up in overcrowded, high-rent locations closer to the center. Industry likewise faced the choice of changing its labor process or suburbanizing.

The absorption of labor and capital surpluses through the reconstruction of Paris had all manner of negative effects—such as increasing displacement and segregation, longer journeys to work, and rising rents and overcrowding—that many at the time regarded as downright pathological. Where contemporaries like Louis Lazare went wrong, however, was in attributing all such pathological effects to the evil genius of Haussmann. In this, of course, critics were engaging in that traditional French practice (by no means yet extinct) of attributing any or all signs of pathology to the defective policies and politics of a supposedly all-powerful state. Exactly how powerful that state was in general, and how powerful Haussmann was in particular, requires, therefore, careful consideration.

CHAPTER SEVEN

THE STATE

But it is precisely with the maintenance of that extensive state machine in its numerous ramifications that the material interests of the French bourgeoisie are interwoven in the closest fashion.

—MARX

The French state at midcentury was in search of a modernization of its structures and practices that would accord with contemporary needs. This was as true for Paris as it was for the nation. Louis Napoleon came to power on the wreckage of an attempt to define those needs from the standpoint of workers and a radicalized bourgeoisie. As the only candidate who seemed capable of imposing order on the "reds," he swept to victory as President of the Republic. As the only person who seemed capable of maintaining that order, he received massive support for constituting the Empire. Yet the Emperor was desperately in need of a stable class alliance that would support him (rather than see him as the best of bad worlds) and in need of a political model that would assure effective control and administration. The model he began with (and was gradually forced to abandon in the 1860s) was of a hierarchically ordered but popularly based authoritarianism. The image he used was of a vast national army headed by a popular leader, in which each person would have his or her place in a project of national development for the benefit of all. Strong discipline imposed by the meritocracy at the top was to be matched by expressions of popular will from the bottom. The task of administration was to command and control.

It is tempting to interpret the gyrations of personnel and policies under the Second Empire as the arbitrary vacillations of an opportunistic dreamer surrounded by venal and grasping advisers. I shall follow Gramsci and Zeldin, who, from opposite ends of the

FIGURE 50 *Louis Napoleon's prob-lem, from the very outset, was to maintain a popular basis for his rule. Daumier, in his celebrated depictions of him as an opportu-nistic figure called Ratapoil, here has him, in 1851 before the coup d'état, attempting to seduce a reluc-tant France depicted, as usual, in the feminine figure of Liberty. She replies to his advances by saying that his passion is too sudden to be believable.*

political spectrum, view the Empire as an important transition in French government and politics that, for all its tentativeness, helped bring the institutions of the nation into closer concord with the modern requirements and contradictions of capitalism.[1] In what follows, I shall focus on how this political transition took place in Paris and what the consequences were for the historical geography of the city.

STATE INTERVENTION IN THE CIRCULATION OF CAPITAL

The idea of "state productive expenditures" derives from the Saint-Simonian doctrine to which the Emperor and some of his key advisers, led by Persigny and including Haussmann, loosely subscribed. Debt-financed expenditures, the argument goes, require no additional taxation and are no added burden on the treasury, provided that the expenditures are "productive" and promote that growth of economic activity, which, at a stable tax rate, expands government revenues sufficiently to cover interest and amortization costs. State-financed public works of the sort that the Emperor asked Haussmann to execute could, in principle at least, help absorb surpluses of capital and labor power, and ensure their perpetual full employment at no extra cost to the taxpayer if they produced economic growth.

The main tax base upon which Haussmann could rely was the *octroi*—a tax on commodities entering Paris. Haussmann was prepared to subsidize and deficit-finance any amount of development in Paris, provided it increased this tax revenue. He would, for example, virtually give land away to developers but, by tightly regulating building style and materials, ensure an expansion of tax receipts on the building materials entering the city. From this, incidentally, derived Haussmann's strong partiality for expensive housing for the rich.

The story of Haussmann's slippery financing has been too well told elsewhere to bear detailed repetition.[2] By 1870 his works had cost some 2.5 billion francs, of which half was financed out of budget surpluses, state subsidies, and resale of lands. He borrowed 60 million by direct public subscription (an innovation) in 1855 and sought another 130 million in 1860, which was finally disposed of only in 1862 when the Pereires' Crédit Mobilier took one-fifth. The loan of 270 million francs authorized after strong debate in 1865 was disposed of only with the active help of the Credit Mobilier. Haussmann needed another 600 million, and the prospects of obtaining another loan were poor. Thus he began to tap the Public Works Fund, which was meant as a floating debt, independent of the city budget, designed to smooth out the receipts and expenditures attached to public works that took a long time to complete. The construction costs were normally paid by the builder, who was then paid by the city in as many as eight annual installments (including interest) after the project was complete. Since the builder had to raise the capital, this was in effect a short-term loan to the city. In 1863, some of the builders ran into financial difficulty and demanded immediate payment on a partially finished project. The city turned to the Crédit Foncier, which, at the Emperor's urging, lent the money to the builders on security of a letter from the city to the builders, stating the expected completion date of the project and the schedule of payment. Haussmann was, in effect, borrowing money from the Crédit Foncier via the intermediary of the builders. And it could all be hidden in the Public Works Fund, which was not open to public scrutiny. By 1868, Haussmann had raised nearly half a billion francs this way.

Given Haussmann's association with the Pereires and the Crédit Mobilier, it is hardly surprising that his misdeeds were first revealed in 1865 by Leon Say, an economist of a liberal (i.e., free-market) persuasion and protégé of the Rothschilds. This gave grand ammunition to those opposed to Empire. Jules Ferry's *Comptes Fantastiques d'Haussmann*, which exposed the whole process and then some, hit the presses to great effect in 1868. A fiscally conservative, unimaginative, and politically motivated bourgeoisie undoubtedly played a key role in Haussmann's dismissal. But there was a much deeper problem here, stemming from the form of state involvement in the circulation of capital. Between 1853 and 1870, "the City's debt had risen from 163 million francs to 2,500 millions, and in 1870 debt charges made up 44.14 percent of the City's budget." City finances thus became incredibly vulnerable to all the shocks, tribulations, and uncertainties that attach to the circulation of interest-bearing capital. Far from controlling the future of Paris, let alone being able to stabilize the economy, Haussmann "was himself dominated by the machine he and his imperial master had created." He was, Sutcliffe concludes, fortunate that national political issues forced him out of power, because an overstretched municipal financial structure "could not have survived the repercussions of the international depression of the 1870s."[3]

FIGURE 51 *Construction workers were everywhere after the demolitions truly got going. Here Daumier has two workers speculate that the reason the Tour St. Jacques (to this day an isolated landmark in the city) is being left standing is because it would require an ascent by balloon to demolish it.*

Here, as in other times and places (New York in the 1970s springs immediately to mind), a state apparatus that set out to solve the grand problems of overaccumulation, through deficit-financing its own expenditures, in the end fell victim to the slippery contradictions embodied in the circulation of interest-bearing money capital. Indeed, there is a sense in which the fate of Haussmann mimics that of the Pereires. In this respect, at least, the Emperor and his advisers modernized the state into the pervasive contradictions of contemporary capitalist finance. They placed the state at the mercy of financial markets and paid the price (as have many states since).

THE MANAGEMENT OF LABOR POWER

"I would rather face an hostile army of 200,000," said the Emperor, "than the threat of insurrection founded on unemployment."[4] To the degree that the 1848 Revolution had been made and unmade in Paris, the question of full employment in the capital was a pressing issue. The quickening pace of public works partially solved the problem. "No longer did bands of insurgents roam the streets but teams of masons, carpenters, and other artisans going to work; if paving stones were pulled up it was not to build barricades but to open the way for water and gas pipes; houses were no longer threatened by arson or fire but by the rich indemnity of expropriation."[5] By the mid-1860s more than a fifth of the working population of Paris was employed in construction. This extraordinary achievement was vulnerable on two counts. First, as Nassau Senior put it,

"A week's interruption of the building trade would terrify the government." Second, the seemingly endless merry-go-round of productive expenditures put such a heavy burden of debt on future labor that it condemned much of the population to perpetual economic growth and forced work in perpetuity. When the public works lagged, as they did for both political and economic reasons after 1868, falling tax receipts and unemployment in the construction trades became a very serious issue. That this had a radicalizing effect on workers who, contrary to bourgeois opinion, were by no means as opposed to Haussmann, as was generally thought—he was their main source of employment, and they knew it—is suggested by the disproportionate number of construction workers who participated in the Commune.[6]

The state had some other strings to its bow to stimulate trade. Imperial splendor demanded that the army get new uniforms and that court dress codes be formally established; the fashion of the day become mandatory for status and reputation throughout the city. The stimulus to the clothing trades from 1852 until the late 1850s was immense. Not all labor surpluses could be absorbed by measures of this sort, however. There were vast labor reserves throughout France that flooded into Paris, particularly in the 1850s, partly in response to the employment opportunities created by the public works. So although the indigency rate (an approximate indicator of the labor surplus) dropped from one in every 16.1 inhabitants to one in 18.4 between 1853 and 1862, the absolute number of indigents at no point declined, while the rate itself rose again to one in 16.9 by 1869.[7]

Haussmann's policy toward this massive industrial reserve army underwent an interesting evolution. Eighteenth-century traditions of city charity as a right, of the city's duty to feed the poor (even from the provinces), were gradually abandoned. Haussmann substituted a more modern neo-Malthusian policy. Indeed, given the pressures on the city budget, the size of the welfare problem, and the shifting forms of financing, he probably had no choice. He argued that the city best fulfilled its duty by providing jobs, not welfare, and that if it looked after job creation, it might reasonably diminish its obligation to provide welfare. If the jobs were provided and poverty continued to exist, it was, he hinted, the fault of the poor themselves, who consequently forfeited their right to state support. This is, of course, an argument with which we continue to be very familiar; it was central to the reform of the welfare system in both the United States and Britain in the 1990s. The state apparatus in Paris conceived of its responsibilities toward the poor, the sick, and the aged in a very different way in 1870 than in 1848. This change of administrative attitude toward welfare, medical care, schooling, and the like contributed, Gaillard suggests, to the sense of loss of rights and of community that lay at the root of the social upheavals from 1868 to 1871.[7] That such neo-Malthusian policies should have provoked such popular response is not surprising. Certainly, the Commune sought to reestablish these rights, and even Haussmann, seeking to shore up support for an ailing regime, found himself having to pay increasing attention to welfare questions as unemployment increased and the Empire struggled to live up to its own propaganda that it provided welfare as a safety net from the cradle to the grave.

Haussmann adopted similar principles with respect to the price of provisions. When prices rose unduly, social protest usually provoked a hurried state subsidy. But Haussmann believed in a free market, at least for the working and middle classes. If price fluctuations tied to variable harvests caused difficulty, then the answer lay in a revolving fund into which bakers or butchers paid when supply prices were low and from which they withdrew when supply prices were high. The burden on the city budget was negligible, and price stability was achieved. Haussmann thus pioneered commodity price-stabilization schemes of the sort that became common in the 1930s. But he preferred to do without them, and abandoned all such schemes as free-market liberalism came to the center of government policy after 1860. By that time the elimination of spatial barriers and the availability of imports from a variety of sources eliminated the vulnerability of the Paris food supply to national harvest conditions. Coupled with better distribution within the city, this brought greater security to the city's food supply.

While no simple guiding principles were established in the administration of the city's immensely complicated social welfare machinery, Haussmann's instincts led him in two quite modern directions that were, at first sight, somewhat inconsistent with the centralized authoritarianism of Empire. First, he sought to privatize welfare functions wherever he could (as in the case of education, where he conceived of the state's role as confined to the schooling of indigents only). Second, he sought a controlled decentralization in order to emphasize local responsibility and initiative. The dispersal of the social welfare burden from Paris to the provinces and the decentralization of responsibility for health care, education, and care of the poor into the *arrondissements* fitted into an administrative schema that, while in no way abandoning hierarchy, connected the expectation of service to local ability to pay. The *arrondissements* therefore displaced the city as the institutional center to which those in need of welfare services had to go to get their needs met.

SURVEILLANCE AND CONTROL

The Second Empire was an authoritarian police state, and its penchant for surveillance and control stretched far and wide. Apart from direct police action, informers, spies, and legal harassment, the imperial authorities sought to control the flow of information, mobilized extraordinary propaganda efforts, and used political power and favors to co-opt and control friend and foe alike.[8] The system worked well in rural France but was harder to impose on the cities. Paris posed severe problems, in part because of its revolutionary tradition and in part because of its sheer size and labyrinthine qualities. While Haussmann and the prefect of police (often at loggerheads over jurisdictional questions) were the main pinions of surveillance and control, various governmental departments (Interior, Justice, etc.) were also involved. And laws were shaped with this end in mind. Censorship of the press had been reimposed under the Second Republic—"all republican journals were forbidden," an English visitor noted ironically, "and those only allowed that represented the Orléanist, Legitimist, or Bonapartist factions."[9] The Empire, in its press laws, simply tightened what the republican "party of order" had already imposed. Even the street singers and entertainers, viewed as peddlers of songs and scenes of socialism and subversion by the authorities, had to be licensed, and their songs officially stamped and approved by the prefect, under a law of 1853. The political content of popular culture was hounded off the streets, as were many of the street entertainers themselves. But the frequency with which contemporaries (like Fournel) encountered such characters and the frequency with which Daumier, for one, took them as subjects suggests that the authorities could never squelch this aspect of popular culture entirely.[10]

The police (whom the workers always referred to as spies) were far more dedicated to collecting information and filing reports on the least hint of political opposition than they were to controlling criminal activity. While they managed to instill considerable fear, they do not appear to have been very effective at their work, in spite of a major administrative reorganization in 1854. The fear arose from the vast network of potential informers. "The police are organized in the workshops as they are in the cities," wrote Proudhon; "no more trust among workers, no more communication. The walls have ears."[11] Lodging houses were kept under strict surveillance, their records of those in residence and their comings and goings were regularly inspected, and the concierge often was co-opted into the police network of informers. And when the emperor struck down the workers' right to association, coalition, and assembly (together with the right to strike) in 1852, he replaced it with a system of *conseils de prud'hommes* (councils of workers and employers to resolve disputes within a trade) and mutual benefit associations for workers. To prevent both from becoming hotbeds of socialism, the

FIGURE 52 *The street entertainers were a crucial element in Parisian street life, but controlling them and preventing them from any political pronouncements proved difficult. Daumier is at his very best in this portrait of street musicians in action.*

Emperor appointed the administrative officers (usually on the advice of the prefect of police), who furnished regular reports. A similar system of control was established when the right to hold public meetings was finally conceded in 1868—"assessors" with power to monitor and close down unduly "political" meetings were appointed and obliged to file extensive reports. The propaganda system was no less elaborate.[12] Controlled flows of news and information through an official and semiofficial press, all manner of official pronouncements, and administrative actions (for many of which the prefect was responsible) sought to convince the popular classes of the merits of those at the top (of the Emperor and Empress, in particular). It was rather as if charitable works and officially sponsored galas, expositions, and fêtes were expected to make up for loss of individual freedom.

Such a system had its limits. It is hard to maintain surveillance and control in an economy where the circulation of capital is given free rein, where competition and technical progress race along side by side, sparking all manner of cultural movements and adaptations. Easier communications throughout Europe turned Brussels into a major center of critical publications, the flow of which into France proved difficult, if not impossible, to stem. The dilemmas of press censorship illustrate the problem. The Parisian press grew from a circulation of 150,000 in 1852 to more than a million in 1870.[13] Though dominated entirely by new money interests, the newspapers and journals were diverse enough to create controversies that were bound to touch on government policies. When Say attacked Haussmann's finances in the name of fiscal prudence, he was eroding the Emperor's authority. Republican opponents like Jules Ferry could opportunistically follow suit. And censorship could not easily be confined to politics; it dealt with public morality, too. Most of the songs rejected by the authorities were bawdy rather than political,[14] and the government got into all kinds of tangles in its prosecutions of Baudelaire, Flaubert, and others for public indecency. The effect was to erode the class alliance that should have been the real foundation of the Emperor's power. The political system was, in short, ill adapted in this regard to a burgeoning capitalism. Since the Empire was founded on a capitalist path to social progress, the shift toward liberal Empire was, as Zeldin insists, present at its very foundation.[15]

The same difficulties arose with attempts to control the popular classes. Propaganda as to the Emperor's merits had to rest on something other than his charity. The formula of "fêtes and bread" did well enough on the fêtes, in which the working classes took genuine delight, but did less well on the bread. Falling real wages in the 1860s made a mockery of claims to social progress and made the fêtes look like ghastly extravaganzas mounted at working-class expense. How, then, could the emperor live up to his own rhetoric that he was not a mere tool of the bourgeoisie? His tactic was to try to co-opt Paris workers by conceding the right to strike (1864) and the rights of public assembly and association (1868). He even promoted collective forms of action. Thus did the French branch of the International Working Men's Association issue from a government-sponsored visit of workers to the London Exposition of 1862 (provoking the natural suspicion that it was a mere tool of Empire). And though popular culture had been lulled by years of repression into a surface state of somnolence, an underground current of political rhetoric quickly surfaced as soon as the opening came in 1868.[16]

The urban transformation also had ambivalent effects on the power to watch and control. Many of the dens and rookeries and narrow, easily barricaded streets were swept

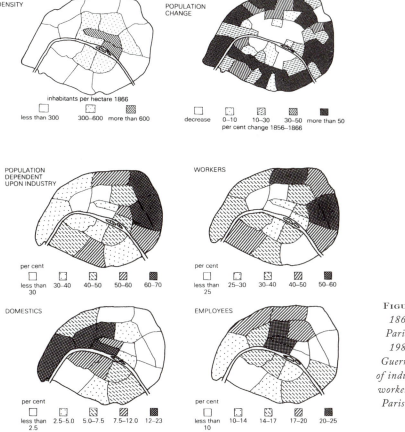

DENSITY

POPULATION
CHANGE

inhabitants per hectare 1866

□ less than 300   ⠂⠂ 300–600   ▨ more than 600

□ decrease   ⠂⠂ 0–10   ▨ 10–30   ▨ 30–50   ▦ more than 50
per cent change 1856–1866

POPULATION
DEPENDENT
UPON INDUSTRY

WORKERS

per cent

□ less than 30   ⠂⠂ 30–40   ▨ 40–50   ▨ 50–60   ▦ 60–70

per cent

□ less than 25   ⠂⠂ 25–30   ▨ 30–40   ▨ 40–50   ▦ 50–60

DOMESTICS

EMPLOYEES

per cent

□ less than 2.5   ⠂⠂ 2.5–5.0   ▨ 5.0–7.5   ▨ 7.5–12.0   ▦ 12–23

per cent

□ less than 10   ⠂⠂ 10–14   ▨ 14–17   ▨ 17–20   ▦ 20–25

FIGURE 53 *Population density in 1866 and population change in Paris, 1856–1866 (after Girard, 1981; Canfora-Argondona and Guerrand, 1976), and distribution of industrially dependent population, workers, employees, and domestics in Paris by* arrondissements *in 1872 (after Chevalier, 1950).*

away and replaced by more easily controlled boulevards. But an uprooted population dispersed from the center, augmented by a flood of immigrants, milled around in new areas like Belleville and Gobelins that became their exclusive preserve. The workers became less of an organized threat, but they became harder to monitor. The tactics and geography of class struggle therefore underwent a radical change.

SHAPING THE SPACES OF SOCIAL REPRODUCTION

"In the space of power, power does not appear as such; it hides under the organization of space."[17] Haussmann clearly understood that his power to shape space was also a power to influence the processes of societal reproduction.

His evident desire to rid Paris of its industrial base and working class, and thus transform it, presumably, into a nonrevolutionary bastion of support for the bourgeois order was far too large a task to complete in a generation (indeed, it was finally realized only in the last years of the twentieth century). Yet he harassed heavy industry, dirty industry, and even light industry to the point where the deindustrialization of much of the city center was an accomplished fact by 1870. And much of the working class was forced out with it, though by no means as far as he wished (figure 53). The city center was given over to monumental representations of imperial power and administration, finance and commerce, and the growing services that spring up around a burgeoning tourist trade. The new boulevards not only provided opportunities for military control, but they also permitted (when lit with gas lighting and properly patrolled) free circulation of the bourgeoisie within the commercial and entertainment quarters. The transition toward an "extroverted" form of urbanism, with all of its social and cultural effects, was assured (it was not so much that consumption increased, which it did, but that its conspicuous qualities became more apparent for all to see). And the growing residential segregation not only protected the bourgeoisie from the real or imagined dangers of the dangerous and criminal classes but also increasingly shaped the city into relatively secure spaces of reproduction of the different social classes. To these ends Haussmann showed a remarkable ability to orchestrate diverse social processes, using regulatory and planning powers and mastering the geography of those neighborhood spill-over effects (in which an investment here enhances the value of another investment there), to reshape the geography of the city.

The effects were not always those Haussmann had in mind, in part because the collective processes he sought to orchestrate took matters in a quite different direction (this was true for industrial production, as we shall later see). But his project was also political from the very start and automatically sparked political counterprojects, not simply within the working class but also among different factions of the bourgeoisie. Thus Michel Chevalier (the Emperor's favorite economist) argued against ridding the city of industry, since this would undermine stable employment and threaten social peace. Until Haussmann had it closed down, Louis Lazare used the influential *Revue Municipale* not only to execrate the speculations of the Pereires but also to castigate Haussmann's works for the way they emphasized the social and geographical divisions between "the old Paris, the Paris of Luxury" and "the new Paris, that of Poverty"—a sure provocation, as he saw it, to social revolt. After that, he wrote books denouncing the social effects of Haussmann's works, but by the time they were published, Haussmann was already gone. Haussmann (and the Emperor) had to seek a coalition of interests in the midst of such warring voices.[18]

THE SEARCH FOR A CLASS ALLIANCE

It was the duty of any prefect to cultivate and consolidate political support for the government in power. Since he had no political party behind him and no natural class alliance to which he could appeal, Napoleon III had to find a deeper social basis for his power than a mere family name and support from the army.[19] Haussmann needed to help conjure up some such class alliance within a politically hostile city and thus give better grounding to imperial power and, by extension, his own.

The drama of his fall tends to conceal how successful Haussmann was at this, under conditions of shifting class configurations (shaped by rapid urban growth and capital accumulation) and stressful modernization, which were bound to stir "blind discontent, implacable jealousies and political animosities." Nonetheless, as kingpin in an incredible "growth machine," he had all kinds of largesse to distribute, around which all manner of interests could congregate. The trouble, of course, is that when the trough runs dry, the interests feed elsewhere. Furthermore, as Marx often noted, the bourgeois is "always inclined to sacrifice the general interest of his class for this or that private motive"—a judgment with which Haussmann concurs, complaining in his *Memoires* of the "prevalence of privatism over public interest." In the absence of a powerful political party or any other means for cultivating expressions of support from some dominant class alliance, Haussmann always remained vulnerable to quick betrayal out of narrow material interests.[20] His slippery financing, from this standpoint, has to be seen as a desperate move to keep the trough full in order to preserve his power.

Haussmann's relation with the landlord class was always difficult, since he took a grander view of spatial structure than that defined by narrow private property rights. And the landlord class was itself fragmented into feudal and modern, large and small, central and peripheral. But Gaillard is probably right in sensing "the progressive tightening of the alliance between the Empire and the Parisian property owners."[21] This, however, had as much to do with the transition in the meaning of property ownership as it did with any fundamental adaptation on the part of government. In any case, property owners of any sort are probably the most likely of all to betray class interests for narrow private gain. Haussmann's alliance with the Pereires was, while it lasted, extremely powerful, but here, too, finance capital was in transition. The downfall of the Pereires and the growing ascendancy of fiscal conservatism in financial circles undermined in the late 1860s what had earlier been a solid pillar of his support. It was, recall, a protégé of Rothschild's who first attacked Haussmann's methods of financing. At the same time, Haussmann's relations with the industrial interests went from bad to worse, so that by the end of Empire they were solidly against him. Here he definitely reaped what he himself had sown in his struggle to rid the city of industry. And commercial interests, though much favored by what Haussmann did, were typically pragmatic, taking what they could but not enthusiastically supportive in return. Most interesting of all is Haussmann's relation to the workers. These forever earned his wrath and denigration by voting solidly republican as early as 1857.[22] And he rarely made attempts to cultivate any populist base. Yet surprisingly little worker agitation was directed at him in the troubled years of 1868–1870, and his dismissal was greeted with dismay and demonstrations in the construction trades. As the grand provider of jobs, he had evidently earned the loyalty of at least part of the working class. And if there were problems with high rents, workers well understood that it was landlords, and not Haussmann, who pocketed the money.

There were deeper sources of discontent that made it peculiarly hard to maintain a stable class alliance within the city. The transformation itself sparked widespread nostalgia and regret (common to aristocrat and worker alike) at the passing of "old Paris," and contributed to that widespread sense of loss of community which Gaillard makes so much of.[23] Old ways and structures were upset. Haussmann knew it, and established institutions to assemble, catalog, and record what was being lost. He established the Bibliothèque Historique de la Ville de Paris, and Marville was employed to record changes in the urban landscape. But nothing clearly emerged to replace what had been lost. And here the failure to establish an elected form of municipal government for the city surely hurt. For Haussmann steadfastly refused to see Paris as a community in the ordinary sense, but treated it as a capital city within which all manner of diverse, shifting, and "nomadic" interests and individuals came and went so as to preclude the formation of any solid or permanent sense of community. It was therefore vital that Paris be administered for and by the nation, and to this end he promoted and defended the Organic Law of 1855, which put all real powers of administration into the hands of an appointed prefect rather than elected officials. Haussmann may have been right about the transitory qualities of the Parisian community, but the denial of popular sovereignty in the capital was a burning issue that pulled many workers and bourgeois into support of the Commune.[24] From this standpoint, Haussmann's failure to sustain a permanent class alliance had less to do with what he did than with how he did it. But then the authoritarian style of his administration had everything to do with the circumstances that gave rise to the coup d'état in the first place. So it stood to reason that he could not long survive the transition to liberal Empire.

The towering figure of Haussmann dominates the state apparatus of Paris throughout the Second Empire. To say that he merely rode out the storm of social forces unleashed through the rapid accumulation of capital is by no means to diminish his stature, because he rode out the storm with consummate artistry and orchestrated its turbulent power with remarkable skill and vision for some sixteen years. It was, however, a storm he neither created nor tamed, but a deep turbulence in the evolution of French economy, politics, and culture, that in the end threw him as mercilessly to the dogs as he threw medieval Paris to the *demolisseurs* (demolishers). In the process the city achieved an aura of capitalist modernity, in both its physical and its administrative infrastructures, that has lasted to this day.

CHAPTER EIGHT

ABSTRACT AND CONCRETE LABOR

Besides the factory operatives, the manufacturing workman and the handicraftsworkers, whom it concentrates in large masses at one spot, and directly commands, capital also sets in motion by means of invisible threads, another army: that of the workers in domestic industries.

—MARX

The collective force and power of workers had proven indispensable to the overthrow of the July Monarchy and their degraded condition subsequently spawned innumerable proposals and movements for social and industrial reform during the 1840s. The question of work therefore lay at the heart of Parisian workers' concerns in 1848. The exact role in this of skilled workers from the craft tradition—a superior class comprising some 40 percent of the workforce, according to Corbon, writing at the midpoint of Empire—is not, however, an easy matter to determine.[1] By the standard account, these workers, confident in their skills but demoralized by chronic insecurity, convinced of the nobility of work as an ideal but constantly distressed by the experience of it, and believing that labor was the source of all wealth, sought a new kind of industrial order that would temper the insecurity of work, alleviate their relative penury, and stave off growing trends toward deskilling and increasing exploitation. Rancière, however, casts doubt upon the power and character of this craft tradition.[2] The evidence he adduces, based largely on the writings of worker poets and authors contributing to the newspaper *L'Atelier*, certainly points to the dangers of romanticizing and homogenizing the craft worker as the bearer of a distinctively proletarian revolutionary consciousness. The workers whose writings and correspondence Rancière studies in detail sought relief from work and had few illusions about the nobility of backbreaking labor. They sought respect from their employers, not

FIGURE 54 *Daumier's* The Worker *captures something of both the self-confidence and the subservient position of Parisian workers who the employer Poulot, for one, believed had a far too high opinion of themselves.*

revolution. They wanted to be treated as equals and as human beings rather than as hired hands. They wanted immediate solutions and personal help with their individual problems. They showed little interest in the Blanquist idea of a dictatorship of the proletariat, and most looked to the Saint-Simonian movement as a source of financial support and employment rather than as a fecund source of ideas for social reform.

But while Rancière's account administers a corrective to the revolutionary romanticism sometimes pressed by Marxist-inspired labor historians, it is not at all clear that his account captures the sentiments of those workers who did fight on the barricades and participated in the deliberations of the Luxembourg Commission, and who actively supported the efforts of Cabet, Considérant, Proudhon, and the communists/socialists of the time. To be sure, most workers seem to have looked for some form of association, autogestion, or mutualism rather than centralized state control. But the recalcitrance of the bourgeoisie in general, and of employers in particular, often forced them (as it did Cabet, Considérant, Leroux, and others) into positions where they had no choice except to take a more revolutionary stance. While there was, evidently, a good deal of confusion and flux with respect to both agenda and means (particularly resort to violence), there is no question that most craft workers looked to the creation of a social republic in 1848 that would support their efforts to reorganize work and reform the social relations of production so as to set the stage for their own social advancement for decades to come.

The evolution of Parisian industry during the Second Empire took a very special path. Paris at midcentury was by far the most important and diversified manufacturing center in the nation. And in spite of its image as a grand center of conspicuous consumption, it in fact remained a working-class city, heavily dependent upon the growth of production. In 1866, for example, 58 percent of its 1.8 million people depended upon industry, whereas only 13 percent depended upon commerce.[3] But there were some very special features of its industrial structure and organization (tables 4, 5, and 6). In 1847, more than half the manufacturing firms had fewer than two employees, only 11 percent employed more than ten, and no more than 425 qualified for the title of "grand enterprises" (more than 500 workers). It was difficult in many cases to distinguish between owners and workers, and Scott shows how the inquiry of 1847–1848 deliberately confused the categories for political reasons.[4] Since the craft workers had in any case evolved hierarchical forms of command, there was little basis within the small enterprises for strong class antagonisms (a condition that prevailed throughout the Second Empire and led a whole wing of the workers' movement, particularly that influenced by Proudhon, to disapprove of strikes, push for association, and confine their opposition to financiers, monopolists, landlords, and the authoritarian state rather than to private property and capital ownership). It was also very difficult to distinguish commerce from manufacturing, since the atelier in the back was often united with the boutique on the street front.

These conditions varied somewhat from industry to industry, as well as with location. Apart from food and provisions (in which the distinction between industry and commerce was particularly hard to define), the textile and clothing trades, together with furniture and metalworking, dominated, cut across by all manner of "articles de Paris" for which the city had become, and would remain, justly famous. Most of the classic sectors for capitalist industrial development were, therefore, absent from the capital; and even textiles, which had been important, was by 1847 mostly dispersed to the provinces, leaving the garment industry behind in Paris. Plainly, most of Parisian industry was oriented to serving its own market. Only in the metalworking and engineering sectors could any semblance of a "modern" form of capitalistic industrial structure be discerned.

This vast economic enterprise could not easily be transformed. Yet it underwent significant evolution in terms of industrial mix, technology, organization, and location. It surged out of the depression of 1848–1850 with a surprising elan that first infected light industry and then, after 1853, spread to the building trades and heavy engineering and metalworking, as well as to the garment industry. During the 1860s the pace of growth slowed, particularly in the large-scale industries, and became more selective as to sector and location.

Table 4 *Employment Structure of Paris, 1847 and 1860*

	1847 (Old City)			1860 (New City)		
Occupation	Firms	Workers	Workers per Firm	Firms	Workers	Workers per Firm
Textiles & clothing	38,305	162,710	4.2	49,875	145,260	2.9
Furniture	7,499	42,843	5.7	10,638	46,375	4.4
Metals & engineering	7,459	55,543	7.4	9,742	68,629	7.0
Graphic arts	2,691	19,132	7.1	3,018	21,600	7.2
Food	2,551	7,551	3.0	2,255	12,767	5.7
Construction	2,012	25,898	12.9	2,676	50,079	18.7
Precision instruments	1,569	5,509	3.5	2,120	7,808	3.7
Chemicals	1,534	9,988	6.5	2,712	14,335	5.3
Transport equipment	530	6,456	12.2	638	7,642	12.0

Source: Daumas and Payen (1976).

Table 5 *Economically Dependent Population of Paris, 1866*

Occupation	Owners	Employees and Workers	Families	Total	%
Textiles & clothing	26,633	182,466	103,964	313,063	25.3
Building	5,673	79,827	71,747	157,247	12.7
Arts and graphics[a]	11,897	73,519	60,449	145,865	11.8
Metals	4,994	42,659	50,053	98,906	8.0
Wood and furniture	5,282	27,882	33,093	66,257	5.3
Transport	9,728	35,022	48,938	93,688	7.6
Commerce	51,017	78,009	101,818	240,840	18.6
Diverse[b]	10,794	50,789	58,435	120,018	9.7
Unclassified	2,073	4,608	5,417	12,098	1.0
Total	128,091	575,981	533,914	1,237,987	(100.0)

Source: Rougerie (1971), 10. (N.B. The total population of Paris in 1866 stood at 1,825,274; see table 1.)

[a] Includes printing, *articles de Paris*, precision instruments, and work with precious metals.

[b] Includes leather, ceramics, chemicals.

TABLE 6 *Business Volume of Parisian Industries, 1847–1848 and 1860*
(billions of francs)

Business	1847–1848	1860
Food and beverages	226.9	1,087.9
Clothing	241.0	454.5
Articles de Paris	128.7	334.7
Building	145.4	315.3
Furniture	137.1	200.0
Chemical and ceramic	74.6	193.6
Precious metals	134.8	183.4
Heavy metals	103.6	163.9
Fabrics and thread	105.8	120.0
Leather and skins	41.8	100.9
Printing	51.2	94.2
Coach building	52.4	93.9

Source: Gaillard (1977), 376.

The Enquêtes of 1847–1848, 1860, and 1872, though flawed, permit a reconstruction of the general path of industrial evolution.[5] The Enquête of 1860 lists 101,000 firms employing 416,000 workers—an increase of 11 percent over 1847, with most of the net gain due to annexation of the suburbs, since comparable data for old Paris indicate a loss of 19,000 workers. But the number of firms increased by 30 percent, indicating a surprising expansion of small firms. However, the number of firms employing fewer than two workers had risen to 62 percent (from 50 percent in 1847–1848), and the number employing more than ten workers had fallen from 11 to 7 percent. This increasing fragmentation was observable in many sectors and was particularly marked in old Paris. In the clothing trades, for example, the number of enterprises increased by 10 percent, while workers employed declined by 20 percent. The figures for the chemical industry were even more startling—45 percent more firms and 5 percent fewer workers. Machine building, the largest-scale industry in 1847–1848, with an average of 63 employees per firm, had fragmented to an average of 24 workers by 1860.

The exact interpretation to be put on this is controversial. On the surface, everything points to the vigorous growth of many very small firms and an increasing fragmentation of industrial structure, a process that continued until the end of the Empire and beyond. Furthermore, this growth and fragmentation of small firms could be seen both close to the center and in peripheral locations. The strong absolute growth of large firms between 1847–1848 and 1860 (the number remained virtually unchanged from 1860 to 1872) was

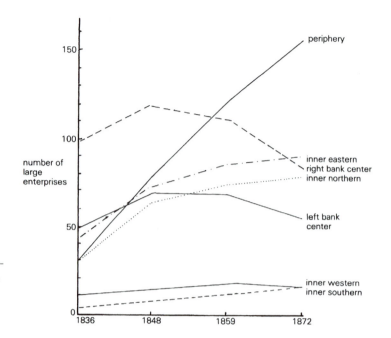

FIGURE 55 *Number of large enter-prises in different sectors of Paris, according to the surveys of 1836, 1848, 1859, and 1872 (after Daumas and Payen, 1976).*

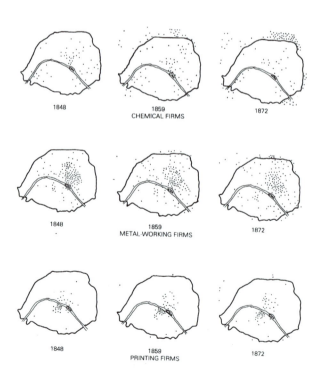

FIGURE 56 *The location of large-scale chemical, metalworking, and printing firms in Paris according to the Enquêtes of 1848, 1859, and 1872 (after Retel, 1977).*

FIGURE 57 *Large factories, like this chemical concern, began to emerge in suburban locations like La Villette in the 1860s.*

accompanied by their suburbanization. But even here the movement was not uniform. Large-scale printing retained its central location on the Left Bank, while metalworking moved only as far as the inner northern and eastern peripheries. Large-scale chemical operations, however, tended to move much farther out.

The case of the chemical industry is interesting to the degree that it captures much of the complex movement at work in Parisian industry during this period. On the one hand, large-scale and often dirty enterprises either were forced out or voluntarily sought out peripheral locations at favored points within the transport network where land was relatively cheap. On the other hand, product innovation meant the proliferation of small firms making specialized products like porcelain, pharmaceuticals, and costume jewelry, artificial flowers, while other industries, mainly in the "articles de Paris" category, generated specialized demands for small quantities of paints, dyes, and the like, which could best be met by small-scale production. Within many industries there was a similar dual movement that saw a growth of some large firms in suburban locations and an increasing fragmentation and specialization of economic activity particularly close to the center.

This highly specialized development had much to do with the maintenance of superior skills of a small group of "superior" workers. The fragmentation and turn to outwork paid by the piece, may also be seen as concessions to the strong predilection of craft workers to conserve their autonomy, independence, and nominal control over their labor process. Yet there was a major transformation of social relations that the raw statistics hide. For what in effect happened, Gaillard convincingly argues, is that there was an increasingly sophisticated detail division of specialized labor in which the products of individuals, small firms, and outworkers and pieceworkers were integrated into a highly efficient production system. Many small firms were nothing more than subcontracting units for larger forms of organization. They therefore functioned more as indentured labor systems beholden to capitalist producers or merchants who controlled them at a distance.[6] By having the work done by the piece at home, the capitalists saved on such overhead costs as premises and energy. Furthermore, by keeping these units perpetually in competition for work, the employers could force down labor costs and maximize their own profits. Workers, even though nominally independent, were forced into subservience and into patterns of self-exploitation that could be as savage and as degrading as anything to be found in the factory system.

Within this a much-hated and oppressive system of foremen, overseers, subcontractors (which had been outlawed under the social legislation of 1848 and reinstated after 1852), and other go-betweens could become all too firmly implanted. So though the craft workers continued to be important, their position underwent a notable degradation. The extreme division of labor helped achieve an unparalleled quality and technical perfection in some spheres, but it yielded neither higher wages nor increasing liberty to the worker. It meant, rather, the gradual subsumption of formerly independent craft workers and owners under the formal domination of a tightly controlled commercial and industrial organization. As a consequence, even Poulot (who spent much of his time criticizing the lazy habits and recalcitrance of his workers in the face of authority) ended up admitting,

> Paris is the city where people work harder than anywhere else in the world. . . . When workers come up to Paris from the provinces, they don't always stay, because so much graft is needed to earn a living. . . . In Paris, there are certain trades which function by piecework, where after twenty years the worker is crippled and worn out, that is if he is still alive.[7]

Behind this general evolution, however, lay a variety of forces that deserve further scrutiny. The reduction of spatial barriers opened up the extensive and valuable Parisian market to provincial and foreign competition (a process further encouraged after the move toward free trade in 1860). But it also meant that Parisian industry had access to geographically more dispersed raw materials and food supplies to feed its laborers and meet its demand for intermediate products at lower cost. Given industry's powerful base in the Parisian market, this meant that Paris could just as easily compete in the provinces and abroad as it could be competed with.

Paris in fact expanded its share of a growing French export trade from around 11 percent in 1848 to 16 percent by the early 1860s.[8] As might be expected, the luxury consumer goods in which Paris specialized were well represented in this vast export surge. But more than half the locomotives and railway equipment and a fifth of the steam engines produced in Paris followed French capital abroad, and even some of the food industry (such as sugar refining) could find a place in provincial markets. The Parisian industrial interest, unlike some of its provincial counterparts, was by no means opposed to free trade, since Parisian manufacturing was evidently capable of dominating provincial and international markets in certain lines of production.

But its advantageous position in relation to this new international division of labor carried some penalties. Parisian industry was more and more exposed to the vagaries of foreign markets. The general expansion of world trade in the period was an enormous

FIGURE 58 *Carpetmaking at Les Gobelins was a typical high-quality artisanal industry that survived during the Second Empire, and benefited from better access to foreign markets (by Doré).*

boon, of course, but industrialists had to be able to adapt quickly to whims of foreign taste, the sudden imposition of tariff barriers, the rise of foreign manufacturing (that had the ugly habit of copying French designs and producing them more cheaply, though with inferior quality), and the interruptions of war (the American Civil War had particularly dire effects, since America was a major export market). Parisian industry also needed to adapt to the peculiar flow requirements of foreign trade. The growth of the American trade, for example, increased problems of seasonal unemployment. The arrival of raw cotton from America in autumn put money into the hands of American buyers, who spent it as fast as they could in order to get their products back to the United States by spring. Three months of intense activity could be followed by nine months of "dead season." The Enquête of 1860 showed that more than one-third of Parisian firms had a dead season, with more than two-thirds of those producing "articles de Paris" and more than half in the furniture, clothing, and jewelry trades experiencing a dead season of between four and six months.[9] I shall take up the problems this posed for the organization of production and labor markets shortly.

Foreign and provincial competition not only challenged Parisian industry in international and provincial markets, but it also looked with a hungry eye at the enormous and expanding consumer and intermediate goods market that Paris offered. External competition became increasingly fierce in the 1860s. At first, the challenge came from mass-produced goods, in which, with cheaper labor and easier access to raw materials, provincial and foreign producers had a distinct cost advantage that falling freight rates made ever more evident. Shoe production thus dispersed into the provinces, to Pas-de-Calais, l'Oise, and similar places. But where mass production went, luxury goods could all too easily follow. The exact process whereby this occurred can best be illustrated by examining the new relations emerging in Paris between industry and commerce.

INDUSTRY IN RELATION TO FINANCE AND COMMERCE

The relative power of industrial, financial, and commercial interests shifted markedly in Paris during the Second Empire. While certain large enterprises remained immune, the mass of small-scale industry was increasingly subjected to the external discipline imposed by financiers and merchants. The latter became, in effect, the agents who ensured the transformation of concrete labor to abstract requirements.

The rise of a new credit system favored the creation of large-scale production and service enterprises in several different ways. Direct financing of factory production using modern forms of technology and industrial organization became feasible. In this, the Pereires pioneered the way, but were quickly followed by a whole gamut of financial institutions. But the indirect effects were just as profound. The changing scale of public works and construction (at home and abroad) and the formation of a mass market for many products (signaled by the rise of the department store, itself a child of the credit system) favored large-scale industry. The absorption of small savings within the new credit structures tended also to dry up small, local, and familiar sources of credit to small businesses without putting anything in their place. The net effect was to redistribute credit availability, putting it more and more out of direct reach of small producers and artisans.

The new credit system was not, therefore, welcomed by most industrialists, who saw the financiers—all too correctly, in the case of the Pereires—as instruments of control and merger. The class relation between producers and money capitalists was typically one of distrust. Indeed, the downfall of the Pereires probably had as much to do with the power of commercial and industrial interests within the Bank of France as it did with the much-vaunted personal antagonism of Rothschild. The lengthy polemics waged against the excessive monopoly power of the financiers toward the end of the Second Empire earned the plaudits of artisans and small businesses, and partly explains the growing bourgeois opposition to the economic policies of the Empire.[10]

Yet the small-scale producers and artisans, faced as they often were with lengthy dead seasons and all manner of settlement dates, had a desperate need for short-term credit. The Bank of France provided discount facilities on commercial paper but served only a very few customers.[11] Only toward the end of the period did other financial institutions arise to begin to fill this gap. What existed in their stead was an informal and parallel financing system based either on kinship ties or on small-scale credits offered between buyers and sellers—a system that spread down even into the lower levels of the working class, who could not have survived if they had not been able to buy on time. And it was out of such a system that a newly consolidating merchant class came to exercise an increasing degree of control over the organization and growth of Parisian industry.

Commerce had always had a special place in the Parisian economy, of course. But at midcentury the distinctions between manufacturing and merchanting were so confused that the expression of a distinctive merchant interest lay with various kinds of specialized traders (in wine, for example). Commerce was, for the most part, the servant of industry. The Second Empire, however, was marked by a growing separation of production from merchanting and a gradual reversal of power relations to the point where much of Parisian industry was increasingly forced to dance to the tune that commerce dictated.[12] The transformation was gradual rather than traumatic, for the most part. Owners simply preferred to keep the boutique and give up the atelier. But they did not give up a direct relation to the producers. They typically became the hub of a network of subcontracting, production on command or by the piece, and of outwork. In this way an increasingly autonomous merchant class became the agent for the formal subsumption of artisan and craft labor under the rule of merchants' capital. "Sometimes," writes Cottereau, "several hundred pseudo-craftworkers and a couple of dozen small workshops were nothing more than the terminal antennae of large clothing interests each with several thousand employees, managed by merchants, industrialists or department stores." Worse still, these new "nodes of capitalist organization. . . . were constantly redistributing work, reorganizing their operations, in order to place as many of them as possible in the hands of a workforce without any recognized skills; laborers, women, children and old people."[13]

The remarkable degree of fragmentation of tasks and specialization in Parisian industry gave it much of its competitive power and reputation for quality in both local and international markets. And the Second Empire saw increasing refinements in this form of organization. Artificial flower making, which already tended to be specialized as to type of flower in different workshops in 1848, was by the end of the Empire organized into a system of workshops producing parts of particular flowers. Maxime du Camp complained of the "infinite division of labor" that called for the coordination of nine different skills to produce a simple knife.[14] That such a system could work at all was entirely due to the efficient organizing skills of the merchant entrepreneurs who supplied the raw materials, organized the detail division of labor among numerous scattered workshops or through piecework at home, supervised quality of product and timing of flows, and absorbed the finally assembled product into well-defined markets.

FIGURE 59 *As early as 1843, Daumier laughed at the organization of the new dry goods stores. The clerk is explaining the intricate route the customer must take to navigate around the store and arrive at his destination in the part of the shop that sells cotton bonnets.*

Yet the very same agents who reorganized Parisian industry to ward off foreign competition also brought foreign and provincial competition into the heart of the Parisian market. Under competitive pressure to maximize profits, the Parisian merchants were by no means loath to search out all manner of different supply sources from the provinces and even from abroad, extending their network of commands and outwork well outside of Paris wherever they found costs (particularly of labor) cheaper. They thus stimulated external competition as much as they organized to repel it, and in some cases actively organized the geographical dispersal of some phases of production to the provinces. Foreign and provincial merchants, once an itinerant or seasonal presence in the city, tended to settle permanently and, making use of international and provincial contacts, organized an increasingly competitive flow of goods into the Parisian market. Examples even exist, as in the hat and glove trade, of the separation of production (which went to the provinces) from design and marketing, which remained in the capital.[15]

There were other developments in merchanting that had a strong impact upon various aspects of Parisian industry. The rise of the large department stores meant the formation of ready-to-wear mass markets. Demand shifted to whatever could be mass-produced profitably, irrespective of its use, value, or qualities. Mass marketing did not necessarily mean mass factory production, but it did imply the organization of small workshop production along different lines (subcontracting being dominant). Worker complaints about the declining concern for quality of product and the deskilling of work in the craft tradition had much to do with the spectacular growth of this kind of trade as large department stores like the Bon Marché (founded in 1852 and with a turnover of 7 million francs by 1869), the Louvre (1855), and Printemps (1865) became centerpieces of Parisian commerce.[16]

By the 1860s, a hierarchically structured credit system was increasingly becoming the powerful nerve center for industrial development, but it had not yet extended down to the small enterprise. The merchants, well served when necessary by both new and old credit structures, stepped in to become the organizing force for much small industry. The increasing autonomy of this merchant class during the Second Empire was signaled by the formation of distinctive merchant quarters, around the Chaussée d'Antin in the northwest center and, to a lesser degree, around Mail et Sentier and in the northeast center (Rue Paradis, then as now, was the thriving center for glass and porcelain ware). It was from here that local, provincial, and international production for the Parisian market and for export was increasingly organized. These quarters also offered special kinds of white-collar employment opportunities, which left an imprint on the division of social space in the city (see figure 53). Special traditions arose in these quarters with respect to politics, education, religion, and the like that led merchants to participate very little in either the formation or the repression of the Commune.

The increasing autonomy of the merchant class and the rise of new financial power spun a complex web of control around much of Parisian industry, while the merchants' concern for profit and their geographical range of operation led them toward a restructuring of Parisian industry to meet the conditions of a new international division of labor. The small-scale producers, once proud and independent craft workers and artisans, were increasingly imprisoned within a network of debts and obligations, of specific commands and controlled supplies; were forced into the position of detail laborers within an overall system of production whose evolution appeared to escape their control. It was within such a system that the processes of deskilling and domination, which had been evident before 1848, could continue to work their way through the system of production. That the workers recognized the nature of the problem is all too clear. The Workers' Commission of 1867 debated the problems at length and put the question of social credit and the liberty of work at the forefront of its social agenda. But by then there had been nearly twenty years in which the association of capital had dominated the noble vision of the association of labor.

INDUSTRY, THE STATE, AND PRIVATE PROPERTY

Haussmann, as we have seen, had no compunction about expelling noxious or unwanted industry (like tanning and some chemicals) from the city center by direct clearance or use of the laws on insalubrity.[17] He also sought by all manner of indirect means (taxation, annexation of the suburbs, orientation of city services) to push most industry, save that of luxury goods and "articles de Paris," out of the city center. His anti-industry policies derived in part from the desire to create an "imperial capital" fit for the whole of Western civilization, but just as important was his concern to rid Paris of the political power of the working class by getting rid of its opportunities for employment. In this he was only partially successful.[18] Though the deindustrialization of the very center was an accomplished fact by 1870, the improvements in communications and in urban infrastructures (gas, water, sewers, etc.) made Paris a very attractive location. Haussmann to some degree counteracted with the one hand what he sought to do with the other. But his failure to attend to the needs of industry and his patent favoring of residential development (for example, in the design of the third network of roads) earned him increasing opposition from industrial interests, which had, in any case, been powerful enough to thwart some of the Emperor's plans for relocation. And to the degree that provincial and international competition picked up in the 1860s, at the same time that Haussmann's campaign against industry intensified, the difficulties of Parisian industry were more and more laid at his door, and a lively opposition to Empire was provoked.

Rent was an important cost that Parisian industry had to bear. The rapidly rising rents in the new financial and commercial quarters (Bourse, Chaussée d'Antin) and in the high-quality residential quarters toward the west and northwest either forced existing industry out or acted (on the western periphery, for example) as a barrier to the implantation of new industry. Rising rents in the center either pushed industry out toward the suburbs or forced it to cluster or intensify its use of space in locations of particular advantage. Metalworking, for example, dispersed a relatively short distance toward the northeast, where it found good communications and access to a superior labor supply (see figure 56). The higher-rent areas closer to the center also proved to be very attractive locations (Haussmann compared them to the vineyards on Mount Vesuvius, which improve in fertility with closeness to the top). This was particularly true for those industries for which immediate access to the luxury consumer goods market (or to industries that supplied such markets) was of vital importance. The attractions of a central location were enhanced by the centralization of commerce in the large department stores, the hotels that served a growing tourist trade, and the central market of Les Halles, which drew all manner of people to it.

The public works and urban investments created an additional market of seemingly endless demand (including that for lavish furniture and decoration), much of it concentrated close to the city center. Many industries had a strong incentive to cling to central locations—pharmaceuticals, toiletries, paints, metalworking (particularly of the ornamental sort), carpentry, and woodworking, as well as the manufacturers of modish clothing and articles de Paris. But the high rents had to be paid. And here the adaptation that saw the growth of outwork paid by the piece made a great deal of sense, because the workers then bore either the high cost of rent themselves (working at home in overcrowded quarters) or the cost of inaccessibility to the center. The merchants could save on rental costs while making sure production was organized into a configuration that flowed neatly into the high points of demand. The independent ateliers that did remain were caught in a cost squeeze, which either forced them into the arms

of the merchants or pushed them to reorganize their internal division of labor and so reduce labor costs. Rising rents in the city center exacted a serious toll on industry and the laborers, and in so doing played a key role in the industrial restructuring of Paris under the Second Empire.

FIGURE 60 *The tanning factories along the highly polluted Bièvre River are captured in this Marville photo from the mid-1860s. These were the kinds of dirty industries that Haussmann sought to expel from the central areas of the city.*

PRODUCTIVITY, EFFICIENCY, AND TECHNOLOGY

There is a general myth, of which historians are only now beginning to disabuse us, that large-scale industry drives out small-scale industry because of the superior efficiency achieved through economies of scale.[19] The persistence of small-scale industry in Paris during the Second Empire appears to refute the myth, for there is no doubt that the small workshops survived precisely because of their superior productivity and efficiency. Yet it is dangerous to push the refutation too far. The industries in which economies of scale

FIGURE 61 *The collective use of steam engines became a feature of Parisian industry during this period. This design, from 1872, illustrates how the system, working through a steam engine in the basement and distributing power to several floors above, allows for the building to be occupied by different businesses.*

could easily be realized (such as textiles and, later on, some aspects of clothing) dispersed to the provinces, and large-scale engineering either suburbanized or went elsewhere. And the small-scale industry that was left behind and that exhibited such vigorous growth achieved economies of scale not through fusion of enterprises but by the organization of interindustrial linkages and the agglomeration of innumerable specialized tasks. It was not size of firm that mattered, but geographical concentration of innumerable producers under the organizing power of merchants and other entrepreneurs. And it was, in effect, the total economies of scale achieved by this kind of industry within the Paris region that formed the basis for its competitive advantage in the new international division of labor.

There is another myth, harder to dispel, that small industry and production by artisans is less innovative when it comes to new products or new labor processes. At the time, Corbon strongly denied this, detecting a very lively interest in new product lines, new techniques, and the applications of science among the "superior" workers and artisans, though he did go on to remark that they tended to admire the application of everything new anywhere but in their own trade.[20] But too much success was to be had from product innovation (particularly in the luxury goods sector) for small owners to let the opportunities pass them by. And new technologies rapidly proliferated. Even steam engines, of feeble horsepower to be sure, were organized into patterns of collective use among the ateliers. And the clothing industry adopted the sewing machine, leatherworking used power cutting knives, cabinetmakers used mechanical cutters, and manufacturers of "articles de Paris" were fairly possessed by a rush to innovate when it came to dyeing, coloring, special preparations, costume jewelry, and the like. Building and construction also saw major innovations (such as the use of mechanical elevators).

The picture that emerges is one of lively innovation and rapid adoption of new labor processes. The objections of the craft workers were not to the new techniques but, judging from the Workers' Commission of 1867 and the writings of workers like Varlin, to the manner in which these techniques were forced on them as part of a process of standardization of product, deskilling, and wage reduction.[21] Here, too, the increasing integration of specialized, detailed division of labor under the command of merchants and entrepreneurs gave special qualities to the transformation of the labor process. The evident technological vigor of small industry in Paris was not necessarily the kind of vigor the workers appreciated. And in this they had good reason: as Poulot (an industrialist with a reputation for innovation) admitted, the three key objectives he had in mind in developing innovations were increasing precision, speeding up production, and "to decrease the free will of the workers."[22]

In this regard the memoire of Xavier-Edouard Lejeune is instructive.[23] Raised in the country by his grandparents, he joined his single mother (the victim, apparently, of a betrayed romance with a bourgeois son of some note) in Paris in 1855, at age ten. He found his mother employing six to eight women in the production of women's coats of high quality with special connections to certain retailing outlets. That year was the high point of the boom in the clothing trades, as the stimulus given by state expenditures and the rise of fashion at the imperial court and throughout Paris took hold. His mother lived in fairly spacious and central accommodations, employed a maid, and entertained relatives and friends. Six years later she employed only one person and had been forced into a number of moves into smaller quarters at much lower rents. She stopped entertaining and dispensed with the maid; Xavier-Edouard did the housework and the shopping for a while, before being sent out to work, for "reasons of economy," in a retail store where he received accommodations and food as well as a small wage. The problem for his mother was the advent of the sewing machine and fiercer market competition under conditions of slacker demand. She was gradually driven into poverty (the account fails to mention her after 1868, but later research showed she still practiced a trade in 1872 but was totally impoverished by 1874, when she was declared insane and incarcerated until she died in 1891). For many small owner-workers, the tale was, I suspect, all too common in its broad outlines.

THE EXPERIENCE OF LABORING

So what was it like, working in Parisian industry during the Second Empire? It is hard to construct any composite picture from such a diversity of laboring experience. Anecdotes abound, and some bear repeating because they probably capture the flavor of the work experience for many.

A recent immigrant from Lorraine in 1865 rents, with his wife and two children, two minuscule rooms in Belleville, toward the periphery of Paris. He leaves every morning at five o'clock, armed with a crust of bread, and walks four miles to the center, where he works fourteen hours a day in a button factory. After the rent is paid, his regular wage leaves him Fr 1 a day (bread costs Fr 0.37 a kilo), so he brings home piecework for his wife, who works long hours at home for almost nothing. "To live, for a laborer, is not to die," was the saying of the time.[24]

It was descriptions of this sort that Zola used to such dramatic effect in *L'Assommoir* (he apparently studied Poulot's text very carefully in preparation for this novel). Coupeau and Gervaise visit Lorilleux and his wife in the tiny, messy, stiflingly hot workroom attached to their living quarters. The couple are working together, drawing gold wire to make column chain. "There is small link, heavy chain, watch chain and twisted rope chain," explains Coupeau, but Lorilleux (who calculates he has spun eight thousand meters since he was twelve and hopes someday "to get from Paris to Versailles") makes only column chain. "The employers supplied the gold in wire form and already in the right alloy, and the workers began by drawing it through the draw plate to get it to the right gauge, taking care to reheat it five or six times during the operation to prevent it from breaking." This work, though it needs great strength, is done by the wife, since it also requires a steady hand and Lorilleux has terrible spasms of coughing. Still relatively young both of them look close to being broken by the exhausting and demanding regime of work. Lorilleux demonstrates how the wire is twisted, cut, and soldered into tiny links, an operation "performed with unbroken regularity, link succeeding link so rapidly that the chain gradually lengthened before Gervaise's eyes without her quite seeing how it was done."

The irony of the production of such specialized components of luxury goods in such dismal and impoverished circumstances was not lost on Zola. And it was only through the tight supervision of the organizers of production that such a system could prevail. Small wonder that the otherwise very moderate workers' delegation of goldsmiths to the 1867 Exposition complained in their report of "an insatiable capitalism," which left them defenseless and unable to protest against the "obvious and destructive evil" occurring "in those large centers of manufacture where accumulated capital, enjoying every freedom, becomes a kind of legalized oppression, regulating labor and passing work out so as to create more specialized jobs."[25] This was, interestingly, written in the year of publication of volume 1 of Marx's *Capital* in Leipzig.

Gervaise later encounters a very different kind of production process when she visits Goujet, the metalworker, after a frightening journey through the industrial segment of northeast Paris. This was, by all accounts, an incredibly impressive industrial zone.

Lejeune in his memoire from the period describes it this way:

> There were factories and manufacturing establishments back into the far corners of court-yards and impasses, there were workshops from the ground floor up into the higher floors of the houses and an incredible density of workers giving an animated and noisy atmosphere to the quarter.

Goujet, in Zola's account, shows Gervaise how he makes hexagonal rivets out of white-hot metal, gently tapping out three hundred twenty-millimeter rivets a day, using a five-pound hammer. But that craft is under challenge, for the boss is installing a new plant:

> The steam engine was in one corner, concealed behind a low brick wall. . . . He raised his voice to shout explanations, then went on to the machines; mechanical shears which devoured bars of iron, taking off a length with each bite and passing them out behind one by one; bolt and rivet machines, lofty and complicated, making a bolt-head in one turn of their powerful screws; trimming machines with cast-iron flywheels and an iron ball that struck the air furiously with each piece the machine trimmed; the thread-cutters worked by women, threading the bolts and nuts, their wheels going clickety-click and shining with oil. . . .The machine was turning out forty-four-millimetre rivets with the ease of an unruf-fled giant. . . . In twelve hours this blasted plant could turn out hundreds of kilogrammes of them. Goujet was not a vindictive man, but at certain moments he would gladly . . . smash up all this iron work in his resentment because its arms were stronger than his. It upset him, even though he appreciated that flesh could not fight against iron. The day would come, of course, when the machines would kill the manual worker; already their day's earnings had dropped from twelve francs to nine, and there was talk of still more cuts to come. There was nothing funny about these great plants that turned out rivets and bolts just like sausages. . . . He turned to Gervaise, who was keeping very close to him, and said with a sad smile, . . . "maybe sometime it will work for universal happiness."[26]

Thus were the abstract forces of capitalism brought to bear on the concrete experience of laboring under the Second Empire.

CHAPTER NINE

THE BUYING AND SELLING
OF LABOR POWER

[Capital] can spring into life, only when the owner of the means of production and subsis-
tence meets in the market with a free laborer selling his labor-power. And this one historical
condition comprises a world's history.

—MARX

The growth of industry and commerce, coupled with the expansion of construction in Paris, put strong pressure on labor markets during the Second Empire. Where was the supply to come from? How and under what conditions were workers prepared to surrender rights over their labor power to others? And how did the quantities and qualities of labor power offered in Paris affect the form and geographical distribution of economic activity?

In 1848, Paris had an enormous surplus of labor power. To those thrown out of employment by the collapse of Parisian industry and trade was added a flood of provincial workers seeking the traditional protections of Paris in times of trouble. The numbers enrolled in the National Workshops rose from 14,000 to over 117,000 between March and June 1848.[1] The repression of the June Days led many to flee the city, but unemployment remained a key problem in both the city and the nation. The labor surpluses in Paris were partially absorbed during the recovery of 1849–1850, but it took the dramatic upsurge of economic activity after 1852 to turn a labor surplus with falling wages into labor scarcity and rising nominal wage rates—though the increases were largely offset by inflation—until the 1860s.[2] The response to this scarcity was a massive immigration wave into the city during the 1850s, followed by increasing absorption of that other segment of the industrial reserve army—women—when nominal wage rates stagnated and real wage rates fell during the 1860s. Thus were the quantitative needs of Parisian industry and commerce broadly satisfied.

FIGURE 62 *The construction trades brought floods of migrant laborers into the city, some of whom came from very specific regions. Here Daumier comments that it is easier to encounter people from Limousin in Paris on the boulevards at six in the evening than it is back in Limoges, the main city of that province.*

The qualities of the labor supply are harder to dissect. Paris had already lost most of its real artisans—workers in control of their own labor process and working independently for market exchange. Cottereau puts them at no more than 5 percent of the economically active population in 1847. But there also were few machine operators. The mass of the workforce was divided between craft workers, who were fully initiated (usually by apprenticeship) into all aspects of a trade; skilled workers, whose skills were confined to specialized tasks within the detail division of labor; and unskilled workers, often itinerant day laborers, grading into the indigent and criminal classes variously referred to as "dangerous classes" or "lumpen-proletariat." Literate and numerate workers also could find employment in the burgeoning white collar occupations spawned by the revolutions in banking and commerce and by the rise of tourism.[3]

The craft workers had evolved means of informal control over labor markets during the preceding half-century.[4] They possessed hidden forms of corporatist organization and were capable of negotiating collectively with owners over rates for the job, conditions of work, and length of employment. Labor markets were often centralized and under collective control, employers hiring from a central assembly point or in a particular locale where workers could exchange information and exert maximum pressure on employers and other workers to respect collective norms. This power did not guarantee steady or secure employment. The ups and downs of trade were felt more as periodic, seasonal, and occasionally prolonged unemployment (the last usually triggering political protest and social unrest) rather than as variations in wage rates. This system of control had the added advantage of easy integration of migrant craft workers into the urban labor market (a relic of the *tour de France* of the *compagnonnage* system that had organized migrating movements of provincial labor for at least two centuries).

It is hard to get any exact estimate of the proportion of Parisian workers operating in labor markets of this kind, but it was plainly substantial. And the craft workers, by their example and their political leadership, undeniably set the tone for the Parisian labor market in the 1840s and were at the heart of the workers' movement of 1848. They were the group with whom the association of capitals had to do battle.

The Second Empire saw a diminishing control over labor markets by craft workers.[5] It also saw redefinitions of skills of the sort Marx describes so well in *Capital* as production moves through the increasing detail and social division of labor to machine and factory production. In some industries, craft skills were eliminated and replaced by specialized skills within a detail division of labor. In others, machine operators replaced craft workers. Some of the specialized skills that arose out of transformations of the labor process were monopolizable, but others were relatively easy to reproduce. Here, too, the tendency was toward deskilling and the use of easily reproducible skills in lower-quality mass-production systems (either factories or integrated workshops). The boundary between skilled and unskilled became more blurred as it became easier, given changes in techniques and organization, to introduce unskilled migrants or women into the workshops. Traditional labor market controls also tended to break down as the Parisian labor market exploded in size and dispersed in space. The centralized hiring points, still a matter of comment in the Enquête of 1847–1848 had all but disappeared by 1870.[6] And most commentators agreed that the labor market had become characterized by a much more pervasive competitive individualism in 1870 than had existed in 1848.

Yet the workers continued to exercise extraordinary power and influence. They remained, according to Denis Poulot's (1980) vivid descriptions of life and customs in the Parisian workshops of 1870, self-confident to the point of arrogance, opinionated, boisterous, and incurably independent to the point of indiscipline (see table 9). They resisted the authority of the capitalists with an ironic intensity that characterized what Poulot, from the perspective of an employer, disparagingly called, "sublimism." They suffered from the incurable belief that Varlin, one of their members, put this way: "Most workers have nothing to learn from owners who are not skilled in their profession and who are only exploiters."[7] They continued to exercise collective pressure on labor markets, largely by staying put in their traditional quarters (even in the face of urban renewal and rising rents). Industries that needed their skills had to go to them (which accounts in part for the persistence of industry close to the center and toward the northeast). Indeed, part of the whole pattern of locational shift and innovation in Parisian industry during the Second Empire must be interpreted as a response to the power of such workers, who could be bypassed only through deskilling and industrial reorganization. And, of course, this group provided much of the political leadership for the workers' movement. It was from the worker quarters that much of the explosive political force of the Commune emanated.

The continued presence of such power and influence is all the more remarkable given the intense repression of the workers' movement after 1852. Denied all rights of association, combination, unionization, public assembly, and going on strike, they were also faced with a battery of laws covering such matters as the *livret* (a kind of work record book, which each worker was supposed to have), jurisdictional disputes (in the event of any conflict of opinion between employer and worker, said the law, that of the employer must prevail), and worker participation in the *conseils de prud'hommes* (trade councils), which always kept them in a minority. They were also faced with a surveillance system that was all too ready to cry conspiracy at the least hint of informal or open discussion. Workers, however, had long been conditioned to this kind of repression and knew only too well how to organize covertly within it. Their resort to irony and disrespectful banter, their sophisticated coding of all manner of signs of resistance, became indispensable weapons in class war. This was the essence of what "sublimism" was all about, and it plainly infuriated employers like Poulot, who saw its eradication as indispensable to industrial progress. But in Paris the workers had another power. Their skills and abilities were indispensable for much of Parisian industry. For this reason legislation on the *livret* remained largely a dead letter among the craft workers.[8]

It was, in the end, transitions in the labor process that did more to undermine their power than any amount of political repression. As the conditions of abstract labor shifted, the concrete labor that the craft workers had to offer became less significant. But workers still had abundant opportunities to parlay their power into new configurations. To the degree that the boundary between master and worker was often highly porous, upward mobility (by marriage or straight succession) was possible, though less so than in earlier times. The hierarchical organization of their own labor system also gave them opportunities to insert themselves as supervisors, foremen, and subcontractors within the detail and social division of labor. And their skill, education, and adaptability allowed them to colonize new trades as these opened up and to monopolize new skills. In so doing, they lost their status as craft workers and became the core of an "aristocracy of labor" that was to be the basis of trade union socialism after 1871. The evidence that this transition was already underway is best represented in the evolution of the French branch of the International after 1864, as it moved from expressing the mutualist ideology emanating from the craft tradition to the revolutionary trade union consciousness of an industrial proletariat.

The pattern of skills and trades underwent a substantial structural revolution between 1848 and 1870. New trades came into being (electrician, for example), while others died out (Haussmann's public works all but eliminated the trade of water carrier, for example). Machine skills came to both factory and workshop—the sewing machine revolutionized the clothing trades, with particularly bad effects, as we have seen—and replaced older crafts. Shop assistants, bank clerks, managers, hotel employees, and bureaucrats also became

Table 7 *Annual Incomes and Daily Wage Rates by Occupation, Paris, 1847–1871*

| | Duvean's Estimates, 1860 | | | Average | Daily | |
Occupation	Annual Wage	Daily Rate	Dead Season (Months)	1847	1860	1871
Men						
Mechanic	1,500	5.00–6.50	3	4.50	4.50	5.00
Carpenter	1,350	5.50–6.00	4	5.00	5.00	6.00
Mason	1,150	4.50–5.50	4	4.00	5.00	5.00
Hatter	1,150	4.00–5.00	3	4.00	5.00	6.50
Jeweler				4.00	5.00	6.00
Bronze worker				4.50	5.00	7.00
Locksmith	1,050	4.00–5.00	4	4.00	4.50	4.50
Printer				4.00	5.00	5.00
Tailor				3.50	4.50	5.00
Joiner	1,000	4.00–5.00	4	3.50	4.00	5.00
Painter	980	4.50–5.00	5	3.50	4.50	6.00
Cobbler	950	3.00–3.50	2½	3.00	3.00	3.50
Bakery worker	900	4.00–5.00	irregular	4.25	5.00	6.60
Team worker	850	2.00–2.50				
Cabinet maker	700	3.00–4.00	4	3.50	4.50	5.00
Day laborer				2.50	3.00	3.25
Construction worker				2.75	3.00	4.00
Women						
Laundress	685	2.00–2.25				
Fashion	640	2.25–3.50				
Flower maker	420	1.50–2.25	3–6			
Mechanic	387	1.50–2.25				
Custom tailor	340	1.00–2.25				

Sources: Duveau (1946), 320–328 (cols. 1–3); and Rougerie (1968a), tables 4 and 6 (cols. 4–6). Simon (1861), 286–287, gives dead season estimates for women's employment.

much more conspicuous in the 1860s as specialized white-collar occupations arose in banking, commerce, tourism, and government. Here lay the seeds for an upwardly mobile petite bourgeoisie that was soon to match the declining shopkeepers in wealth and power. And it was into this flux that provincial immigrants and women were inserted and craft workers were transformed to create radically new structures within the labor market.

All sources agree that wage rates rose by some 20 percent or more during the Second Empire and that the increases were widely spread across different occupations (table 7), including those dominated by women. The wage rates, which remained fairly standardized, though less so at the end of the Empire than at its beginning, are much easier to tabulate than are worker incomes, because of unstable employment and the notorious dead season. Duveau draws upon numerous contemporary monographs to get rough estimates of the dead season and annual worker incomes. The latter varied from Fr 700 to Fr 1,500 for men and Fr 345 to Fr 685 for women, depending upon occupation. To the degree that these figures refer to conditions at roughly the midpoint of the Empire, they presumably underestimate annual incomes toward the end of the period.[9]

The movement of real wages is very different. The rise in the cost of living almost offset the rise in nominal wages. If the cost of workers' necessities is used as a standard then the rise in nominal wage rates would be more than offset. The latter calculation is particularly tricky because the Second Empire also saw revolutions in consumption habits that affected workers as well as the bourgeoisie.[10] However this may be, all sources agree that prices rose during the Second Empire, fundamentally affecting the workers' standard of living. Thomas[11] gives the following estimates of annual living costs (in francs) for a family of four:

Years	Housing	Food/Heating, etc.	Total
1852–1853	121	931	1,051
1854–1862	170	1,052	1,222
1864–1873	220	1,075	1,295

These costs, spearheaded by rent increases that were a never-ending source of complaint, increased by 20 percent. When we compare these costs with Duveau's estimates of annual incomes (see table 7), we see that only mechanics and carpenters averaged enough to support a family of four. All other groups needed a supplementary source of income, that of the woman, if basic family needs were to be met. This condition was universal enough to command widespread comment and concern before the Workers' Commission of 1867. The budgets there drawn up (excluding the more fanciful ones) indicated annual needs of between Fr 1,670 and Fr 2,000 for a family of four, although a carpenter in that year with 337 days' work (a most unusual occurrence) could get only Fr 1,470. The single male, who could meet his basic needs for Fr 700 or so, was, under such circumstances, ill-advised to form a family unless with a woman who worked. Women, however, simply could not survive alone on the wages they received. This disparity was to have enormous social effects upon working-class life.

There were, however, some shifts in timing and pattern within this overall picture of movement in the nominal and real wages. Duveau, for example, detects an increasing polarization within the working class between a small but growing group of privileged workers whose incomes more than kept pace with the cost of living (and who might even aspire to property ownership) and the increasing mass of workers in the "unhappy" category who simply could not make ends meet no matter how hard they tried. Such a trend is hard to confirm. But contemporary accounts certainly give the impression that at least some workers were sufficiently well off either to accumulate some small savings or to choose freely not to work on Mondays and to spend lavishly at the cabarets.[12]

How hard it was to make ends meet depended, however, on the economy. Conditions appear to have been very difficult before 1857. Bad harvests and the inflationary effects of deficit financing and inflows of gold from California and Australia combined to generate strong price rises in the face of stagnating wages. Conditions improved rapidly thereafter as labor shortages forced wages up and improved transport brought prices down. The rough equilibrium between wage movements and cost of living shifts that appears to have prevailed in the early 1860s came unstuck after 1866 when financial difficulties (the collapse of the Crédit Mobilier) and the cessation of the public works combined with fiercer external competition to make life extremely hard for much of the Paris working class. This general picture (confirmed by Rougerie 1968a; Duveau 1946; and Thomas n.d.) undoubtedly contained innumerable nuances depending upon occupation, sex, and location. Some of the forces shaping these nuances deserve deeper scrutiny.

TEMPORAL AND SPATIAL FRAGMENTATION IN THE LABOR MARKET

In Paris, as elsewhere, the struggle for command over the laborer's time was royally fought. Legislation of March 1848 to restrict the Parisian workday to ten hours had been rolled back to twelve by September, and then so riddled with exceptions that on this score the worker had almost no protection. Duveau puts the average workday at eleven hours for much of the Second Empire but notes tremendous variation between craft workers (who still often took "Saint Monday" off) and those who worked fourteen-hour days in some of the small sweatshops.[13] But the biggest problem of all was insecurity of employment, for which Second Empire Paris was notorious. The dead season in some sectors was so long that even craft workers producing high-quality products for high wages during one part of the year were forced to supplement their incomes by participating in mass production at low wages for the rest of the year. It is very hard, therefore, to translate standard rates for a job into any sense of worker incomes. Furthermore, there existed a fluid conduit for the translation of craft workers for one part of the year into mere skilled laborers for the other part. Though the problem of the dead season tended to diminish in aggregate, there were many contemporary observers who saw its increase in certain trades as a major problem in the closing years of the Second Empire.[14] The instability of employment in certain crafts may well have made regular factory employment more attractive, even at lower wages and with diminished control over the labor process. Certainly one of the attractions of Paris to prospective employers was the availability of qualified labor power at low cost during the dead season.

The Parisian labor market also became more fragmented geographically. The growth and dispersal of population, housing, and employment was accompanied by an increasing separation of work and home. Lazare, a contemporary observer of some note, makes much of the increasing journey to work (mostly on foot and over long distances) as a growing burden on workers, particularly recent immigrants forced to settle on the periphery. A worker named Tartaret complained in testimony to the Workers' Commission of 1867 that many workers now had to walk three hours a day to get to work and back.[15] Cheaper transport systems oriented to workers' needs or a shorter working day to compensate for increased travel time emerged as issues. The craft workers who clung to central locations had few complaints on this score, however, and focused their wrath on high rents instead. The increasing dispersal and fragmentation of the labor market had a variety of effects. Another contemporary, Cochin, worried that the emergence of new employment centers, each with its own tradition, style, and ties, would turn Paris into a city of inhabitants, not citizens. Certainly wage differentials between one part of the city and another (between center and suburb, particularly) became more marked. But geographical fragmentation also increased the sense of separation of workers and owners who often used to live under the same roof, accelerated the breakup of the apprenticeship system, and made the informal systems of labor market control harder to maintain. Though some, like the carpenters, kept their corporatist traditions intact until after the Commune, other trades witnessed a severe erosion of their collective power because of geographical spread and fragmentation.

The Parisian labor market had never been totally centralized, of course, and French workers had a well-earned reputation for individualism, as Poulot's *Le Sublime* so well illustrates. But something more was needed than corporatist tradition to cope with the new geographical patterns and the rising individualism. The shift within the Paris branch of the International from mutualism toward revolutionary trade unionism can be read as exactly such an adaptation.

IMMIGRATION

The rapid increase in population from just under 1.3 million in 1851 to nearly 2 million on the eve of the siege of Paris in 1870 (see table 1) was largely fueled by a massive immigration wave of between 400,000 and 450,000 people.[16] Much of the labor reserve in Paris came from the provinces. Its movement was in part to be attributed to depressed rural conditions in the 1850s—provoked in part by changing space relations, which destroyed some rural industries, broke down local self-sufficiency, and generated a slow modernization process in French agriculture.[17] When this was put up against the tremendous boom in employment opportunities created by the public works in Paris and the revival of Parisian industry, it is not hard to understand the fundamental impulse behind the immigration. The Parisian labor market had for many years spread its tentacles out into the provinces, mainly to the north but in some special cases, such as the celebrated migrations of stonemasons from the Creuse and Limousin, deep into rural France. But the coming of the railroads shifted the field of recruitment outward to give it even greater geographical coherence and range. Furthermore, the diversity and size of the Parisian labor market made it an attractive destination, no matter what the differences in wage rate. When rural conditions improved in the 1860s and Parisian wages stagnated, immigration continued, though at a slower rate than the vast flood of the 1850s.

The integration of immigrants into the Parisian labor market was a complex affair.[18] To begin with, there was little relation between the skills the immigrants possessed and the jobs they took up in Paris. Many were unskilled, at least in the jobs that Paris offered, and had to find their own paths to job opportunities. The continuing shortages of skilled labor provided an incentive toward technical and organizational change in Parisian industry, even in the face of the vast immigration wave. And the immigrants proved, for the most part, adept at adopting the new skills that opened up. There were, to be sure, certain exceptions. The traditional seasonal migrations of skilled construction workers became a more and more permanent affair, with the stonemasons' lodging houses still operating as employment exchanges and reception points for new immigrants. Privileged paths of integration also existed for those of particular regional origins (from Auvergne, or even Germans in the Faubourg Saint-Antoine). In some cases, Parisian industries experiencing shortages of skilled labor recruited directly—woodworkers and metalworkers from Alsace, for example. But with the exception of the construction trades, much in demand because of the public works and therefore in the forefront of the immigration wave, it seems that the immigrants did not possess the qualities needed to sustain traditional forms of labor but were quick to form the new qualities required for new labor processes.

This mass influx of largely unskilled but adaptable immigrants created all kinds of opportunities for Parisian industry. There were many dirty jobs to be had—the white lead works were a notorious enough death trap that the workers were shunned on the street— and the growth of mass production opened up many semiskilled jobs for which the new immigrants could be relatively easily trained. And to the degree that most of these immigrants found housing on the periphery, they increased the attraction of suburban locations for certain newer industries. The mass of the unskilled immigrants therefore underwent a socialization process into the ways of industrial capitalism very different from that achieved through the transformation of craft workers. Thus there arose a formidable social division within the Parisian labor market, one that was to have pronounced political effects signaled by the low participation of suburban industrial workers in the events of the Commune.

THE EMPLOYMENT OF WOMEN

The employment of women—that other great reservoir of surplus labor—underwent some most peculiar gyrations after 1848. Women accounted for 41.2 percent of the workforce (not including domestics) in 1847–1848, declined to 31 percent in 1860, and went back up to 41.3 percent by 1872.[19] The declining participation in the 1850s is partly a statistical aberration, since the industrial mix in the suburbs annexed in 1860 was more oriented to male employment. But there was still a very real relative decline, explained by the heavy predominance of males in the immigration wave that hit Paris in the 1850s and the deindustrialization and depopulation of the city center that had been the main bastion of women's jobs. Rising male salaries may also have diminished the incentive for married women to engage in what was in any case poorly paid work—women's rates were less than half those of men for comparable work. And the young single women who did immigrate probably entered as domestic servants brought in from the country estates of the nobility, meaning that most of them ended up on the western, nonindustrial side of the city. The east-west division of working-class Paris therefore took the demographic form of a predominantly male east and a predominantly female west.

The general reversal of women's participation after 1860 had equally cogent explanations. The increasing competitive pressure on Parisian industry, particularly with respect to labor costs, made the employment of lower-paid women not only attractive but imperative in certain sectors. And in the face of declining immigration, that vast captive labor reserve of women that had been dispersed to the periphery during the 1850s must have been eyed hungrily by many an employer. Women's wage rates, already low, were a third less in the suburbs than in the center. Not only did their employment exert a downward pressure on wage rates, but they could be used directly to confront the power of craft workers in certain trades. The use of women to break one of the first major (illegal) strikes in the printing workshops in 1862 made a deep impression upon employers and workers alike.[20] And although men, partly as a consequence, typically inveighed against the employment of women, they were increasingly forced to recognize in the 1860s that the male wage was insufficient to support a family. To the degree that the immigrants of the 1850s formed families in the 1860s, the employment of women became more and more of a sheer economic necessity.

Within these general trends, of course, there were innumerable nuances, depending upon technological and organizational changes and product innovations that opened up some occupations (particularly machine tending of the sort that Zola describes) and eliminated others. Considerable debate also arose over the education and position of women and the organization of their labor.[21] On the one hand, the Parisian convents became centers of tightly organized, low-paid, and highly competitive women's labor—a fact that created considerable resentment in male workers and fueled the anticlerical sentiment that was to flourish under the Commune. In the late 1860s small groups of socialist feminists tried to revive the experiments of 1848 with women's cooperatives for production and consumption, before becoming a major organizing force during the Commune.[22] This brings us, however, to broader questions on the position of women that deserve consideration in their own right.

CHAPTER TEN

THE CONDITION
OF WOMEN

The change in an historical epoch can always be determined by women's progress towards freedom.

—MARX

"The worst destiny for a woman," wrote Michelet in *La Femme* (published in 1859), "is to live alone." He cites the disproportionate number of young women whose bodies were never reclaimed from the public hospitals as grisly support for his thesis on the inevitable fate of a woman who lived outside the protection of the family.[1] He used this distressing fact of life in Second Empire Paris as a basis for moral judgment. But he also thereby gave expression to a pervasive fear in bourgeois circles; that of the unsubmissive, independent woman. For the bourgeois, the term *femmes isolées* signaled "the domain of poverty, a world of turbulent sexuality, subversive independence and dangerous insubordination. . . . In their association with prostitution, these women carried 'the moral leprosy' that made large cities 'permanent centers of infection'; they permitted expression of or simply expressed those 'tumultuous passions' that, in time of political upheaval—as in the revolution of 1848—threatened to overturn the entire social order."[2] Thus, as we shall later see, was constructed a strong connection among gender, sexuality, and revolution.

Legally considered a minor under the Code Napoléon, it was difficult though not impossible for a woman to make her own way in life, economically or socially, without some kind of protection from father, husband, kin, lover, pimp, institutions (like convents and schools), or employer. That such "protection" was open to all manner of abuse (social, economic, sexual) was all too evident, though there were many men who took their paternalistic responsibilities seriously, while women found innumerable ways, individually and

FIGURE 63 *Daumier's* La Muse de la Brasserie *not only seems to have inspired Manet's famous paining of the barmaid at the Folles Bergères, but also indicates one of the roles that women increasingly played in the fête impériale. In the bars as well as in the department stores the overt display of sexuality in relation to commodification became standard practice during these years.*

sometimes collectively, to carve out special positions for themselves within the overall constraints that hemmed them in.

Consider, first, the possibility of some reasonable economic independence through gainful employment. Women's wages (see table 7) were for the most part insufficient to meet even basic needs. Simon's study from 1861 depicts a woman working at home for twelve hours a day with the shortest possible dead season and receiving, at generous estimate, an annual income of Fr 500. After deducting the basic costs of rent and clothing, she is left with 59 centimes a day for food—enough for some bread and milk. And this presumes that she remains healthy, able to work at full capacity. Employment in the workshops or in services and retailing (street vending and food preparation, for example) offered equally dismal prospects.[3] And those trades in which women were predominantly employed, like the 70,000 specialist washerwomen and laundresses found in Paris in 1870, were likewise badly remunerated.

A skilled dressmaker, seamstress, or bookbinder could occasionally achieve economic independence.[4] A scattering of independent women (mostly single), running their own small businesses could be found particularly among dressmakers, seamstresses, and laundresses, but their livelihoods were precarious because they had little access to capital or credit when things became difficult. The steady displacement of custom-made by ready-to-wear clothing in the garment trade seems also to have diminished one of the few areas where independent women entrepreneurs could successfully compete. The new department stores, which purveyed the ready-to-wear clothing, offered a new kind of opportunity for attractive and well-turned-out women, closely chaperoned within a paternalistic system of control. These opportunities expanded after an 1869 strike of commerce workers that led employers to rely more heavily on more "docile" women's labor.

Domestic employment, by far the most important occupation for women in the city (111,496 in 1861), had special characteristics. It offered adequate food, problematic shelter, and less intense conditions of labor. But the hours were long (often fifteen to eighteen hours a day, on call all week) and conditions of living were strictly regulated (domestics, like all women, were viewed legally as minors and subject to strict supervision). Though they might often change employers, they could never escape the condition of virtual enslavement to the employer's whims. And that sometimes meant sexual whims (tales of domestics required to take care of the sexual needs of sons who might otherwise fulfill them under less controlled conditions abounded). Since unwanted pregnancy was cause for instant dismissal, that meant abortion or prostitution. "Fallen" domestics accounted for most of the prostitutes and most of the illegitimate births, and probably made up the majority of the unclaimed bodies that Michelet cited. Yet the position of domestic, if the dangers could be avoided, was not unattractive, given the alternatives. Money wages, though low, could be put by (domestics were the largest group of small savers), and some kind of training and even education procured; faithful domestics could, further, expect a pension or legacy in old age. Domestic service was also a reasonably protected path for the socialization of young rural women into the dangers of urban life (they concentrated in the safer bourgeois quarters of the west). While it was hard to marry, and even harder to have children, and stay in service, a prudent young domestic who put something by as a dowry and had learned skills of household management was not a bad marriage prospect for the shopkeeper or artisan. Most domestics were, therefore, rather young (40 percent were under twenty-five years of age).

Educated women could aspire to be governesses, companions, and schoolteachers, occupations again giving little liberty of action and for which the remuneration was generally poor—four thousand schoolmistresses earned less than Fr 400 a year.[5] Only women of independent means (those who married under the system called *le regime dotal* retained certain rights and protection of property brought as dowry into marriage) could avoid the economic basis for social domination by the institutions and customs of a male-dominated society.[6] To be a well-endowed widow was a privilege that many might hope for but that few attained. Married women who separated, like George Sand, could regain

FIGURE 64 *Gustave Doré's depictions of a corridor at the Opéra (a favorite site for acquiring a mistress) and in the Café Concert depict spaces where women's roles were defined by sexual positioning.*

control over their property only after a legal struggle that usually rested on extorting concessions from a husband who had the legal power to put his wife in jail for up to three years if she left without his agreement.

So what, then, could a single working woman do, living on bread and a little milk and working twelve hours a day? There were, most bourgeois commentators agreed, two basic options: supplement their income through prostitution or establish a liaison (formal or informal) with a man. Prostitution was extremely widespread—thirty-four thousand women were proported to be engaged in the activity in 1850s Paris—and treated with the usual total hypocrisy by the bourgeoisie.[7] In regulated establishments—brothels and other licensed places—the activities and health of prostitutes could be monitored by the authorities. The big problem was the large number of women working on their own account who were not registered (there were four thousand or so registered prostitutes in the early 1850s). The term *femmes isolées* applied (as Scott points out) to unregulated prostitutes as well as to women working independently as dressmakers or seamstresses, thereby suggesting an association between the two.

Prostitution shaded into a wide range of other activities, from the lower-class dance halls to the higher-class opera and theater, and merged into the profession of "mistress." For the woman, the temptations were enormous, though the probability of parlaying good looks into a share of a banker's fortune (like Zola's Nana) was very low. Besides, there was too much competition at the top, since the high points of courtesan and bourgeois life were already well occupied. (Did the Marquis of Hertford really pay a million francs for one night with that exquisite beauty and sometime mistress of Napoleon III, the Countess of Castiglione?) But in a large city like Paris, where a certain anonymity could easily be preserved, all kinds of liaisons were possible, none of them without their dangers. It was customary, for example, for the large numbers of students from the provinces to take mistresses, thus giving rise to the curious profession of grisette. One close English observer of student life, while falling over backward not to condone the condition, ended up conveying a certain admiration for such women. They looked after their students faithfully and well, even managed the budget, in return for relief from dull and ill-remunerated employment. While they might, like the ill-fated Fantine in Hugo's *Les Misérables*, be left totally in the lurch when the student returned to provincial responsibilities, and while marriage was out of the question, they sometimes received support for children and perhaps some sort of payoff (being set up with a shop being a favorite—many of the independent women owners got their start this way) in return for their faithful service.

Some regretted the gradual displacement of grisettes by "lorettes."[8] Named after the quarter of Notre Dame de Lorette (where they were presumably concentrated), lorettes were women of pleasure who used their powers of seduction for shorter-term gain (meals, entertainment, and gifts as well as money). Lejeune, in his memoire about life as department store salesboy in the 1850s, provides one instance of how they worked. Called at the last minute to substitute for an older salesman, he took items for sale to a potential customer's house and was greeted on entry by a woman in a diaphanous neg-ligée. Obviously surprised, the woman explained she had not the money right then, and suggested he leave the items for her consideration and ask the other salesman to come for payment later. Lejeune picked up the items and left the house in a hurry. This role of lorette, remarked the English visitor, appeared an appropriate response to a legal system that seemed to have been constructed solely for "the protection of men of pleasure." Given the open flauntings of mistresses (it was a sign of affluence in the middle class to be able to support one) and the innumerable intersections between the bourgeoisie and the demimonde of the cafés and boulevards, the theaters and the Opera, the possibilities and temptations were infinite. Haussmann, for example, had a fairly open and longstanding liaison with an actress at the Opera who thrived on his protection.

Most prostitution was, however, out of desperation and sheer hunger (more like Gervaise's stumbling on the boulevards after three days without food in Zola's *L'Assommoir* than the spectacular rise and fall of her daughter Nana in the novel of that name). Prostitution was for the most part quite simply as extensive and ghastly as the poverty that bred it. Only an occasional madame was talented enough to turn it into a reasonable business—in 1870 some 15 percent of the bordello owners were women—and even then it was hard to keep the pimps at bay.[9] But for a woman living on her own with a budget that allowed only for bread and a little milk, the offer of a good evening out or a cheap jewel was more than a little tempting. And for married women with families in the direst straits, prostitution was too often the only option. The industrialist Poulot even worried that working-class women (including wives) were taking to the streets in a spirit of class vengeance and class war.

Compared to this, any kind of reasonably secure liaison with a man of means must have appeared like true economic emancipation. "In order to have enough to live on," said Paule Minck, women "take a lover and cynically admit it."[10] The trouble was that the woman had an economic need for the man, whereas for the man a wife and children were economic liabilities, unless the woman worked. Out of that inequality all kinds of rela-tions arose. Within the working class of Paris, concubinage was as common as marriage. This was so in part because marriage was expensive (the license was costly) and hemmed in by all manner of legalities (consent of parents was obligatory under age twenty-five). Before 1860 many got married in the Thirteenth Arrondissement (the joke being that there were only twelve). The relatively rare marriages among the working classes either arose for religious or economic reasons or occurred because of longstanding family con-nections, often reaching back into the province of origin. Concubinage sometimes meant temporary liaisons, but many were relatively permanent, marriages in all but name. The problem was that, economically powerless entering a relationship and legally powerless to get out of it with any benefits, women were exposed to all manner of exploitation by the dominant males. Either their outside income was indispensable (in which case women were thrown into the workshops, where sexual harassment and violent abuse were all too common[11]), or their labor power was absorbed as assistants and helpers of men working at

FIGURE 65 *The occupations of grisette and lorette were favorite topics for Gavarni. On the left, the student being looked after by his grisette says that when he becomes Minister of Justice, he will prevent women from preventing students from studying (to which she replies that he would then be deprived of conversation). On the right, the lorette replies to the visiting gallant's remark that she is as beautiful as always, and that this is, of course, her station in life.*

home (in the manner Zola describes in the gold trade in *L'Assommoir*). They might be taken in and given protection, but then put to work (their labor power was cheaper than that of an apprentice under such conditions) and abandoned if they became pregnant. And they were generally expected to manage the household as well, though the burdens of work often precluded their effective participation as wives and mothers.

This was the focus of both male and female objections to the appalling conditions and burdens of labor in many fields of Parisian industry throughout the Second Empire. Tailor delegates to the London Exposition of 1862 complained, for example, that the system of homework to which they were increasingly subjected did not help, as bourgeois theorists proclaimed, shape a more rewarding family life. Working sixteen to eighteen hours a day and aided by wives working without compensation, there was no time for domestic functions. "While the wife rests, the husband does his share and prepares the wife's tasks; when he finishes or rather succumbs to exhaustion, the wife gets up and the husband takes her place. . . . How can a woman in these deplorable circumstances educate and raise her children decently?"[12] Worse still, as their male companions became exhausted, sick, and destroyed (often at a relatively early age) through exposure to savage conditions in many of the workshops, the women were increasingly relied upon to support them as well as the rest of the family out of a pittance of a wage. To be a worker's widow at an early age was probably the worst of all situations in which a woman could find herself.

Women had no real recourse if abandoned for another woman or for the companionship of the cabaret or the wine house. Imprisonment within failed relationships was a severe enough problem that most women speakers at the public meetings after 1868 emphasized the right to divorce and free union.[13] But it was by no means evident that such concentration on legal forms had any meaning for working-class women whose daily life was nothing but a very basic struggle for existence. But there were many affective relationships established between men and women, within or without marriage, and often under the most impoverished of economic circumstances. Most men spoke warmly of the values of family life before the Workers' Commission of 1867, and the few socialist feminists who survived into the Second Empire out of the vigorous movement that peaked in 1848, likewise coupled demands for the right to work at equal remuneration with a recognition of the importance of the family (and of the distinctive role of the women as mothers) in social life. Poulot observed as many supportive relationships among his workers as more casual liaisons and contested marriages. The women, he complained, could end up playing the game of "sublimism" just as well as the men, and often formed strong partnerships against the employers. The social inquiries of Le Play showed that women often controlled the household budget, even allocating the man his lunch money. This practice, which employers sought to enhance by giving take-home pay slips, led Poulot to characterize the "good wife" as one who knew how to economize and manage household expenditures while encouraging sober and industrious habits on the part of her mate. Employers sought an alliance with the wives in their struggle to control their workers (which also explains employer interest in the education of women). But such a strategy rarely worked, and solidarity between husband and wife in the face of employer exploitation appears to have been quite general.[14]

The "good wife" had a number of important ideal roles in bourgeois thought. Increasing constraints on women's access to public life, the separation of home and workplace, and the growing disorder and chaos of urban life revolutionized the role of bourgeois women in nineteenth-century Paris.[15] Bourgeois women became not only managers and governors of the household (a role eschewed by their aristocratic forebears) but also took on the role of creators of order, particularly a spatial and temporal order, within the interior space of the household. The latter became more and more strictly their preserve; they managed the servants, kept the accounts, and imposed a strict discipline on the inner organization of the household. The discipline was simultaneously an expression of capitalist rationality and a kind of structured and controlled response to the perceived disorder and uncontrolled passions that reigned not only in the streets but also in the marketplace. This outer space of excessive stimulation and passion was supposed to be closed to them. "A contained woman, contained in a corset, contained in a house, was

FIGURE 66 *The good wife and the bourgeois family, as Daumier depicts them here, achieve a certain serenity and paternalistic calm that can also be found in many impressionist paintings.*

an orderly woman." She was, as Michelet portrayed her, supposed to be the guardian of a different kind of private intimacy and caring within the household different from that exhibited in the marketplace.[16]

This was the arena on which the two most celebrated women impressionist artists—Berthe Morisot and Mary Cassatt—concentrated their attention. But it would be an error to conclude that this reflected the general condition of women as opposed to a small group of women who seemed just as dedicated to promoting the ideals of feminine domesticity and motherhood as Michelet or Simon. Pollock may exaggerate somewhat when she claims that Morisot's and Cassatt's art reflected the fact that "a range of places was closed to them while open to their male colleagues who could move freely with men and women in the socially fluid public world of the streets, popular entertainment and commercial or casual sexual exchange." That they ought not be in these other places, according to bourgeois opinion, and that they reflected this in their art is undeniable; that the spaces were actually closed to them is another matter.[17]

Daumier conveys a completely different sense of the varied roles of women in different class positions in Parisian public spaces and society. Some bourgeois women tried to stay close to the worlds of work and power, even dabbling in the stock market (though they could not trade on their own account, they lurked in the corridors outside and had agents buy in their name). And as shoppers and consumers as well as exhibitors of fashion, they played, as we shall see, a key role in consumer culture and the presentation and public display of commodities as spectacle. Moreover, the salons of Second Empire Paris were as renowned, if not more so, than their predecessors, as centers of political, financial, and cultural intrigue. But that was not supposed to be the path of "the good bourgeois wife" who, like Olivia Haussmann, simply ruled competently over the household. It was within this interior space that a kind of "domestic feminism" could arise, a center of considerable women's power. Perhaps it was this that the women impressionist painters were seeking to capture and even celebrate.

Within the household the woman also acquired an extremely important role as educator—this in spite of Proudhon's influential protest that the education of children ought to be under the authority of the father. The education of women in turn became the focus of intense public debate and concern. The church saw its almost exclusive grip on the education of girls as essential to the perpetuation of its moral influence, while bourgeois reformers, like Jules Simon and Victor Duruy, thought that social progress depended crucially upon more liberal and thorough education of women of all social classes. The respect accorded the mother was quite extraordinary. Le Play records, for example, that respect for the mother was a key element in the carpenters' corporation's ritual. And the *mère terrible* lurks in the background of almost every piece of poetry and fiction of the period (witness Baudelaire and Flaubert). If the various manuals of the time are anything to go by, it also seems that the role of sexual partner was not to be neglected; the incidence of painful gynecological diseases (afflicting perhaps as much as 80 percent of Parisian women) was so great as to be a serious barrier to a regular sexual partnership.[18] Venereal diseases also took a terrible toll in life and pain.

These roles appear to have carried over into even the lowest strata of working-class life.[19] Of course, they had to be much modified by the fact that the working-class wife (or equivalent) was expected, besides taking care of the household, to supplement the family income as seamstress or outworker, by retailing food, taking in laundry, or acting as the man's assistant in the atelier or the shop. Better-off workers could hope to set their wives up as corner grocers, wine sellers, laundresses, and so forth. But some women appear to have had considerable control over household management and accounts, education, health care, and even family limitation.

In those roles they appear to have been trusted and often highly valued companions. Most feminist proposals for reform followed Flora Tristan in seeing the family as a central institution for the construction of the good life, but recognized that family life of a fulfilling sort was impossible under the social relations and prevailing economic conditions of capitalism. It was also generally recognized that the status of working-class women, as "proletarians of the proletariat" in Tristan's memorable phrase, meant that the tensions between gender and class, between feminism and socialism, were relatively muted in these years. The Women's Union was to play a very important role in the Paris Commune.

The issue of family limitation opens up the thorny problem of abortion. Domestics, mistresses, and actresses had strong incentives to terminate unwanted pregnancies. So, too, did working-class women whose contribution to the family income was at stake and who often appear to have had the tacit approval of men who saw "little sense in breeding their own competition." The Parisian birthrate was extremely low, compared to the national average. Later observers considered that abortion was already a large-scale business by the 1850s, and the widespread knowledge of all kinds of methods of inducing abortion (some folkloric and others more powerful, even dangerous) later in the century surely had its roots in earlier times.[20] But here, too, women appear to have exercised a certain amount of control over their own bodies, consistent with the thesis of a domestic rather than a strongly public and political feminism.

Conventional family structures, whether legally sanctified or not, survived and allowed women all the possibilities and limitations inherent in such a situation. Many marriages within the bourgeoisie were pure business ventures, a habit that spread down to shopkeepers and *petits commercants* with particularly vicious effects. But working-class relationships appear to have been far more supportive than bourgeois opinion (like that of Zola) allowed. Poulot complained that his many attempts to get the wives on his side in class struggle all too frequently backfired. The wineshops on Saturday nights were regularly overflowing with whole families celebrating whatever advantage they had taken that week over employers. Most women who participated in the Siege and the Commune, far from being enraged, bestial furies, as the bourgeoisie so often described them, were simply being supportive of their men in very traditional ways. And to the degree that an alternative feminist politics was evident in the women's clubs and associations then set up, it was oriented not only to the right to divorce and to work, but also toward establishing an economic basis for the emancipation of women through the collective organization of production and consumption. The rank and file of the women involved in the Commune were the seamstresses, dressmakers, finishers, cutters, washerwomen, trimmers, and artificial flower makers (the domestics hardly participated at all), who had had long experience (since most of them were over forty years of age) of the economic basis of their own domination and who, like men, saw collectivist and cooperative politics as their answer.[21]

But if a single theme stands out during the Second Empire, it is that of increasing women's control over the interior space of the household, coupled with the increasing commodification of women in public life. One has only to read Balzac to realize that this was not entirely new, any more than land or financial speculation was new. But, as in these other cases, the Second Empire saw a quantum leap onto a different plane of practices. Both the monetization and the commodification of sexual relations and personal liaisons in all classes, and the increasing significance of women within the domestic economy of the household as well as in the labor market, betokened a sea change in the role of women in society. But it was a sea change blocked by traditional legal structures of male domination and economic organization. Yet within the increasing monetization of social relations, a guerrilla war was unfolding, a war in which domestics learned how to use and even swindle their employers; prostitutes to short-change their clients; lorettes to replace grisettes; wives or companions to put tighter clamps on the circulation of revenues; bourgeois women to take the lead in shaping fashionable consumer culture; and working women to take up the challenge of new kinds of factory work and service roles, and to explore alternative forms of organization that could form an economic basis for their future emancipation. It was as if women learned that if they were a valued commodity with a money value, then they could use the democracy of money as a tool for their own liberation, whether as consumers or producers.

CHAPTER ELEVEN

THE REPRODUCTION
OF LABOR POWER

Variable capital is therefore only a particular historical form of the labor—fund which the laborer requires for maintenance of himself and his family, and which, whatever the system of social production, he himself must produce and reproduce.

—MARX

The reproduction of labor power, for which women then, as now, bore heavy responsibility, has two aspects. There is first the question of food, sleep, shelter, and relaxation sufficient to return the laborer refreshed enough to be able to work the next day. There are then the longer-term needs, which attach to the next generation of workers through having, rearing, and educating children.

It is probably fair to say that on the average the resources available to the mass of male workers were barely sufficient for daily needs and quite insufficient for long-term needs of child-rearing. This general judgment—which, to be sure, needs much nuancing—is consistent with many of the basic facts of Parisian demography during the Second Empire. In 1866, for example, only a third of the total population could claim Paris as their place of birth. Even in the 1860s, past the peak of the great immigration wave, natural population growth was nine thousand a year, compared to an annual immigration of eighteen thousand.[1] The long-term reproduction of labor power appears to have been very much a provincial affair. Paris met its demand for labor, as Marx once put it, "by the constant absorption of primitive and physically uncorrupted elements from the country." The links with the provinces were more intricate, however, than the bare facts of immigration. Children were often sent back to the provinces to be brought up, and even the working class engaged in that common French practice of putting their children out to rural wet nurses, which, given the high death rate, was more akin to organized infanticide

FIGURE 67 *Daumier's*
La Soupe depicts
family reproduc-
tive relations within
the working class.
Contrasted with
the serenity of the
bourgeois family
(fig. 66), the woman
hastily and hungrily
consumes a soup
while suckling an
infant at her breast
(hardly in the manner
depicted in Daumier's
Republic, fig. 23).

than to the reproduction of labor power.[2] Paris was, in any case, full of single males (60 percent of males between twenty-one and thirty-six in 1850). Marriages, if contracted at all, occurred relatively late (29.5 years for men in 1853, rising to nearly 32 years in 1861), and the average number of children per household stood at 2.40, compared to 3.23 in the provinces, with an illegitimacy rate of 28 percent compared to 8 percent elsewhere. Furthermore, the natural population growth there was almost entirely due to the young age structure of the population, itself a function of immigration.

The demographic picture did shift somewhat toward the end of the Second Empire. Household formation picked up in the 1860s and shifted outward to the suburbs, leaving the center single and older in age structure. The chronic slum poverty of the center, which affected mainly new immigrants and the old, was now matched by the suburbanization of family poverty, affecting the young (figure 69). The changing age structure triggered by the vast immigration wave of mainly young unmarried people in the 1850s worked its way through the demographics of the city, quarter by quarter. The idea that those who drew so freely on this labor power had some sort of responsibility or self-interest in its reproduction dawned slowly on the bourgeoisie. And even those, like the Emperor, who saw that bourgeois failure in this regard had had something to do with the events of 1848, were unable to define a basis, let alone a consensus, for intervention. Bourgeois reformers were nevertheless much preoccupied with the question. Fecund with ideas, though short on their application, their inquiries and polemics yielded much information and many ideas that, after the trauma of the Commune, became the basis for social reform under the Third Republic. How and why the configuration of class forces stymied their efforts in housing, nutrition, education, health care, and social welfare deserves careful reconstruction.

HOUSING

The Second Empire witnessed a radical transformation in the system of housing provision. Bourgeois housing was largely captured by the new system of finance, land development, and construction, with the effect of increasing residential segregation within the city. A parallel system of small-time speculative building to meet the demand for working-class housing also sprang up on open land at the periphery. But though the system of housing provision changed, worker incomes remained relatively low, putting fairly strict upper limits on the housing they could afford. A relatively well-off family with stable employment and two people working might make Fr 2,000 a year in 1868 and be able to afford not much more than Fr 350 a year rent. How much and what quality of housing could be provided for Fr 350 or less? Under the best of conditions, the answer was not much; and under the worst, where land and construction were expensive and landlords aggressively sought their 8 percent or more, housing conditions were nothing short of dreadful.

Rapidly rising rents placed an increasing burden on the working population. As early as 1855, Leon Say signaled 20 to 30 percent rises all over the city, so that a single room could not be had for much less than Fr 150. Corbon put rents on working-class housing in 1862 at 70 percent higher than before 1848, and Thomas has housing costs increasing by 50 percent in each decade of the Empire. The statistical series assembled by Flaus indicates a lower figure of between 50 and 62 percent for the whole period, with rents less than Fr 100 increasing by only 19.5 percent. But there were few rents less than Fr 100 to be had; the rent of a single room for registered indigents averaged between Fr 100 and Fr 200 in 1866. A report on the rents paid by these forty thousand or so indigent families put the average at Fr 113 in 1856, rising to Fr 141 in 1866, even after the annexation of the suburbs had brought the cheaper suburban housing into the sample. There is a strong consensus that rising rents outpaced workers' nominal incomes, particularly during the 1860s.[3] The rental increases were consistent with the general rise in property values and affected all social classes. Those living on fixed incomes or even off the stagnant rents of rural estates, and who could afford to pay no more than Fr 700 or so, had a particularly hard time of it. Innumerable cases of hardship and of forced relocation could be found within this segment of the bourgeoisie. But for those who participated in the economic gains of the Second Empire, the rising rents posed no problem. For the more than half-million people who lived by their labor in the city, it was an entirely different story.

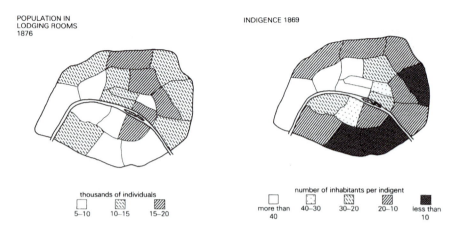

thousands of individuals

□ 5–10 ▨ 10–15 ▨ 15–20

number of inhabitants per indigent

□ more than 40 ⬚ 40–30 ▨ 30–20 ▨ 20–10 ■ less than 10

FIGURE 68 *The total population living in lodging rooms in 1876 and the indigence rate in Paris in 1869 (after Gaillard, 1977).*

Workers could adapt to this situation in a number of ways. There is evidence, largely anecdotal, that they spent an increasing proportion of their budget on housing. Workers may have been spending as much as one-seventh of their income on housing in 1860, compared to one-tenth in earlier times, and by 1870 the figure may have gone as high as 30 percent.[4] They could also save on space. For a family already confined to one room (and that was true for two-thirds of the indigents surveyed in 1866), doubling up came hard, but it was not impossible and far from uncommon for the poorer families. It was easier for single people, and many lodging houses did indeed take on the aspect of barracks, with multiple beds per room for low-paid single workers. It was also possible to seek out lower-cost accommodations on the periphery, thus often trading off a long journey to work on foot for a lower rent. But the pressures were such that the rents for speculative housing on the periphery, though lower, were by no means that much lower, particularly given the strong penchant that suburban builders and property owners had for getting their cut of the Parisian property boom by profiteering at the worker's expense. The last resort was to populate one of the innumerable shantytowns that sprang up, sometimes temporarily, on vacant lots on the periphery or even close to the center.

The paucity of worker incomes relative to rents left its indelible stamp upon the city's housing situation. And it was partly out of this history that Engels fashioned his famous argument that the bourgeoisie has only one way of solving the housing question: by moving it around. There is no better illustration of that thesis than Paris under Haussmann. The Health Commissioners complained of the temporary shantytowns that arose next door to the new construction sites in the city center. Conditions there, to which everyone turned a blind eye, were simply horrifying.[5] The proliferation and overcrowding of lodging houses close to the center; the construction of poorly ventilated, cramped, and poorly serviced dwelling houses that became almost instant slums; and the celebrated "additions," which in some cases transformed the interior courts behind Haussmann's splendid facades into highly profitable working-class slums, were all a direct concession that worker incomes were insufficient to afford decent housing. Far from ridding the city of slums, Haussmann's works, insofar as they assisted the general rise in rents at a time of stagnant worker incomes, accelerated the process of slum formation, even in the heart of the city. On a simple traverse from the city center to the fortifications, Louis Lazare counted no fewer than 269 alleys, courtyards, dwelling houses, and shantytowns constructed without any municipal control whatsoever. Though much of the housing for impoverished families was in the suburban semicircle running around the east of the city, with particular concentrations in the southeast and northeast, there was intense overcrowding of single workers in the lodging houses close to the city center, and there were patches of poor housing even within the interstices of the predominantly bourgeois west.

Such a dismal housing situation could not but have had social effects. It presumably accentuated what was already a strong barrier to family formation, and both Simon and Poulot attributed what they saw as the instability and promiscuity of working-class life to

FIGURE 69 *Daumier takes landlords to task for using their power to exclude unwanted elements, such as children and pets, who are then forced to spend their nights on the streets.*

high rents and inadequate housing (thus avoiding, in Poulot's case, the implication that perhaps the low wages he paid had something to do with it). There was also considerable evidence to connect inadequate and insalubrious housing to the persistent though declining threat of epidemics of cholera and typhoid. Sheer lack of space also forced much social life onto the streets, a tendency exacerbated by the general lack of cooking facilities. This forced eating and drinking into the cafés and cabarets, which consequently became collective centers of political agitation and consciousness formation.

With bourgeois reformers deeply aware of and nervous about such a condition and an Emperor who recognized that the consolidation of working-class support through the "extinction of pauperism" (to cite a tract the Emperor had written in 1844) was important to his rule, it is surprising that so little in the way of tangible reform was accomplished. Laws on insalubrity, passed under the Second Republic at the urging of a Catholic reformist, either were used selectively by Haussmann for his own purposes or remained a dead letter—less than 18 percent of the total housing stock was inspected in eighteen years.[6] The plan to build a series of *cités ouvrières* (large-scale working-class housing that drew some inspiration from Fourier's ideas for collective working-class housing, the *phalanstère*) was launched in 1849, with Louis Napoleon subscribing some of the funds, but quickly ground to a halt in the face of virulent conservative opposition, which saw *cités ouvrières* as breeding grounds for socialist consciousness and as potential hearths of revolution. The workers, however, viewed them more as prisons, since the gates were locked at 10 o'clock and life was strictly regimented within. Proposals for individualized housing, more acceptable to the conservative right and the Proudhonists of the left, generated many designs (there was even a competition at the Paris Exposition of 1867) but little action, since the proposal to subsidize the provision of low-income housing had generated only sixty-three units by 1870, and the one cooperative society (to which the Emperor again generously subscribed) had built no more than forty-one units by that same date.

The failure of action in spite of the Emperor's evident interest (he gave personal financial support to both collectivist and individualized initiatives, inspired articles and government programs, and was responsible for the translation of English tracts on the problem) was partly a matter of confused ideologies. Fourier, with his collectivist model, and Proudhon, who came out very strongly in favor of individual home ownership for workers, split the left. Proudhon's influence was so strong that no challenge was mounted to property ownership under the Commune, when resentment against landlords was at its height. With such a wide consensus stretching from Le Play on the Catholic right to Proudhon on the socialist left, the only real option was to take care of the housing problem within the framework of private property. But home ownership for the workers was not feasible except with government subsidy. And at that point the government ran up against the powerful class interest of landlords, to whom it was increasingly beholden as a basis for its political power, and a general attachment to freedom of the market, which, for someone like Haussmann, was a cardinal principle of action. Powerful class forces compounded ideological confusion to stymie any action on the housing problem over and beyond the slum clearance that Haussmann masterminded. It was only after the Commune, when the reformers saw that the pitiful slums and inner court-yards were better breeding grounds for revolutionary action than any *cités ouvrières* could ever have been, that housing reform began to have any teeth.

NUTRITION

The "revolution in consumption" facilitated by failing transport costs of agricultural prod-ucts and by economies of scale and efficiency within the Parisian distribution system did not entirely pass the worker by, even though it also meant an increased "stratification of diet and taste" across the social classes.[7] Bread, meat, and wine formed the basis of a distinctive work-ing-class diet (quite different from that in the provinces) and was increasingly supplemented and diversified by fresh vegetables and dairy products. Meat was rarely eaten by itself, of course, but was incorporated in soups and stews, which formed the heart of the main meal. To the degree that diversity and security of food supply improved, there is evidence that standards of nutrition improved at the same time that the cost of living rose. That Paris was still vulnerable to harvest failure became all too evident in 1868–1869, when there was a repeat of the very difficult phase of high prices of 1853–1855. It then became evident, too, that restricted working-class incomes made it difficult for the mass of the population, as opposed to the bourgeoisie, to take advantage of the more diversified food base.

The system of food distribution had some important characteristics. The large lodging-house population and the lack of interior cooking facilities for many families (63 percent of indigents had only a fireplace for food preparation) forced much food consumption and preparation onto the streets and into the restaurants and cafés. The periodicity of worker incomes (during the dead season in particular) meant that much food was purchased on credit. Yet the food typically entered the highly centralized mar-kets (Les Halles) or abattoirs (La Vilette) or wine depots (Bercy) in bulk. The break-down of bulk via a system of retailers, street vendors, and the like also rested on credit. This opened up innumerable possibilities for small-scale entrepreneurial activity, often organized by women, though here, as in other aspects of life, usually under the ultimate control of men.

This intricate system of intermediation had interesting social consequences. Workers evidently viewed it ambivalently. On the one hand, it provided many opportunities for supplementary employment (particularly of women), and even a chance of upward mobil-ity into the petit-bourgeois world of the shopkeeper. On the other hand, the intermediar-ies made what were often close to life-and-death decisions as to when and when not to extend credit, and were often viewed as petty exploiters. It was to circumvent this that the workers' movement began to build a substantial consumer coopertive movement in the 1860s, and many of these cooperatives had considerable success. Nathalie Lemel joined with the indefatigable Varlin to found La Marmite, a food cooperative to which workers could subscribe Fr 50 annually and then have rights to cheap, well-prepared food on a daily basis at much lower cost than in the restaurants. By 1870 there were three branches doing a very busy trade.[8] Lemel and Varlin had dual objectives. Not only did they seek to take care of the needs of those who had no place to cook for themselves, but they also saw the cooperatives as centers of political organization and collective action.

In this they were simply confirming the slowly dawning fears of bourgeois reformers: that the mass of the population of Paris, deprived of the facilities and comforts necessary to a stable family life, were being forced onto the streets and into places where they could all too easily fall prey to political agitation and ideologies of collective action. That the cabarets, cafés, and wineshops provided the premises for the elaboration of scathing criticism of the social order and plans for its reorganization was all too evident to Poulot. That they were hearths for the formation and articulation of working-class consciousness and culture became all too apparent as political agitation mounted after 1867. The emphasis that bourgeois republicans like Jules Simon put upon the virtues of stable family life (in a decent house with adequate cooking facilities) was in part a response to the dangers that lurked when food, drink, and politics became part of a collective working-class culture.

EDUCATION

The social reformers of the Second Republic had envisaged a system of free, secular, and compulsory state primary education for both sexes. What they got, after the victory of the "party of order," was the Falloux Law of 1850, which promoted a dual system of education—one religious and the other provided by the state—while bringing all teaching under the supervision of local boards in which the traditional power of the university was now matched by that of the church and of elected and appointed officials. It is generally conceded that the law brought few benefits and many liabilities. Coupled with niggardly state educational budgets, it contributed to the dismal record of educational achievement during the Second Empire.[9]

Problems arose in part because educational policy lay at the mercy of church-state relations. Anxious to rally Catholics to his cause, the Emperor not only supported the Falloux Law but was reluctant to undermine its spirit until 1863, when, already at loggerheads with the Pope over his Italian policy, he appointed Duruy, a liberal freethinker and reformer, as Minister of Education. Duruy struggled against great odds and with only limited success to give a greater dynamism to the state sector and thus undermine the power of the church. His moves toward free and compulsory primary education and toward state education for girls were often vitiated by legislative tampering and meager educational budgets. But there were all kinds of other conflicts. Apart from the interminable philosophical and theological debates (religion versus materialism, for example), there was no clear consensus within the bourgeoisie as to the objectives of education. Some saw it as a means of social control that should therefore inculcate respect for authority, the family, and traditional religious values—a total antidote to socialist ideology, which some teachers had been rash enough to promote in the heady days of 1848. Even traditionally anticlerical republicans were content to see a hefty dose of religion in education if it could protect bourgeois values (hence the support many of them gave to the Falloux Law). The trouble was that the religious values promoted within the church were, for the most part, of an extraordinarily conservative and backward variety. As late as the 1830s the church had preached against interest and credit, and by the 1850s it was little enamored of materialist science. The church's backwardness in such matters in part accounts for the violent anticlericalism of many of the students (particularly medical students) who made up the core of the Blanquist revolutionary movement.[10]

Others, however, saw education as a way to bring the mass of the population into the spirit of modern times by inculcating ideals of free scientific inquiry and of materialist science and rationality appropriate to a world of scientific progress and universal suffrage. The problem was how to do it. Some, like Proudhon, were deeply antagonistic to state-controlled education (it should always remain under the control of the father, said Proudhon), while others feared that without centralized state control there would be nothing to stop the spread of subversive propaganda. Duruy struggled for responsible and progressive education, and was simultaneously appreciated and vilified on all sides. Given such confusions, it is not surprising that the net outcome was meager progress for educational provision and equally meager progress in educational content. Yet the debate in the 1860s over the role of education was to have a lasting influence on French political life.[11] Progressive Catholics and republicans alike were, in education as in housing and other facets of social welfare, striving to define a philosophy and practice that would give mass education a new meaning in bourgeois society. The debate was vital, even if the achievements before 1870 were minimal.

To the degree that Paris drew its labor power from the four corners of France, the general failure to improve education had a serious impact upon the quality of labor power to be had there. The general decline in illiteracy throughout France was helpful, of course, but it still left around 20 percent of Parisians illiterate by 1872; and even many of those who could read and write had only the most rudimentary form of education, leaving them with marginal abilities when it came to any kind of skill demanding formal schooling. There was little in the educational system of Paris to offset this dismal national picture. The government initially sided with those who saw education simply as a means of control. State and religious schools developed equally side by side.[12] Haussmann's budget allocations to education were parsimonious in the extreme when compared with his lavish expenditures on public works. He looked to religious and private schools to meet the needs of new immigrants and the newly forming suburban communities, and did his best to limit free schooling to the children of indigents, so payment to attend state schools was commonly demanded. Teachers' pay, around Fr 1,500 a year, was barely sufficient to make ends meet for a single person, and certainly insufficient to raise a family. For purely budgetary reasons Haussmann (and quite a few taxpayers) preferred to leave schooling to the private sector, particularly to the religious institutions, where teachers' pay was even lower (around Fr 800).

This picture began to change only after 1868, when Duruy finally forced through the principle of free public education and Greard set about reforming educational provision in Paris. But by then Haussmann's laissez-faire and privatist strategy had shaped a very distinctive map of educational provision in the city. The annexed suburbs formed what can only be described as an educational wasteland of few and inadequate public schools and weak religious or private development, since this was hardly an area of affluent parents who could afford to pay. Haussmann's neglect of schooling here is best evidenced by the fact that he spent only four million francs on new schools in the annexed zone between 1860 and 1864, compared to forty-eight million for the new *mairies*, sixty-nine million for new roads, and five and one-half million for new churches. The rate of school attendance was low and illiteracy higher than the city average. Here were to be found those "ragged schools" in which were assembled "children of all ages who had nothing in common save their . . . degree of ignorance." Here was the space of social reproduction of an impoverished and educationally marginalized working class. In the bourgeois quarters of the west, Haussmann's system worked, since the public schools were used free by the poor quite separately from the private and religious schooling preferred by the bourgeoisie. In some of the central quarters populated by craft workers, petit bourgeois, and those in commerce, the public schools were seen as a common vehicle for educating all children in technical and practical skills, which the Catholic schools found it difficult to impart. Thus the increasing social segregation of space in the city was reflected in the map of educational provision.[13]

The qualities of this educational system also varied greatly. While there were progressive Catholic schools (and the church put special emphasis upon its efforts in education in Paris), the state sector usually had an advantage in science and other modern subjects. However, the tight surveillance of teachers made possible by the supervisory boards set up in 1850 kept the whole of the educational system biased toward control and religious indoctrination rather than enlightened materialism. But to the degree that the Catholic schools preached intolerance as well as respect for traditional values they became less and less popular with the liberal bourgeoisie, many of whom turned to the Protestant schools. The education of girls was left, until Duruy's reforms of the late 1860s, almost exclusively in the hands of the church. Interestingly enough, it was here that the question of the proper balance between moral teachings and vocational skills became most explicit as the issue of women's role came to the fore.

The failures of the formal educational system to produce a labor force equipped with modern technical skills would not have been so serious were it not for a breakdown of other, more traditional modes of skill formation. The apprenticeship system, already in serious trouble by 1848, went into a generalized crisis in the Second Empire.[14] In some trades, given the pressures of competition and fragmentation of tasks, apprenticeship degenerated into cheap child labor and nothing else. The geographical dispersal of the labor market and the increasing separation of workplace and residence created a further strain within a system that had always been open to abuse unless there was close surveillance and control by all parties involved. The system seems to have survived reasonably well in only a few trades, such as jewelry. Furthermore, even some of the traditional provincial centers of skill formation for the Parisian labor market were more and more cut off as seasonal migrations gave way to permanent settlement. There therefore arose, on the part of both employers and the working class, a demand for a school system that could replace the apprenticeship system through vocational training and skill formation in educational institutions. The few private institutions that were formed in the 1860s realized some success, thus pioneering the way for educational reform after the Commune. But it was mainly the children of the petite bourgeoisie or well-off workers who could afford the time or money to attend them. The same limitation affected the popular adult education courses that were established in central city areas in the 1860s.

The rudiments of working-class education then, as now, were imparted in the home, where, according to most bourgeois observers and in spite of Proudhon's injunctions, the woman usually played the main role. Simon's strong interest in the education of women in part derived from what he saw as the need to improve the quality (moral as well as technical) of the education that mothers could impart. Thereafter, children's education ran up against the conflict "the more they earn, the less they learn"—a vital problem for households close to the margin of existence. Much of the uneducated working class proved hostile to compulsory education and the apprenticeship system for this very simple reason. A different attitude prevailed among craft workers, who venerated the apprenticeship system and bewailed its degeneration. It was from this sector of the working class that the demand for free, compulsory, and vocationally oriented education was most strongly voiced. And they were prepared to take matters into their own hands. There was no lack in Paris of dissident free-thinkers and students anxious, as the Blanquists were, to offer education for political reasons or, more frequently, for small sums of cash. Varlin, for example, both educated himself and learned principles of moral and political economy from a part—time teacher.[15] Herein, as the more savvy members of the bourgeoisie like Poulot realized, lay a serious threat: the autodidacts among the craft workers, with their freethinking and critical spirit (their "sublimism"), might lead the mass of uneducated laborers in political revolt. That the freethinking students who formed the core of the Blanquist revolutionary movement, who joined the International, or who adhered to the popular radical press could take on similar radicalizing roles also became all too apparent in the numerous public meetings to which many an uneducated worker was drawn after 1868. And it was, after all, in the educational wasteland of the periphery that the anarchist Louise Michel began her extraordinary and turbulent career as a teacher. From this standpoint, the bourgeoisie was to reap the harvest of its own failure in the field of educational reform and investment—a lesson it was to take to heart after the Commune, as education became the cornerstone of its effort to stabilize the Third Republic.

THE POLICING OF THE FAMILY

What really went on in the heart of the family, whether legally constituted or not, is for the most part shrouded in mystery. How effective the kinship system was in integrating immigrants into Parisian life and culture and in providing some kind of social security is likewise open to debate. The occasional biographies and autobiographies (such as those of Nadaud, Varlin, Louise Michel, and Edouard Moreau) indicate the tremendous importance of family (or free union) and kin within the social networks of Parisian life. Yet we are dealing here not only with politically active people, but also with educated craft workers or petit bourgeois professionals or shopkeepers whose social condition, as we have seen, was quite different from that of the mass of uneducated immigrants. Many of the latter, however, drew their mates from their province of origin and presumably imported into Paris as many systems of family and kin relations as existed in provincial France.[16] For the first generation of such immigrants, the Parisian melting pot probably had little meaning, and through the formation of distinctive colonies from Brittany, Creuse, Auvergne, and Alsace, they could even preserve provincial cultures within the overall frame of Parisian life. Yet there are many indications also of a too rapid melting into the alienation and anomie of large-scale urban culture. The unclaimed bodies from the hospitals, the high rates of children apprehended for vagabondage, the orphans and abandoned children, all point to the breakdown of traditional security systems embedded in the family and kinship organization in the face of insecurity of employment, wretched living conditions, and all the other pathologies and temptations (drink, prostitution) of Parisian life.

FIGURE 70 *Most of the time Daumier depicts family life as anything but idyllic, as in this disastrous episode. This is in marked contrast to the idealized serenity that often characterizes the women impressionist painters of the period, such as Cassatt and Morisot.*

Within the family and kinship systems that did survive, it appears that the older woman acquired a certain prestige, based upon her capacities as mother, nurse, and educator, as the manager of the reproduction of labor power within the home. This was a role that many men clearly valued, that bourgeois reformers sought to encourage as a pillar of social stability, and that the church sought to colonize through the education of girls as purveyors of religious values and morality. Such a role was doubly important because one of the key values that women were expected to inculcate was respect for the authority of the father within the home and of church or state outside the home. That such an ideology was hegemonic is suggested by the fact that the farthest most radical feminists went was to claim mutual respect within free union. For it was, as we saw earlier, almost impossible for a woman to survive, economically or socially, outside of a liaison with a man.

Even though women may have controlled the purse strings, there was all too often too little in the purse to provide for the proper reproduction of labor power. The dead season meant terrible seasonal strains on income, and rent payment dates (customarily three or six months in advance) put a similar strain on expenditures. It was hard for families to stay together under such material conditions without some other forms of support. The numbers with savings in the *caisses d'epargne* (set up in 1818 and consolidated in 1837 to promote working-class thrift) expanded enormously, but the average amount put by fell to around Fr 250 per depositor by 1870—enough for a rainy day or two but not much more. The other resource—to farm out children to kin—probably was equally limited insofar as most kin were in the same financial boat.[17] Where the kinship system was probably most effective, however, was in tracking down employment opportunities for those in immediate need. Outside of this, the family had to look to state or charitable support.

Paris had traditionally been the welfare capital of France, with a tradition of religious and state charity as a right that all indigents could claim. This system, under attack by conservative republicans in the Second Republic, was steadily dismantled by Haussmann, whose neo-Malthusian attitudes to the welfare question we have already noted. The idea, of course, was to reduce the fiscal burden and to force welfare provision back within the framework of family responsibilities—a strategy (then, as now) that would have made more sense if families had had the financial resources to meet the burden. As it was, hospitals and medical care could not be so easily displaced, and the poverty problem was such as to keep support for indigents a major item in the city budget.

Haussmann's strategy of decentralization and localization of responsibility for welfare provision simply kept pace, in the end, with the rapid suburbanization of family and child poverty. The only other strategy was to look to the formation of mutual benefit societies and other forms of mutual aid within the working class. The government took several steps to encourage such organizations but was terrified that they might become centers of secret political mobilization—which, of course, they did. Their considerable growth and their attempted surveillance and control by the government forms an interesting chapter in the struggle for political rights and economic security. Women found it hard to gain access to such societies, and they could not independently draw upon their benefits—a limitation that in part undermined the fundamental aim of support to the family. But the government's insistence on strict surveillance and control also limited the development of the societies in important ways. Here, as with the surveillance system that attached to welfare for indigents, the authoritarian state was stepping crudely down a road toward the policing of the family, which was to be trodden with much greater sophistication by subsequent generations of bourgeois reformers.

CHAPTER TWELVE

CONSUMERISM, SPECTACLE, AND LEISURE

The relations connecting the labor of one individual with that of the rest appear, not as direct social relations between individuals at work, but as what they really are, material relations between persons and social relations between things.

—MARX

The spectacle of Empire initially had a purely political aspect that focused on the populism of the Napoleonic legend and the presentation of imperial power. The plan for Paris to assume the mantle of imperial Rome and become the head and heart of civilization in Europe was part of Haussmann's mandate. Court ceremonies, imperial marriages, burials and visits of foreign dignitaries, military parades (preferably with the Emperor riding in the vanguard after some victorious venture, as in the return from Italy in 1859) all provided occasions to mobilize spectacle in support of imperial power. Haussmann's appointment to Paris in part depended on his successful orchestration of Louis Napoleon's spectacular entry into Bordeaux in the autumn of 1852, shortly before the Empire was declared. Haussmann was a master at organizing spectacles of this sort, and transformed the Hotel de Ville into a perpetual center of spectacle with balls and galas for every occasion. Boulevard openings—Sebastopol (1858), Malesherbes (1861), and Prince Eugene (1862)—were elaborately staged and decorated events as were the unveilings of monuments (St. Michel Fountain in 1860). All such events were turned into spectacular celebrations in which an adoring public could applaud imperial munificence, grace, and power. Popular support for the Emperor was likewise mobilized through galas, fêtes, and balls (even the women of Les Halles, known for their republicanism, organized a grand public ball to celebrate the advent of Empire in 1852). August 15 was declared a day of the *fête imperial*.

FIGURE 71 *Daumier, as early as 1849, picked up the idea that spectacle might be good for the popular classes after a day's hard work.*

The more permanent monumentality that accompanied the reconstruction of the urban fabric (the design of spaces and perspectives to focus on significant symbols of imperial power) helped support the legitimacy of the new regime. The drama of the public works and the flamboyance of the new architecture emphasized the purposive yet festive atmosphere within which the imperial regime sought to envelop itself. The universal expositions of 1855 and 1867 added their weight to the glory of Empire. Yet there was, as Van Zanten (1994, 211) notes, a rapid falling off in this theatricality after 1862 as imperial power gradually faded before that of capital and commerce as driving forces in the reconstruction of Paris. Haussmann thereafter increasingly lost mastery of the urban process. The architect Garnier, in the midst of the universal exposition of 1867 and on the eve of the fête of August 15, had to organize the unveiling of the newly completed facade of his new opera house with no public help or participation.[1]

Spectacle, even that of the city itself, has always been fundamental to urban life, and its political aspects have long played an important role in the construction of legitimacy and social control. There had been no lack of spectacle under the July Monarchy, but much of it escaped social control by the authorities. Sunday excursions took the workers outside the city limits to the bars and dance halls of places like Belleville, culminating in a ribald and riotous evening descent back into the city center. The fear lurked that spectacle of this sort could all too easily lead to riot and revolution. This was particularly true of the Carnaval in the week preceding Lent during the 1840s, characterized as "the last, exuberant fling of a pre-industrial theatre of excess which cut hard against the nascent ideologies of the metropolitan city." The "promiscuous mixing and reversals," the cross-dressing, the temporary loss of class distinctions, threatened the social order. Carnaval "too rudely mocked the careful modulations between spectacle and urban menace staked out across the city. In making gestures, looks and appearances both more explicit and more explicitly counterfeit, in mixing them pell-mell as if no ill would come of the brew, it called the bluff of the Boulevard des Italiens, the Chaussée d'Antin." The authorities and those bourgeois who were not drawn into the frenzy were fearful and horrified.[2] The macabre carnavelsque way in which the bodies of those shot down on the Boulevard des Capucines on that February evening of 1848 were paraded around the city as an incitement to revolution drew upon such traditions. This, then, was what the socially controlled spectacles of the

FIGURE 72 *Military parades played a vital role in the construction of imperial spectacle. This one, in May 1852, preceded the formal declaration of Empire.*

Second Empire set out to displace. The aim was to transform active players into passive spectators. The Belleville Carnaval declined during the Second Empire through a mix of displacement, active repression, and administrative shifts (such as the incorporation of Belleville into the city through the annexation of 1860). The troublesome image of "the descent from Belleville" remained, however, and when it was finally resurrected in the late 1860s, it was with the clear intent of ending Empire and making revolution.

But Second Empire spectacle went far beyond imperial pomp. To begin with, it sought directly to celebrate the birth of the modern. This was particularly true of the Universal Expositions. These were, as Benjamin remarks, "places of pilgrimage to the fetish Commodity," occasions on which "the phantasmagoria of capitalist culture attained its most radiant unfurling."[3] But they were also celebrations of modern technologies. In many respects, imperial spectacle dovetailed neatly with commodification and the deepening power of the circulation of capital over daily life. The new boulevards, besides generating employment, facilitated circulation of commodities, money, and people. The expositions drew massive crowds from the provinces and from abroad, stimulating consumer demand. And all those spectacles took skill, labor, commodities, and money to mount. The stimulus to the economy was therefore considerable.

Haussmann worked at all these levels simultaneously. The new boulevards created their own forms of spectacle, through the hustle and bustle of carts and public conveyances over newly macadamized surfaces (which some radicals thought were designed to prevent them from converting cobblestones into barricades). The arrival of the new department stores and cafés, both of which spilled out onto the sidewalks of the new boulevards, made the boundary between public and private spaces porous. The proliferation of cabarets, circuses, concerts and theaters, and popular opera houses produced a frenzy of popular entertainment (the frivolity of Second Empire culture was strongly associated with Offenbach's popular spoofs on Italian opera in the form of the opera bouffe). The transformation of parks like the Bois de Boulogne, Monceau, and even squares like that at the Temple into places of sociality and leisure likewise helped to emphasize an extrovert form of urbanization that emphasized public show of private opulence. The sociality of the masses of people drawn to the boulevards was now as much controlled by the imperatives of commerce as by police power.

The increasing power of the commodity itself as spectacle was nowhere better expressed than in the new department stores. The Bon Marché, opening in 1852, was the pioneer; it was followed by the Louvre in 1855 (though prototypes went back to the 1840s). Such high turnover stores needed a large clientele drawn from all over the city, and the new boulevards facilitated such movement. The shop windows were organized as an enticement to stop and gaze. The commodities visibly piled high inside the department stores became a spectacle in their own right. The stores were open to the street and encouraged entry of the public without obligation to buy. An army of ushers and salespeople (particularly seductive young men and women) patrolled behavior in the interior space at the same time they sought to cater to consumer desires. The sexuality involved in

FIGURE 73 *Boulevard openings—
Sebastapol in 1858 (top, anonymous)
and Prince Eugene in 1862 (bottom,
Thorigny and Lix)—were also occasions
for display.*

FIGURE 74
*Excursions to the
Bois de Boulogne by
day and to the Opéra
by night (both by
Guerrard) kept every-
one who could afford
it, entertained.*

Figure 75 *Galas and balls were arranged as celebratory events, often concentrated around August 15. Even the women of Les Halles and Les Marches des Innocents (historically Republic sympathizers) organized an event in August 1853 to celebrate the coming of Empire. Later on, the gardens of the Tuileries were regularly packed for the August 15 fête and the firework displays.*

this was blatant. Women therefore had a much more important role, as both buyers and sellers. Mouret, the fictional proprietor of a store like the Bon Marché in Zola's retrospective novel *Au Bonheur des Dames*, explains "the techniques of modern business" to a baron (modeled, rather obviously, on Haussmann). Of supreme importance, says Mouret,

was the exploitation of Woman. Everything else led up to it, the ceaseless renewal of capital, the system of piling up goods, the low prices that attracted people, the marked prices that reassured them. It was Woman the shops were competing for so fiercely, it was Woman they were continually snaring with their bargains, after dazzling her with their displays. They had awoken new desire in her weak flesh, they were an immense temptation to which she inevitably yielded, succumbing in the first place to purchases for the house, then seduced by coquetry and, finally consumed by desire. By increasing sales tenfold, by making luxury democratic, shops were becoming a terrible agency for spending, ravaging households, working hand in hand with the latest extravagances in fashion, growing ever more expensive. . . . "Get the women," he said to the Baron, laughing impudently as he did so, "and you'll sell the world.[4]

FIGURE 76 *Leisure days in the countryside became a feature of Second Empire life, but here Daumier comments on the competitive trauma of getting there on overcrowded trains. Note the contrast with the restful scenes typically presented by the impressionist painters.*

The art of enticement began with window display (sparking a new line of skilled and well-paid employment). Mouret was depicted as "the best window dresser in Paris, a revolutionary window dresser who had founded the school of the brutal and gigantic in the art of display."

The role of the boulevards, already established under the July Monarchy as important centers of public display, was reemphasized and rendered far more extensive. Their theatricality fused with the performative world inside the many theaters, cafés, and other places of entertainment that sprang up along them to create spaces for the display of bourgeois affluence, conspicuous consumption, and feminine fashion. The boulevards, in short, became public spaces where the fetish of the commodity reigned supreme. The new rail communications also facilitated the rise of new leisure forms. Many more tourists and foreigners came in, and excursions for weekends at the coast or in the country (favorite topics for impressionist painters, though Daumier put more emphasis upon the trauma of getting there on overcrowded "pleasure trains") became exceedingly popular.

FIGURE 77 *The cartoonist Cham took up the consequences of replacing cobblestone streets with macadamized surfaces. Here the woman is carefully stacking the displaced cobblestones at the side of the road, "in case they might be needed for barricades."*

The symbiotic relation between commercial and public spaces and their private appropriation through consumption became crucial. The spectacle of the commodity came to dominate across the public/private divide and effectively unified the two. And while the role of bourgeois women was in some ways enhanced by this progression from the arcades to the department stores, it was still their lot to be exploited, though this time as consumers rather than as managers of the household. It became a fashionable necessity for them to stroll the boulevards, window-shop, buy, and display their acquisitions in the public space rather than squirrel them away in the home or in the boudoir. They, too, became a part of the spectacle (particularly when the fashion turned to enormous crinoline dresses) that fed upon itself and defined public spaces as exhibition sites for commodities and commerce overlain with an aura of sexual desire and sexual exchange. This was, obviously, in deep contradiction to the cult of bourgeois domesticity that sought to confine women to the home. The other effect, Sennett claims, was depoliticization:

FIGURE 78 *The fashion for crinoline dresses afforded Daumier multiple opportunities for humorous commentary.*

The capitalist order had the power to throw the materials of appearance into a permanently problematical, permanently "mystifying" state. . . . In "public," one observed, one expressed oneself, in terms of what one wanted to buy, to think, to approve of, not as a result of continuous interaction, but after a period of passive, silent, focused attention. By contrast, "private" meant a world where one could express oneself directly as one was touched by another person; private meant a world where interaction reigned, but it must be in secret[5]

Yet in important ways the private world mirrored the public even as it inverted it. Baudelaire, for example, fully acknowledged the power of the spectacle over interior states of mind. "In certain almost supernatural inner states," he wrote, "the depth of life is almost entirely revealed in the spectacle, however ordinary, that we have before our eyes, and which becomes the symbol of it."[6]

Who were all these consumers? Increasing mechanization (e.g., the advent of the sewing machine), falling costs of raw materials, improving efficiencies in both production and consumption, and a rising rate of exploitation of labor power cheapened many commodities,

FIGURE 79 *Boulevard life—around the famous café Tortoni's (by Guerrard) and around the new grand hotels (anonymous)—became part of the consumerist urbanism that took over during the Second Empire.*

clothing in particular. This broadened the consumer base for certain products down to the lower middle classes and even to the better-paid (or single) workers. The older segregations remained—Tortoni's and the Boulevard des Italiens still centered the haute bourgeoisie and the Boulevard du Temple the anxious middle classes, but mass consumerism backed by the democracy of money proliferated all over the place at the same time that it muddled some of the spaces (such as the Champs Elysée). The mixing that went on in the exterior spaces—the boulevards and the public gardens (such as the Tuileries)—was hard to control, despite the evolution of a more segregated residential ecology within the city. Policing the public space became difficult. The boundary between respectable women and women of easy virtue called for stricter surveillance, and the politics of street life—the itinerant musicians and pamphleteers—was a focus of considerable police activity. From this there arose a sense of insecurity and vulnerability, of bourgeois anxiety, even of anomie, behind the turbulent mask of spectacle and commodification in the public spaces.

Consider, for example, how this anxiety is expressed in Baudelaire's prose poem *The Eyes of the Poor*.[7] He opens by asking his lover if she understands why he suddenly hates her so. Throughout the day they had shared their thoughts and feelings in the utmost intimacy, almost as if they were one. And then that evening:

> You wanted to sit down in front of a new café forming the corner of a new boulevard still littered with rubbish but that already displayed proudly its unfinished splendors. The café was dazzling. Even the gas burned with all the ardor of a debut, and lighted with all its might the blinding whitness of the wall, the expanse of mirrors, the gold cornices and moldings . . . nymphs and goddesses bearing on their heads piles of fruits, pates, and game . . . all history and all mythology pandering to gluttony.

But then on the street they see a gray-bearded man about forty with two children dressed in rags, staring at the café in admiration of its beauty. The eyes of the father said: "All the gold of the poor world must have found its way onto those walls," and the eyes of the little boy said, "But it is a house where only people who are not like us can go." The boy stares, awestruck. Baudelaire says:

> Song writers say that pleasure ennobles the soul and softens the heart. The song was right that evening as far as I was concerned. Not only was I touched by this family of eyes, but I was even a little ashamed of our glasses and decanters, too big for our thirst. I turned my eyes to look into yours, dear love, to read my thoughts in them; and as I plunged my eyes into your eyes, so beautiful and curiously soft, into those green eyes, home of Caprice and governed by the Moon, you said: "Those people are insufferable with their great saucer eyes. Can't you tell the proprietor to send them away?"

"So you see," the poet concludes, "how difficult it is to understand one another, my dear angel, how incommunicable thought is, even between two people in love."

The public space of the new boulevard provides the setting, but it acquires its qualities in part through the commercial and private activities that illuminate and spill outward onto it. The boundary between public and private spaces is depicted as porous. The poem signals ambiguity of proprietorship, of aesthetics, of social relations, and a point of contestation for control over public space. The poet's lover wants someone to assert proprietorship over the public space. The café is not exactly a private space either: a selected public is allowed in for commercial and consumption purposes. The poor family sees it as a space of exclusion, internalizing the gold that has been taken from them. They cannot ignore it, and are forced to confront it in the same way that those in the café cannot ignore them. The poet sees them as part of the spectacle of modernity, a sign of those "thousand uprooted lives" that constitute Paris. He appreciates the differences and the mixing. She wants the poor evicted, just as Cavaignac cleared the revolutionaries off the boulevards in the June days of 1848. She looks for safety and exclusion through segregation.

The spectacle, Clark insists, "is never an image mounted securely in place, it is always an account of the world competing with others, and meeting the resistance of different, sometimes tenacious forms of social practice."[8] Haussmannization, he maintains, failed "to put together an account of anomie with that of social division, it [failed] to map one form of control upon another." And it is this failure that is highlighted in *The Eyes of the Poor*. The social control of commodification and spectacle ("all history and all mythology pandering to gluttony") runs up against the clear signs of exploitation of the poor to spark either anger ("send them away") or guilt ("I felt a little ashamed at our decanters and glasses too big for our thirst"). The sense of bourgeois anxiety and insecurity in the midst of the spectacle is palpable. The anxiety in part reflected the rise of new senses of class distinctions based on consumption and appearances rather than on relations to production. Class divisions stood out more than ever, the mask now became more significant than the reality as daily life came to mimic the facades displayed at the masked ball or during Carnaval. "Faces are eclipsed by clothes, feelings by landscapes," wrote Goncourt.[9]

How this all played out in terms of political identifications within the bourgeoisie is a matter of conjecture. But I suspect that Sennett has it roughly right when he argues that presentation of self in the public sphere came to substitute for representation, and that the presentation of self was more and more reduced to a matter of commodification and spectacle. The public sphere became, as a result, more and more mystified. In the spectacle few people play an active role. While, therefore, the public persona was a participant in the sense that individuals became bearers of the spectacle (if only as the walking mannequins of fashion), they were passive in the sense that it was what they were bearers of (i.e., commodities) which mattered, rather than what they might stand for politically or socially. By the same token, the withdrawal into family life on the part of the bourgeoisie became more marked, for it was there and only there that intimacy, trust, and authenticity seemed possible. But the price of that was extreme secrecy, isolation, and constant fear of exposure, to say nothing of fierce pressures on bourgeois women to conform to these new requirements while straddling the contradiction between their role as bearers of commodity values and their role as guardian of all that was left of intimacy and warmth within the bourgeois household.

The mass of workers, condemned for the most part to live on miserable wages and faced with notoriously unstable conditions of employment, had to live and consume somewhere else. A predominantly immigrant male population resorted for its sustenance to the innumerable small eating and drinking establishments and turned to the cafés, dance halls, cabarets, and drinking establishments for its pleasures. Transformed into what Balzac called "the parliament of the people," a place where all "the notables of the quarter gather," the working-class cafés came in for a lot of regulation and surveillance during the Second Empire. But the inexorable increase in their numbers (from four thousand in 1851 to forty-two thousand in 1885) guaranteed their burgeoning importance in social and political life. "The café may have become the most stable and accessible space in many a worker's existence." And women and families were by no means excluded—many marriages took place in cafés (with the owner acting as witness). The café or wineshop therefore performed an institutional as well as a political and social role in working-class life. Workers "who frequently changed dwellings often stayed in the same neighborhood and continued to patronize the same café." The café or wineshop, in short, became a center through which working-class solidarities were forged on a neighborhood basis.[10] For the working-class women the washhouses that proliferated after 1850 likewise became exclusive centers of social interaction, intimacy and solidarity, gossip, and occasional conflict (of the sort so graphically described in Zola's *L'Assomoir*[11]).

More fortunate male workers could construct a rather different life. Concentrated in the center, they relied upon small-scale commercial establishments as centers of sociality, political discussions, and pleasure (often to excess, as many contemporary commentators, like Poulot, complained). The dingy private and commercial spaces in these areas cast a shadow over public space, while the roiling turbulence of proletarian street life could do little to reassure the anxious bourgeoisie that they lived in a secure world. Such spaces were to be feared, and most bourgeois steadfastly avoided them. The Second Empire authorities sought to regulate them, but there was a limit to this, and housing scarcity and cramped conditions ensured that the street and the café were always in demand as centers of sociality in working-class quarters.

The Second Empire began with tremendous emphasis upon imperial spectacle, but as time went on, it was more and more the spectacle of the commodity that prevailed. Not everyone appreciated these changes. Ernest Renan, a man of letters of some renown, inveighed against them at length and assailed the weakness of women in the face of the sordid commercial temptations that beset them. The Goncourt brothers were equally horrified, Edmond writing in their diary for 1860:

Our Paris, the Paris in which we were born, the Paris of the manners of 1830 and 1848, is disappearing. And it is not disappearing materially but morally. Social life is beginning to undergo a great change. I can see women, children, husbands and wives, whole families in the café. The home is dying. Life is threatening to become public. The club for the upper classes, the café for the lower—this is what society and the common people are coming to. All this makes me feel like a traveler in my spiritual homeland. I am a stranger to what is coming and what is here, as for example, to these new boulevards that have nothing of Balzac's world about them, but make one think of London or some Babylon of the future."[12]

How, then, to distinguish oneself in the midst of that restless crowd of purchasers that confronted the rising ride of commodities on the boulevards? Benjamin's stunning analysis of Baudelaire's fascination with the man in the crowd—the flaneur and the dandy, swept along in the crowd, intoxicated by it, yet somehow apart from it—provides one interesting masculine reference point.[13] The rising tide of commodity and money circulation cannot be held back. The anonymity of the crowd and of money circulation can hide all kinds of personal secrets. Chance encounters within the crowd help us penetrate the fetishism. These were the moments that Baudelaire relished, though not without anxiety. The prostitute, the ragpicker, the impoverished and obsolete old clown, a worthy old man in rags, the beautiful mysterious woman, all become vital characters in an urban drama. The poet is startled by an encounter in a public park: "It is impossible not to be gripped by the spectacle of this sickly population which swallows the dust of factories, breathes in particles of cotton, and lets its tissues be permeated by white lead, mercury and all the poisons needed for the production of masterpieces."[14] Open to chance encounters, the poet can reconstruct, at least for the male bourgeois man of pleasure, the innumerable interrelations between the medley of hands that money touches. The insecurity was something to be reveled in rather than feared.

But there were more disquieting signs at work within the culture of governance and pacification by spectacle. When, for example, Louis Napoleon invited the workers from the various trades to report collectively to him on their impressions of the wondrous new technologies on display at the Universal Exposition of 1867, the workers failed to be impressed by the spectacle and pointed instead to the degradation of labor and of skills, as well as to the inferiority of the product. It was better, they generally concluded, to form worker associations (that magical term could now once more be used) supplemented by new technologies to improve efficiency as well as to ameliorate conditions of labor. And when someone remembered the poor unfortunate Baudin, the democratic-socialist deputy senselessly shot down on one of the few barricades erected to protest the coup d' état of 1851, the result was a campaign to erect a monument by public subscription as part of a more general argument to counter the imperial monumentality that Haussmann had imposed. It was at this time that the idea of a monumental statue of liberty to be placed somewhere was first mooted as a political gesture with obvious implications. Even more troublesome was the habit of turning funerals of almost anyone who had the remotest connection to 1848 or the resistance of 1851 into spectacular political occasions for fiery graveside rhetoric. And when Napoleon's nephew killed Victor Noir, a republican journalist, in an argument in 1869, the burial was attended by at least twenty-thousand people. The whole symbolic order turned back upon itself as the return from Père Lachaise Cemetery and the descent from Belleville fused into a threatening spectacle that augured ill for the regime as a harbinger of revolution. Theatricality and spectacle could be turned to account by both sides, and as the Empire weakened, the center of gravity of spectacle shifted not only toward commodification but also toward political opposition.

CHAPTER THIRTEEN
COMMUNITY AND CLASS

The Commune was therefore to serve as a lever for uprooting the economical foundations upon which rest the existence of classes, and therefore of class rule.

—MARX

Individuals develop allegiances broader than those given by the individualism of money and loyalty to family and kin. Class and community define two such broader social configurations. There is a tendency in modern times to see these as mutually exclusive categories that give rise to antagonistic forms of consciousness and political action. This plainly was not so in Paris, neither before (see chapter 2) nor during the Second Empire. That many felt at home with the idea that there was a community of class as well as a class of community was not an ideological aberration; it had a real material base. What was perhaps more surprising was the way many evidently felt not only that community and class provided compatible categories and identities, but also that their synthesis was the ideal toward which any progressive civil society must strive. This was the basic idea of communism in the 1840s, and the idea of association—so fundamental within the workers' movement and in the ideals of Saint-Simon that underlay the practices of finance capital—either ignored or unified the distinction. Yet it was also true that the conceptions and realities of both community and class underwent a very rapid evolution as the Second Empire progressed. Haussmann's works and the transformation of the Parisian land and property market upset traditional notions of community as much as they upset the socio-spatial structure, and transformations in financial structures and labor processes had no less an impact upon the material basis of class relations. It is only in terms of such confusions that the extraordinary alliance of forces which produced the Paris Commune—the greatest class-based communal uprising in capitalist history—can be fully appreciated.

FIGURE 80 *Daumier used the class distinctions set up on the railways to explore the physiognomy of classes.*

To put things this way is, of course, to invite controversy. Gould rejects the idea that class had anything to do with the Commune. It was, he says, a struggle to gain municipal liberties in the face of an oppressive state, and therefore purely communitarian in inspiration. There have, over the years, been many such attempts to "municipalize" the revolutionary tradition in France.[1] Cobb, to take one well-known example, disputed Soboul's class-driven account of 1789, and Castells, abandoning his earlier Marxist-inspired formulations, interpreted the Commune as an urban social movement in *The City and the Grassroots*. And there are, in addition, numerous books, such as Ferguson's, which so highlight the revolutionary tradition of the city as to turn it into a social force that in and of itself played a critical role in political and cultural change. Against this, I shall argue that there had long been local, neighborhood, and even communitarian identifications of class. Those Marxists who refuse to acknowledge the importance of community in the shaping of class solidarities are seriously in error. But by the same token, those who argue that community solidarities have nothing to do with class are similarly blinded. Signs of class and of class consciousness are just as important in the living space as in the working space. Class positioning may be expressed through modes of consumption as well as through relations to production.

CLASS

Daumard's reconstruction of the fortunes left by Parisians in 1847 yields a vivid picture of the distribution of wealth by socioeconomic category (table 8).[2] Four major groupings stand out. At the top sat the haute bourgeoisie of business (merchants, bankers, directors, and a few large-scale industrialists), landed gentry, and high state functionaries. Accounting for only 5 percent of the sample population, they had 75.8 percent of the inherited wealth. The lower classes (constituting the last four categories) made up three-quarters of the population but collectively accounted for 0.6 percent of the wealth. Between lay an upper middle class of civil servants, lawyers, professionals, and upper management combined with pensioners and those living off interest. Shopkeepers, once the backbone of the middle class, were, as we have already noted, on the way down the social scale (with almost the same proportion of the population, their share of wealth fell from 13.7 percent in 1820 to 5.8 percent by 1847). But they still were a notch above the lower middle class of employees and lower-level managers (mainly white-collar) and the self-employed (mainly craft workers and artisans). The disparities of wealth within this class structure were enormous.

We can look at this class structure another way. To begin with, what Marx called "the old contrast between town and country, the rivalry between capital and landed property" is very much in evidence. The disproportionate presence of rural gentry and state functionaries is directly connected with the centralized role of Paris in national life. The peasant class is not actively seen, but its presence is everywhere felt, not only as the reserve of labor power upon which Paris could draw, but also as the source of the taxes that sup-

TABLE 8 *Inherited Wealth by Socioprofessional Categories, 1847*

Category	Index of Average Value of Wealth per Recorded Death	% Leaving No Wealth	% of Recorded Deaths	% of Total Wealth
Business (commerce, finance, etc.)	7,623	26.3	1.0	13.8
Land and property owners	7,177	8.6	3.7	54.0
High functionaries	7,091	13.0	0.6	8.0
Liberal professions and managers	1,469	39.4	2.0	5.6
Middle functionaries	887	16.9	1.7	3.2
Rentiers and pensioners	709	38.2	5.7	8.3
Shopkeepers	467	35.7	6.1	5.8
State and private employees	71	52.8	2.7	0.4
Home workers	61	48.5	1.8	
0.2Clergy	15	75.9	0.4	0.1
Domestics	13	81.6	6.9	0.2
Withous attribution (and Diverse)	4	79.2	29.1	0.1
Workers	2	92.8	30.2	0.2
Manual laborers	1	80.5	8.1	0.0
All categories	503	72.6	100.0	100.0

Note: I have combined certain minor categories from differently constructed tables without, I think, violating the overall picture.

Source: Daumard (1973), 196–201.

ported government and the unearned incomes that the property owners spent so liberally. When we add in pensioners and rentiers (living off interest), we find nearly a tenth of the population of Paris, controlling more than 70 percent of the wealth, lived off unearned incomes. Here lay much of the enormous effective demand that Parisian industry was so well placed to satisfy. The dominance of the "idle rich" or "consuming classes" had tremendous implications for Parisian life, economy, and politics, as did the overblown role of state functionaries. We find only a fifth of the haute bourgeoisie engaged in economically gainful activities. This had a great effect on the comportment of the bourgeoisie, its social attitudes, and its internal divisions.

The internal divisions within the mass of the lower class (74.3 percent in Daumard's 1847 sample) are harder to discern. The differences between craft, skilled, unskilled, casual, and domestic laborers were obviously relevant, though Poulot later preferred distinctions based on attitudes toward work, and work skill and discipline (table 9). Contemporaries often dwelt (with considerable fear) on that most contentious of all social divisions: between the laboring and the "dangerous" classes. Before 1848, much of the bourgeoisie lumped them together.[3] The workers' movement of 1848 defined a different reality without totally dispelling the illusion. But it left open how to classify the miscellaneous mass of street vendors, ragpickers and scavengers, street musicians and jugglers, errand boys and pickpockets, occasional laborers at home or in the workshop. For Haussmann, these were the "true nomads" of Paris, floating from job to job and slum to slum, bereft of any municipal sentiment or loyalties. For Thiers, they constituted the "vile multitude" who saw the erection of barricades and the overthrow of government as pure theater and festival. Marx was hardly more charitable. The "whole indefinite, disintegrated mass" of "vagabonds, discharged soldiers, discharged jailbirds, escaped galley slaves, swindlers, mountebanks, lazaroni, pickpockets, tricksters, gamblers, maquereaux, brothel keepers, porters, literati, organ grinders, ragpickers, knife grinders, tinkers, beggars,"—"scum, offal, refuse of all classes"—made up a lumpenproletariat, an important support for Napoleon's coup d'état.[4]

Corbon, a contemporary observer, tried to take some of the drama out of the contrasts.[5] The "useless class" accounted for only a fifth of the lower classes, and many of them, like the ragpickers, were so impoverished as to be both passive and "inoffensive" (except for the sight of their poverty); they were not socialized to regular labor, produced and consumed almost nothing, and lacked intelligence, ambition, or concern for public affairs. The "vicious" group among them might be shiftless and perverse, but again had to be distinguished from the minority of truly offensive "dangerous classes" made so much of in the novels of Hugo, Sue, and Balzac, and given such political prominence by analysts as diverse as Thiers and Marx. Then, as now, the question of how to define "marginality" or the "informal sector" and its economic and political role was contentious and confusing. Given the insecurity of employment, the boundary between the "street people" and the workers must have been highly porous. The large number of women trapped in poverty and forced to make a living off the street also gave a strong gender component to the actual constitution of this lowest layer in the population (and, as we will later see, compounded sexual fears with fear of revolution). The street people—living off rather than in the city—were, however, a vital force in Parisian economy, life, and culture.

The boundary between these lower classes and the socioeconomic groups that lay above them was also confused and rendered porous by social and economic insecurity. Hugo remarked, for example, on "that indeterminate layer of society, sandwiched between the middle and lower classes, which consists of riff-raff who have risen in the world and more cultivated persons who have sunk, and which combines the worst qualities of both, having neither the generosity of the worker nor the respectable honesty of the bourgeois."[6] Many shopkeepers (whose aggregate position, we have seen, was in strong decline) were close to this margin of survival. Locked in a network of debt, they were forced to cheat, scrimp, and cut corners in order not to lose the little they had built up out of a lifetime of hard work. Ruthlessly exploiting the people they served, they could also latch onto revolution in the hope for economic improvement. Many of the workshop

TABLE 9 *An Abbreviated Reconstitution of Poulot's Typology of Parisian Workers, 1870*

	True Workers	Workers	Mixed Workers
Work habits and skills	Skilled workers, not always as capable as the "sublimes"—they agree to everything the owner demands in order to win promotion. They work nights and Sundays willingly, and never absent themselves on Mondays. They cannot be diverted from their duties by comrades, friends, or family.	No more reasonably skilled, but willing to work nights and Sundays, and never absent themselves on Mondays. They are motivated solely by monetary gain.	Least skilled, and incapable of supervising anyone. They simply follow the flow of the rest and will sometimes take Mondays off with them.
Drink and society	Of an "exemplary sobriety." They never get drunk and control their bad humor or sadness by keeping it to themselves. They seek consolation in work. They refuse the camaraderie of the workshop and are often rejected by their workmates for that reason.	The get "pickled" occasionally, but usually at home on Sundays. They rarely drink with workmates because their women would not permit it.	They get drunk most often at home but also with workmates, and celebrate paydays, Monday mornings, and collective events.
Life before marriage	They prefer professional prostitutes rather than seduction, and marry without practicing concubinage.	They sleep around with laundresses, domestic servants, etc. and thereby avoid the cost of rent or having to live in with the masters. When they marry, they often desert their mistresses and look for a good housekeeper from their native region.	They are either celibate in rooming houses or marry a shrewish wife . . . or pass to "sublimism."
Economic condition	They are the most well off, have savings, and participate in mutual benefit societies from which they try to exclude the "sublimes." Their wives are often concierges or small-scale retailers.	They sometimes have some surplus money to pay off their debts. Their wives are often concierges or small-scale retailers.	They have permanent difficulties making ends meet.
Family life	They act as heads of households, regard their women as inferior by nature. They put strong barriers between their family and work life.	The wife usually manages the household and often controls the friendships and behaviors of the husband.	The wife is a rough policewoman feared by her mate. She has a tight hold on the purse strings and is the main barrier between the worker and "sublimism."
Politics	True democrats, they are against both the Empire and socialism. They share Proudhon's views on "just aspirations to ownership" and look to association between capital and labor. They read the republican opposition journals, rarely attend political meetings, and disapprove of utopian schemes and worked demagoguery. They defend the Republic and are scorned by socialists.	They do not really understand socialist rhetoric and reject the more advanced ideas. They like to go to public meetings, where they can be persuaded by the demagogues.	They follow the ideas of the "sons of God" and read what they recommend. They often go to the public meetings and defer entirely to the ideas of the the leaders.

Note: This is an abridged version of a more complete typology in Rifkin and Thomas (1988), 104–111.

Simple "Sublimes"	True Sublimes	"Sons of God" and Sublimes of Sublimes
Skilled workers, capable of directing a team, but often see "ripping off" the boss as a duty. Will quit work rather than submit to strict discipline, and therefore move a lot from master to master. Always take Mondays off and refuse Sunday and nightwork.	Elite workers of exceptional skill and indispensable to the point where they can openly defy their bosses without fear of reprisal. often earn a living working only 3 ½ days a week.	The most able to direct production teams with great personal influence over others. They organize collective resistance to the bosses and dictate rhythms of work. The sublime of sublimes never submits to workshop discipline, works at home, but is the "prophet of resistance" within the workforce.
Lose at least one day every two weeks through drinking and are often drunk on Saturdays and Mondays, but spend Sunday with their families.	Truly alcoholics. Unable to function in or out of the workplace without eau-de-vie.	Get drunk only on feast days and with friends and family. They love to drink and discuss politics, and can get drunk more on the politics than the drink.
They are either celibate, living in rooming houses, or in concubinage. They marry to make sure they have children to look after them in old age.	They guard their freedom jealously and live alone or in free union. They marry only to have children to care for them in old age.	Play "Don Juan" until their late 30s, and seduce with ease the wives and daughters of workers on their team. Marry late and to ensure children to care for them in old age, but often live in free union. Wives usually also work.
In permanent economic difficulty and live from day to day. Frequently in debt, they make a virtue out of not paying off debts. The wives are usually workers also.	Always in economic difficulty and lack the resources to support a family, even though the companion usually works, too.	Not in so great difficulty but make it a point of principle not to pay off debts to retailers or landlords.
If the wife has "bourgeois" attitudes, there is a lot of conflict. If she does not work, she has to resort to welfare to survive. Wives who work tend to share the men's attitudes toward bosses and work, and express their solidarity openly.	If the wife is not also a sublime, there is permanent conflict with a lot of violent and drunken beatings and brawling. If the wife is a sublime, there is common understanding in the midst of many rows. The wife will "take to the streets" and is proud to so support the children at the expense of the exploiters.	The woman companion asserts more and more control as the man grows older and loses vigor.
They reflect on socialism every payday and consider themselves exploited by bosses and landlords, who are considered thieves. They sometimes go to public meetings, nearly always with a "son of God."	They rarely talk politics, never read or go to public meetings, but listen very attentively to the commentaries of the "sons of God."	Read the press daily and offer profound commentary on politics, to which others listen with respect. They dream of solutions to the social problem, are against Proudhon, and animate the workers' movement. Prepared for martyrdom. The sublime of sublimes is more reflective, a "man of principle" who acts as prophet and guru to the workers' movement. Prepared to do battle against the Republic, they are the most respected orators at meetings.

owners were in a similar position. There were few large-scale factories in 1848, so the material conditions for the direct confrontation between capital and labor in production were not powerfully present. The distinction between workers and masters in the small-scale workshops that dominated Parisian industry was often ill-defined, and they worked closely enough together for bonds of sympathy and cooperation often to be as strong as daily antagonisms.[7] Both resented the new mass-production techniques and the "confection" system of subcontracting, and felt as oppressed by the power of high finance and commerce as they were angry at and envious of the idle rich—who, in return, as Poulot complained, looked upon those who worked with their hands for a living with equal measures of disgust and disdain. An often radical petite bourgeoisie of small masters, threatened by new production processes and indebtedness, was much more important for Parisian political life than any class of capitalist industrialists.

The bourgeoisie also registered some confusions. *La bohème* was more than a dissipated group of youthful students, posturing and impoverished. It really comprised an assortment of dissident bourgeois, often individualistic in the extreme—seeking identities as writers, journalists, painters, artists of all kinds—who often made a virtue of their failure and mocked the rigidities of bourgeois life and culture. Courbet's café companions often bore more resemblance to Poulot's "sublime" workers than they did to any other layer of the bourgeoisie. And a large number of students (mostly of provincial origin and usually living on a meager allowance) added to the confusions of class. Skeptical, ambitious, contemptuous of tradition and even of bourgeois culture, they helped make Paris "a vast laboratory of ideas" and the foyer of utopian schemes and ideologies.[8] Relatively impoverished, they were forced into some kind of contact with the street people and some workers, and knew only too well the rapacity of the shopkeeper and the loan shark. They formed the core of many a revolutionary conspiracy (the Blanquists, for example), were active in the International, and were likely to launch their own spontaneous movements of protest into the streets of the Left Bank. And they often merged with the disgruntled layers of *la bohème*. A strong dissident movement within the bourgeoisie, which sometimes encompassed relatively well-off lawyers and professionals as well as successful writers and artists, had its roots in these layers of the population.

This class structure underwent a certain transformation during the Second Empire. While data are lacking to make exact comparisons, most observers agree that if there was any change at all in the lopsided distribution of wealth, it was toward greater rather than less inequality. Important shifts occurred within the class fragments, however. Business activities (banking, commerce, limited companies) became relatively more important within the haute bourgeoisie, drawing to their side not only those state functionaries (like Haussmann) bitten with the Saint-Simonian vision but also a segment of the propertied class that found diversification into the stock market and Parisian property more remunerative than relatively stagnant rural rents. But if traditional landed property became rather less prominent, divisions between finance, commerce, and industry became more so, while rivalries among fractions (such as that between the Rothschilds and the Pereires) assumed greater importance. The haute bourgeoisie was no less divided in 1870 than it was in 1848, but the divisions were along different lines.

There were similar important mutations within the working class. Transformations in the labor process and in industrial structure had their effects. The consolidation of large-scale industry in sectors such as printing, engineering, and even commerce (the large department stores) set the stage for more direct confrontation between labor and capital in the workplace, signaled by the printers' strike of 1862 and the commerce workers' strike of 1869. The reorganization and deskilling of craft work also exacerbated the sense of external domination either by the small masters or by the innumerable intermediaries who controlled the highly fragmented production system. Strikes by tailors and bronze workers in 1867, by tanners and woodworkers in 1869, and by the iron founders at Cail in 1870 registered the growing confrontation between capital and labor, even in trades where outwork and small-scale production were the rule. The prospects for craft workers to become small masters seem to have diminished as the latter were either proletarianized or forced to separate themselves out as a distinct layer of bosses, with all that this entailed.

But if Paris had a rather more conventional sort of proletariat in 1870 than it did in 1848, the working classes were still highly differentiated. "The crucible in which workers were forged was subtle," says Duveau; "the city created a unity out of working class life, but its traditions were as multiple as they were nuanced."[9] And nothing was done to assuage the condition of that dead weight of an industrial reserve army and of the underemployed. Living close to the margin of existence, their numbers augmented by migration, they merged into a massive informal sector whose prospects looked increasingly dismal as Haussmann shifted the state apparatus toward a more neo-Malthusian stance with respect to welfare provision. But with nearly a million people living at or below the poverty level (according to Haussmann's own estimates), there were limits to how far even he could afford to go. A surge of unemployment in 1867 thus provoked the Emperor into opening an extensive network of soup kitchens to feed the hungry.

The internal composition of the middle classes also shifted. While the liberal professions, managers, and civil servants participated in the fruits of economic progress, the rentiers and pensioners had a harder time of it as rising living costs and rents in Paris eroded some of their wealth (unless, of course, they switched to more speculative investments, in which case, if Zola's *L'Argent* (*Money*) is anywhere near accurate, they were as likely to lose their fortunes to the stock exchange wolves as to augment their stagnant rural rents). The shopkeepers, if their diminishing hold on Parisian property is anything to go by, continued their descent into the lower middle class or even lower, except for those who found new ways of selling (like the grand department stores and the specialized boutiques, which catered to the upper classes and the flood of tourists). This is the sort of transition that Zola records in such excruciating detail in *The Ladies' Paradise*. At the same time, the boom in banking and finance created a host of intermediate white-collar occupations, some of which were relatively well paid.

The class structure of Paris was in full mutation during the Second Empire. By 1870 the lineaments of old patterns of class relations—traditional landowners, craft workers and artisans, shopkeepers, and government employees—could still be easily discerned. But another kind of class structure was now being more firmly impressed upon it, itself confused between the state-monopoly capitalism practiced by much of the new haute bourgeoisie and the growing subsumption of all labor (craft and skilled) under capitalist relations of production and exchange in the vast fields of small-scale Parisian industry and commerce. Deskilling was at work undermining craft worker power. And economic power was shifting within these frames. The financiers consolidated their power over industry and commerce, at least in Paris, while a small group of workers began to acquire the status of privileged aristocracy of labor within a mass of growing unskilled labor and impoverishment. Such shifts produced abundant tensions, all of which crystallized in the fierce class struggles fought out in Paris between 1868 and 1871.

COMMUNITY

Then, as now, the ideals and realities of community were hard to sort out. As far as Paris was concerned, Haussmann would have nothing to do with the ideal, and if the reality existed, he was blind to it. The Parisian population was simply a "floating and agitated ocean" of immigrants, nomads, and fortune—and pleasure-seekers of all types (not only workers but also students, lawyers, merchants, etc.), who could not possibly acquire any stable or loyal sense of community.[10] Paris was simply the national capital, "centralization itself," and had to be treated as such. Haussmann was not alone in this view. Many in the haute bourgeoisie, from Thiers to Rothschild, thought of Paris only as "the geographical key to a national power struggle" whose internal agitations and propensity for revolution disqualified it for consideration as a genuine community of any standing.[11] Yet many who fought and died in the siege of Paris and in the Paris Commune did so out of some fierce sense of loyalty to the city. Like Courbet, they defended their participation in the Commune with the simple argument that Paris was their homeland and that their community deserved at least that modicum of freedom accorded to others. And it would be hard to read the *Paris Guide* of 1867, the collective work of some 125 of the city's most prestigious authors, without succumbing to the powerful imagery of a city to which many confessed a passionate and abiding loyalty. But the *Guide* also tells us how many Parisians conceived of community on a smaller scale of neighborhoods, quarters, and even the new *arrondissements* created only seven years before. That kind of loyalty was also important. During the Commune, many preferred to defend their quarters rather than the city walls, thus giving the forces of reaction surprisingly easy access to the city.

"Community" means different things to different people. It is hard not to impose meanings and thus do violence to the ways in which people feel and act. Haussmann's judgments, for example, were based on a comparison with a rural image of community. He knew all too well that the "community of money" prevailed in Paris, rather than the tight network of interpersonal relations that characterized much of rural life. And he had a visceral aversion to any version of community that invoked the socialist ideal of a nurturing body politic. Yet while Haussmann denied the possibility of community of one sort, he strove to implant another, founded in the glory of Empire and oozing with symbols of authority, benevolence, power, and progress, to which he hoped the "nomads" of Paris would rally. He used, as we have seen, the public works (their monumentalism in particular); the Universal Expositions; the grand galas, fêtes, and fireworks; the pomp and circumstance of royal visits and court life; and all the trappings of what became known as the *fête impériale* to construct a sense of community compatible with authoritarian rule, free-market capitalism, and the new international order.

Haussmann tried, in short, to sell a new and more modern conception of community in which the power of money was celebrated as spectacle and display on the grand boulevards, in the *grands magasins*, in the cafés and at the races, and above all in those spectacular "celebrations of the commodity fetish," the Universal Expositions. No matter that some found it hollow and superficial, a construction to be revolted against during the Commune, as Gaillard insists.[12] It was a remarkable attempt, and much of the population evidently bought it, not only for the Second Empire but also well beyond. In his decentralization of functions within the *arrondissements* and in the symbolism with which he invested them (the new *mairies*, for example), Haussmann also tried to forge local loyalties, albeit within a hierarchical system of control. Again, he was surprisingly successful. Loyalties to the new *arrondissements* built quickly and have lasted as a powerful force to this day. They were vital during the Commune, perhaps because the *arrondissements*

FIGURE 81 *The cartoonist Darjou here responds to Haussmann's comment that Paris is not a community but a city of nomads by pointing out that displacement by Haussmann's works has been a primary cause of nomadism.*

were the units of National Guard enrollment, and the latter, perhaps not by accident, turned out to be the great agent of direct, local democracy. Haussmann's impositions from above became the means of expression of grassroots democracy from below.

That sentiment of direct, local democracy had deep historical roots. It was expressed in the Parisian sections of 1789 and in the political clubs of 1848, as well as in the manner of organizing public meetings after 1868. There was strong continuity in this political culture, which saw local community and democracy as integral to each other. That ideology carried over to the economic sphere, where Proudhon's ideas on mutualism, cooperation, federation, and free association had a great deal of credibility. But Proudhon emerged as such an influential thinker precisely because he articulated that sense of community through economic organization which appealed so strongly to the craft worker tradition and even to small owners. And Paris had long been divided into distinctive quarters, urban villages, each with its own distinctive qualities of population, forms of economic activity, and even styles of life. The neighborhood wineshop, as has frequently been emphasized, was a key institution for forging neighborhood solidarities. In addition, the flood of immigrants often had their distinctive "receiving areas" within the city based upon their place of origin or their trade, and the "nomads" of Paris seem often to have used their kinship networks as guides to the city's labyrinths.

There is a thesis, held in rather different versions by writers as diverse as Lefebvre and Gaillard, that Haussmann's transformations, land speculation, and imperial rule disrupted the traditional sense of community and failed to put anything solid in its place. Others argue that the administration's refusal of any measure of self-governance that would give political expression to the sense of community was the major thorn in Parisians' side. The Commune can then be interpreted as an attempt by an alliance of classes to recapture the sense of community that had been lost, to reappropriate the central city space from which they had been expelled, and to reassert their rights as citizens of Paris.[13]

The thesis is not implausible, but it needs considerable nuancing to make it stick. It is, for example, fanciful to argue that the notion of community had been more stable and solidly implanted in 1848. There was sufficient disarray in evidence then for the thesis of Haussmann's disruptions to be easily dismissed as a romanticized retrospective reconstruction. What is clearer is that the realities and ideologies of the construction of community underwent a dramatic transformation in Second Empire Paris. And the same processes that were transforming class relations were having equally powerful impacts upon community. The community of money was dissolving all other bonds of social solidarity, particularly among the bourgeoisie (a process that Balzac had complained about as early as the 1830s).

Haussmann's urbanization was conceived on a new and grander spatial scale. He simultaneously linked communities that had formerly been isolated from each other. At the same time, this linking allowed such communities specialized roles within the urban matrix. Spatial specialization in social reproduction became more significant, as did spatial specialization in production and service provision. True, Haussmann's programs also wiped out some communities (Ile de la Cité, for example), punched gaping holes through others, and sponsored much gentrification, dislocation, and removal.

This provoked a great deal of nostalgia for a lost past on the part of all social classes, whether directly affected or not. Nadar, a photographer, confessed it made him feel a stranger in what should have been his own country. "They have destroyed everything, even memory," he lamented.[14] But however great the sense of loss or the "grieving for a lost home" on the part of the many displaced, collective memories in practice were sur-

prisingly short and human adjustment rather rapid. Chevalier notes how memories and images of the old Ile de la Cité were eradicated almost instantaneously after its destruction.[15] The loss of community, which many bourgeois observers lamented, probably was generated primarily by the breakdown of traditional systems of social control consequent upon rapid population growth, increased residential segregation, and the failure of social provision (everything from churches to schools) to keep up with the rapid reorganization of the space of social reproduction. Haussmann's neo-Malthusianism with regard to social welfare, plus the insistence upon authoritarian rule rather than municipal self-government, undoubtedly exacerbated the dangers. The problem was not that Belleville was not a community but that it became the sort of community that the bourgeoisie feared, and the police could not penetrate, the government could not regulate, and where the popular classes, with all their unruly passions and political resentments, held the upper hand. This is what truly lay behind the prefect of police's complaint of 1855:[16]

> The circumstances which compel workers to move out of the center of Paris have generally, it is pointed out, had a deplorable effect on their behavior and morality. In the old days they used to live on the upper floors of buildings whose lower floors were occupied by the families of businessmen and other fairly well-to-do persons. A species of solidarity grew up among the tenants of a single building. Neighbors helped each other in small ways. When sick or unemployed, the workers might find a great deal of help, while on the other hand, a sort of human respect imbued working class habits with a certain regularity. Having moved north of the Saint Martin canal or even beyond the barrières, the workers now live where there are no bourgeois families and are thus deprived of their assistance at the same time as they are emancipated from the curb on them previously exercised by neighbors of this kind.

FIGURE 82 The clearances on the Ile de la Cité, here recorded in a late 1860s photo, were extensive even by present-day standards.

The growth and transformation of industry, commerce, and finance; immigration and suburbanization; the breakdown of controls in the labor market and the apprenticeship system; the transformation of land and property markets; growing spatial segregation and specialization of quarters (of commerce, craft work, working-class reproduction, etc.); reorganization of housing, social welfare provision, and education—all of these taken together, under the overwhelming power of the money calculus, promoted vital shifts in the meaning and experience of community. Whatever the sense of community had been in 1848, it was radically changed, but no less coherent or viable (as the Commune was to prove), in 1870. Let us probe these differences a little more deeply.

THE COMMUNITY OF CLASS AND THE CLASS OF COMMUNITY

The workers' movement of June 1848 was crushed by a National Guard drawn from over three hundred provincial centers. The bourgeoisie who moved within the commercial orbit of Paris had the advantage of "much better communications over long distances than the working class, which possessed strong local solidarity but little capacity for regional or national action."[17] The bourgeoisie used its far-flung spatial network of commercial contacts to preserve its economic and political power.

Behind this incident lie a problem and a principle of some importance. Does "community" entail a territorial coherence—and if so, how are boundaries fixed? Or can "community" mean simply a community of interest without regard to particular spatial boundaries? What we see, in effect, is the bourgeoisie defining a community of class interest sprawled over space. This was, for example, the secret of Rothschild's success (with his far-flung family network of correspondents in the different national capitals). But armed with the lessons of 1848, and following their class interests, the haute bourgeoisie in business and administration (such as Pereire, Thiers, and Haussmann) increasingly thought and acted along such lines. Thiers mobilized to repress the Commune in exactly the same way as had been done in 1848. The bourgeoisie had discovered that it could use its superior command over space to crush class movements, no matter how intense local solidarity was in particular places.

The workers were also pressed to redefine community in terms of class and space. Their movement of 1848 had been marked by xenophobia against foreign workers coupled with intense sympathy for oppressed peoples everywhere (solidarity with Poland sparked major street unrest in Paris in May 1848). The new space relations and changing international division of labor prompted writers like Corbon to argue that the labor question now had no local solution but had to be looked at from a European perspective, at least.[18] The problem was, then, to make this internationalist perspective compatible with the mutualist and corporatist sentiments that infused the working-class tradition. The tradition of *compagnonnage* and the *tour de France* provided some kind of basis for thinking about new kinds of worker organization that could command space in a fashion comparable to the bourgeoisie. This was the problem the newborn International Working

Men's Association faced. The effect was to create an enormous and uncontrollable panic within the ranks of the bourgeoisie, precisely because the International set out to define a community of class "across all provinces, industrial centers and states" and thus match the power the bourgeoisie had found so effective in 1848.[19]

In practice, the bourgeoisie trembled without good reason. The relative weakness of the International's connections, coupled with the powerful residue of a highly localized mutualism, became all too apparent in the War of 1870 and the Commune. In contrast, the creation of the citywide Fédération des Chambres Syndicales Ouvrières in 1869—an umbrella organization (under Varlin's leadership) for the newly legalized trade unions— helped build a worker perspective on labor questions on a citywide scale consistent with Haussmann's urbanization. This kind of organization synthesized powerful traditions of localized mutualism and direct democracy into citywide strategies of class struggle over the labor process and conditions of employment. This was to be part of the volatile mix that gave the Commune so much of its force.

The space over which community was defined altered as the scale of urbanization changed and spatial barriers were reduced. But it also shifted in response to new class configurations and struggles in which the participants learned that control over space and spatial networks was a source of social power. At this point the evolutions of class and community intersected to create new and intriguing possibilities and configurations.

The new communities of class were paralleled by new forms of the class of community. The social space of Paris had always been segregated. The glitter and affluence of the center had long contrasted with the dreary impoverishment of the suburb; the predominantly bourgeois west, with the working-class east; the progressive Right Bank, with the traditionalist though student-ridden Left Bank.[20] Within this overall pattern there had been considerable spatial mixing. Dismal slums intermingled with opulent town houses; the businesses of craft workers and artisans mingled with aristocratic residences on the Left Bank and in the Marais; and, though diminished, the celebrated vertical segregation (rich bourgeois on the second floor above the boutique and worker families in the garret) still brought some social contact between the classes. Masters and employees in industry and commerce also had traditionally lived close to each other, particularly within the city center, and this pattern continued to hold in spite of Haussmann's efforts at deindustrialization.

While it would be untrue to say that Haussmann created spatial segregation in the city, his works, coupled with the land-use sorting effect of rent in the context of changed land and property markets, produced a greater degree of spatial segregation, much of it based on class distinctions. Slum removal and building speculation consolidated bourgeois quarters to the west, while the separate system of land development on the northern and eastern peripheries produced tracts of low-income housing unrelieved by any intermingling with the upper classes. In Belleville, La Villette, and Montmartre this produced a vast zone of generic rather than occupationally specific working-class concentrations that were to play a crucial role in the agitation that led up to the Commune. Land-use competition also consolidated the business and financial quarters, and industrial and

FIGURE 83 *To meet their needs, working-class people had to search out either peripheral housing (often of a temporary nature) or the more substantial inner courtyards within the center, where overcrowding was chronic.*

commercial activities also tended toward a tighter spatial clustering in selected areas of the center—printing on the Left Bank, metalworking on the inner northeast, leather and skins around Arts et Métiers, ready-to-wear clothing just off the grand boulevards. And each type of employment quarter often gave social shape to the surrounding residential quarters—the concentrations of white-collar employees to the north of the business center, the craft workers to the northeast center, the printers and bookbinders (a very militant group) on the Left Bank. Zones and wedges, centers and peripheries, and even the fine mesh of quarters were much more clearly class or occupationally defined in 1870 than they had been in 1848.

Though this had much to do with the spatial scale of the process that Haussmann unleashed, it was also a reflection of fundamental transformations of the labor process, the industrial structure, and an emergent pattern of class relations in which craft and occupation were playing in aggregate a less significant role. The consolidation of commercial and financial power, the rising affluence of certain segments of the haute and middle bourgeoisie, the growing separation of workers and masters, and increasing specialization in the division of labor that permitted deskilling were all registered in the production of new communities of class. Old patterns could still be discerned—the intermingling on the Left Bank was as confused as ever—but it was now overlaid with a fiercer and more definite structuring of the spaces of social reproduction. Spatial organization and the sense of community that went with it were caught up in the processes of reproduction of class configurations. As Sennett perceptively concludes, "localism and lower class fused" during the Second Empire, not because workers necessarily wanted it that way but because social forces imposed such identifications upon them.[21]

Exactly how the community of class worked is best illuminated by Poulot's jaundiced account of "sublimism" among Parisian workers. As a significant industrialist and employer, he was infuriated by insubordination in the workplace and attitudes of anti-authoritarianism and class opposition. He considered failures of family formation to be a major part of the problem (hence his attempt to co-opt the women and promote "respectable" forms of family life). The neighborhood wine bars were a problem. Workers and even whole families habitually gathered there to voice complaints that could not be heard under the oppressive conditions of the workshop or in the isolation of subcontracted work at home. The fact that patronage of the wine bar was mostly neighborhood rather than trade-based,[22] allowed a perspective to build on the condition of the working class in general rather than on conditions of labor within a particular trade. There were also tensions in and around what the wine bar was about for, as Sennett notes: "When the café became a place of speech among peers at work, it threatened the social order; when the café became a place where alcoholism destroyed speech, it maintained the social order." It was for this reason that socialists like Varlin cultivated cooperative eating establishments (La Marmite) as political spaces for the articulation of socialist ideals. What Poulot recognized, and what has often proven to be the case, is that class solidarities and identifications are far stronger when backed, if not sparked, by community organization (the case of mining communities is paradigmatic in this regard). Class identifications are forged as much in the community as they are in the workplace. Poulot's frustration was that he could assert some level of control over the workplace but not in the space of community.

Gould disagrees with this perspective. "The rebuilding of central Paris, the geographical dispersion of workers in a number of industrializing trades, and the significant expansion of the population in the new peripheral *arrondissements*," he writes, "created the conditions for a mode of social protest in which the collective identity of community was largely divorced from the work-based identities of craft and its more elusive cousin, class." The neighborhood was a "basis for a collective identity that had little to do with the world of labor." The Commune was, therefore, "predicated on identification with the urban community rather than with craft and class."[23] Gould claims to have arrived at this conclusion solely on the basis of "neutral" empirical evidence, and rails at those of us who supposedly superimpose a class interpretation upon recalcitrant facts.

Gould is quite correct to insist that the new peripheral spaces (such as Belleville), which played such an important role in the Commune, were less defined by craft, but is quite in error to assume a lack of relation to "its more elusive cousin, class." The evidence he adduces is that Belleville did not significantly increase its class concentration between 1848 and 1872 (it merely remained stable, by his own account, at the astounding level of 80 percent classified as workers in a vastly increased population in 1872). Poulot, for one, would doubtless appreciate Gould's insistence on the importance of neighborhood networks and institutions in the creation of social solidarities, but would have been astonished to learn that these had nothing to do with class. The main evidence that Gould presents for cross-class solidarities is the class composition of witnesses at working-class weddings—the witnesses for workers are disproportionately in the categories of owners and employers. From this he concludes that social networks in the neighborhood had no class basis. Gould conveniently ignores the fact that concubinage was the rule and marriage the exception (in 1881, Poulot went to great lengths to found a society for the promotion of working-class marriages precisely for this reason). Most workers did not get married because it was too expensive and too complicated. Those who did, were almost certainly seeking some upward mobility and respectability, and were therefore far more likely to want "respectable" witnesses (such as doctors, lawyers, local notables).

The distinction between workers and small owners was, as we have repeatedly noted, porous, and this was not the primary class divide—bankers and financiers, landlords, merchant capitalists, the industrialists, and the whole oppressive network of subcontractors constituted the main class enemy for the workers, and I doubt very much if any of them ever turned up as witnesses in Gould's data. That the witnesses were part of the local social network is undeniable, but the meaning to be ascribed to that is also open to question. The wineshop and café owners, according to Haine, frequently acted as witnesses for their clients, but this is hardly evidence of lack of class solidarity because those establishments were often centers for the articulation of class-consciousness.[24] Gould is, however, quite correct to point to the issue of municipal liberties as a crucial demand both before and dur-

FIGURE 84 *Working-class street life around Les Halles (by Le Couteux) and night-life in the wineshops (by Crepon) was a far cry from bourgeois respectability. Note how women and children seem fully integrated into the wineshop scene.*

ing the Commune. But the evidence is strong on both sides—bourgeoisie as well as workers—that this was conceptualized as a class demand, albeit one that overlapped (sometime uneasily) with the more radical forms of bourgeois political republicanism.

Contrary to Gould's unsubstantiated opinion that "there is no evidence" that the socialist content of the public meetings which occurred after 1868 was having any effect, we have Varlin's confident assertion as early as 1869 that eight months of public discussion had revealed that "the communist system is more and more favored by people who are working themselves to death in workshops, and whose only wage is the struggle against hunger," and Millière's thoughtful press articles in 1870 on the prospects and dangers of "the social commune" as a solution to the problems of working class life.[25] Control of the body politic had, as we have seen, been seriously contested along class lines ever since the 1830s, if not before, and the association between "communism" and "commune" was actively being revived. That the demand for municipal self-governance was so salient in a city where the working class constituted a clear majority can hardly be taken as evidence of a lack of class interest. And if the Commune was solely about municipal liberty, why did the republican bourgeoisie (who generally favored it) flee the city so fast and why did the monarchists (who had long campaigned for political decentralization) provide the core of military leadership that dealt so savagely with the communards as "reds" in the bloody week of May 1871?

Interestingly, much of the evidence that Gould mobilizes about the salience of spatial propinquity in social (class) relations, and the importance of neighborhood institutions and of the new *arrondissements* as loci of social solidarity, is perfectly consistent with the account I am offering here. The Commune was indeed a different kind of event from 1848, and in part it was so because of the radical reorganization of the living spaces that haussmannization accomplished along with the equally radical transformations in labor processes, in the organization of capital accumulation, and in the deployment of state powers. The community of class and the class of community became more and more salient features of Second Empire daily life and politics, and without the close intermingling of these elements the Commune would not have taken the form it did.

CHAPTER FOURTEEN
Natural Relations

That man's physical and spiritual life is linked to nature means simply that nature is linked to itself, for man is a part of nature.

—Marx

Haussmannization did not leave the pastoral longings of Balzac's utopianism unrequited. Nor did it ignore the legitimacy to be conferred by appeal to the medieval, Gothic, and Christian origins of the French state (the architect and great restorer of Gothic cathedrals, Viollet-le-Duc, twice decorated Notre Dame, once (hurriedly) to celebrate the declaration of Empire and once, at Haussmann's invitation, to celebrate Louis Napoleon's marriage). Haussmann also responded to the emphasis upon health and hygiene, upon the revitalization of the human body and the psyche through access to the curative powers of "pure" nature, which had lain behind a series of proposals made by the "hygienists" of the 1830s. And he acted upon proposals, most explicitly laid out by Meynadier in 1843, for parks and open spaces within the city (to function as the "lungs" of the city). Personally dedicated to dealing with these issues, Haussmann invited his talented advisers (particularly Alphand and Belgrand) to come up with remedies. The Bois de Boulogne (known as a "pitiless desert" during the July Monarchy and a particular object of Louis Napoleon's interest for revitalization), Vincennes, Luxembourg, the spectacular Buttes Chaumont (carved out of a garbage dump), Parc Monceau, and even smaller spaces such as the Square du Temple were either created from scratch or completely reengineered, mostly under Alphand's creative guidance, to bring a certain concept of nature into the city.

It was, of course, a constructed concept of nature that was at work here, and it was fashioned according to very distinctive criteria. Grottoes and waterfalls, lakes and rustic places to dine, restful walks and bowers, were all craftily engineered within these distinc-

FIGURE 85 *The opening up of neighborhoods to sunlight and fresh air allows this inhabitant, as Daumier records it, to know whether the plant he is growing will be a rose or a gillyflower.*

tive spaces of the city, emphasizing pastoral and arcadian visions, Gothic designs and romantic conceptions of the restorative powers of access to a pristine, nonthreatening (therefore tamed), but still purifying nature.[1] These strategies served several purposes. They brought "the spectacle of nature" into the city and thereby contributed to the luster of the imperial regime. They also co-opted the politicized romanticism of the 1840s and sought to transform it into a passive and more contemplative relation to nature within the open spaces of the city.

There was much in this that appealed to a distinctive cultural tradition, common to both workers and bourgeois alike, that stretched back at least to the Restoration if not before. But this was not an autonomous cultural development that had no relation to the evolving paths of capitalism.[2] The commodification of nature (and of access to nature) and the spreading influence of finance capital and credit had much to do with developments during the July Monarchy. Concerns over the consequences of overcrowding, insalubrity, and the casualization of an increasingly impoverished labor force—all products of what Marx called "the manufacturing" period of capitalist development that typically preceded machinery and modern industry—had brought the question of the relation to

FIGURE 86 *The transformation of the Bois de Boulogne from a "pitiless desert" under the July Monarchy into a site of pastoral image (above, in Marville's photo) accompanied by innumerable Gothic touches was one of Alphand's supreme achievements, along with the extraordinary reengineering of the old city dump to make the spectacular park of Buttes Chaumont (below, by Charpentier and Benoist).*

FIGURE 87 *The redesign of the Square du Temple (which conveniently erases all popular memory of the place where the King and his family were imprisoned for several months before their executions in 1793) brought vegetation and running water into the very heart of the city. It actually combined the park by Alphand, a mairie by Hittorff, and a covered market by Baltard into a total re-orchestration of an urban space around leisure, administration, and the market.*

nature center stage during the Restoration and after. Romanticism (of the Lamartine and Georges Sand variety) and pastoral utopianism (of the sort that Balzac articulated) were both in part a response and a reaction to these degraded conditions of urban life. The Fourierists were particulary emphatic about restoring the relation to nature as a central tenet of their utopian plans. In a more practical register, the hygienists of the July Monarchy (Villermé, Frègier, and Parent-Duchatalet) produced more and more evidence of the vile living conditions in which much of the urban population in both Paris and the provinces were confined. While they looked to cleanliness and public health measures as remedies (particularly for the scourge of cholera), there was plenty of grist in these reports to feed sentiments that varied from Fourierist disgust with the failures of civilization to a romantic longing for return to some healthier relation to living nature. The conditions that gave rise to such sentiments had everything to do with the gathering pace of capitalist development.

Haussmann, as was his wont, altered the scale of the response to these questions, and thereby changed the stakes in the remedies he produced:

> In 1850 there were forty-seven acres of municipal parks. When he was forced from office, twenty years later, there were 4,500 acres. He added eighteen squares to the city—an additional seven in the annexed zone—and nearly doubled the number of trees lining avenues and boulevards, with some of the grander streets given a double row of trees on each side. In addition he planted trees on all public land. . . . The greening of Paris was a political act for Haussmann.[3]

FIGURE 88 *Most of Marville's photos of old Paris seem to have been taken shortly after a rain shower, for there are invariably runnels of liquid in the street. But these runnels are, for the most part, indicators of raw sewage. Much work was needed to remedy this unhealthy situation.*

This was the era of the chestnut with its spring blossoms and its fall foliage. If Alphand provided the genius for overall design (particularly of the Bois de Boulogne), then the horticulturalist he summoned from Bordeaux, Barillet-Deschamps, provided innumerable romantic touches for those who ventured into the parks and squares of the city.

With respect to water and sewage, however, Haussmann had very little choice, because it was obvious in 1850 that Paris lagged far behind British and American cities, and even some of the other cities of Europe (such as Berlin), in its level of provision. The disgusting conditions described by Fannie Trollope during her visit in 1835 had scarcely been touched by 1848. "But great and manifold as are the evils entailed by the scarcity of water in the bedrooms and kitchens of Paris," she wrote, "there is another deficiency greater still and infinitely worse in its effects. The want of drains and sewers is the great defect of all the cities in France and a tremendous defect it is."[4] Most of Marville's street photos of the 1850s make it seem as if it has just stopped raining, but the runnels visible in the streets are signs of raw sewage, not rainwater. The cholera outbreak of 1848–1849 and another in 1855 raised the stakes even higher, for though the causes were not yet known, it was generally presumed that insalubrious conditions had much to do with it.

FIGURE 89 *The new sewers were wide and spacious enough (top, by Valentin) for the bourgeoisie and visiting royalty to be taken on tours of them (bottom, by Pelcoq). The tours were partly designed to reassure the bourgeoisie that there were no sinister forces, of the sort that Hugo had described in* Les Misérables, *lurking underground.*

The story of Haussmann's reshaping of Paris underground has been told many times over, and it is generally applauded as dramatic, spectacular, and even heroic.[5] Water provision certainly improved. In 1850 Paris had a daily inflow of twenty-seven million gallons, which amounted to twenty-six gallons a day per inhabitant if it had been distributed equally (which it was not). By 1870 this was increased to fifty gallons a day per inhabitant (still far less than London), with works in hand that would shortly raise it to sixty-four. On the distribution side Haussmann was less successful. Half the houses did not have running water in 1870, and the distribution system to commercial establishments was weakly articulated. Belgrand, with Haussmann's support, also decided to separate the supply of drinking water from nonpotable water for the fountains, street cleaning, and industrial uses. Initially, this helped reduce the costs of provision of fresh potable water. But the struggle to identify and procure adequate supplies of fresh potable water of good quality in the Paris region was drawn out and beset by many technical difficulties. Haussmann emerged victorious. Fittingly, the aqueducts that brought pure water from the springs of Dhuis and Vanne some distance from Paris could be modeled on those of imperial Rome, and thus contribute in their own way to the propagation of an imperial aura. They came to Paris at sufficient height, furthermore, to allow the whole city to be serviced by gravitational flow.

Increased flows of water entailed paying more attention to sewage disposal. It was still the case in 1850 that the street was the main sewer. In 1852 (before Haussmann) the prefecture had already directed that "sewer hookups be installed in all new buildings and buildings undergoing major renovation on streets with sewers." But to be effective, this required that all Paris streets have sewers. Haussmann's response was typical. "While the length of city streets doubled during the Second Empire (from 424 kms to 850 kms) the sewer system grew more than fivefold (from 143 kms to 773 kms)."[6] Even more important, the sewers constructed were capacious enough to house easily repaired water pipes and other underground infrastructures (electricity cables in later times). Paris underground became a spectacle to behold. Tours were laid on for visiting dignitaries and a bourgeoisie hitherto fearful of all that lay underground, including the low species of underclass life that lurked there (Hugo's famous description of the Paris sewers in *Les Misérables* emphasized that idea). In a rather famous passage in his report to the Municipal Council, Hausmann wrote:

> These underground galleries would be the organs of the metropolis and function like those of the human body without ever seeing the light of day. Pure and fresh water, along with light and heat, would circulate like the diverse fluids whose movement and replenishment sustain life itself. These liquids would work unseen and maintain public health without disrupting the smooth running of the city and without spoiling its exterior beauty.[7]

Gandy interprets this as a discursive throwback to premodern conceptions (of nature as alive rather than as dead) and sets out to show how "the circulatory dynamics of economic exchange were to overwhelm organic conceptions of urban order and institute a new set of relationships between nature and urban society."[8] This, he argues, was not accomplished by Haussmann, but had to wait until the end of the nineteenth century. Haussmann's language here may of course just have been tactical, drawing upon the long tradition of biological reasoning and organic metaphors that suffused the work of the hygienists of the July Monarchy, but it is just as likely that, at a moment when mechanical engineering language was not settled upon as the technical language of modernity, he was drawn to the metaphor of circulation and metabolism as a purely practical matter (much as contemporary environmentalists have revived the concept of metabolism as fundamental to the idea of sustainable urban development). The careful scientific inquiries and reports of Belgrand, and the memoranda that Haussmann produced to persuade a skeptical and always cautious Municipal Council, are largely devoid of such organic rhetoric, and analyze matters in a mechanical way. They do, however, emphasize the idea of circulation, and this metaphor did double duty. On the one hand, it could emphasize the cleansing functions of the free circulation of air, of sunlight, of water, and of sewage in the construction of a healthy urban environment at the same time that it evoked a connection with the free circulation of money, people, and commodities throughout the city, as if these were also entirely natural functions. The circulation of capital could thereby be rendered "natural" and the reshaping of the metropolis (its boulevards, park spaces, squares, and monuments) could be interpreted as in accord with natural design.

CHAPTER FIFTEEN

SCIENCE AND SENTIMENT, MODERNITY AND TRADITION

Upon the different forms of property, upon the social conditions of existence, rises an entire superstructure of distinct and peculiarly formed sentiments, illusions, modes of thought and views of life.

—MARX

To try to peer inside consciousness is ever a perilous exercise. Yet something has to be said about the hopes and dreams, the fears and imaginings that inspired people to action. But how to reconstruct the thoughts and feelings of Parisians of more than a century ago? To be sure, there is a vast literary record (popular and erudite), which, when complemented by cartoons, paintings, sculpture, architecture, engineering, and the like, tells us how at least some people felt, thought, and acted. Yet many left no such tangible mark. The mass of the population remains mute. It takes a careful study of language—words, gestures, popular songs, theater, and mass publications (with titles like *La Science pour Tous*; *Le Roger Bontemps*; *La Semaine des Enfants*)—to get even a fragmentary sense of popular thought and culture.[1]

The Second Empire had the reputation of being an age of positivism. Yet, by modern standards, it was a curious kind of positivism, beset by doubt, ambiguity, and tension. Thinkers were "attempting in differing ways and to differing extents to reconcile aspirations and convictions that [were] incompatible."[2] What was true for the intelligentsia, the artists, and the academicians was also profoundly true for many workers; though passionately interested in progress, they frequently resisted its applications in the labor process. Wrote Corbon: "the worker who reads, writes, has the spirit of a poet, who has great material and spiritual aspirations, the devotee of progress, becomes, in fact, a reactionary, retrograde and obscurantist, when it comes to his own trade."[3] For the craft work-

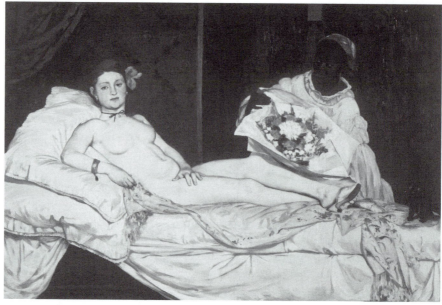

FIGURE 90 *The way in which modernity echoed tradition is beautifully set up with Manet's Olympia, which clearly used Titian's Venus d'Urbino for its model. But the obedient dog is replaced by an uncontrollable cat (a symbol of the powerful Masonic movement among the middle classes), the retainer is much more of this world and her power is more ambiguous, and the nude appears less of a courtesan and, as many critics at the time complained, more like a common prostitute.*

ers, of course, their art was their science, and their deskilling was no sign of progress, as leaders like Varlin were ceaselessly to complain. Since Paris was the hearth of intellectual ferment, not only for the cream of the country's intelligentsia but also for the "organic intellectuals" of the working class, it experienced these tensions and ambiguities with double force. There were also innumerable intersections in which the sense of increasing submission of the worker to the money power of capitalism was mirrored by the prostitution of the skills of writer and artist to the dictates of the market. Here was the unity of experience that put *la bohème* on the side of workers in revolution.

Most were struck by the virtues of science. The achievements of medicine had particular importance. Not only were the medical students often in the avant-garde in the political and scientific movements of the 1860s, but the image of the cool dissection of something as personal as the human body became a paradigm of what science was all about. And if the human body could be dissected, then why not do the same thing to the body politic? Science was not so much a method as an attitude given over to the struggle to demystify things, to penetrate and dissect their inner essence. Such an attitude even underlay the movement toward "art for art's sake." Not only scientists but writers, poets, economists, artists, historians, and philosophers could aspire to science. "It was free of conventional morality and of any didactive motive; it was 'pure' in the sense they wished their art to be 'pure,' [and] its objectivity and impartiality resembled their determination to avoid sentimentality and an open display of personal feeling." It was every writer's ambition, as Sainte-Beuve wrote in praise of *Madame Bovary*, to wield "the pen as others wield the scalpel." Flaubert, the son of a doctor, was fascinated by the dissection of cadavers all his life. "It's a strange thing, the way I'm attracted by medical studies," he wrote, but "that's the way the intellectual wind is blowing nowadays." Maxime du Camp, one of Flaubert's closest friends in his early years, subsequently wrote an "anatomical dissection" of the "body" of Paris in a six-volume study (and, as Edmond Goncourt remarked in his journal, pretty much dissected Flaubert in his *Mémoires* in similar fashion). Delacroix was moved to observe that science, "as demonstrated by a man like Chopin is art itself, pure reason embellished by genius." Many artists saw themselves as working in a spirit analogous to that of a scientist like Pasteur, who was then penetrating the mysteries of fermentation.[4]

Others, sensing the widening gap, sought to close it. "The time is not far off," wrote Baudelaire, "when it will be understood that any literature which refuses to march fraternally between science and philosophy is a homicidal, suicidal literature." Hugo thought likewise: "It is through science that we shall realize that sublime vision of poets; social beauty. . . . At the stage which civilization has reached, the exact is a necessary element in what is splendid, and artistic feeling is not only served but completed by the scientific approach; the dream must know how to calculate."[5] Craft workers like Varlin would surely have agreed; that was, after all, why they set out to educate themselves. The historian Michelet was even more programmatic. He sought "the poetry of truth, purity itself, [that] which penetrates the real to find its essence . . . and so breaks the foolish barrier which separates the literature of liberty from that of science."[6]

Confusions and ambiguities arose because few were ready to separate science from sentiment. While a scientific posture helped liberate thinkers from the traps of romanticism, utopianism, and, above all, the mysticism of received religion, it did not absolve them from considering the directions of social progress and the relation to tradition. "A little science takes you away from religion; a lot brings you back to it," said Flaubert. Saint-Simon had earlier led the way by insisting that his new science of society could go nowhere without the power of a renovated Christianity to drive its moral purpose. Auguste Comte (who collaborated with Saint-Simon in his early days) followed suit. The systematizer of an abstract, systematic, and theoretical positivism in the 1830s converted to a more humanistic strain of thought in the 1840s. From 1849 until his death in 1857, tract after tract dedicated to the foundation of positivist churches of humanity issued forth from his house close by the Place Sorbonne.

Those most concerned with constructing a science of society did not want to separate fact from value. Prior to 1848, social science had been divided between the grand systematizers like Comte, Saint-Simon, and Fourier, whose abstractions and speculations might inspire, and the empiricists, who, like the hygienists of the 1840s, confined themselves to moving but Malthusian descriptions of the awful pathologies and depravities to which the poor were exposed and the dangerous classes prone. Neither tactic yielded incisive social science. It took Proudhon to make the connection between capitalism, pauperism, and crime more explicit in the French context, and Marx's *Capital*, the first volume of which came out in German only in 1867, made the connections even clearer. The medical students who later formed the core of the Blanquist movement likewise used their materialist scalpels to great effect in the dissection of society and its ills. But other, less encouraging trends could be observed. Le Play combined positivism with empiricism to construct a new kind of social science during the 1850s in order to support the Catholic cause. His extensive studies of family budgets and family life were dedicated to securing the Christian concept of the family as the basis of the social order. The liberal political economists were no less assiduous in shaping their "objective" social science to political ends.[7]

These confused crosscurrents are hard to understand without reference to the complex evolution of class relations and alliances that produced 1848, the conservative Republic, and the Empire. In the Revolution of 1848, as we have seen, progressive social democrats were joined on the barricades by a motley assortment of *la bohème* (Courbet and Baudelaire, for example), romantics (Lamartine, George Sand), utopian socialists (Cabet, Blanc), and Jacobins (Blanqui, Delescluze), as well as by an equally motley assortment of workers, students, street people, and representatives of "the dangerous classes." The bitter days of June shattered that alliance in all manner of ways. Whatever their actual role may have been, the powerful ideological stamp that the romantics and the socialist utopians put upon the rhetoric of 1848 was totally discredited with the June repression. "Poets cannot cope," quipped Flaubert. Proudhon found the demagoguery on the barricades vapid and utopian, totally lacking in practicality. Yet romanticism and utopianism had been the first line of defense against the subordination of all modes of thought to religion. Some other means of defense and protest had to be found:

> Utopianism was now, generally speaking, displaced by positivism; the mystic belief in the virtue of the people and hopes for a spiritual regeneration gave way to a more guarded pessimism about mankind. Men began to look on the world in a different way, for splendid illusions had been shattered before their eyes, and their very style of talking and writing changed.[8]

Herein lies the significance of Courbet's sudden breakthrough into realism (called "socialist" by many) in art, Baudelaire's fierce and uncompromising embrace of a modernity given a much more tragic dimension by the violence of 1848, and Proudhon's initial confusion followed by total rejection of utopian schemes. Courbet, Baudelaire, and Proudhon could, and did, make common cause.[9] Their disillusionment with romanticism and utopianism was typical of a social response to 1848 that looked to realism and practical science as means to liberate human sentiments. They may have remained romantics at heart, but they were romantics armed with scalpels, ready to take shelter from the authoritarianism of religion and Empire behind the shield of positivism and detached science. The respectable bourgeoisie drew a similar sort of conclusion, though for quite different reasons. Professional schools should be organized, wrote one, to train competent workers, foremen, managers of factories "for the combats of production" instead of producing "unemployed bacheliers embittered by their impotence, born petitioners of every public office, disturbing the state by their pretensions."[10]

It would seem that the Empire, with its concerns for industrial and social progress, would have welcomed this turn to realism and science, would have encouraged and co-opted it. And on the surface it did just that, through promotion of Universal Expositions dedicated to lauding new technologies, the establishment of worker commissions to examine the fruits and applications of technological change, and the like. Yet the Second Empire did nothing to reverse and, until 1864, even exacerbated what most commentators agree was a serious decline of French science from its pinnacle early in the century into relative mediocrity by the end.[11] Little was done to support research—Pasteur, for example, had a hard time obtaining funds—while government policies (denying students free speech on political questions, for example) often threw the universities into such turmoil that student protests were forced onto the streets or into underground conspiracies like the Blanquist. Science and positivism, free thought and materialism, became forms of protest. The mysticism of religion, the censorious authoritarianism and the frivolity of Second Empire culture were its main targets.

The contradictions in imperial policy also have to be understood in terms of the shaky class alliance upon which Louis Napoleon had to rest his power. It was, indeed, his genius and misfortune that he sought the implantation of modernity in the name of tradition, that he used the authoritarianism of Empire to champion the freedoms and liberties of private capital accumulation. He could occupy such an odd niche in history precisely because the instability of class relations in 1848 gave him the chance to rally the disillusioned and fearful of all classes around a legend that promised stability, security, and perhaps national glory. Yet he knew he had to move forward. "March at the head of the ideas of your century," he wrote, "and those ideas follow and support you. March behind them and they drag you after them. March against them, and they overthrow you."[12] The problem, however, was that Napoleon had to seek support from a Catholic Church that was reactionary and uncultured at the base and led by a Pope who totally rejected reconciliation with progress, liberalism, and modern civilization. To be sure, there were progressive Catholics, unloved by Rome, who, like Montalembert, supported the coup d'état but later so deplored the alliance of Catholics with Empire that they were hauled before the public prosecutor. But the net effect, at least until the breakdown of the alliance in the 1860s, was to surrender much of education to those who thought of it solely as a means for social control by the inculcation of traditional values rather than as a fount of social progress. That, combined with censorship, transformed the free-thought movement in the universities into a major criticism of Empire.

The Empire also was vulnerable because it uncomfortably straddled the break between modernity and tradition. It sought social and technological progress, and therefore had to confront in thought as well as in action the power of traditional classes and conceptions (religion, monarchical authority, and artisanal pride). The Empire was also founded on legend; but the legend could not bear too close an inspection. There were two principal embarrassments: the manner of the First Empire's emergence from the First Republic, and its ultimate collapse. The censors sought to impose a tactful silence on such matters, banning popular performances and plays (even one by Alexander Dumas) that referred to them. Victor Hugo, thundering against the iniquities of Napoleon "le petit" from the safety of exile, took up the cudgels. He inserted a brilliant but, from the standpoint of plot, quite gratuitous description of the defeat at Waterloo into *Les Misérables*, editorializing as he did so that for Napoleon I to have won at Waterloo "would have been counter to the tide of the nineteenth century," that it would have been "fatal to civilization" to have "so large a world contained within the mind of a single man," and that "a great man had to disappear in order that a great century might be born." *Les Misérables*, though published in Brussels, was "in everyone's hands" in the Paris of 1862, and Hugo's message was surely not lost on his readers.[13]

This kind of exploitation of tradition was not new. The grapplings of historians and writers like Michelet, Thiers, and Lamartine with the meaning of the French Revolution had played a major role in the politics of the 1840s. Republicans used history and tradition after 1851 to make political points. They were as much concerned to invent tradition as to represent a certain version of it. This is not to accuse them of distortion, but of reading the historical record in such a way as to mobilize tradition to a particular political purpose. It was almost as if the dead weight of tradition were such that social progress had to depend on its evocation, even when it did not weigh "like a nightmare on the brain of the living," as Marx puts it in the *Eighteenth Brumaire*.[14] In this respect, artists, poets, novelists, and historians made common cause. Many of Manet's paintings of the Second Empire period, for example, portray modern life through the overt re-creation of classical themes (he took the controversial *Olympia* of 1863 directly from Titian's *Venus d'Urbino*). He did so, Fried suggests, in a way that echoed Michelet's political and republican tracts of 1846–1948 while answering Baudelaire's plea for an art that represented the heroism of modern life.[15]

The experience of craft workers was no different. Their resistance had forced much of Parisian industry to all manner of adaptations. They had defended their work and their lifestyle fiercely, and had used corporatist tactics to do so. When the Emperor invited them to inspect the virtues of technological progress and document their reactions to the Universal Exposition of 1867, they responded with a defense of craft traditions.[16] Yet their power was being eroded and sometimes swamped by competition and technological change within the new international division of labor. This posed enormous problems for the "organic intellectuals" of the working-class movement as well as for revolutionary socialists who sought a path to the future but had to do so on the basis of fiercely held ideological traditions (stemming, in the Blanquist case, from the French Revolution). And the mass in-migration of often unskilled workers, clinging to bastardized rural traditions and parochial perspectives, did not help matters. But the coup d'état had also revealed significant pockets of rural revolutionary consciousness and resistance, from which were reimported revolutionary sentiments that Paris had hitherto prided itself upon exporting to a supposedly backward countryside. That the countryside was itself a site of class relations and contestations, and hence a breeding ground for class politics, was a fact that most Parisians, as we have seen (chapter 1), preferred to deny.

The problem, however, was that the new material circumstances and class relations in Parisian industry and commerce required a line of political analysis and action for which there was no tradition. The International, which began rooted in mutualist and corporatist traditions, had to invent a new tradition to deal with the class struggles of 1868–1871. This put a forward-looking and modernist gloss on some of what happened in the Commune. It was, sadly, more successful after the martyrdom of many of its members in 1871 than before. Consciousness is as much rooted in the past and its interpretations as in the present.

The modernity that Haussmann created was itself powerfully rooted in tradition. The "creative destruction" necessitated by the demolitions and reconstructions had its precedents in the revolutionary spirit. Though Haussmann would never evoke it, the creative destruction of the barricades of 1848 helped pave his way. And his willingness to act decisively was admired by many. Wrote About in the *Paris Guide* of 1867, "Like the great destroyers of the eighteenth century who made a tabula rasa of the human spirit, I applaud and admire this creative destruction. " Haussmann was not, however, above the struggle between modernity and tradition, science and sentiment. Subsequently lauded or condemned as the apostle of modernity in urban planning, he could do what he did in part because of his deep claims upon tradition. "If Voltaire could enjoy the spectacle of Paris today, surpassing as it does all his wishes," he wrote in his *Mémoires*, "he would not understand why Parisians, his sons, the heirs of his fine spirit, have attacked it, criticized it and fettered it. " He appealed directly to the tradition of Enlightenment rationality and even more particularly to the expressed desire of writers as diverse as Voltaire, Diderot, Rousseau, and Saint-Simon—and even of socialists like Louis Blanc and Fourier—to impose rationality and order upon the chaotic anarchy of a recalcitrant city. The Haussmannization of Paris, suggests Vidler, carried the "techniques of rationalist analysis and the formal instruments of the ancien regime, as refurbished by the First Empire and its institutions, to their logical extreme."[17] It was, I suspect, in part because of these roots in tradition that Haussmann's works gained the acceptance they did. In addition to About, several authors in the influential *Paris Guide* of 1867 (written by eminent authors to highlight the Universal Exposition of that year) praised Haussmann's works in exactly these terms.

But Paris had also long been dubbed a sick city. Haussmann could therefore also appear in the guise of surgeon:

> After the prolonged pathology, the drawn-out agony of the patient, the body of Paris, was to be delivered of its illnesses, its cancers, and epidemics once and for all by the total act of surgery. "Cutting" and "piercing' were the adjectives used to describe the operation; where the terrain was particularly obstructed a "disembowelling" had to be performed in order that arteries be reconstituted and flows reinstated. The metaphors were repeated again and again by the pathologists, the surgeons, and even by their critics, becoming so firmly embedded in the unconscious analogies of urban planning that from that time the metaphor and the scientific nature of the action were confused and fused.[18]

The metaphors of "hygienic science" and "surgery" were powerful and appealing. Haussmann's representational strategy when approaching the metabolic functions of the city—the circulation of air, water, sewage—was to cast the city as a living body whose vital functions must be cleansed. The Bois de Boulogne and Vincennes were fondly referred to as the giant lungs of the city. But Haussmann more generally saw the city dispassionately as an artifact that could be understood and shaped according to mechanical, natural scientific principles and techniques. The towers from which the triangulation of Paris proceeded symbolized a new spatial perspective on the city as a whole, as did Haussmann's attachment to the geometry of the straight line and the accuracy of leveling to engineer the flows of water and sewage. The engineering science he put to work was exact, brilliant, and demanding; "the dream" of Voltaire and Diderot had, as Hugo would have it, "learned to calculate," or, as Carmona prefers to put it, the dreamer (Louis Napoleon) found someone (Haussmann) who could calculate. But Haussmann also tried, as we have seen, to pander to sentiment, even to engineer it—hence the elaborate street furnishings (benches, gas lights, kiosks), monuments, and fountains (like that in the Place Saint-Michel), the widespread planting of trees along the boulevards, and the construction of Gothic grottoes in the parks. He sought to reimport romance into the details of a grand design that spelled out the twin ideals of Enlightenment rationality and imperial authority.

But if the body of the city was being radically reengineered, what was happening to its soul? The responses to this question were clamorous and contentious. Baudelaire, for example, who knew only too well the "natural pleasure in destruction," could not and did not protest the transformation of Paris. His celebrated line "Alas, a city's face changes faster than the heart of a mortal" was critically directed more at the incapacity to come to terms with the present than at the changes then occurring. And for those concerned with hygiene (and in particular the containment of cholera that did serious damage in 1848–1849, then reappeared, less virulently, in 1853–1855 and 1865), the reengineering could be welcomed as a form of purification of both the body and the soul. But there were many who were visceral in their condemnation. Paris was dying under the surgeon's knife, it was becoming Babylon (or, worse still, becoming Americanized or like London!). Its true soul and essence were being destroyed not only by the physical changes but also by the moral decay of the *fête impériale*.

Lamentations, more often than not laced with nostalgia, were everywhere to be heard. The destruction of old Paris and the evisceration of all memory were frequently evoked. Zola inserts a telling scene in *La Curée* (*The Kill*). A former workman member of a commission to assess compensation for expropriation visits a neighborhood where he once lived as a youth. He is seized with emotion when he sees the wallpaper of his old room and the cupboard where he "put by three hundred francs, sou by sou," exposed in a building under demolition. This was a theme that Daumier invoked more than once. Saccard, on the other hand, "seemed enraptured by this walk through devastations. . . . He followed the cutting with the secret joys of authorship, as if he himself had struck the first blows of the pickaxe with his iron fingers. And he skipped over the puddles, reflecting that three millions were awaiting him beneath a heap of building rubbish, at the end of this stream of greasy mire." Nowhere is the brazen joy of creative destruction better invoked than in this extraordinary novel of Haussmanization in all its crudity.[19]

But nostalgia can be a powerful political weapon. The royalist writer Louis Veuillot invoked it to great effect in his influential *Les Odeurs de Paris*. Contemplating the destruction of the house in which his father had been born, he writes: "I have been chased away; another has come to settle there and my house has been razed to the ground; a sordid pavement covers everything. City without a past, full of spirits without memories, of hearts without tears, of souls without love! City of uprooted multitudes, moveable heaps of human rubble, you can grow and even become the capital of the world, but you will never have any citizens." Jules Ferry (1868), in his dissection of Haussmann's creative accounting, wept copious (and certainly opportunistic, if not crocodile) tears "for the old Paris, the Paris of Voltaire, of Diderot and of Desmoulins, the Paris of 1830 and of 1848," when confronted with "the magnificent but intolerable new residences, the affluent crowds, the intolerable vulgarity, the appalling materialism, that we are leaving to our descendants."[20] Haussmann almost certainly had this passage in mind when he defended his works as being precisely in the tradition of Voltaire and Diderot. In one of his last works, published in 1865, Proudhon saw a city destroyed physically by force and madness, but insisted that its spirit had not

FIGURE 91 *The spectacle of the demolitions—for the Boulevard de Sebastapol (above by Linton and Thorigny) and the rue de Rennes (below, by Cosson, Smeeton, and Provost)—was frequently recorded in lithographs of the time.*

FIGURE 92 *In these two cartoons, Daumier takes up the theme of nostalgia for what has been lost through the changes that Haussmann wrought. In the first the man is surprised to find his house demolished, and comments that he seems to have lost his wife, too. In the second, the man complains of the insensitivity of Limousin workers, who have no respect for memory as they tear down the room in which he spent his honeymoon.*

been laid low, that the Paris of old, buried beneath the new, the indigenous population rendered invisible by the flood of cosmopolitans and foreigners, would arise phantom-like from the past and evoke the cause of liberty. For Fournel, as well as for many others, the problem was the monotony, the homogeneity, and the boredom imposed by Haussmann's geometrical attachment to the straight line. Paris would soon be nothing other than a giant *phalanstère*, Fournel complained, in which everything would have been equalized and flattened to the same level. The Paris of multiplicity and diversity was being erased and replaced by a single city. There was only one street in Paris—the Rue de Rivoli—and it was being replicated everywhere, said Fournel, which perhaps explains Hugo's cryptic response when asked in exile if he missed Paris: "Paris is an idea," he said, and as for the rest, it is "the Rue de Rivoli, and I have always loathed the Rue de Rivoli."[21]

It is not clear, of course, how much of this was a genuinely felt sense of loss and how much merely a tactical move (as I suspect it was in Ferry's case) by monarchists or republicans to invoke some past golden age as a means to attack imperial rule. But Haussmann's works were only one focus. The disappearance of older trades, the rise of new employment and ownership structures, the emergence of the credit institutions, the dominance of speculation, the sense of time-space compression, the transformations in public life and spectacle, the gross consumerism (lamented in the Goncourts's journal), the instability of neighborhoods through immigration and suburbanization—all gave rise to a grumbling sense of loss that could easily erupt into full-fledged anger at the way the new Paris was superseding the old. Those who got left behind, like Baudelaire's old clown,

FIGURE 93 *The Rue de Rivoli, with its very straight-line alignment, was often viewed as symptomatic of everything that Haussmann was about. Hence Hugo's comment from exile that Paris was still a great idea, but it all seemed to have physically become like the Rue de Rivoli, and "I loath the Rue de Rivoli."*

were unlikely to be mollified by tales of modernity and progress as both necessary and emancipatory for daily life.

How to read all of this was the problem. Certainly something had gotten lost. But what was it, and should it really be the focus of that much regret? Consider, in this light, Baudelaire's prose poem *Loss of a Halo*.[22] Baudelaire records a conversation between a poet and a friend who surprise each other in some place of ill repute (much as actually happened, according to the Goncourts's journal, when Baudelaire, coming out of a bordello, bumped into St. Beuve, who was going in, St. Beuve was so entranced that he changed his mind and went drinking with Baudelaire instead). The poet explains that, terrified of horses and vehicles, he hurried across the boulevard, "splashing through the mud, in the midst of seething chaos, with death galloping at me from every side" (a tension given visual form in Daumier's splendid rendition of "the new Paris"—see figure 27). A sudden move caused his halo to slip off his head and fall into "the mire of the macadam." Too frightened to pick it up, he left it there but finds he enjoys its loss because now he can "go about incognito, be as low as I please and indulge in debauch like ordinary mortals." Besides, he takes a certain delight in the thought that "some bad poet" might pick it up and put it on.

Much has been said about *Loss of a Halo*. Wohlfarth records "the shock of recognition" in the image when juxtaposed with the *Communist Manifesto*: "The bourgeoisie has stripped of its halo every occupation hitherto honored and looked up to with reverent awe." Capitalism "has converted the physician, the lawyer, the priest, the poet, the man of science, into its paid wage laborers." To Wohlfarth, the poem signifies "the writer's plight amidst the blind, cut-throat laissez-faire of the capitalistic city: the traffic reduces the poet in his traditional guise to obsolescence and confronts him with the alternative of saving his skin or his halo." What better way to summarize the dilemma of the craft workers in the revolution of 1848? But Berman takes interpretation in another direction.[23] He focuses on the traffic:

> The archetypal modern man, as we see him here, is a pedestrian thrown into the maelstrom of modern city traffic, a man alone contending against an agglomeration of mass and energy that is heavy, fast and lethal. The burgeoning street and boulevard traffic knows no spatial or temporal bounds, spills over into every urban space, imposes its tempo on everybody's time, transforms the whole modern environment into "moving chaos." . . . This makes the boulevard a perfect symbol of capitalism's inner contradictions: rationality in each individual capitalist unit leading to anarchic rationality in the social system that brings all these units together.

But those who are willing to throw themselves into this maelstrom, to lose their halo, acquire a new kind of power and freedom. Baudelaire, says Berman, "wants works of art that will be born in the midst of the traffic, that will spring from its anarchic energy . . . so that 'Loss of a Halo' turns out to be a declaration of something gained." Only a bad poet will try to pick up the halo of tradition and put it on. And behind that experience

Berman sees Haussmann, that archetype of the capitalist developer, the archangel of creative destruction. The poem is itself a creative product of the transformation of Paris, as is Daumier's representation.

Wohlfarth sees it differently. It is no accident that the poet ends up in a place of ill repute. Here "Baudelaire foresees the increasing commercialization of bourgeois society as a cold orgy of self-prostitution." That image also echoes Marx on the degradation of labor under capitalism, as well as his thoughts on the penetration of money relations into social life: "Universal prostitution appears as a necessary phase in the development of the social character of personal talents, capacities, abilities, activities."[24] Baudelaire's fascination with the prostitute—simultaneously commodity and person through whom money seems to flow in the act of sex—and the dissolution of any other sense of community save that defined by the circulation of money is beautifully captured in his "Crepuscule du Soir":

> Against the lamplight, whose shivering is the wind's,
> Prostitution spreads its light and life in the streets:
> Like an anthill opening its issue it penetrates
> Mysteriously everywhere by its own occult route;
> Like an enemy mining the foundations of a fort,
> Or a worm in an apple, eating what all should eat,
> It circulates securely in the city's clogged heart.[25]

The city itself has become prostituted to the circulation of money and capital (see the Gavarni cartoon, figure 40). Or, as Wohlfarth concludes, the place of ill repute is the city itself, an old whore to whom the poet "like old lecher to old mistress goes," as the epilogue to *Paris Spleen* puts it. Having dubbed the city "brothel and hospital, prison, purgatory, hell," Baudelaire declares: "Infamous City, I adore you."

The tension that Haussmannization could never resolve, of course, was transforming Paris into the city of capital under the aegis of imperial authority. That project was bound to provoke political and sentimental responses. Haussmann delivered up the city to the capitalists, speculators, and moneychangers. He gave it over to an orgy of self-prostitution. There were those among his critics who felt they had been excluded from the orgy, and those who thought the whole process distasteful and obscene. It is in such a context that Baudelaire's images of the city as a whore take on their particular meaning. The Second Empire was a moment of transition in the always contested imagery of Paris. The city had long been depicted as a woman. Balzac (see chapter 1) saw her as mysterious, capricious, and often venal, but also as natural, slovenly, and unpredictable, particularly in revolution. The image in Zola is very different. She is now a fallen and brutalized woman, "disemboweled and bleeding," the "prey of speculation, the victim of all-consuming greed."[26] Could so brutalized a woman do anything other than rise up in revolution? Here the imagery of gender and of Paris formed a strange connection—one that boded ill, as we shall see, for both women and the city in 1871.

CHAPTER SIXTEEN

RHETORIC AND REPRESENTATION

It is always necessary to distinguish between the material transformation of the economic conditions of production, which can be determined with the precision of natural science, and the legal, political, religious, artistic or philosophic—in short, ideological forms in which men become conscious of conflict and fight it out.

—MARX

How did people view each other, represent themselves and others to themselves and others? How did they picture the contours of Parisian society, comprehend their social and spatial position and the radical transformations then in progress? And how were these representations transposed, used, and shaped in the rhetoric of political discourse? These are easy and important questions to pose but tough ones to answer.

The experience of 1848 provides a benchmark against which much that followed has to be understood. "Order" and "disorder" were code words, but behind them lay some unforgettable experiences. De Tocqueville's are illustrative. On May 15, when the National Assembly was invaded by the political clubs, "a man appeared at the rostrum whom I never saw save on that day, but whose memory has always filled me with disgust and horror. His cheeks were pale and faded, his lips white; he looked ill, evil, foul, with a dirty pallor and the appearance of a mouldering corpse; no linen as far as one could see, an old black frock-coat thrown about spindly and emaciated limbs; he might have lived in a sewer and have just emerged from it. I was told that this was Blanqui." Again, on June 24, de Tocqueville encounters an old woman in the street with a vegetable cart that impedes his path. He orders her "sharply to make room."

FIGURE 94 *Paris, so often represented as a woman, is here depicted as bound down and swarmed over by myriad construction workers.*

Instead of doing so, she left her cart and rushed at me with such sudden frenzy that I had trouble defending myself. I shuddered at the frightful and hideous expression on her face, which reflected demagogic passions and the fury of civil war. . . . It is as though these great public emotions create a burning atmosphere in which private feelings seethe and boil.[1]

The bourgeoisie feared not only the collapse of public order but also the horror of uncaged emotions, unbridled passions, prostitutes and libidinous women, the explosion of evil from the subterranean Paris of sewers, the haunt of the dangerous classes. The fear of disorder was inordinate. No wonder that the "party of order" took such a Draconian path to repression, creating first a Republic without republicans and then caving in to Empire as the only hope. Yet the Empire was anything but orderly, and had to be kept in shape by active surveillance and police repression. So who or what was to blame for the disorder? Workers pointed (if they were permitted to speak their mind at all) to the anarchy of free-market capitalism, with its periodic bouts of speculation, market collapse, and unemployment; its unbridled greed and money passion; its undermining of job security, skills, and worker

268

dignity; and its fierce waging of class war in the name of the general good. But they also blamed immigrants and foreigners, unfair competition, heartless bureaucracy and an uncaring state that accorded them neither dignity or rights. The bourgeoisie blamed irresponsible and feckless government, subversives, bohemians, debauched women, freethinkers, socialists, cosmopolitan foreigners, and utopians who might incite the "vile multitude" to riot and revolution at the slightest provocation. Both sides might rally to the defense of order, but the "order" they had in mind varied from craft workers defending their skills through association to landlords and bankers defending their different kinds of property rights. An English visitor was surprised to find that the "society" his hosts proclaimed to be so threatened referred exclusively to the fashionable circles in which they moved.[2] The same words evidently carried very different meanings; the challenge is to interpret those meanings correctly.

That task is made difficult by the political repression and censorship. All manner of hidden and allegorical meanings, of veiled references and subtle innuendos, entered into political discourse and appear to have been widely understood. Catholicism had left a legacy of appreciation for symbolism and allegory that could be put to political use (including by the church, once it moved into opposition to Empire after 1860). Corporatist traditions within the labor force and the Masonic movement (with all their rituals of initiation) provided all kinds of codes and languages. And the rewriting of history, particularly of the revolutionary period, was used to shape popular imagery. The censors were aware of such problems—they rejected a simple song that mentioned a bonnet, presumably because it might be taken as a reference to the republican cap of liberty.[3] But what could the authorities do when critics of Empire turned funerals, fêtes, and other public events into occasions for spontaneous mass demonstrations? The problem was not simply that twenty-five thousand workers could turn up at twenty-four hours' notice for the funeral of a republican leader's wife, but that any burial with its tradition of graveside discourse could turn into a mass political meeting.

The means of representation and communication were multiplying rapidly. The explosion in newspaper circulation was accompanied by political diversification and the rise of skilled editors who knew how to skirt the censor. Others preferred to confront, make their point, and be closed down in a blaze of glory. By the late 1860s, newspapers and journals were opening up every month. When an influential newspaper like *Le Rappel* was controlled by no less fierce a critic than the exiled Victor Hugo, the government was surely in trouble. The penny press also exploded as the popular taste for education, romance, and travel came together with a commercial apparatus capable of exploiting it. Much of the material was innocuous enough to appear as pablum for the masses. But some of it, like the pamphlets on French history, had strong political overtones. By 1860, this penny literature was more numerous and popular than the daily press. Worse still, all such publications relied heavily on illustrations. Drawings and cartoons—Daumier's work being just one example among many—were extraordinary vehicles for political satire and polemic. Nor could Courbet's gallant thrust of 1848–1851 to create an art of and for the people easily be forgotten.[4]

The salons continued to be political events to which the popular classes were drawn as much as the bourgeoisie (who sought to raise the entry price one day a week so as not to have to rub shoulders with a riffraff of smelly and sweaty workers). And while the government could ban performances of Victor Hugo's plays, they could not stop *Les Misérables* from being in almost everyone's hands almost immediately after it was published in 1862, in Belgium. And herein lay another problem. The improved transport and communications systems and the flood of foreign visitors (a tenfold increase of visitors from England between 1855 and 1863) made the flow of foreign news and commentary much greater at the same time that it increased the capacity to smuggle in any number of political tracts produced by those in exile. The Emperor's decision to offer amnesty to the exiles in 1859 hinged not so much on magnanimity as on the idea that it was easier to keep them under surveillance in France than it was abroad. Realizing this only too well, Proudhon for a while, and Louis Blanc and Hugo for the rest of the Empire, preferred to remain abroad.

It is invidious, perhaps, to select any dominant themes out of the swirl and confusions of images, representations, and political rhetoric. Yet there are some that stand out, that cry out for further explication. Within each we shall see manifested that overriding concern for the tension between order and disorder, as well as between modernity and tradition.

FIGURE 95 *The salons for new art drew huge crowds. They were so popular that the bourgeoisie insisted on payment for entry so they would not have to mix with the populace at large. On those days when entrance was free (as this Daumier cartoon illustrates), the crowds were overwhelming.*

THE GEOGRAPHICAL IMAGINATION

The spreading tentacles of the rail net and the growing regularity and speed of maritime and telegraph connections shook perceptions of space and place to their very roots. Information, commodities, money, and people moved around the world with much greater facility in 1870 than in 1850. Increasing competition and dependence within the international division of labor liberated Paris from local constraints but rendered the city vulnerable to far-off events (the American Civil War, for example, which disrupted the inflow of raw cotton and the outflow of Paris-made goods to an important market). Foreign ventures (the consolidation of colonial power in North Africa, the Italian campaigns, the Crimean War, the abortive attempt to impose Maximilian as Emperor of Mexico, the construction of the Suez Canal) had local reverberations. The changing mix of commodities in the market (from basic foods to exotic luxuries) gave daily testimony to shifts in space relations. A burgeoning press (fed news through the telegraph) placed information on people's lunch tables about everything from foreign investment, price movements, and profit opportunities to geopolitical confrontations to bizarre stories of foreign habits. With the photograph, space and time seemed to collapse into one simple image. Every new conquest of space—the opening of rail links or of the Suez Canal—became an occasion for enormous celebration, as did the Universal Expositions, which highlighted new geographical connections as well as new technologies.

It was not necessary to leave Paris to experience the shock of transformed space relations. The geographies of the mind had therefore to adapt and learn to appreciate the world of geographical variation and of "otherness" that now constituted the global space of political-economic activity. This meant, inter alia, coming to terms with the social and spatial relations concealed by the market exchange of things (consider, for example, Flaubert's description of the cosmopolitan range of objects in Rosanette's room in *Sentimental Education*, quoted on p. 87). The mass of travelogues and popular geographies that swamped the penny press indicated plenty of public curiosity.[5] But travel and travel literature can just as easily confirm prejudices and feed fears as broaden the mind. So how was "the other" broadly understood in the midst of such rapid transformations? The question is important because, as we shall see, the construction of "the other" in broadly racist and exclusionary terms was to have devastating effects upon internal politics as well as across the colonial empire that France was beginning to assemble overseas.

The French geographical imagination had long been encumbered with heavy doses of environmentalism and racism. Montesquieu and Rousseau had agreed that liberty was not the fruit of all climates, and therefore not within the reach of all peoples. "Despotism is suited to hot climates, barbarism, to cold, and good government, to temperate regions."[6] By 1870 this had been converted by writers like Gobineau, whose influential "Essay on the Inequality of Human Races" appeared in 1855, proclaiming the superiority of the Nordic races, into a simple grid of interpretation in which categories like "civilized," "barbarian," and "savage" were superimposed upon the map of the world.[7] The savage could, on occasion, be depicted as noble, but popular imagination had long seen Rousseau's ideal displaced by the tales of Fenimore Cooper (often referred to by Balzac) and depictions of savage practices that had peoples living in such a state of nature as to render them subhuman, and therefore ineligible for consideration in any regime of rights or citizenship. Barbarians, on the other hand, possessed sufficiently well-articulated forms of political organization to be a force to be reckoned with. But their values and practices (especially when non-Christian) were such as to make them antagonistic to civilization.

This interpretive grid could loosely be thrown over the whole world as well as over Paris itself. The bourgeoisie routinely depicted the workers living on the "frontiers" of Belleville as savages. Critics of Haussmann on occasion accused him of producing such a result by promoting social segregation. "A city whose neighborhoods would be divided between, on the one hand, those blessed with good fortune, wealth, and elegance, and on the other, the population condemned to work for its livelihood, such a city would no longer be a Christian city, it would become a city of barbarians."[8] If the workers were "savages," a "vile multitude," mere criminal and "dangerous classes," as the bourgeoisie was wont to depict them, then 1848 had showed all too clearly the kind of danger they posed and the kind of savagery they had in mind. Victor Hugo, however, proudly proclaimed the workers, "the savages of civilization." But the general drift of this association, in 1848 as well as in 1871, was that the forces of "civilization" and "order" assumed a moral right to shoot the revolutionaries down like the dogs and savages they were presumed to be. Representing "the other" of working-class Paris in such racialized terms explains how class war could be conducted with such extraordinary ferocity and violence. It was not uncommon for the aristocracy and monarchists to justify their right to rule in terms of the supposed racial superiority of the (Nordic) Franks over the (Celtic) Gauls (workers and peasants).[9] And it was no accident that it was Cavaignac, a general who had learned his trade in the colonial wars against the "barbarians" in Algeria, who led the ruthlessly violent repression of 1848.

Michelet, one of the most influential historians of the time, saw civilization as the product of "the struggle of reason, spirit, the West, the male to separate themselves and establish their authority over their origins in nature, matter, the East, the female." Eroticized racist and gendered imagery of this sort, reinforced by painters like Delacroix and many Romantic writers, produced what Said calls "orientalism."[10] The Orient was seen as the womb from which civilization had issued forth, but also as the locus of irrational and erotic femininity and the seat of barbaric practices. That imagery remained untouched by the increasing ease of human contact. When Flaubert journeyed up the Nile in 1849, he went, like many before him, with only one thing in mind: to "find another home" in the voluptuous sensuality of the Oriental woman. His subsequent writings confirmed the image. Hitzman interprets all this as "unconscious projections onto aspects of the ancient world of underlying anxieties about the mère terrible."[11] It could also be an expression of deep fears (similar to those which Hugo and De Tocqueville recorded in the difficult days of 1848 and which erupted again in 1871 around the Commune) of "destructive, castrating female sexuality." It is hard to read Flaubert's *Salammbo* (with its graphic scenes of awful cathartic violence) and his letters to his mother without giving such interpretations some credence.

But it is too simple to let matters rest there. For, as Said points out, the Orient posed threats other than imagined licentious sex, disturbing though that may have been to the bourgeois fantasy of family and its accompanying cult of domesticity. A European and very capitalistic "rationality of time, space, and personal identity" confronted "unimaginable antiquity, inhuman beauty, boundless distance." Michelet and the Saint-Simonians thus justified the penetration (and the sexuality of the term was flagrant) of the Orient by railroads, canals, and commerce, and the domination of an irrational Orient in the name of a superior Enlightenment rationality. The submission of East to West was as necessary to the progress of civilization as the submission of female to male authority and control. In *L'Argent* (*Money*) Zola had a fictional Saccard (loosely based on the real-life Pereires) set out to transform the Orient according to Western standards and Western commercial and capitalistic ideals (see above, p. 122).[12] Flaubert, however, did not take this tack. Critical of bourgeois values and culture, he used the myth of the Orient, as did the many avid readers of tales of harems, princes, and the Arabian Nights in the penny press, to explore the "other" in his own personality and the underside of bourgeois culture. Reflecting on his Egyptian journey, he wrote:

> The thing we all lack is not style, nor the dexterity of finger and bow known as talent.
> We have a large orchestra, a rich palette, a variety of resources. We know more tricks and
> dodges, probably, than were ever known before. No, what we lack is the intrinsic principle,
> the soul of the thing, the very idea of the subject. We take notes, we make journeys; empti-
> ness! emptiness! We become scholars, archaeologists, historians, doctors, cobblers, people of
> taste. What is the good of all that? Where is the heart, the verve, the sap? Where to start out
> from? Where to go? We're good at sucking, we play a lot of tongue games, we pet for hours:
> but—the real thing! To ejaculate, beget the child![13]

So what, then, could "the very idea of the subject" be? "Travelling makes one modest," Flaubert observed. Remarkably, he did not appropriate the idea of the Orient for himself. He saw through the myth of it as a peculiarly Western neurosis. In his novel *Salammbo*, with its Orientalist setting, he dramatically prophesied the searing rage of male hysteria that erupted in the violence of the 1871 Commune.

But such modes of interpretation were not universal. Elisée Reclus, for example, sought a very different kind of geographical understanding of the world than did Michelet or Flaubert. Reclus believed in the potential harmony not only of "man" with nature "but also of all the different cultures that populated the earth." Behind that there lay a utopian vision. "Humanity, until now divided into distinct currents, will be no more than a single river, and, reunited into a single flow, we will descend together toward the great sea where all life will lose itself and be renovated." Free of the psychodrama imposed by the "progressive" Michelet, this admirer of Proudhon, fellow conspirator with Bakunin, participant in the Commune, and future collaborator with Kropotkin, produced a geographical vision that had all the flavor of the Parisian craft workers' optimistic mutualism. He supported the International Working Men's Association's project to unite workers of the world in common struggle. Reclus's geographical thought, presented in voluminous writings from the 1860s (only now being recovered from the obscurity in which they have for too long languished), provides a different way of understanding and presenting "the other" in the full splendor of personal dignity and potential harmony.[14] This was far more consistent with the view from the Paris workshop than the racially charged imperialism characteristic of the affluent salons of the Faubourg St. Germain.

The case of Orientalism illustrates, however, a general point. The same processes that increased knowledge of the world rendered its misrepresentation all the more likely. Images of the city-country and Paris-provinces relation within a changing national economy of space were confused by class interests and prejudices. While it had long been fashionable (as Balzac showed) to affect a certain denial of rural and provincial life in bourgeois circles, the country was the secure base for a lot of those unearned revenues that circulated into Paris. The country also appeared (sometimes wrongly) as a peaceful haven of submission and reaction, compared to the rebellious incoherence of Paris. That was where the threatened bourgeois (and even their artists and writers like Delacroix, Flaubert, and George Sand) fled when matters got out of hand, and it was from there that the army and National Guard were mobilized to crush Parisian revolts in 1848 and 1871. Provincial France was the secure if invisible rock upon which Parisian life and French politics were founded. Bucolic images of rurality in the novels of George Sand reassured. Even the

FIGURE 96 *Relations between the countryside and the city were changing rapidly as the new modes of communication came into being and as Haussmann set out to annex large tracts of the suburbs into Paris. In this Daumier cartoon, two peasants celebrate the fact that they have suddenly become Parisians.*

worker poets (many from the provinces) whom she encouraged appeared naive enough in their socialism to be unthreatening.

The extensive rural resistance to the coup d'état of 1851 came, therefore, as a shock. It indicated class relations, discontent, and revolutionary sentiment in the countryside. And this was the sentiment that Courbet brought to the salon of 1851, particularly in his painting *Burial at Ornans*. The trouble was that he rendered explicit the class relations in rural and provincial France, and did so with a fierce realism that earned him the name of "the Proudhon of painting."[15] It was from that countryside, rich with the ambiguities of its own class experience, that new workers poured into Paris, carrying with them from Limousin, Creuse and Var, from Seine-et-Oise and Doubs, their own particular brands of revolutionary sentiment. Many a leader of the workers' movement of 1868–1871 had, like Varlin, provincial and rural origins. But by the end of the Second Empire there was also a strange reversal: even the popular classes could take excursions to the countryside, a frontier where the commodification of access to nature as a consumption good was becoming as important as the search for open land for new industrial and housing development.[16] It was in this environment that the impressionists did so much of their work.

The interior transformation of Paris and the beginnings of suburbanization were likewise perceived and understood through political lenses. Subsequent commentators have replicated the consequent ambiguities without always understanding them. On the one hand, Berman treats Baudelaire's "The Eyes of the Poor" as an image of how Haussmann's boulevards "inadvertently broke down the self-enclosed and hermetically sealed world of traditional urban poverty," thus making a fact of "the misery that was once a mystery." On the other hand, many saw increasing spatial segregation due to Haussmannization as the crux of the problem. Both propositions may be true. The construction of an extroverted, public, and collectivized style of urbanism under the Second Empire altered the balance between public and private spaces in the city. Public investments were organized around private gain, and public spaces were appropriated for private use; exteriors became interiors for the bourgeoisie, while panoramas, dioramas, and photography brought the exterior into the interior.[17] The boulevards lit by gas lights, dazzling shop window displays, and cafés open to the street (an innovation of the Second Empire) became, as we have seen, corridors of homage to the power of money and commodities, play spaces for the bourgeoisie. When Baudelaire's lover in "The Eyes of the Poor" suggests the proprietor send the ragged man and his children packing, it is the sense of proprietorship over public space that is really significant, rather than the all-too-familiar encounter with poverty (see above, p. 133).

The irony, of course, was that the new means of communication (boulevards, streets, omnibuses) and illumination opened up the city to scrutiny in a way that had not been possible before. The urban space was experienced, therefore, in a radically different way. Frédéric Moreau, the hero of Flaubert's *Sentimental Education*, moves from space to space in Paris and its suburbs, collecting experiences of quite different qualities as he goes. The sensation of space is quite different from that in Balzac. The same disaggregations may be there, but what is special is the way that Frédéric moves so freely, even into and out of the spaces of the 1848 Revolution. He glides as easily from space to space and relationship to relationship as money and commodities change hands. And he does so with the same cynicism and lassitude. Yet there is a hidden bound in Frédéric's wanderings, in much the same way that the circulation of money concentrates in certain zones rather than in others. Frédéric has no reason to be in Belleville or even in the parts of eastern Paris where artisanal industry holds sway. It is solely in bourgeois Paris and its environs that Frédéric moves. For Flaubert, the segregations were so naturalized as to be almost unnoticeable, and it would take the ethnographic inquiries of Zola to bring them back into the heart of literature.

The bourgeoisie did not welcome encounters with "the other" of the working or dangerous classes (like the lover in "The Eyes of the Poor"). And they had another fear: the crowd might hide subversive elements or suddenly become an unruly mob. The fears were well grounded. Prostitutes circulated easily within the crowds along the boulevards, in defiance of all police attempts to control and evict them. When Blanqui decided to review his secret army, the word went out, and two thousand troops, all unknown to each other and to him, paraded past him in the midst of a crowd on the Champ-de-Mars that did not even notice.[18] Spaces and the crowd had to be controlled if the bourgeoisie was to maintain its class position and power. The dilemma in 1868–1871, as in 1848, was that the republican bourgeoisie had to open its space in order to achieve its own revolution. Weakened, it could not resist the rising pressure of the working-class and revolutionary movements. It was for this reason that the reoccupation of central Paris by the popular classes—the descent from Belleville—took on such symbolic importance. For it occurred in a context where the poor and the working class were being chased, in imagination as well as in fact, from the strategic spaces and even off the boulevards now viewed as bourgeois interiors. The more space was opened up physically, the more it had to be partitioned and closed off through social practices of forced ghettoization and racially charged exclusions. Zola, writing in retrospect, presents as closed those same Parisian spaces that Flaubert had seen as open. Thus did the geographical imagination of the bourgeoisie seek to impose sociospatial exclusions and order upon the spaces that Haussmann's works had opened up.

CENTRALIZATION AND DECENTRALIZATION

The relations between a traditionally centralized state, civil society, and individual liberties had long been the fulcrum of French political debate. Monarchy and religion had made common cause around the idea of respect for authority within a hierarchically ordered state and civil society. The Jacobins looked to a strong, centralized power but sought to root its legitimacy in the sovereign will of a people liberated from hierarchy in civil society. They attacked the workers' corporations that restrained the liberty of labor with the same vehemence they attacked religion. The Second Empire tried to have the best of both worlds, using universal suffrage to legitimize the Emperor, from whom all authority then flowed. But there were strong currents of criticism of such forms of centralization. An English visitor considered the political system "a coarse form of communism" and wondered how his compatriots could so laud the practical application of a doctrine that, in its theoretical form, "smites them with so much horror."[19] The enemies of Empire increasingly focused their attacks, therefore, upon its excessive centralization. Much depended, however, upon whether it was economic, political, or territorial centralization of power that was the focus of complaint.

The Second Empire saw the state enhance direct economic control and indirect economic influence through the formation of strong institutions for the centralization of capital. The connection between the Pereires and Haussmann was typical of an organizational form close to state monopoly or finance capitalism. Because they controlled banking, transport, communications, the press, urban services, and property speculation, there were few arenas of economic life outside the orbit of finance capital and the state. This sparked debate over the nature of capitalism and the relative virtues of competition and monopoly. The debate pitted what might loosely be called Saint-Simonian ideology and practice against the doctrines of the free-market economists. While the Saint-Simonians never developed a coherent economic theory, they did cultivate an attitude of mind that, being both pragmatic and broadly oriented to social questions, led many of them to adapt their ideas, albeit always around the general theme of production, in diverse ways. The Emperor may have entered the Empire as "Saint-Simon on horseback" (to use Sainte-Beuve's famous phrase), but he left it as a liberal free trader. Chevalier, an original member of the sect and then professor of economics, negotiated the free-trade agreement with Britain in 1860 and then embraced liberalism. And the practices of the Pereires evolved in pragmatic and often self-interested ways. But Saint-Simonian doctrine gave legitimacy to imperial economic policy and the centralization of capital.

Free-market economists like Bastiat and Say, by contrast, advocated greater market liberty and competition (supposed virtues already forced on the working class in 1852). As private property rights were reasserted against state power in Paris in the late 1850s, and as fears of the Pereires' power mounted, free-market ideology was mobilized as part of an attack upon imperial policy. In the hands of industrialists or bankers like Rothschild, the arguments appeared hypocritical and self-serving. But the 1860s saw a growing consensus, within both the bourgeoisie and the workers' movement, that the excessive centralization of economic power had to be checked. Though the solutions they might offer were very different, a powerful class alliance (joining Proudhonists like Duchêne and Rothschild's protégé Say) could form around the theme of opposition to the further centralization of capital. The downfall of the Pereires and of Haussmann, the transition to liberal Empire, and the increasing credibility of the "economists" (liberals) testified to the growing power of that alliance.

The question of political decentralization stirred similar passions. The Second Empire produced a tightly controlled hierarchy of power from the Emperor down to the prefects and subprefects, appointed mayors and local councils, appointed heads of mutual benefit societies, worker-employer commissions, and the like. Local democracy was negligible. But local autonomy outside of Paris was partly protected by inaccessibility. The new transport and communications system, often pushed hard by local elites, had the ironic effect of making central government control easier and thus reducing local autonomy. Increasing spatial integration was accompanied by a rising clamor for some degree of local self-government. Legitimists, Orléanists, republicans, and socialists all took to championing the cause of local liberties during the 1860s. All of them, even the Bonapartists, trumpeted the importance of the commune as a central political institution. But Bonapartists supported it as a local vehicle for central administration; royalists supported it, provided it empowered local notables and the clergy; republicans supported it, as a central institution of local democracy (governed by the local bourgeois or, among democrats, by the people); communists supported it because it was within the commune that political solidarities were formed; and mutualists like Proudhon supported it as the basis of federal governance. Historians debated it endlessly, usually through discussion of the relative merits of the Jacobin Robespierre and the more democratically minded Girondists, almost always coming down on the side of the latter. By the late 1860s "decentralization had assumed all the appearances of a national crusade." It certainly became the centerpiece of attack against Haussmann.[20]

It is hard to differentiate, however, between purely opportunistic arguments of those out of power (the monarchist case is particularly suspect) and deeply held beliefs of someone like Proudhon, who looked to the withering away of the state through the federation of independent and autonomous associations as his ideal, and who in any case saw political reorganization as irrelevant in the absence of a fundamental reorganization of production against the centralization of capital. But whatever the basis, the fight for political decentralization was real enough, and it put the question of self-government for Paris squarely on the agenda. The fact that hardly anyone was against the idea of the commune (with a small "c") was to play a crucial role in the way so many disparate forces rallied to support the Paris Commune of 1871.

But that posed another problem. For was not Paris, as Haussmann insisted, "centralization itself"? Fearful of the immense centralization of economic, political, administrative, and cultural power in Paris, many a provincial who supported decentralization demurred when it came to self—government for so influential a city, one that had also been prone to radical if not "red" political leanings. And there were many in the Parisian bourgeoisie, like Thiers, who shared those fears. This was the sort of coalition that behaved in such an inflammatory way toward the Paris Commune. Nonetheless, there were many Parisians who supported the cause of decentralization but who also proudly held that Paris was "the head, the brain, and the heart of Europe"—a view "which may explain," an English visitor wryly observed, "why Europe sometimes plays such strange antics."[21] Proudhon thus wanted Paris to "discard the crown of capital" but nevertheless to "take the lead as a free and independent commune in the crusade for a federated nation." Blanqui agreed that the revolution had to begin in Paris, but, Jacobin that he was, he thought of a revolutionary Paris conquering, ruling over, and bringing enlightenment to the backward provincials. That Blanquists and mutualists fought side by side to create and defend the Commune was, therefore, nowhere nearly as odd as it may have seemed.

Clearly, there was a sense in which the Commune was a rising for municipal liberty. That it was exclusively so in the social democratic sense, as Greenberg argues, or that it was purely about community and in no way about class, as Gould insists, is, however, beyond the bounds of credibility. Certainly, different factions saw the Commune very differently. For mutualists and communists, it was the shield behind which they could begin their more solid work of reorganizing production, distribution, and consumption, in alliance with other movements in other centers. For the Blanquists it was the first step in the political liberation of France, if not the world. For the republican mayors of the *arrondissements*, it was the first step in integrating Parts into a republican system of government and, if necessary, a defensive weapon to be used against monarchist reaction. For all of them it was easier to define what the Commune was against than what it was for. And the paradox, of course, was that the strong sentiment for decentralization in the provinces could so easily be mobilized to crush a movement of decentralization within a city where so much power was centralized.

TWO CITIES, TWO PEOPLES

Four o'clock. The other Paris awakes, the Paris of work. The two cities hardly know each other, the one that rises at midday and the one that beds down at eight. They rarely look each other in the eye and then—all too often—only on the sad and somber days of revolution. They live far from each other; they speak a different language. There is no love lost between them; they are two peoples.[22]

No matter how intricate the class structure and the division of social space in actuality, the simplistic image of Paris as a city divided into two classes and two spaces erupts again and again in representations of the time. It was an image with a long history. Before 1848, the "other Paris" was seen in terms of "dangerous classes," whose utter destitution sometimes inspired pity, but more often horror, disgust, and loathing. Terms like "savage" and "barbarian," and epithets like "animal," gave racial coloration to bourgeois imagery, justifying the murderous violence with which the bourgeoisie often approached workers and the impoverished.[23] "Equality asserted itself triumphantly," wrote Flaubert of 1848; "an equality of brute beasts, a common level of bloody atrocities; for the fanaticism of the rich counterbalanced the frenzy of the poor, the aristocracy shared the fury of the rabble, and the cotton nightcap was just as savage as the red bonnet."[24] Though 1848 may have proved there were differences between the laboring and the dangerous classes, it had also promised, then denied, real political power to the workers. Power shifted—relatively permanently, as it turned out—to the bourgeois side of the barricades. Thereafter, many in the bourgeoisie felt free to tar all those who had been on the other side with the same brush. The imagery previously applied to the dangerous classes now clung not only to the laboring classes but even to their defenders, like Blanqui. Furthermore, everyone knew where the barricades had been erected, what part of the city belonged to "the other." A barricade makes for a simple dividing line. The experience of 1848 lived on in simplified, polarized representations of social and physical space.

Bourgeois representations of what existed "on the other side" were colored by the nature of their contacts. Most of the haute bourgeoisie were either economically inactive (in Paris) or in government service, and the economically active tended to concentrate in high finance. Industrialists who actually dealt with workers (like Poulot) were few and far between, and in any case were considered inferior. Yet Paris was a working-class city, increasingly organized so that the conspicuous consumers could, as Lazare put it, "long savor the taste of the honey without being troubled by the buzzing of the bees."[25] The imagery of what existed "on the other side" was not built out of human contact, save casual and usually unfortunate street encounters (of the sort described in Baudelaire's "The Eyes of the Poor"). The reports of bourgeois reformers (of no matter what political persuasion) on conditions in working-class Paris fueled rather than assuaged the imagery by dwelling upon the destitution and degradation. Living in such animal conditions, could the people be anything other than animals? That sort of racial reasoning was not far from the surface in influential circles and filtered with ease into literary representations. It was standard fare in response to the Commune. In all cities, wrote the poet Théophile Gautier, there were closed caverns for

FIGURE 97 *The distribution of barricades in Paris during the June uprising of 1848 illustrates how strong the political division was between the east and the west of the city (after Girard, 1981).*

wild animals, stinking beasts, venomous beasts, all the refractory perversities that civilization has been unable to tame, those who love blood, who are as amused by burning down as by fireworks, who delight in thievery, those for whom attacks against decency pass for gestures of love, all the monsters of the heart and the crippled of spirit; a population from another world, unused to daylight, craving trapped in the depths of subterranean shadows. One day, when the animal tamer inadvertently leaves his keys in the gate of this zoo, these ferocious creatures go about a terrified city with savage cries. The cages open, the hyenas of '93 and the gorillas of the Commune pour forth.[26]

The venomous violence of such sentiments was all too common. It is hard to read influential journals like the *Revue des Deux Mondes* during the 1860s without blanching.

And the violence has a curious quality to it, rather as if there is an inner longing to exorcise a devil, to burn out some excruciating sore on society, to seek some ultimate denouement, a catharsis. "There are but three beings worthy of respect: the priest, the warrior and the poet," wrote Baudelaire, "to know, to kill and to create. " Flaubert confessed that the riot was the only thing he understood in politics: "I despise modern tyranny because it seems to me stupid, weak and without the courage of its convictions." He added, "I have a deep cult of ancient tyranny which I regard as mankind's finest manifestation."[27] The scenes of murderous violence toward conquered people in *Salammbo* led to accusations of sadism. But it was exactly such scenes that were to be acted out against the Commune, a brutal bloodletting justified by Goncourt as a bleeding white by killing off the combative reds. Fearfully recalling the Reign of Terror, it seems the bourgeoisie built images and representations to justify launching its own preemptive terror against the other Paris.

Revolutionaries, particularly those drawn from the ranks of students and *la bohème*, played the image in reverse. They saw the workers as noble, skilled, self-reliant, intelligent, generous, and capable of leadership. Their "other Paris," to the west, was populated by speculators, stock-exchange wolves, rentiers, parasites, and vampires, who sucked the lifeblood of the workers and destroyed their dignity and self-respect. Crushed under the burden of the idle rich, working-class Paris had every right to rise up in revolution. The Blanquists took that idea even farther. They saw Paris as the revolutionary hearth from which liberation had to spread not only to the rest of France but to the rest of the world, as it had in 1789. It was, furthermore, in the "other" Paris, more particularly in Belleville and the quarter of Père Lachaise, that the revolution would have its origin.[28] It was into this quarter that those with Blanquist sympathies, like the influential Gustave Flourens (a professor of human anatomy, killed in the early days of the Commune), moved to cultivate their revolutionary base. And there is more than a hint of that same sense of violent revolutionary catharsis in the Blanquist rhetoric (drawing, as it did, so explicitly on the ideals of Hebertist revolutionary purity of 1793).

Not everyone was caught in such polarized imagery. Yet even those who sought to soften its edges often ended up reinforcing the general argument. Contemporary writers like Audiganne, Corbon, and Poulot at least had intimate contact with the Parisian workers and provide us with a composite character sketch. Writes Audiganne:

> Paris workers are extremely sociable, open, with grand ideas and strong philanthropic concerns, expressed as mutual aid and reciprocal tolerance. On the other hand, they have an irresistible taste for dissipation and expenditure, an ardent thirst for pleasure, and a passionate love of change. . . . They participate in riots with the same enthusiasm as they do in fêtes, delighted to break the monotony of their daily life without concern for the consequences. The cult of equality and nationality is their hallmark.[29]

The irresponsibility of Parisian workers was, of course, anathema to the rather puritanical radical bourgeoisie (Poulot, for example). But many commentators who knew them, like the socialist Vallés, who moved to working-class Paris out of sympathy for the oppressed, were amazed at the warmth and generosity they found there. All the more reason, therefore, to regret both the polarization of opinion and the weight of oppression that fell on working-class Paris. But in arguing for relief of the latter, reformers could not help but reinforce the former. Corbon lamented the perpetuation and deepening of class divisions and argued that although the poor did not resent wealth as such, their own perilous condition, taken together with the increasing affluence of the rich, was certain to pose a threat to the security of the wealthy. That threat, moreover, had a geopolitical expression. "The transformation of Paris, having forcibly removed the working population from the center towards the extremities, has made two cities of the capital—one rich, one poor. . . . The deprived classes form an immense cordon around the well-off." Lazare resorted to the same threatening imagery: "The flood of poverty rose in Belleville," he wrote, "while the river of luxury flowed at full crest in the new quarters of Paris."[30] The haute bourgeoisie suspected, with good reason, that the "reds" were submerging themselves in that flood of poverty in Belleville. To the degree that they could not and would not even set foot in the place, such accounts could only exacerbate their fears. There dwelt "the dregs of the people," editorialized newspapers like *Le Figaro* and *Le Moniteur*. There you found, wrote the journalist Sarcey, "the deepest depths of poverty and of hatred where ferments of envy, of sloth and anger, bubble without cease."[31]

COMMUNISTS, CAPITALISTS, AND THE DREAM OF ASSOCIATION

Feared though he was by the bourgeoisie, Blanqui never succeeded in establishing a mass base within the working class. Indeed, there were periods when he seemed totally without influence, except as a remote, uncompromising, and incarcerated symbol. Only in the 1860s did the Blanquist movement spring to life, and then mainly among militant, atheist intellectuals, and students, drawn to the nobility of his suffering and the purity of his cause.[32] During the active class struggles of 1868–1871, the Blanquists, partly out of their dedicated concern for education and their willingness to swim in the "rivers of poverty" that flowed in the "other Paris," did acquire an important following. Their lack of mass influence was partly a matter of choice. The experience of 1848 and the foundation of Empire through universal suffrage made them suspicious of mass democracy under conditions of ignorance and bourgeois domination of the instruments of mass communication. Their roots in the pure forms of the French revolutionary tradition (as represented by Babeuf, Hébert, and Buonarotti) held them to an insurrectionary Jacobin politics. Under conditions of tight police surveillance, this meant the formation of closed cells, impenetrable to infiltration but also closed to mass participation. Dictatorship of the proletariat through insurrectionary violence was their aim.

Their influence was also checked by circumstances of class structure that did not fit easily with the message they sought to convey. While insurrection against a state apparatus controlled by the haute bourgeoisie made a great deal of sense, it could not address the question of the organization of work in a city where the small workshop and the putting-out system dominated, and where the line between capital and labor in production was still somewhat blurred even by the end of Empire. The Parisian workshops had, in fact, been fertile breeding grounds, as we saw in chapter 2, for all kinds of socialist, communalist, and communist ideologies ever since the early 1830s, and they continued to be so.

The communist slogan "From each according to his capacity and to each according to his need" sounded seductive to the mass of the impoverished, and had a powerful hold among craft workers faced with insecurity of employment and the ravages of technological change. But the communists were, as Corbon noted, of two sorts. There were those who sought to impose their system on the whole of society through an increase in state power vis-à-vis private property. They had looked in 1848 to the formation of national workshops as a prelude to state ownership, a guaranteed right to work, and equality of distribution. From this standpoint socialists like Louis Blanc, Raspail, and Barbès could make common cause with Blanqui (interpersonal rivalries permitting) to seize state power in the abortive movements of April 16 and May 15, 1848. Others, like the Cabetists (Icarians) and the Fourierists, sought to live out their doctrines in their own daily lives, hoping by their example to persuade people of the virtues of collective organization and communism. After the frustration of 1848, these latter groups chose emigration or were forced into exile, mostly to the United States, as their only hope.

Proudhon, however, drew quite different conclusions from the experience of 1848. He felt the insurrectionary movements offered nothing but the replacement of one regime of repression and domination by another. The problem of work could not be solved through political channels. The state was the enemy no matter who controlled it. This put Proudhon at odds not only with Blanquists and communists but also with all those who saw the political republic as a necessary prelude to social change. The struggle to liberate the worker was to begin in the workshop with the implementation of practical plans rather than utopian schemes. Cooperation and mutualism meant a new conception of workers' democracy in the labor process, and it was to be backed by mutual credit and banking, mutual insurance and benefit societies, cooperative housing schemes, and the like. The virtue of such a program was that it avoided state intervention and could lay a basis for the withering away of the state. Just as important, it could bypass class confrontation in the workshops and rally small masters (threatened by competition, changing conditions of credit and marketing, etc.) to the cause.

Proudhon supported private property in housing, retailing, and so forth, provided it was open to all; objected to strikes and unions; and was suspicious of the idea of association, since by 1860 it was becoming part of an ideology of class struggle. His ideas were influential. We thus find Clément, the shoemakers' representative to the Workers' Commission of 1867, defying and condemning those who looked to strikes, class struggle, and other forms of confrontation to advance the workers' cause.[33] The power of private property could be undermined and class struggle avoided, he argued, "by laborers working in solidarity, coming together, learning to know each other, living in the family," building up their own capital and thus eliminating the power of external ownership over their lives.

But within the debates that swirled around the organization of labor in Second Empire Paris, one concept exercised a peculiar power and fascination: association. It acquired its central position in part because of its deep roots in tradition but also by virtue of its ambiguity. It had been central to Saint-Simonian thought in the 1830s as well as to the Fourierism and workers' socialism that cut their teeth in the same period (see chapter 2). Initially it was an idea that sought to overcome class conflict and the social anarchy, selfish greed, and social inequalities engendered by private property capitalism. In the hands of the Saint-Simonians, it meant the association of all capitals, great and small, mobilized to such productive and socially desirable ends that the whole of civil society, including the workers themselves, would be embraced within the harmony of social progress. The Pereires were schooled in that ideology in the 1830s and put it to use in the 1850s to try to construct a kind of democratic state-monopoly capitalism. The idea of association therefore had a certain legitimacy and was actively supported by the government. Even Marx, who mocked the idea that the association of capitals could do anything other than spark orgies of speculation, conceded that it might constitute a "form of transition to a new mode of production," thus endowing the Pereires "with the pleasant character mixture of swindler and prophet."[34]

In the hands of the workers' movement, the idea underwent a significant evolution. In its earliest manifestations in the 1830s, it meant producer associations, mutual benefit societies, and other forms of which Proudhon was later to approve. But repression followed by the ravages of technological change and capitalist exploitation later turned "association" into a code word for class and corporatist resistance. The first sense seems to have remained dominant in Paris at least until 1848–1851. The provisional government decree of 1848 that guaranteed the right to work also guaranteed the right of workers to associate "in order to enjoy the legitimate benefits of their labor." The phrase is ambiguous. Does it mean the right to form trade unions or the right to found producer cooperatives? In practice, it rallied all those craft workers who, understanding that wealth was founded on labor, saw the free association of workers in production as the means to capture the benefits of their own labor and simultaneously to ensure the peaceful reorganization of society under the control of the direct producers.[35]

The vicious repression of all forms of worker organization in 1851 (save the mutual benefit societies and those under strict imperial control) drove such hopes underground, from whence Proudhon strove to resurrect them in their voluntaristic rather than state-directed form. But Corbon thought the idea steadily lost ground after 1848, not as a noble vision of some socialist future, but as a practical matter. Given the reorganization of the labor process and the increasing schism between capital and labor in Parisian industry, collective means had to be found to resist the deskilling of labor and sagging real incomes. Corbon noted the revival of corporatist sentiments during the 1860s and the mobilization

of corporatist forms (abolished in the French Revolution) to defend working-class interests and to challenge the liberty of labor markets.[36] "Association" then meant the right to
form unions to negotiate collectively regarding wage rates and work conditions. The two
meanings ran along side by side in the late 1860s. Liberty of association was one of the
demands of all workers at the Workers' Commission meetings of 1867. But they either
meant different things by it or consciously chose to straddle the ambiguity in order to
make good political use of it.

DREAMING THE SOCIALIST CITY

In 1869, Moilin published a utopian tract, *Paris en l'An 2000*.[37] A dedicated and learned
doctor (he had been the assistant to Claude Bernard, an eminent physician) he had
acquired a significant reputation for his care of the poor in the First Arrondissement
during the cholera epidemics. During the 1860s he became enamored of a socialist future
based on order and social justice, and at times ran into difficulty with the authorities
because of his ideas. He envisaged a socialist government that would reshape the city
by the year 2000 to promote the well-being of all. The state would own all the property,
eliminating property speculation and landlordism. The reshaping of the city was placed in
the hands of architects, who would remove dilapidated slums and unhygienic structures.
But the process would be gradual and avoid the brutality and class biases of Haussmann's
demolitions. The urban fabric would ultimately be dominated by structures reminiscent
of Fourier's *phalanstères*, square blocks of housing with a central space of gardens and
courtyards for social and common activities. Connectivity within the city would be
assured by second-floor arcades linked together with bridges and passages and serviced
with elevators. This provided connected shopping and walking spaces and a sheltered
system of communication for the whole of the urban population (ideal for the flaneur).
Workshops were located on the ground floor and, light and airy in design, ensured work
under the very best environmental conditions.

The whole of the Ile de la Cité and the Ile St. Louis were occupied by an immense
structure, the Palais Internationale (shades of Perreymond—see above, pp. 83–85), into
which flowed aerial railways and which functioned as a reception station into something
like a permanent world exposition to celebrate universal fraternity and the unity of
humanity. Here also were located government functions and a temple of socialism (replacing Notre Dame) that was the center of ritual and worship in the new order. Innumerable
civic activities took place here through which a sense of identity with the city was forged
for everyone. A balcony high up on this structure permitted people to look out over the
whole city and appreciate its unity. Immense columns surrounding the palace supported a
huge covering dome, made practicable by the new architecture in glass and iron.

By the year 2000, income inequality had been much reduced (no more than 1
to 5) and, thanks to public ownership, equality had entered into the organization of
work. Social habits of generosity, mutual support, and equality of engagement had been

achieved by reforms in education and apprenticeship. Ownership of property was rare, rents were modest, and housing blocks were characterized by the greatest possible diversity of people. Domestic service had been abolished. Many women worked according to their aptitudes, but they still did not have political rights (a concession to Proudhon?) and the family was still the basis of the social order (though divorce was recognized and prostitution forbidden). The intellectual world was marked by lively discussions and debates within the Academy of Paris (to which women and the young could be elected by universal suffrage). The strong taste for exhibitions, balls, concerts, theaters, journals, and for competition and achievement of marks of distinction (the Medal of the Republic being most valued), continued to be an important feature of cultural life. Huge cafés (where one did not drink too much) were centers of sociality and conversation. Parisians had not forgotten how to pursue their pleasures, and the arts of the lounger and the flaneur were much appreciated. As Benjamin noted rather dismissively, Moilin not only derived much from Fourier but envisaged the ideal city largely in terms of consumption and democratized *fête impérial* rather than of organized production.

The art of utopian thought, so thoroughly crushed in 1848, was here resuscitated twenty years later. Moilin was to play a very minor part in the Commune of 1871—he was an acting mayor of his *arrondissement* for the first three days in March. But he was arrested by the Versaille forces on May 27, brought before a summary court-martial in the Luxembourg Gardens, and instantly condemned to death, not because of his actions, the judgment said, but because "he was one of the leaders of the Socialist party, dangerous through his talents, his character and his influence over the masses; one of those men, in short, of whom a prudent and wise government must rid itself when it finds a legitimate occasion to do so."[38] He was given a respite of twelve hours to marry his pregnant companion, and then shot in the Gardens on the morning of May 28, 1871.

GENDER, SEXUALITY, AND REVOLUTION

Shortly before the Commune, Edmond de Goncourt noted in his journal, "They speak of the nervous over-excitation of women . . . of the fear of having to suppress riots of women." After the Commune that fear became a legend of "sinister females," of "amazons and viragos," inspiring and inflaming men by their obscene and unashamed immodesty, . . . clothing undone, their bosoms almost bare," inciting and leading the torching of Paris. Contemplating the bodies of women dragged from houses and barricades and summarily shot, Houssaye wrote: "Not one of these women had a human face; only the image of crime and vice. They were bodies without souls, deserving of a thousand deaths, even before having touched the petrol. There is only one word to portray them: hideous."[39]

This imagery of the bestiality and barbarism of women in the midst of riot and revolution, of the role of "women incendiaries" in the Commune, lived powerfully on, even though the military tribunals could find hardly any evidence for it—and not for want of trying.[40] Zola, drawing heavily upon Maxime du Camp's descriptions of the Commune, inserted into *Germinal* a horrendous scene of lynching and castration of the village shop-keeper by enraged women. Images of this sort were far from uncommon. They can be traced throughout the whole of the Second Empire. What, then, was this all about?

The connection between women, liberty, and the Republic (and hence with revolution) had long been in the making (as we saw in chapter 2). The imagery was so powerful that the manner in which women were depicted became, as we have seen, a tense focus of iconographic rivalry. In the June Days of 1848, the *London Examiner* reported an incident that reads like a reenactment of Delacroix's painting *Liberty Leading the People* (though with a less than happy outcome):

> One of the females, a young woman neatly dressed, picked up the flag, and leaping over the barricade, rushed towards the national guards, uttering language of provocation . . . a shot reached her and she was killed. The other female then advanced, took the flag, and began to throw stones at the national guards . . . [who] killed the second female.

Victor Hugo recorded the same incident. But he called both the women "prostitutes, beautiful, dishevelled, terrifying." Uttering obscenities, they pulled up their dresses to the waist, crying, "Cowards! Fire, if you dare, at the belly of a woman." "That was how this war began," adds Hugo somberly.[41] De Tocqueville, as we have seen, likewise gave vent to all the bourgeois fears of the unsubmissive and uncontrollable woman as an agent of revolution, and Flaubert's depiction of the prostitute posing as liberty in the Tuileries in 1848 continued the tradition. On the other side of the English Channel, Charles Dickens propagated the same idea (though it was, of course, depicted as peculiarly French) in his portrayal of Madame Defarge and "La Vengeance" in *A Tale of Two Cities*.

Events of the sort that Hugo describes put the allegory into motion. And the symbolism was surely not lost: Had not the Republic shot down Liberty on the barricades? The iconography thereafter split along lines exactly demarcated by the distinction between the social and the political republic. The "cautious Republic of order and reconciliation" needed a quite different representation from the "impetuous and rebellious" image of the people's Republic: "It began to look as if soon the camps of those clad in workers' clothes would have one Republic with a red cap and a gaping bodice, while the camp of dark-suited gentlemen would have another, a ladylike Republic behatted with foliage and draped in robes from top to toe."[42] After 1848, the respectable republicans set out to domesticate the image (Bartholdi first discussed his plans for the Statue of Liberty that now stands in New York Harbor in the late 1860s). The workers clung to a more revolutionary image. They formed "Mariannist conspiracies" mainly in rural areas, although one was broken up in Paris in 1855. The emancipation of women, the nationalization of land and "all that lies therein," and guarantees of adequate living, employment, and education for all were part of its program. Such sentiments evidently died hard. When women observers came to the Workers' Commission of 1867, a worker was moved to cry out: "Madame, on seeing you enter, I believed I saw liberty enter. Whenever women sit down with men at these meetings, there commences the reign of liberty and justice. Vive la Femme! Vive la Liberté!"[43]

That women belonged exclusively in the home was a fiercely held belief among the bourgeoisie. Even radical republicans, like Michelet, and socialists espoused it. Proudhon's notes for *Pornocratie* contain "every cruelly reactionary notion ever used against female emancipation by the most extreme anti-feminist."[44] Reinforced by a cult of domesticity (which broadly paralleled the taming of the image of liberty), its material underpinnings lay in a conception of marriage as a business enterprise, in the increasing separation of workplace from residence, and in the crucial importance of a well-managed domestic economy to bourgeois success. It also had much to do with a system of property and inheritance that made the habits and morals of the aristocracy impractical except under conditions of enormous wealth. Bourgeois republicans were trapped between the specter of collapse into the dissolute ways of the working class and the noblesse oblige of the aristocracy. For them, control over women was deemed essential to the preservation of class position. What is more, most women seem to have accepted that equation. Even George Sand took to lauding the virtues of the family in the 1860s, and after the Commune felt free to direct the most vitriolic barbs against the communards, even though she had never stirred from her rural estate. Those women like d'Hericourt who dissented were not paid much attention, and there was little sign of an independent feminist politics—the question of women's suffrage (much debated in England) did not come up. Only toward the end of Empire did a group of women (Louise Michel, Paule Minck, Andrée Leo, and Elizabeth Dmitrieff)—begin to speak out on women's rights and organize groups such as the Union des Femmes that played such an important role in the Commune.[45]

FIGURE 98 *Daumier picks up on bourgeois fears of feminism and of the political consequences of women engaging with politics in this 1848 depiction of women threatening to storm the National Assembly to obtain the right to divorce.*

It is tempting to speculate on the social-psychological meaning of all this. The image of liberty as a terrifying and uncontrollable woman of the sort de Tocqueville encountered—worse still, a public whore—in a phallocratic society where the preservation of bourgeois private property and class position depended on the control of women must have shaken the bourgeois male psyche to the core. Manet's representations of women (in *Olympia* and *Déjeuner sur l'Herbe*) seem to have provoked bourgeois wrath precisely because the women appeared to be common prostitutes with an insufficiently submissive gaze.[46] Hertz suggests that castration fears (of the sort that Zola made so explicit in *Germinal*) combined with class antagonism to produce "male hysteria under political pressure."[47] It is hard to explain the extraordinary violence of male rhetoric against women who participated in revolutionary action in any other way. It is hard even to grapple with conventional republican representations.

Michelet's *La Femme*, first published in 1859, was a very influential tract by a celebrated republican historian. When the Workers' Commission of 1867 turned its attention to women, a certain Dr. Dupas spelled out a crude version of Michelet's ideas at length. The woman, he argued, is not equal to the man in physical strength, intellect, moral concerns, or devotion to public affairs, but her love and devotion as wife and mother surpass a thousandfold anything that men are capable of. Men are representatives of civilization, and women are creatures of nature ("Woman is natural. that is to say abominable," sputtered Baudelaire, while Manet's *Déjeuner sur l'Herbe* seems simultaneously to represent and to parody the opposition that Michelet made so much of).

The opposition between men and women could have a creative or a destructive resolution. In the absence of male restraint, the unclean side of woman's nature (represented by menstruation) could dominate and erupt into violent hysteria (which is presumably what Hugo, de Tocqueville, and the anti-communards thought they saw in the midst of revolution). Woman at work and outside the restraint of men, Dupas continued, put a moral blot on society; this unhappy situation exposed society to the degradation and hysteria produced in the workshop. The only positive resolution lay in the union of male and female under the domination of men (the man is "1" and the woman is "0," he explained, and the only way to multiply their social power was to put the "1" in front of the "0"; that way you got 10). But it was essential that the woman be given respect and sympathy. And here was the crux of Michelet's message. The woman was to be cast in the role of suffering madonna, whose natural burdens could be relieved and whose infinite capacity for love and devotion could be released only under conditions of respectful and paternalistic male control.[48] It is significant, I think, that not a single worker spoke up in support of such a view, and most condemned it outright.

Jules Simon also appeared before the Workers' Commission, but he took a quite different tack. He deplored the fact that women worked, since that tended to destroy the family, led to the neglect of children, and deprived the man of a stable, caring, and loving home environment where he could replenish his body and his soul. Some way had to be found to preserve the family. Yet Simon knew that for most of the working class, women's work was a necessity. He also knew that industry needed women's labor power. He attacked the idea that women should be banned from the workplace on the grounds that this interfered with a precious liberty (that of the market) and that women needed employment. The problem was to find respectable and well-remunerated employment and so to prevent the slide into debauchery and prostitution. The answer lay in free education provided by the state. This would allow women to increase the value of their labor power (a human capital argument) at the same time that they would improve their skills as educators within the family. The educational reforms of the late 1860s did open up this possibility, and apparently were appreciated by workers and even the more militant feminists. Simon was popular enough to draw a massive working-class vote for his election in 1869, and his ideas were appreciated by militant feminists. But as several workers pointed out at the commission meetings, the improved education of women would increase the range of jobs for which women could compete and would push wages down. Simon did indeed have the support of the industrial interest, who saw merit in his proposals from their own standpoint.[49]

So what did workers think? Fribourg, a member of the International, spoke up at the Workers' Commission for what was probably the majority, echoing Proudhon. The latter held that women belonged at home, under the authority of men. Though there was more than a touch of misogyny in Proudhon's writings, worker sentiment did not rest on the kinds of arguments that Michelet or Dupas advanced. It drew, in the first instance, on a tradition in which the man had the legal and moral right to dispose of the family labor power. It also drew upon the desire to protect the family and the authority of the male as the grand provider. Men should therefore be paid more than women. But in Second Empire Paris it was also fueled by intense hostility to competition from women's labor power, whether mobilized by the convents or directly in the workshops. The printers' strike of 1862 was, in this regard, a cause célèbre; the introduction of women at a third less pay to break the strike was exactly what the male workers feared. The short-run solution was to raise men's wages to cover family needs and to legislate women out of the workshops. The printers petitioned the Emperor to do just that. And in so doing they were not loath to use the sorts of arguments advanced by Michelet. They pointed to the hysteria generated by exposure to the workshop and argued, probably correctly, that the nature of the work and the toxic substances to which women were exposed induced a high rate of stillbirths and spontaeous abortions among the women employed there. So strongly were such views held that the French delegation to the Geneva meetings of the International in 1866 forced passage of a resolution banning women from the workshops and confining them to the home.

Socialist feminists like Paule Minck militated against such attitudes within the Parisian branch of the International. "We want to be treated neither as madonnas nor as slaves," she argued at a public meeting in 1868, "but as ordinary human beings, different but equal, with the right to work at equal pay and to associate for our own economic emancipation." She had male allies like Varlin, who rebutted Fribourg before the Workers' Commission: "Women's right to work was the only means to their true liberation," and those who refused it "simply wanted to keep them under the domination of men." Varlin, at least, was as good as his word, and wrote the right of women to work at equal pay into the constitution of the bookbinders' union.[50] The shoemakers, however, thought it sufficiently progressive to permit women into their union only if they asked no questions except in writing or through a male member.

Representations and rhetoric flew past each other at the Workers' Commission meetings without touching. The real tragedy of that was already etched into women's daily lives. The grisly aftermath of the Commune illustrates the violence and horror unleashed when class and gender antagonism reinforce each other. Many of the women dragged before the military tribunals had simply acted as ambulance or canteen helpers, and were totally mystified by the rhetoric and charges of heinous crimes directed against them. They had lived by the nobility of one vision only to be judged by the hysterical rhetoric of another.

When private representations enter into public rhetoric, they become means and motivations for both individual and collective action. It is always easier, of course, to reconstruct what people said, much harder to guess how they thought. And individual variation in this sphere is often so great that any general statement must appear misleading. Yet within the numerous conflicting eddies of ideas, broad themes stand out to suggest motivations. The final testing ground must lie, however, in action. For there is much that can be thought that never acquires the status of material force, since it stays forever locked in the realm of dreams. The themes we have here examined were not of that sort. The experience of the Commune saw all of them enter into social life, often with a vengeance. And there is enough evidence of the ordering of daily life in Second Empire Paris to make it at least reasonable to infer that the manner of the rhetoric and representation, as well as of the science and the sentiment, were more than just idle moments for the few. What ought, however, to be added is another category, that of silences—the silences of that multitude whose ideas we cannot trace and the strategic silences of those we can.

CHAPTER SEVENTEEN

The Geopolitics of
Urban Transformation

Mankind . . . inevitably sets itself only such tasks as it is able to solve, since closer examina-
tion will always show that the problem itself arises only when the material conditions for its
solution are already present or at least in the course of formation.

—Marx

"When the imperial mantle finally falls on the shoulders of Louis Bonaparte," Marx predicted in 1852, "the bronze statue of Napoleon will crash from the top of the Vendôme Column."[1] On May 16, 1871, the hated symbol collapsed before a Communard crowd, temporarily diverted from the threatening gunfire of the forces of reaction encircling Paris. Between the prediction and the event lay eighteen years of "ferocious farce."

The ferocity had dual, sometimes complementary, but in the end conflictual, origins. The Empire, to protect both itself and the civil society over which it reigned, resorted to an arbitrariness of state power that touched everyone, from the street entertainers hounded off the boulevards to the bankers excluded from the lucrative city loan business. But the accelerating power of the circulation and accumulation of capital was also at work, transforming labor processes, spatial integrations, credit relations, living conditions, and class relations with the same ferocity that it assumed in the creative destruction of the Parisian built environment. In the aftermath of 1848, the arbitrariness of state power appeared to be a crucial prop to private property and capital. But the farther the Empire degenerated into open farce, the more evident it became that modernity could not be produced out of imperial tradition, that there was and could be no stable class basis of imperial power, and that the supposed omnipotence of government sat ill with the omniscience of market rationality. The schism between the Saint-Simonians and the liberal political economists therefore symbolized a deep antagonism between political and economic processes.

FIGURE 99 *Daumier's view of the history of the Second Empire has the traditional feminine figure of Liberty bound hand and foot and placed between the cannons of the coup d'état of 1851 and those of the Emperor's defeat at Sedan in 1870.*

Napoleon III's strategy for maintaining power was simple: "Satisfy the interests of the most numerous classes and attach to oneself the upper classes."[2] Unfortunately, the explosive force of capital accumulation tended to undermine such a strategy. The growing gap between the rich (who supported the Empire precisely because it offered protection against socialistic demands) and the poor led to mounting antagonism between them. Every move the Emperor made to attach to the one simply alienated the other. Besides, the workers remembered as fact (adorned with growing fictions) that there had once been a Republic that they had helped to produce and that had voiced their social concerns. The demand for liberty and equality in the market also tended to emphasize a republican political ideology within segments of the bourgeoisie. This was as much at odds with the authoritarianism of Empire as it was antagonistic to plans for the social republic.

FIGURE 100 *The toppling of the Vendôme Column by the Communards occurred on May 16th, 1871. In this photo by Braquehais, the painter Courbet (who was later ordered to pay for the reconstruction of the column out of his own pocket) may well be the middle figure among those at the back. The column had a checkered history. Chaudet's imperial statue (made from captured Austrian canon) was taken off and melted down with the restoration of the monarchy in 1815, and used to remake the destroyed statue of Henry IV on the Pont-Neuf. The figure of Napoleon as Caesar was replaced atop the column by a simple fleur-de-lis. The July Monarchy, anxious to link itself to the revolution and Napoleon's populism, put Napoleon back on top of the column in 1834, but as a citizen-soldier in a campaign cloak. In 1863, Seurre's representation was replaced by Dumont's figure of Napoleon as Caesar, in antique dress and holding a Roman symbol of victory. This was the version toppled by the Communards.*

The split between political and social conceptions of the Republic—so evident in 1848—continued to be of great significance. It could be and was used to great effect to divide and rule. But that gave no secure class basis to political power. The Empire was, however, so caught up in the maelstrom of capitalistic progress that it could not satisfy the traditionalists and the conservatives (particularly the Catholics) who objected to the new materialism and the new class configurations that were in the course of formation. The consensus behind imperial authority was hard to sustain and threatened to evaporate entirely when problems of overaccumulation and devaluation once more arose. The contradictions of capitalist growth were therefore matched by unstable political lurchings from this or that side of the class spectrum or from this or that faction. When, in 1862, the Emperor honored James Rothschild with a visit to his country house (to the immense chagrin of the Pereires), and when, in the same year, he granted two hundred thousand francs to workers to send their elected delegates to London (where Karl Marx so eagerly awaited them and from whence they returned to form the Paris branch of the First International), something was plainly amiss. Such shifting, far from alleviating matters, only added anxiety about what was to replace the Empire if and when it should fall.

The monarchists, though extremely powerful, offered no real alternative. Divided among themselves, they gathered around them ultraconservative Catholics, traditionalists, and almost every reactionary sentiment antagonistic to capitalistic progress. With a strong base in rural France, their influence in Paris tended to shrink during the Second Empire and in the end was confined mainly to the very traditional salons of the aristocratic Left Bank. While the Empire had its supporters, particularly among the finance capitalists, state functionaries, and bourgeois property owners of western Paris who were well satisfied with Haussmann's works, the centers of business, commerce, and professional services (like law) on the Right Bank became bastions of republicanism, usually tempered by pragmatic financial opportunism that gave the Empire many opportunities to co-opt them. The Café de Madrid on the Boulevard Montmartre was the geopolitical meeting point of this kind of republicanism with the more déclassé and sometimes bohemian sentiments of writers drawn to that area as a center of press and communications power. The republicanism of the Left Bank was of a rather different order. The product of students and academics, it was less pragmatic and more revolutionary and utopian, capable of spinning off in all kinds of directions into alliances with workers and artisans or into its own forms of revolutionary and conspiratorial politics. Working-class Paris, sprawled in a vast peripheral zone from northwest through the east to southwest (with its thickest concentration in the northeast), was solidly republican, but with strong social concerns and not a few resentments at the betrayal suffered at the hands of bourgeois republicanism in 1848.

The struggle that unfolded in Paris during the 1860s and presaged the Commune was of epic proportions. It was a struggle to give political meaning to concepts of community and class; to identify the true bases of class alliances and antagonisms; to find political, economic, organizational, and physical spaces in which to mobilize and from which to press demands. It was, in all these senses, a geopolitical struggle for the transformation of the Parisian economy, as well as of the city's politics and culture.

The parting of the ways between capital and Empire was not registered by dramatic confrontation but by the slow erosion of the organic links between them. The counterattack of Parisian property owners against the conditions of expropriation, the resistance of the Bank of France to the cheap credit that the Saint-Simonians sought, the growing resentment of industrialists at Haussmann's harassment, and the increasing domination of small owners and shopkeepers by finance capital signaled growing disaffection of this or that fragment of the bourgeoisie. Though some, like the property owners, partially returned to the imperial fold, others were more and more alienated. Ironically, the more successfully the Empire repressed the workers, the freer the bourgeois opposition felt to express itself. Yet the more that opposition grew, the greater the political space within which workers could operate. On the one hand, bourgeois republican rhetoric shielded them, while on the other, the growth of bourgeois opposition forced the Empire to curry the workers' favor as part of its populist base.

The reconstruction of the republican party was one of the most signal achievements of the Second Empire. And while it depended upon the coming together of many different currents of opinion in many parts of the country, what happened in Paris was crucial. Powerfully but incoherently implanted within the liberal professions (which saw the Republic perhaps as a means to acquire an autonomous class power) and with strong potential support in business, industry, and commerce, bourgeois republicanism needed a much sharper definition than it had achieved in 1848. The rambunctious, explosive image of femininity on the barricades had to be corseted, tamed, and made thoroughly respectable. The déclassé republicanism of students, intellectuals, writers, and artists had somehow to be confronted and controlled. But the bourgeois republicans also needed working-class support if they were to succeed. How to gain that support without making any but the mildest concessions to social conceptions of the Republic that typically threatened private property, money power, the circulation of capital, and even patriarchy and the family was the fledgling republican party's most pressing problem. On questions of political liberty, legality, freedom of expression, and representative government (locally, as in the nation), it was possible to make common cause. Bourgeois republicans therefore tried to keep such issues at the center of political

FIGURE 101 *Daumier here depicts one of the minor contradictions facing the "good bourgeois" at a time when they were facing many serious political complications.*

debate. Questions of freedom of association, workers' rights, and representation were touchier. And debate over the social republic had to be buried within a reformist rhetoric on relatively safe questions like improved education. Bourgeois republicanism tended to become violent in its defense of patriarchy and vicious in its attitudes toward socialism. But the terms of alliance with the working class always had to be open to negotiation at the same time that the battle between social and political conceptions of the Republic had to be fought out unto death, as it turned out, in the bloodbath of the Commune.

The revival of working-class politics in the early 1860s initially rested upon the reassertion of traditional institutional rights. The mutual benefit societies, in spite of imperial regulation, had early become the legal front for all kinds of covert worker organization. Their direct subversion into trade union forms (they were at the root of most strike activity) provoked innumerable prosecutions in the 1850s. But their indirect use for political purposes was quite uncontrollable. Herein lay, for example, the significance of funerals, since this was a key benefit and brought all members together to listen to a graveside discourse that often became a political speech. The Empire became less willing to attack the mutual benefit societies because it increasingly needed them as a means to canvass and to mobilize working-class support. There is considerable evidence that associations and coalitions existed in practice without prosecution by the early 1860s.[3] The mutual benefit societies became centers of consciousness formation and means for organizing the collective expression of demands. The corporatist forms hidden within them became more explicit as craft workers sought to protect themselves against the ravages of technological and organizational change and the flood of unskilled immigration. This use of the mutual benefit frame had important effects. It helped bridge the separation between working and living, and preserved a unity of concern for production and consumption questions. In the context of Parisian industry, it also reinforced the search for alternatives down mutualist, cooperative paths. Both consciousness and political action were to draw much of their strength from that sense of unity.

The wave of institution-building and modernization, upon which later administrations were to draw, became most marked after 1862. The Emperor, under increasing attack from upper-class royalists in alliance with conservative Catholics and threatened on the other flank by the revival of bourgeois republicanism, was forced to seek support from a working class that even his own prefects were telling him was in dire straits. But imperial initiatives to draw workers to the side of industrial progress and Empire sparked little grassroots response save a lengthy explanation from Tolain, which earned him an interview with the Emperor and the right to form a workers's commission made up of presidents of mutual benefit societies, thus recognizing the latter's de facto corporatist and professional role. Ironically, the commission meetings began at the very moment of one of the first major strikes of Parisian craft workers, that of the printers in 1862. The printers' leaders were imprisoned for the crime of coalition, even though public sympathy (including that of many republicans) was with them. When the Emperor pardoned them, he in effect rendered the laws against coalition and association moot. He did so as the workers he had helped send to the fateful London exposition were returning, telling tales of better working conditions and wages achieved in Britain through trade unions.

But, curiously, neither side was yet willing to recognize the realities of class struggle. The opening given to working-class politics in the early 1860s initially provoked a wave of mutualist sentiments. The mutual benefit societies flourished in numbers and membership, while schemes for mutual credit (such as the Credit au Travail), consumer cooperatives (two founded in 1864), and cooperative housing burst out all over (some even drew the Emperor's private support). The International's statutes were approved by the government in 1864. At the same time, the Empire engaged Emile Ollivier (later to head the liberal Empire of 1869) to rewrite the law on combinations. The law, designed to avoid organized class struggle, gave the working class the right to strike but not the right to organize or assemble. The bookbinders and bronze workers, followed by the stonecutters, promptly celebrated by striking for shorter hours without wage reductions. But the labor movement's main focus was on organizing rights and conditions of labor rather than on wage levels in the early 1860s. Proudhon was, at this point, at the height of his influence, inveighing against strikes and unions (he almost seemed to approve of Ollivier's law) and pushing for mutualist worker democracy (as well as for all women to return to the domestic sphere, where they belonged). The French delegates to the International's meetings of 1866 in Geneva, led by Tolain, carried with them a veritable charter for Proudhonism and mutualism, thus testifying to the deep hold of such ideas over craft worker consciousness.

The workers' movement had its setbacks, too. Attempts to create an independent workers' press were quickly quashed, in part through bourgeois republican opposition. The attempt to define an independent political space likewise failed. In 1864 the craft workers, with some radical republican support, issued the Manifesto of the Sixty, which focused on workers' rights as a political issue. The general effect was to raise the fearful specter of class struggle and provoke the unfounded but not unreasonable suspicion that the workers' movement was being used by the Empire to frustrate bourgeois republican aspirations. When Tolain, a signer of the Manifesto and a founder of the Parisian branch of the International, ran as an independent workers' candidate in 1863 to emphasize the distinctiveness of the workers' cause, he was vilified in the republican press and so squeezed by opposition from that quarter that he received fewer than five hundred votes in a parliamentary election that saw the bourgeois republicans sweep to power in much of Paris.

The recession of 1867–1868 marked a radical realignment of class forces as well as a turning point in worker militancy and rhetoric. What became known as the "million-aires' strike" saw the massive accumulation of surplus capital in the coffers of the Bank of France, stagnation in public works and in the upper-class Parisian property market, and fiercer international competition and rising unemployment in the face of strongly rising prices. The downfall of the Pereires, a jittery stock market, and the growing likelihood of geopolitical conflict with Prussia undermined the sense of security that the authoritarianism of Empire had earlier been able to impart. The spectacle of the 1867 Universal Exposition diverted attention at one level, though many noted the irony that it celebrated the commodity fetish and consumerism at a time of shrinking real incomes, and that it brought competitive commodities as well as the king of Prussia into the very heart of Paris at a time of heightened international competition and geopolitical tension.

The workers' movement then became much more militant and switched to real wages rather than organizational rights as its main focus of concern. Within the International this was marked by the eclipse of the mutualists like Tolain and Fribourg and their replacement by communists like Varlin and Malon, whose attitudes, given their youth, were less affected by memories of 1848 and more forged out of the actualities of class conflict through the 1860s. The persecution of the International at that point only helped the process of transition by removing the original leaders, giving it greater and greater credibility among Parisian workers, and forcing it into the underground, where it encountered militant Blanquists—themselves turning to the organization of the working class as part of their revolutionary strategy. Yet even though Varlin, for one, moved rapidly to a more and more collectivist politics, striving to organize and federate unions into agents of mass working-class action, he still clung to certain mutualist principles of organization as the basis for the transition to socialism.[4] The craft workers straddled the ambiguity between class organization and mutualism without, apparently, being too aware of the tension between them.

The year 1867 saw important strikes by bronze workers (supported for the first time by international funds), tailors, and construction workers oriented primarily toward higher wages. In that same year generalized discontent over living standards spilled over into street demonstrations that touched the unorganized and unskilled workers. For the first time since 1848, the unorganized of Belleville descended into the space of inner-city craft workers to express their discontent. Barricades appeared sporadically, only to be swept away by the forces of order almost immediately. The bourgeoisie was not beguiled, either, by the important concessions made to it. The return to quasi-parliamentary government (symbolized by the restoration of the speaker's tribune in the legislature) opened up a forum for complaint. And there was much to complain about. The free-speech movement of the early 1860s had already turned the Left Bank into a hotbed of student and intellectual unrest. Industrialists complained about Haussmann, and workshop masters and shopkeepers complained fiercely about conditions of credit and the power of the grand monopolies that the state had done so much to support. The recession and Prussia's defeat of Austria at Sadoya (to say nothing of the unhappy Mexican venture) shook the confidence of everyone in a government that had come to power on the promise of peace and prosperity, and that now looked like it could not deliver on either. Those bourgeois like Thiers who had long felt excluded from the grand feast of state wealth and power stood ready to mobilize the agitation and unrest to their own advantage. Even the monarchists could find causes, like that of decentralization, around which they sought to rally popular discontent.

All of this was mere prelude to the awesome struggles of 1868–1871. But it was an important prelude because it posed the question of what class alliance could emerge that would be capable of replacing the Empire. Could the monarchists wean away enough support from the bourgeois center to stymie the republican thrust? Could the bourgeois republicans control the working-class movement to keep the political republic out of the clutches of the socialists? Could the radical freethinkers and déclassé republicans enter into alliance with a workers' movement that overcame its craft worker bias and reached out to encompass the unskilled and thus create a revolutionary and socialist republic? Could the Empire divide and rule and manipulate each and every one of these factions through co-optation and its police and provocateur power? In practice, the Empire was forced into more and more concessions. It relaxed press censorship (May 1868) and permitted public meetings on "nonpolitical" topics (June 1868). The right to form unions was conceded in 1869. But the state in no way relinquished its powers of provocation and repression.

The International's leaders looked to collaborate with the republican bourgeois opposition, and were promptly arrested as early as the end of 1867. The respectable republicans ignored the call for a class alliance. The workers were equally critical of such a tactic, since they remembered only too well how the political republic had betrayed them in 1848. The second wave of the International's leaders sought an independent space within which they could build the strength of their own movement. Varlin led the bookbinders' mutual benefit society and transformed it into a vigorous and coherent union in 1869. He helped to found an extensive system of consumer cooperatives (La Marmite) in 1867, bringing cheap food, politics, and consumption together in a more coherent way than the wineshop or the cabaret, which the mass of workers who lived in boardinghouses otherwise patronized. He vigorously defended equal rights for women in the workplace and within workers' organizations. He headed the movement to federate the numerous Parisian unions (perhaps twenty thousand strong) in 1869 and played a leading role in the International's efforts to unify working-class action over national and international space. It was exactly such a broad geopolitical conception of the struggle that terrified the "honest bourgeois." The problem for Varlin was to integrate the restless

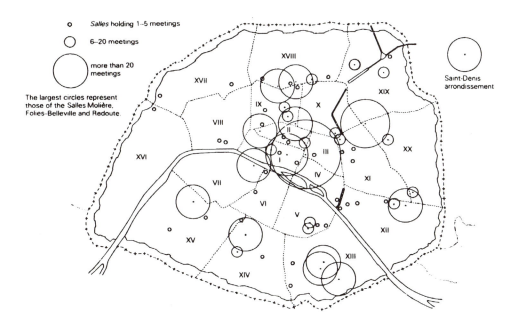

FIGURE 102 *The location and frequency of public meetings in Paris, 1868–1870.*

mass of unorganized and unskilled workers into a movement that had always had a craft-worker base. The scaffolding he and others had erected by 1870 was by no means sufficient to that task. Recognizing that weakness, he sought tactical alliances with the radical and often revolutionary fringe of the bourgeoisie.

There had always been such a fringe within *la bohème* and within the student movement. The Blanquists had set about organizing such discontent around their own program. But the relaxation of press censorship revealed a much wider swath of disaffection. Rochefort, a newspaper proprietor, became the instant hero of the popular and disaffected classes with *La Lanterne*, a newspaper full of radical critique and revolutionary rhetoric (which earned Rochefort periodic stays in jail and which horrified the conservative bourgeoisie). Recognizing the power of this movement, Varlin established a tactical alliance to try to ensure that social questions were properly integrated into any radical republican program. The radical republicans, for their part, had to erase the memory of betrayal in 1848. They made the attempt in 1868 by recalling the death of a republican representative, Baudin, on the barricades of 1851. They proposed a massive pilgrimage to his tomb on the Day of the Dead. The government tried to bar their way, and those who did get into the cemetery of Montmartre had a hard time finding the grave. Hence there arose the idea of a public subscription. The government's prosecution of those engaged in the affair only drew more attention to the "crime" of the coup d'état while allowing a young lawyer, Gambetta, to become another instant hero of the radical cause. The symbolic resurrection of Baudin, the creation of tradition, was, in a way, a stroke of genius. It focused on the illegitimacy of Empire in such a way as to symbolize the bourgeois role in the heart of the space of worker struggle (this was the special virtue of the cemetery of Montmartre). It was by gestures of this sort that the radical bourgeoisie reached out to embrace the "other Paris" in symbolic unity.

The "nonpolitical" public meetings, which began on June 28, 1868, were extraordinary affairs. Heavily concentrated in the zones of disaffection, no amount of government surveillance could prevent them from turning into occasions for mass education and political consciousness-raising.[5] The geopolitics was highly predictive of the Commune. Not only were the meetings unevenly spread across the Parisian space, but specialization of audience, topic, and place was quickly established. The political economists and bourgeois reformers who looked to the meetings as opportunities for mass education about their cause were outgunned and often shouted down in the meeting halls of the "other Paris." An assortment of radicals, feminists, socialists, Blanquists, and other revolutionaries dominated what became regular political theater in many quarters of the city. The political economists and reformers were forced to withdraw to the relative safety of the Left Bank and Right Bank center, leaving the north and northeast of the city entirely to the radicals, socialists, and revolutionaries. It seemed that the "other Paris" was now the exclusive space for popular political agitation. That trend was reinforced by a sudden resurgence of popular street culture, revolutionary songs and ballads suddenly bursting from a murky underground where they had lain dormant for almost two decades.

This kind of agitation was as disturbing to the respectable bourgeois as it was to the supporters of Empire. Could the Empire rally the disaffected in the name of law and order? Only if it made major concessions. The year 1869 therefore began with official disavowal of Haussmann's slippery financing in the face of fiscally conservative bourgeois critics. The appearance of Jules Ferry's severe attack on the prefect in the *Comptes Fantastiques d'Haussmann* in 1868 charged him with all kinds of improprieties. The aftermath was curious. First, it forced Haussmann to reduce public works activities and depressed the construction trade and Parisian industry even further, thus exacerbating social discontent. Second, none of those who attacked him denied the utility of his works, and many of them pleaded for completion of this or that part of his project in 1869 or, like Rothschild, were only too happy to lend the city money as it needed it. It increasingly appeared that Haussmann was a mere surrogate target for the Emperor and that the exclusivity of his seeming patronage was what was at stake.

The subsequent election campaign of May 1869 was surrounded with political agitation. A riot ensued when Ollivier tried to take the theme of support for liberal Empire into the center of Paris. The crowd at Châtelet moved noisily to the Faubourg Saint-Antoine, the traditional hearth of revolution, before dispersing. The next day a crowd of twenty thousand moved around the craft worker quarters; and the day after that a crowd of fifteen thousand tried to move from the Sorbonne, where it had assembled, to the Bastille, but found its way blocked. During this phase, Haussmann's boulevards were turned into a battleground. Hitherto appropriated by bourgeois strollers and consumers, they were suddenly taken over by a surging mass of discontented workers, students, shopkeepers, and street people. On June 12 a crowd even penetrated as far as the Opéra and set up the first real barricade. The bourgeois response was to try and reassert their rights to boulevard space by chasing off undesirables. Even the Emperor saw the symbolic value of passing along the contested terrain between the Opéra and the Port-Saint-Denis, though he was greeted with glacial silence as he passed.

FIGURE 103 *Haussmann's fall was accompanied by a campaign to discredit his creative accounting, amid speculation to the effect that he had robbed the public treasury. In this cartoon by Mailly he is branded as a thief, as the man who sold Paris for purposes of destruction. There is little evidence, however, that he personally profited from the works he set in motion.*

But the crowds upon the boulevards hid secrets. It was never clear, for example, whether the violent agitations and the "white blouses" were signs of secret police activity or not. Certainly, they had abundant opportunities to stir up threats to law and order and scare the respectable bourgeois back into the imperial fold. It was never clear, either, just how revolutionary in spirit the crowds were. Large crowds of twenty thousand or more frequently dispersed when asked to do so by law-abiding republicans. And the huge demonstration of over one hundred thousand people, which assembled after the Emperor's nephew shot a radical journalist, Victor Noir, dispersed quietly at Rochefort's request rather than confront the forces of order that barred their way into central Paris. Yet the day before, Rochefort had more than hinted that the day of revolution was near. The Blanquists had also wanted to start the insurrection at that moment, but found little support. The times were very unsettled but the leadership was uncertain. Could the ambiguity and dispersal of opposition sentiment be overcome and transformed into revolution?

The elections of May and June 1869 indicated otherwise. Only in Belleville was a radical sympathizer elected, and Gambetta was a politician who could bridge moderate socialist and left bourgeois opinion with skill and authenticity. Elsewhere, the political republicans swept the board; it even took a very conservative Thiers to narrowly overcome the Empire's candidate in the bourgeois west. The plebiscite a year later was harder to interpret, but the abstentions (urged by the radical left) did not increase markedly, and although the "no" votes prevailed, the Empire still received a surprising number of affirmative votes. It would take, it seemed, a much more thorough organization and education of the popular classes to bring the social republic into being. And it was exactly on such a task that the socialists spent their efforts. The public meetings provided a basis for neighborhood organizations, while the themes broached there encouraged the formation of trade unions, consumer cooperatives, producers' cooperatives, feminist organizations, and the like. These formed the organizational infrastructure that would be used to such good effect in the Commune. And there is no question as to their revolutionary political orientation, though there was much room for disagreement, interpersonal feuds, and neighborhood conflicts. But this form of opposition had a different orientation than that on the streets. Strikes in commerce, tanning, and woodworking, and the building of links between unions and neighborhoods, proceeded with a different rhythm and had more definite targets at the same time that they were relatively more immune to police infiltration. Here was the grand dividing line between the socialists, who urged the patient building of a revolutionary movement, and the Blanquists, who looked to spontaneous, violent insurrection.

But by 1870 it was plain that the mass of the bourgeoisie was looking for a legal way out of the impasse of Empire, was shifting away from any coalition with the "reds." And it used its ownership and influence within the press to hammer home the message of law and order to workers and petite bourgeoisie alike. The discontent, however, daily became more threatening as living conditions deteriorated and the economy stagnated. Conflict in Belleville in February 1870 left several dead, many arrested, and considerable property damage (usually that of unpopular shopkeepers and landlords). A major strike at the locomotive works at Cail signaled a level of anger as well as worker organization that had hitherto not been apparent. The ferment of discontent seemed uncontainable as the Empire lost its nerve and the bourgeoisie held its ground. Though conditions were des-

perate, the International's leaders (unlike the Blanquists') thought the political conditions were not yet ripe for social revolution. They were, as the Commune was to show only too well, right in that judgment. What is extraordinary is how far, wide, and deep they had ranged in the construction of a revolutionary organization capable of uniting many disparate elements within the dispersed space of Paris (as well as France). The tragedy, in the end, was that a conjuncture of events forced them to put their efforts on the line so prematurely in defense of a losing cause. That conjuncture was less accidental, however, than might be supposed. For all the signs were there that the "honest bourgeois"—led by Thiers—not only were concerned to have done with Empire and seize the fruits of political power but also were determined to have done with the "reds" once and for all and to subject them to their own vile brand of "final solution." Thus was the final act of ferocious farce left until that bloody week in May 1871 when some thirty thousand Communards died.

Exactly what happened in the Commune is beyond our ken. But much of it was rooted in the processes and effects of the transformation of Paris in the Second Empire. The organization of municipal workshops for women; the encouragement given to producer and consumer cooperatives; the suspension of the night work in the bakeries;

FIGURE 104 *The strike of the workers at the large factory of Cail in 1870 was both extensive enough and significant enough to make it into the bourgeois press.*

and the moratorium on rent payments, debt collections, and the sale of items from the municipal pawnshop at Mont-de-Piété reflected the sore points that had bothered working-class Paris for years. The assemblies of craft workers; the strengthening of unions; the vigor of the neighborhood clubs that grew out of the public meeting places of 1868–1870 and that were to play a crucial role in the defense of quarters; the setting up of the Union of Women; and the attempt to pull together working political organizations that bridged the tensions between centralization and decentralization, between hierarchy and democracy (the Committee of the Twenty Arrondissements, the Central Committee of the National Guard, and the Commune itself) all testified to the vigorous pursuit of new organizational forms generated from the nexus of the old. The creation of a Ministry of Labor and strong measures toward free and nonreligious primary and professional education testified to the depth of social concern.

But the Commune never challenged private property or money power in earnest. It requisitioned only abandoned workshops and dwellings, and prostrated itself before the legitimacy of the Bank of France (an episode that Marx and Lenin noted well). The majority sought principled and mutually acceptable accommodation rather than confrontation (even some of the Blanquists in practice went in that direction). But much of the opposition to the Commune was also given. The schism between the "moderate" republican mayors of the *arrondissements* (who got short shrift in Versailles when they tried to mediate) and the Commune grew as tensions rose. The bourgeoisie, which had deigned to remain to brave the rigors of the Prussian siege of 1870, quickly showed its teeth in mobilizing the "Friends of Order" demonstration of March 21 and 22, 1871, and thereafter turned western Paris into an easy point of penetration for the forces of reaction. The map of voting patterns for the Commune was predictable enough. The difference this time was that hegemonic power now lay with a worker-based movement.

Thiers's decision to relocate the National Assembly from Bordeaux to Versailles after signing a humiliating surrender to the Prussians, and his withdrawal of all executive functions from Paris after his failure to disarm Paris on March 18, 1871, crystallized the forces of rural reaction in a way that the Commune's faint calls for urban and rural solidarity could not match. His mobilization of rural ignorance and fear, fed by vicious propaganda, into an army prepared to give no quarter (were they not charged, after all, with chasing the red devils out of a sinful and atheistic Paris?), showed he meant to have a cathartic resolution, come what may. Once the possibility of a quick, preemptive strike against Versailles was lost, there was little the Commune could do except await its fate. The stress of that brought out divisions and fed interior discontents and rivalries within the uneasy class and factional alliance that produced the Commune. Splits between radical bourgeois, each armed with his own splendid theory of revolution; between practical patriots and peddlers of rhetoric and dreams; between workers bewildered by events and leaders of craft unions trying to render consistent and compelling interpretations; between loyalties to quarter, city, and nation; between centralizers and decentralizers, all gave the Commune an air of incoherence and a political practice riddled with internal

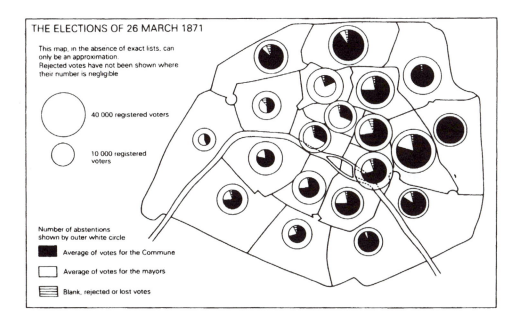

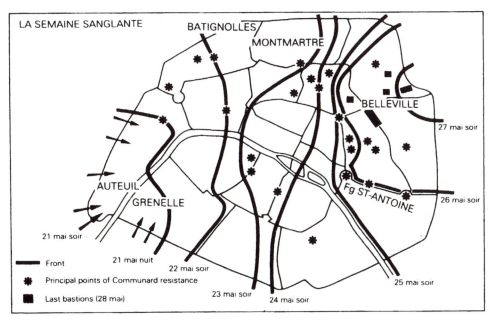

FIGURE 105 *The elections of March 26, 1871, and the phases of reoccupation of Paris during the "bloody week" of May 1871 illustrate all too clearly the east-west imbalance in political affiliations within the city. The low number of voters in the west reflects the fact that many of the more affluent citizens of the city had fled to their rural retreats.*

conflict. But such divisions had been long in the making; their roots lay deep in tradition, and their evolution had been confused by the turn to capitalist modernity and the clash between the politics of Empire and the economy of capital. Once more, as Marx had written in the *Eighteenth Brumaire*, "The tradition of all the dead generations weighs like a nightmare on the brain of the living," but this time it was the working-class movement that internalized the nightmare. The Commune was a high price to pay to discredit pure Proudhonism and the pure Jacobinism drawn from the reconstructed spirit of 1789. The tragedy was that an alternative modernity, one that was central to what the Commune was striving for, was killed in the womb of a bourgeois society that never looked beyond the political to the social republic as a potential fulfillment of its aspirations.

The Commune was a singular, unique, and dramatic event, perhaps the most extraordinary of its kind in capitalist urban history. It took war, the desperation of the Prussian siege, and the humiliation of defeat to light the spark. But the raw materials for the Commune were put together by the slow rhythms of the capitalist transformation of the city's historical geography. I have tried in this work to lay bare the complex modes of transformation in the economy and in social organization, politics, and culture that altered the visage of Paris in ineluctable ways. At each point along the way, we find people like Thiers and Varlin, like Paule Minck and Jules Michelet, like Haussmann and Louis Lazare, like Louis Napoleon, Proudhon, and Blanqui, like the Pereires and the Rothschilds, swirling within the crowd of street singers and poets, ragpickers and craft workers, bankers and prostitutes, domestics and idle rich, students and grisettes, tourists, shopkeepers, and pawnbrokers, cabaret owners and property speculators, landlords, lawyers, and professors. Somehow all were contained within the same urban space, occasionally confronting each other on the boulevards or the barricades, and all of them struggling in their own ways to shape and control the social conditions of their own historical and geographical existence. That they did not do so under historical and geographical conditions of their own choosing is self-evident. The Commune was produced out of a search to transform the power and social relations within a particular class configuration constituted within a particular space of a capitalist world that was itself in the full flood of dramatic transition. We have much to learn from the study of such struggles. And there is much to admire, much that inspires there, too.

PART THREE

CODA

CHAPTER EIGHTEEN

THE BUILDING OF THE BASILICA OF SACRÉ-COEUR

Strategically placed atop a hill known as the Butte Montmartre, the Basilica of Sacré-Coeur occupies a commanding position over Paris. Its five white marble domes and the campanile that rises beside them can be seen from every quarter of the city. Occasional glimpses of it can be caught from within the dense and cavernous network of streets that makes up old Paris. It stands out, spectacular and grand, to the young mothers parading their children in the Jardins de Luxembourg, to the tourists who painfully plod to the top of Notre Dame or who painlessly float up the escalators of the Centre Beaubourg, to the commuters crossing the Seine by metro at Grenelle or pouring into the Gare du Nord, to the Algerian immigrants who on Sunday afternoons wander to the top of the rock in the Parc des Buttes Chaumont. It can be seen clearly by the old men playing *boule* in the Place du Colonel Fabien, on the edge of the traditional working class quarters of Belleville and La Villette—places that have an important role to play in our story.

On cold winter days when the wind whips the fallen leaves among the aging tombstones of the Père Lachaise cemetery, the basilica can be seen from the steps of the tomb of Adolphe Thiers, first president of the Third Republic of France. Though now almost hidden by the modern office complex of La Défense, it can be seen from more than twenty kilometers away in the Pavillion Henry IV in St. Germain-en-Laye, where Adolphe Thiers died. But by a quirk of topography, it cannot be seen from the famous Mur des Fédérés, in that same Père Lachaise cemetery, where, on May 27, 1871, some of the last few remaining soldiers of the Commune were rounded up after a fierce fight among the tombstones and summarily shot. You cannot see Sacré-Coeur from that ivy-covered wall now shaded by an aging chestnut. That place of pilgrimage for socialists, workers, and their leaders is hidden from a place of pilgrimage for the Catholic faithful by the brow of the hill on which stands the grim tomb of Adolphe Thiers.

FIGURE 106
*The Basilica of
Sacré-Coeur*

Few would argue that the Basilica of Sacré-Coeur is beautiful or elegant. But most would concede that it is striking and distinctive, that its distinctive and unique style achieves a kind of haughty grandeur that demands respect from the city spread out at its feet. On sunny days it glistens from afar, and even on the gloomiest of days its domes seem to capture the smallest particles of light and radiate them outward in a white marble glow. Floodlit by night, it appears suspended in space, sepulchral and ethereal. Thus does Sacré-Coeur project an image of saintly grandeur, of perpetual remembrance. But remembrance of what?

The visitor drawn to the basilica in search of an answer to that question must first ascend the steep hillside of Montmartre. Those who pause to catch their breath will see spread out before them a marvelous vista of rooftops, chimneys, domes, towers, monuments—a vista of old Paris that has not changed much since that dull and foggy October morning in 1872 when the archbishop of Paris climbed that steep slope. When he reached the top, the sun miraculously chased both fog and cloud away to reveal the splendid panorama of Paris spread out before him. The archbishop marveled for a moment before crying aloud: "It is here, it is here where the martyrs are, it is here that the Sacred Heart must reign so that it can beckon all to it!"[1] So who are the martyrs commemorated here in the grandeur of this basilica?

The visitor who enters that hallowed place will most probably first be struck by the immense painting of Jesus that covers the dome of the apse. Portrayed with arms stretched wide, the figure of Christ bears an image of the Sacred Heart upon his breast. Beneath, two words stand out directly from the Latin motto—GALLIA POENITENS. And beneath this stern admonition that "France Repents," stands a large gold casket containing the image of the Sacred Heart of Jesus, burning with passion, suffused with blood, and surrounded with thorns. Illuminated day and night, it is here that pilgrims come to pray. Opposite a life-size statue of Saint Marguerite Marie Alacoque, at the entry to the basilica, words from a letter written by that saintly person—date, 1689; place, Paray-le-Monial—tell us more about the cult of the Sacred Heart:

THE ETERNAL FATHER WISHING REPARATION FOR THE BITTERNESS AND ANGUISH THAT THE ADORABLE HEART OF HIS DIVINE SON HAD EXPERIENCED AMONG THE HUMILIATIONS AND OUTRAGES OF HIS PASSION DESIRES AN EDIFICE WHERE THE IMAGE OF THIS DIVINE HEART CAN RECEIVE VENERATION AND HOMAGE.

Prayer to the Sacred Heart of Jesus, which, according to the Scriptures, had been exposed when a centurion thrust a lance through Jesus' side during his suffering upon the cross, was not unknown before the seventeenth century. But Marguerite Marie, beset by visions, transformed the worship of the Sacred Heart into a distinctive cult within the Catholic Church. Although her life was full of trials and suffering, her manner severe and rigorous, the predominant image of Christ that the cult projected was warm and loving, full of repentance and suffused with a gentle mysticism.[2] Marguerite Marie and her disciples set about propagating the cult with great zeal. She wrote to Louis XIV, for example, claiming to bring a message from Christ in which the King was asked to repent, to save France by dedicating himself to the Sacred Heart, to place its image upon his standard, and to build a chapel to its glorification. It is from that letter of 1689 that the words now etched in stone within the basilica are taken.

The cult diffused slowly. It was not exactly in tune with eighteenth-century French rationalism, which strongly influenced modes of belief among Catholics, and it stood in direct opposition to the hard, rigorous, and self-disciplined image of Jesus projected by the Jansenists. But by the end of the eighteenth century it had some important and potentially influential adherents. Louis XVI privately took devotion to the Sacred Heart for himself and his family. Imprisoned during the French Revolution, he vowed that within three months of his deliverance he would publicly dedicate himself to the Sacred Heart and thereby save France (from what, exactly, he did not say, nor did he need to). And he vowed to build a chapel for the worship of the Sacred Heart. The manner of Louis XVI's deliverance did not permit him to fulfill that vow. Marie Antoinette did no better. The queen delivered up her last prayers to the Sacred Heart before keeping her appointment with the guillotine.

These incidents are of interest because they presage an association, important for our story, between the cult of the Sacred Heart and the reactionary monarchism of the ancien régime. This put adherents to the cult in firm opposition to the principles of the French Revolution. Believers in the principles of liberty, equality, and fraternity, who were in any case prone to awesome anticlerical sentiments and practices, were, in return, scarcely enamored of such a cult. Revolutionary France was no safe place to attempt to propagate it. Even the bones and other relics of Marguerite Marie, now displayed in Paray-le-Monial, had to be carefully hidden during those years.

The restoration of the monarchy in 1815 changed all that. The Bourbon monarchs sought, under the watchful eye of the European powers, to restore whatever they could of the old social order. The theme of repentance for the excesses of the revolutionary era ran strong. Louis XVIII did not fulfill his dead brother's vow to the Sacred Heart, but he did build, with his own moneys, the Chapel of Expiation on the spot where his brother and his family had been so unceremoniously interred—GALLIA POENITENS.

A society for the propagation of the cult of the Sacred Heart was founded, however, and proceedings for the glorification of Marguerite Marie were transmitted to Rome in 1819. The link between conservative monarchism and the cult of the Sacred Heart was further consolidated, and the cult spread among conservative Catholics. But it was still viewed with some suspicion by the liberal, progressive wing of French Catholicism. But now another enemy was ravaging the land, disturbing the social order. France was undergoing the stress and tensions of capitalist industrialization. In fits and starts under the July Monarchy, and then in a great surge in the early years of the Second Empire of Napoleon III, France saw a radical transformation in certain sectors of its economy, in its institutional structures, and in its social order. From the standpoint of conservative Catholics, this transformation threatened much that was sacred in French life, since it brought within its train a crass and heartless materialism, an ostentatious and morally decadent bourgeois culture, and a sharpening of class tensions. The cult of the Sacred Heart now assembled under its banner not only those devotees drawn by temperament or circumstance to the image of a gentle and forgiving Christ, not only those who dreamed of a restoration of the political order of yesteryear, but also all those who felt threatened by the materialist values of the new social order, in which money had become the Holy

Grail, the papacy of finance capital threatened the authority of the Pope, and mammon threatened to supplant God as the primary object of worship.

To these general conditions, French Catholics could also add some more specific complaints in the 1860s. Napoleon III had finally come down (after considerable vacillation) on the side of Italian unification, committing himself politically and militarily to the liberation of the central Italian states from the temporal power of the Pope. The latter did not take kindly to such politics and under military pressure retired to the Vatican, refusing to come out until his temporal power was restored. From that vantage point, the Pope delivered searing condemnations of French policy and the moral decadence which, he felt, was sweeping over France. In this manner he hoped to rally French Catholics in the active pursuit of his cause. The moment was propitious. Marguerite Marie was beatified by Pius IX in 1864, and the cult of the Sacred Heart became a rallying cry for all forms of conservative opposition. The era of grand pilgrimages to Paray-le-Monial, in the south of France, began. The pilgrims, many carried to their destination by the new railroads that the barons of grand finance had helped to build, came to express repentance for both public and private transgressions. They repented for the materialism and decadent opulence of France. They repented for the restrictions placed upon the temporal power of the Pope. They repented for the passing of the traditional values embodied in an old and venerable social order. GALLIA POENITENS.

Just inside the main door of the Basilica of Sacré-Coeur in Paris, the visitor can read the following inscription:

THE YEAR OF OUR LORD 1875 THE 16TH JUNE IN THE REIGN OF HIS HOLINESS POPE PIUS IX IN ACCOMPLISHMENT OF A VOW FORMULATED DURING THE WAR OF 1870–71 BY ALEXANDER LEGENTIL AND HUBERT ROHAULT DE FLEURY RATIFIED BY HIS GRACE MSGR. GUIBERT ARCHBISHOP OF PARIS; IN EXECUTION OF THE VOTE OF THE NATIONAL ASSEMBLY OF THE 23RD JULY 1873 ACCORDING TO THE DESIGN OF THE ARCHITECT ABADIE; THE FIRST STONE OF THIS BASILICA ERECTED TO THE SACRED HEART OF JESUS WAS SOLEMNLY PUT IN PLACE BY HIS EMINENCE CARDINAL GUIBERT. . . .

Let us flesh out that capsule history and find out what lies behind it. As Bismarck's battalions rolled to victory after victory over the French in the summer of 1870, an impending sense of doom swept over France. Many interpreted the defeats as righteous vengeance inflicted by divine will upon an errant and morally decadent France. It was in this spirit that Empress Eugénie was urged to walk with her family and court, all dressed in mourning, from the Palace of the Tuileries to Notre Dame, to publicly dedicate themselves to the Sacred Heart. Though the Empress received the suggestion favorably, it was, once more, too late. On September 2, Napoleon III was defeated and captured at Sedan; on September 4, the Republic was proclaimed on the steps of the Hôtel de Ville and a

Government of National Defense was formed. On that day also Empress Eugénie took flight from Paris, having prudently, and at the Emperor's urging, already packed her bags and sent her more valuable possessions on to England.

The defeat at Sedan ended the Empire but not the war. The Prussian armies rolled on, and by September 20 they had encircled Paris and put that city under a siege that was to last until January 28 of the following year. Like many other respectable bourgeois citizens, Alexander Legentil fled Paris at the approach of the Prussian armies and took refuge in the provinces. Languishing in Poitiers and agonizing over the fate of Paris, he vowed in early December that "if God saved Paris and France and delivered the sovereign pontiff, he would contribute according to his means to the construction in Paris of a sanctuary dedicated to the Sacred Heart." He sought other adherents to this vow, and soon had the ardent support of Hubert Rohault de Fleury.[3] The terms of Legentil's vow did not, however, guarantee it a very warm reception, for, as he soon discovered, the provinces "were then possessed of hateful sentiments towards Paris." Such a state of affairs was not unusual, and we can usefully digress for a moment to consider its basis.

Under the ancien régime, the French state apparatus had acquired a strongly centralized character that was consolidated under the French Revolution and Empire. This centralization thereafter became the basis of French political organization and gave Paris a peculiarly important role in relation to the rest of France. The administrative, economic, and cultural predominance of Paris was assured. But the events of 1789 also showed that Parisians had the power to make and break governments. They proved adept at using that power and were not loath, as a result, to regard themselves as privileged beings with a right and a duty to foist all that they deemed "progressive" upon a supposedly backward, conservative, and predominantly rural France. The Parisian bourgeoisie, of no matter what political persuasion, tended to despise the narrowness of provincial life (even though they often depended upon the rents they accrued there to live comfortably in the city) and found the peasant disgusting and incomprehensible. From the other end of the telescope, Paris was generally seen as a center of power, domination, and opportunity. It was both envied and hated. To the antagonism generated by the excessive centralization of power and authority in Paris were added all of the vaguer small town and rural antagonisms toward any large city as a center of privilege, material success, moral decadence, vice, and social unrest. What was special in France was the way in which the tensions emanating from the "urban-rural contradiction" were so intensely focused upon the relation between Paris and the rest of France.

Under the Second Empire these tensions sharpened considerably. Paris experienced a vast economic boom as the railways made it the hub of a process of national spatial integration. The city was brought into a new relationship with an emerging global economy. Its share of an expanding French export trade increased dramatically, and its population grew rapidly, largely through a massive immigration of rural laborers. Concentration of wealth and power proceeded apace as Paris became the center of financial, speculative, and commercial operations. The contrasts between Parisian wealth and dynamism and, with a few exceptions (such as Marseille, Lyon, Bordeaux, and Mulhouse), provincial lethargy and backwardness became more and more marked. Furthermore, the contrasts between affluence and poverty within the city became ever more startling and were increasingly expressed in terms of a geographical segregation between the affluent bourgeois quarters of the west and the working-class quarters of the north, east, and south. Belleville became a foreign territory into which the bourgeois citizens of the west rarely dared to venture. The population of that place, which more than doubled between 1853 and 1870, was pictured in the bourgeois press in the most denigrating and fearful of terms. As economic growth slowed in the 1860s and as the authority of Empire began to fail, Paris became a cauldron of social unrest, vulnerable to agitators of any stripe. And to top it all, Haussmann, as we have seen, had embellished Paris with spacious boulevards, parks, and gardens, monumental architecture of all sorts. He had done this at immense cost and by the slipperiest of financial means, a feat that scarcely recommended itself to the frugal provincial mind. The image of public opulence that Haussmann projected was matched by the conspicuous consumption of the bourgeoisie, many of whom had grown rich speculating on the benefits of Haussmann's state-financed improvements.

Small wonder, then, that provincial and rural Catholics were in no frame of mind to dig into their pockets to embellish Paris with yet another monument, no matter how pious its purpose. But there were even more specific objections that emerged in response to Legentil's proposal. The Parisians had with their customary presumptuousness proclaimed a republic when provincial and rural sentiment was heavily infused with monarchism. Furthermore, those who had remained behind to face the rigors of the siege were showing themselves remarkably intransigent and bellicose, declaring they would favor a fight to the bitter end, when provincial sentiment showed a strong disposition to end the conflict with Prussia. And then the rumors and hints of a new materialist politics among the working class in Paris, spiced with a variety of manifestations of revolutionary fervor, gave the impression that the city had, in the absence of its more respectable bourgeois citizenry, fallen prey to radical and even socialist philosophy. Since the only means of communication between a besieged Paris and the nonoccupied territories was pigeon or balloon, abundant opportunities arose for misunderstanding, which the rural foes of republicanism and the urban foes of monarchism were not beyond exploiting.

Legentil therefore found it politic to drop any specific mention of Paris in his vow. But toward the end of February 1871 the Pope endorsed it, and from then on, the movement gathered some strength. And so on March 19, a pamphlet appeared that set out the arguments for the vow at some length.[4] The spirit of the work had to be national, the authors urged, because the French people had to make national amends for what were national crimes. They confirmed their intention to build the monument in Paris. To the objection that the city should not be further embellished, they replied, "Were Paris reduced to cinders, we would still want to avow our national faults and to proclaim the justice of God on its ruins."

FIGURE 107 *The fires that raged in Paris during the closing days of the Commune left behind an enormous train of destruction. Among the many photos available (mostly anonymous), we find one of the Rue Royale with the fires still smoldering. Many of the major public buildings, such as the Hotel de Ville, the Ministry of Finance, and the Palace of the Tuileries were reduced to ruins. The palace was eventually torn down by the Republican administration that came to power in the 1880s, in part because of the cost to rebuild it, but also because it was a hated symbol of royal and Napoleonic power.*

The timing and phrasing of the pamphlet proved fortuitously prophetic. On March 18, Parisians had taken their first irrevocable steps toward establishing self-government under the Commune. The real or imagined sins of the Communards were subsequently to shock and outrage bourgeois and, even more vociferously, provincial opinion. And since much of Paris was indeed reduced to cinders in the course of a civil war of incredible ferocity, the notion of building a basilica of expiation upon these ashes became more and more appealing. As Rohault de Fleury noted, with evident satisfaction, "In the months to come, the image of Paris reduced to cinders struck home many times."[5] Let us rehearse a little of that history.

The origins of the Paris Commune lie in a series of events that ran into each other in complex ways. Precisely because of its political importance within the country, Paris had long been denied any representative form of municipal government and had been directly administered by the national government. For much of the nineteenth century, a predominantly republican Paris was chafing under the rule of monarchists (either Bourbon "legitimists" or "Orléanists") or authoritarian Bonapartists. The demand for a democratic form of municipal government, often referred to by all parties, as we have seen, as a "commune," was long-standing and commanded widespread support within the city.

The Government of National Defense set up on September 4, 1870, was neither radical nor revolutionary, but it was republican.[6] It also turned out to be timid and inept. It labored under certain difficulties, of course, but these were hardly sufficient to excuse its weak performance. It did not, for example, command the respect of the monarchists and lived in perpetual fear of the reactionaries of the right. When the Army of the East, under General Bazaine, capitulated to the Prussians at Metz on October 27, the general left the impression that he did so because, being monarchist, he could not bring himself to fight for a republican government. Some of his officers who resisted the capitulation saw Bazaine putting his political preferences above the honor of France. This was a matter that was to dog French politics for several years. Rossel, who was later to command the armed forces of the Commune for a while (and who was to be arbitrarily sentenced to death and executed for so doing), was one of the officers shocked to the core by Bazaine's evident lack of patriotism.[7]

But the tensions between the different factions of the ruling class were nothing compared to the real or imagined antagonisms between a traditional and remarkably obdurate bourgeoisie and a working class that was beginning to find its feet and assert itself. Rightly or wrongly, the bourgeoisie was greatly alarmed during the 1860s by the emergence of working-class organization and political clubs, by the activities of the Paris branch of the International Working Men's Association, by the effervescence of thought within the working class and the reemergence of anarchist and socialist philosophies. And the working class—although by no means as well organized or as unified as its opponents feared—was certainly displaying abundant signs of an emergent class consciousness.

The Government of National Defense could not stem the tide of Prussian victories or break the siege of Paris without widespread working-class support. And the leaders of the left were only too willing to give it in spite of their initial opposition to the Emperor's war. Blanqui promised the government "energetic and absolute support," and even the International's leaders, having dutifully appealed to the German workers not to participate in a fratricidal struggle, plunged into organizing for the defense of Paris. Belleville, the center of working-class agitation, rallied spectacularly to the national cause, all in the name of the Republic.[8]

The bourgeoisie sensed a trap. They saw themselves, wrote a contemporary commentator drawn from their ranks, caught between the Prussians and those whom they called "the reds." "I do not know," he went on, "which of these two evils terrified them most; they hated the foreigner but they feared the Bellevillois much more."[9] No matter how much they wanted to defeat the foreigner, they could not bring themselves to do so with the battalions of the working class in the vanguard. For what was not to be the last time in French history, the bourgeoisie chose to capitulate to the Germans, leaving the left as the dominant force within a patriotic front. In 1871, fear of the "enemy within" was to prevail over national pride.

The failure of the French to break the siege of Paris was first interpreted as the product of Prussian superiority and French military ineptitude. But as sortie after sortie promised victory, only to be turned into disaster, honest patriots began to wonder if the powers that be were not playing tricks that bordered on betrayal and treason. The government was increasingly viewed as a "Government of National Defection"—a phrase Marx was later to use with crushing effect in his passionate defense of the Commune.[10] The government was equally reluctant to respond to the Parisian demand for municipal democracy. Since many of the respectable bourgeois had fled, it looked as if elections would deliver municipal power into the hands of the left. Given the suspicions of the monarchists of the right, the Government of National Defense felt it could not afford to concede what had long been demanded. And so it procrastinated endlessly.

As early as October 31, these various threads came together to generate an insurrectionary movement in Paris. Shortly after Bazaine's ignominious surrender, word got out that the government was negotiating the terms of an armistice with the Prussians. The population of Paris took to the streets and, as the feared Bellevillois descended en masse, took several members of the government prisoner, agreeing to release them only on the verbal assurance that there would be municipal elections and no capitulation. This incident was guaranteed to raise the hackles of the right. It was the immediate cause of the "hateful sentiments towards Paris" that Legentil encountered in December. The government lived to fight another day. But, as events turned out, they were to fight much more effectively against the Bellevillois than they ever fought against the Prussians.

So the siege of Paris dragged on. Worsening conditions in the city now added their uncertain effects to a socially unstable situation.[11] The government proved inept and insensitive to the needs of the population, and thereby added fuel to the smoldering fires of discontent. The people lived off cats or dogs, while the more privileged partook of pieces of Pollux, the young elephant from the zoo (forty francs a pound for the trunk).

The price of rats—the "taste is a cross between pork and partridge"—rose from sixty centimes to four francs apiece. The government failed to take the elementary precaution of rationing bread until January, when it was much too late. Supplies dwindled, and the adulteration of bread with bone meal became a chronic problem which was made even less palatable by the fact that it was human bones from the catacombs which were being dredged up for the occasion. While the common people were thus consuming their ancestors without knowing it, the luxuries of café life were kept going, supplied by hoarding merchants at exorbitant prices. The rich who stayed behind continued to indulge their pleasures according to their custom, although they paid dearly for it. In callous disregard for the feelings of the less privileged, the government did nothing to curb profiteering or the continuation of conspicuous consumption by the rich.

By the end of December, radical opposition to the Government of National Defense was growing. It led to the publication of the celebrated Affiche Rouge of January 7. Signed by the central committee of the twenty Parisian *arrondissements*, it accused the

FIGURE 108 *The cartoonist Cham joined with an aging Daumier to try and extract some humor from the desolate months of the 1870 siege of Paris. Here we see Parisians queuing for their nightly share of rat meat; Cham also advises his viewers to take care, when eating mouse, that the cat does not give pursuit.*

FIGURE 109 *Thiers had been a frequent subject for Daumier ever since the 1840s. His sudden reappearance on the political stage in 1870 provided another chance for critical comment. In the figure to the left (published on February 24, 1871), Thiers is seen orchestrating the newly elected National Assembly in Bordeaux (but "one can't see the prompter"), and on the right (published on April 21, after the Commune has been declared) we see Thiers frenetically whipping on his horses, harnessed to the coach of state, in the direction of Versailles. Paris, depicted in the statuesque figure of Liberty, is left with horses straining in the opposite direction, but with head turned disapprovingly towards thiers. The breakup of the state is ominously foretold.*

government of leading the country to the edge of an abyss by its indecision, inertia, and foot-dragging; suggested that the government knew not how to administer or to fight; and insisted that the perpetuation of such a regime could end only in capitulation to the Prussians. It proclaimed a program for a general requisition of resources, rationing, and mass attack. It closed with the celebrated appeal "Make way for the people! Make way for the Commune!"[12] Placarded all over Paris, the appeal had its effect. The military responded decisively and organized one last mass sortie, which was spectacular for its military ineptitude and the carnage left behind. "Everyone understood," wrote Lissagaray, "that they had been sent out to be sacrificed."[13] The evidence of treason and betrayal was by now overwhelming for those close to the action. It pushed many an honest patriot from the bourgeoisie, who put love of country above class interest, into an alliance with the dissident radicals and the working class.

Parisians accepted the inevitable armistice at the end of January with sullen passivity. It provided for national elections to a constituent assembly that would negotiate and ratify a peace agreement. It specified that the French army would lay down its arms, but permitted the National Guard of Paris, which could not easily be disarmed, to remain a fighting force. Supplies came into a starving city under the watchful eyes of the Prussian troops. Most of the remaining bourgeoisie fled to their rural retreats, while the influx of impoverished, unpaid, and demoralized soldiers into the city added to the social and political stresses there. In the February elections, the city returned its quota of radical republicans (Louis Blanc, Hugo, Gambetta, and even Garibaldi). But rural and provincial France voted solidly for peace. Since the left was antagonistic to capitulation, the republicans from the Government of National Defense were seriously compromised by their management of the war, and the Bonapartists were discredited, the peace vote went to the monarchists. Republican Paris was appalled to find itself faced with a monarchist majority in the National Assembly. Thiers, by then seventy-three years old, was elected President in part because of his long experience in politics and in part because the monarchists did not want to be responsible for signing what was bound to be an ignoble peace agreement.

Thiers signed a preliminary peace agreement on February 26 (rather too close to the anniversary of the February Revolution of 1848 for comfort). He ceded Alsace and Lorraine to Germany. Worse still, in Parisians eyes, he agreed to the symbolic occupation of Paris by the Prussian troops on March 1, which could easily have become a bloodbath since many in Paris threatened an armed fight. Only the organizational power of the left (who understood that the Prussians would destroy them, and thus do Thiers's work for him) and a shadowy new group called the Central Committee of the National Guard prevented a debacle. The Prussians paraded down the Champs Elysée, watched in stony silence by the crowds, with all the major monuments shrouded in black crepe. The humiliation was not easy to forgive, and Thiers was held partly to blame. Thiers also agreed to a huge war indemnity. He was enough of a patriot on this point to resist Bismarck's suggestion that Prussian bankers float the loan required. Thiers reserved that privilege for the French, and turned this year of troubles into one of the most profitable ones ever for the gentlemen of French high finance.[14] The latter informed Thiers that if he was to raise the money, he must first deal with "those rascals in Paris." This he was uniquely equipped to do. As Minister of the Interior under Louis Philippe, he had, in 1834, been responsible for the savage repression of one of the first genuine working-class movements in French history. Ever contemptuous of "the vile multitude," he had long had a plan for dealing with them—a plan he had proposed to Louis Philippe in 1848 and which he was now finally in a position to put into effect. He would use the conservatism of the country to smash the radicalism of the city.

On the morning of March 18, the population of Paris awoke to find that the remains of the French army had been sent to Paris to relieve that city of its cannons, obviously a first step toward the disarmament of a populace which had, since September 4, joined the National Guard in massive numbers. The populace of working-class Paris set out spontaneously to reclaim the cannons as their own (had they not, after all, forged them out of metals they had collected during the siege?). On the hill of Montmartre, weary French soldiers stood guard over the powerful battery of cannons assembled there, facing an increasingly restive and angry crowd. General Lecomte ordered his troops to fire. He ordered once, twice, thrice. The soldiers had not the heart to do it, raised their rifle butts in the air, and fraternized joyfully with the crowd. An infuriated mob took General Lecomte prisoner. They stumbled across General Thomas, remembered and hated for his role in the savage killings of the June Days of 1848. The two generals were taken to the garden of no. 6, Rue des Rosiers and, amid considerable confusion and angry argument, put up against a wall and shot.

This incident is of crucial importance. The conservatives now had their martyrs. Thiers could brand the insubordinate population of Paris as murderers and assassins. The hilltop of Montmartre had been a place of martyrdom for Christian saints long before.

FIGURE 110 *The cannons of Montmartre, depicted in this remarkable photo, were mainly created in the Parisian workshops during the siege out of melted-down materials contributed by the populace. They were the flash point of contention that sparked the break between Paris and Versailles.*

Conservative Catholics could now add the names of Lecomte and Clément Thomas to that list. In the months and years to come, as the struggle to build the Basilica of Sacré-Coeur unfolded, frequent appeal was to be made to the need to commemorate these "martyrs of yesterday who died in order to defend and save Christian society."[15] The phrase was actually used in the official legislation passed by the National Assembly in 1873 in support of the building of the basilica. On that sixteenth day of June in 1875 when the foundation stone was laid, Rohault de Fleury rejoiced that the basilica was to be built on a site which, "after having been such a saintly place had become, it would seem, the place chosen by Satan and where was accomplished the first act of that horrible saturnalia which caused so much ruination and which gave the church two such glorious martyrs." "Yes," he continued, "it is here where Sacré-Coeur will be raised up that the Commune began, here where generals Clément Thomas and Lecomte were assassinated." He rejoiced in the "multitude of good Christians who now stood adoring a God who knows only too well how to confound the evil-minded, cast down their designs and to place a cradle where they thought to dig a grave." He contrasted this multitude of the faithful with a "hillside, lined with intoxicated demons, inhabited by a population apparently hostile to all religious ideas and animated, above all, by a hatred of the Church."[16] GALLIA POENITENS.

Thiers's response to the events of March 18 was to order a complete withdrawal of military and government personnel from Paris. From the safe distance of Versailles, he prepared methodically for the invasion and reduction of Paris. Bismarck proved not at all reluctant to allow the reconstitution of a French army sufficient to the task of putting down the radicals in Paris, and released prisoners and material for that purpose. But, just in case, he kept large numbers of Prussian troops stationed around the city. They were to be silent witnesses to the events that followed.

Left to their own devices, and somewhat surprised by the turn of events, the Parisians, under the leadership of the Central Committee of the National Guard, not only took over all the abandoned administrative apparatus and set it running again with remarkable speed and efficiency (even the theaters reopened), but they also arranged for elections on March 26. The Commune was declared a political fact on March 28.[17] It was a day of joyous celebration for the common people of Paris and a day of consternation for the bourgeoisie. But the politics of the Commune were hardly coherent. While a substantial number of workers took their places as elected representatives of the people for the first time in French history, the Commune was still dominated by radical elements from the bourgeoisie. Composed as it was of diverse political currents shading from middle-of-the-road republican through the Jacobins, the Proudhonists, the socialists of the International, and the Blanquist revolutionaries, there was a good deal of factionalism and plenty of contentious argumentation as to what radical or socialist path to take. It was riddled with nostalgia for what might have been, yet in some respects pointed toward a more egalitarian modernist future in which principles of association and of socially organized administration and production could be actively explored. Much of this proved moot, however, since whatever pretensions to modernity the Communards may have had were about to be overwhelmed by a tidal wave of reactionary conservativism. Thiers attacked in early April, and the second siege of Paris began. Rural and provincial France was being put to work to destroy working-class Paris.

What followed was disastrous for the Commune. When the Versailles forces finally broke through the outer defense of Paris—which Thiers had had constructed in the 1840s—they swept quickly through the bourgeois sections of western Paris and cut slowly and ruthlessly down the grand boulevards that Haussmann had constructed into the working-class quarters of the city. Barricades were everywhere, but the military was prepared to deploy cannons to blast them apart and incendiary shells to destroy buildings that housed hostile forces. So began one of the most vicious bloodlettings in an often bloody French history. The Versailles forces gave no quarter. To the deaths in the street fighting—which were not, by most accounts, very extensive—were added an incredible number of arbitrary executions without judgment. Moilin was put to death for his socialist utopian views; a republican deputy and critic of the Commune, Millière, was put to death (after being forced to his knees on the steps of the Pantheon and told to beg forgiveness for his sins—for the first time in his life he cried, "Vive la Commune" instead)

FIGURE 111 *Barricade of the Communards on the Rue d'Allemagne, March 1871.*

FIGURE 112 *Some three hundred of the last Communards captured at the end of the "bloody week" of May 1871 were arbitrarily shot at the Mur des Fedérés in Père Lachaise cemetery, turning the wall into a place of pilgrimage for decades to come. Gouache by Alfred Darjon.*

because an army captain happened not to like his newspaper articles. The Luxembourg Gardens, the barracks at Lobau, the celebrated and still venerated wall in the cemetery of Père Lachaise, echoed ceaselessly to the sound of gunfire as the executioners went to work. Between twenty and thirty thousand communards died thus. GALLIA POENITENS—with vengeance.

Out of this sad history there is one incident that commands our attention. On the morning of May 28, an exhausted Eugène Varlin—bookbinder; union and food cooperative organizer under the Second Empire; member of the National Guard; intelligent, respected, and scrupulously honest, committed socialist; member of the Commune and brave soldier—was recognized and arrested. He was taken to that same house on Rue des Rosiers where Lecomte and Clément Thomas died. Varlin's fate was worse. Sentenced to die, he was paraded around the hillside of Montmartre, some say for ten minutes and others for hours, abused, beaten, and humiliated by a fickle mob. He was finally propped up against a wall (his face already smashed in and one eye out of its socket) and shot. He was just thirty-two years old. They

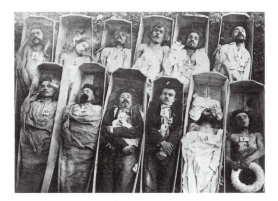

FIGURE 113 *Communards shot by the Versailles forces (photo attributed to Disdéri). Someone has placed a white wreath in the hands of the young woman at the bottom right (a symbol of Liberty, once again about to be interred?).*

had to shoot twice to kill him. In between fusillades he cried, evidently unrepentant, "Vive la Commune!" His biographer called it "the Calvary of Eugène Varlin." The left can have its martyrs, too. And it is on that spot that Sacré-Coeur is built.[18]

The "bloody week," as it was called, also involved an enormous destruction of property. The Communards, to be sure, were not enamored of the privileges of private property and were not averse to destroying hated symbols. The Vendôme Column—which Napoleon III had doted upon—was toppled in a grand ceremony on the May 16 to symbolize the end of authoritarian rule. The painter Courbet was later held responsible for this act, and condemned to pay for the reconstruction of the monument out of his own pocket. The Communards also decreed, but never carried out, the destruction of the Chapel of Expiation, by which Louis XVIII had sought to impress upon Parisians their guilt in executing his brother. And when Thiers had shown his true colors, the Communards took a certain delight in dismantling his Parisian residence, stone by stone, in a symbolic gesture that Goncourt felt had an "excellent bad effect." But the wholesale burning of Paris was another matter entirely. To the buildings set afire in the course of the bombardment were added those deliberately fired for strategic reasons by the retreating Communards. From this arose the myth of the "incendiaries" of the Commune who recklessly took revenge, it was said, by burning everything they could. The false myth of the hideous woman *petroleuse* was circulated by the Versailles press, and women under suspicion were arbitrarily shot on the spot. A bourgeois diarist, Audéoud, complacently recorded how he denounced a well-dressed woman in the Rue Blanche as a *petroleuse* because she was carrying two bottles (filled with what we will never know). When she pushed a lunging and rather drunken soldier away, the soldier shot her in the back.[19]

FIGURE 114 *The toppling of the Vendôme Column, here depicted by Meaulle and Viers, created a lot of interest, illustrating how buildings and monuments were deeply political symbols to Parisians.*

No matter what the truth of the matter, the myth of the incendiaries was strong. Within a year, the Pope describing the Communards as "devils risen up from hell bringing the fires of the inferno to the streets of Paris." The ashes of the city became a symbol of the Commune's crimes against the church and were to fertilize the soil from which the energy to build Sacré-Coeur was to spring. No wonder that Hubert Rohault de Fleury congratulated himself upon that felicitous choice of words—"were Paris to be reduced to cinders." That phrase could strike home with redoubled force, he noted, "as the incendiaries of the Commune came to terrorize the world."[20]

The aftermath of the Commune was anything but pleasant. Bodies littered the streets and the stench became unbearable. To take just one example, the three hundred or so bodies unceremoniously dumped into the lake in Haussmann's beautiful new park at Buttes Chaumont (once a site for hanging petty criminals and later a municipal dump) had to be dragged out after they surfaced, horribly bloated, several days later; they were burned in a funeral pyre that lasted for days. Audéoud delighted in the sight of all the bodies "riddled with bullets, befouled and rotting," and took "the stink of their corpses" as "an odor of peace, and if the all-too sensitive nostril revolts, the soul rejoices." "We, too," he went on, "have become cruel and pitiless and we should find it a pleasure to bathe and wash our hands in their blood." But the bloodletting began to turn the stomachs of many within the bourgeoisie until all but the most sadistic of them had to cry "Stop!" The celebrated diarist Edmond de Goncourt tried to convince himself of the justice of it all when he wrote: "It is good that there was neither conciliation nor bargain. The solution was brutal. It was by pure force. The solution has held people back from cowardly compromises . . . the bloodletting was a bleeding white; such a purge, by killing off the combative part of the population defers the next revolution by a whole generation. The old society has twenty years of quiet ahead of it, if the powers that be dare all that they may dare at this time."[21] These sentiments were exactly those of Thiers. But when de Goncourt later passed through Belleville and saw the "faces of ugly silence," he could not help but feel that here was a "vanquished but unsubjugated district." Was there no other way to purge the threat of revolution?

The experience of 1870–1871, taken together with the confrontation between Napoleon III and the decadent "festive materialism" of the Second Empire, plunged Catholics into a phase of widespread soul-searching. The majority of them accepted the notion that France had sinned, and this gave rise to manifestations of expiation and a movement of piety that was both mystical and spectacular. The intransigent and ultramontane Catholics unquestionably favored a return to law and order and a political solution founded on respect for authority. And it was the monarchists, generally themselves intransigent Catholics, who held out the promise for law and order. Liberal Catholics found all of this disturbing, but they were in no position to mobilize their forces since even the Pope dismissed them as the "veritable scourge" of France. There was little to stop the consolidation of the bond between monarchism and intransigent Catholicism. And it was this powerful alliance that was to guarantee the building of Sacré-Coeur.

The immediate problem for the progenitors of the vow was, however, to operationalize a pious wish. This required official action. Legentil and Rohault de Fleury sought the support of the newly appointed Archbishop of Paris. Monseigneur Guibert, a compatriot of Thiers from Tours, had required some persuading to take the position in Paris. The three previous archbishops had suffered violent deaths: the first during the insurrection of 1848, the second by the hand of an assassin in 1863, and the third during the Commune. The Communards had early decided to take hostages in response to the butchery promised by Versailles. The Archbishop was held as a prime hostage for whom

FIGURE 115 *This view, from the hilltop of Montmartre, of Paris burning in the final days of the Commune captures something of what Rohault de Fleury had in mind when he commented on how fortuitously appropriate it had been to make the vow to build Sacré-Coeur even if "Paris were reduced to ashes."*

the Communards sought the exchange of Blanqui. Thiers refused that negotiation, apparently having decided that a dead and martyred Archbishop (who was a liberal Catholic in any case) was more valuable to him than a live one exchanged for a dynamic and aggressive Blanqui. During "the bloody week," certain segments among the Communards took whatever vengeance they could. On May 24, with the Versaille forces hacking their way into Paris in the bloodiest and most brutal fashion, executing anyone they suspected of having played an active role in the Commune, the Archbishop was shot. In that final week, seventy-four hostages were shot, of whom twenty-four were priests. That awesome anticlericalism was as alive under the Commune as it had been in 1789. But with the massive purge that left more than twenty thousand Communards dead, nearly forty thousand imprisoned, and countless others in flight, Thiers could write reassuringly on June 14 to Monsignor Guibert: "The 'reds,' totally vanquished, will not recommence their activities tomorrow; one does not engage twice in fifty years in such an immense fight as they have just lost."[32] Reassured, Monsignor Guibert came to Paris.

FIGURE 116 *Remorse and revulsion for what happened in the Commune were initially confined to republicans of a social democratic persuasion. Manet (top) was deeply moved by the events, and drew several representations mourning the deaths on the barricades. Daumier (bottom), in one of his last drawings, commented sadly and poignantly on "when workers fight each other."*

The new Archbishop was much impressed with the movement to build a monument to the Sacred Heart. On January 18, 1872, he formally accepted responsibility for the undertaking. He wrote to Legentil and Rohault de Fleury thus:

> You have considered from their true perspective the ills of our country. . . . The conspiracy against God and Christ has prevailed in a multitude of hearts and in punishment for an almost universal apostasy, society has been subjected to all the horrors of war with a victorious foreigner and an even more horrible war amongst the children of the same country. Having become, by our prevarication, rebels against heaven, we have fallen during our troubles into the abyss of anarchy. The land of France presents the terrifying image of a place where no order prevails, while the future offers still more terrors to come. . . . This temple, erected as a public act of contrition and reparation . . . will stand amongst us as a protest against other monuments and works of art erected for the glorification of vice and impiety.[23]

By July 1872, the ultraconservative Pope Pius IX, still awaiting his deliverance from captivity in the Vatican, formally endorsed the vow. An immense propaganda campaign unfolded, and the movement gathered momentum. By the end of the year, more than a million francs were promised, and all that remained was to translate the vow into its material, physical representation.

The first step was to choose a site. Legentil wanted to use the foundations of the still-to-be-completed Opera House, which he considered "a scandalous monument of extravagance, indecency and bad taste."[24] The initial restrained design of that building by Charles Rohault de Fleury (no relation of Hubert) had, in 1860, been dropped at the insistence of Count Walewski ("who had the dubious distinction of being the illegitimate son of Napoleon and the husband of Napoleon III's current favorite"[25]). The design that replaced it, by Garnier (which exists today), most definitely qualified in the eyes of Legentil as a "monument to vice and impiety," and nothing could be more appropriate than to efface the memory of Empire by constructing the basilica on that spot. This would have meant, of course, tearing down the façade that had been completed in 1867. It probably escaped Legentil's attention that the Communards had, in the same spirit, toppled the Vendôme Column.

By late October 1872, however, the Archbishop had taken matters into his own hands and selected the heights of Montmartre because it was only from there that the symbolic domination of Paris could be assured. Since the land on that site was in part public property, the consent or active support of the government was necessary if it was to be acquired. The government was considering the construction of a military fortress on that spot. The Archbishop pointed out, however, that a military fortress could well be very unpopular, while a fortification of the sort he was proposing might be less offensive and more sure. Thiers and his ministers, apparently persuaded that ideological protection might be preferable to military, encouraged the Archbishop to pursue the matter formally. This the latter did in a letter of March 5, 1873. He requested that the government pass a special law declaring the construction of the basilica a work of public utility. This would permit the laws of expropriation to be used to procure the site.

Such a law ran counter to a long-standing sentiment in favor of the separation of church and state. Yet conservative Catholic sentiment for the project was very strong. Thiers procrastinated, but his indecision was shortly rendered moot. The monarchists had decided that their time had come. On May 24, 1873, they drove Thiers from power and replaced him with the archconservative royalist Marshal MacMahon, who just two years before, had led the armed forces of Versailles in the bloody repression of the Commune. France was plunged, once more, into political ferment; a monarchist restoration seemed imminent.

The MacMahon government quickly reported out the law, which then became part of its program to establish the rule of moral order in which those of wealth and privilege—who therefore had an active stake in the preservation of society—would, under the leadership of the king and in alliance with the authority of the church, have both the right and the duty to protect France from the social perils to which it had recently been exposed, thereby preventing the country from falling into the abyss of anarchy. Large-scale demonstrations were mobilized by the church as part of a campaign to reestablish some sense of moral order. The largest of these demonstrations took place on June 29, 1873, at Paray-le-Monial. Thirty thousand pilgrims, including fifty members of the National Assembly, journeyed there to dedicate themselves publicly to the Sacred Heart.[26]

It was in this atmosphere that the committee formed to report on the law presented its findings on July 11 to the National Assembly; a quarter of the committee members were adherents to the vow. The committee found that the proposal to build a basilica of expiation was unquestionably a work of public utility. It was right and proper to build such a monument on the heights of Montmartre for all to see, because it was there that the blood of martyrs—including those of yesterday—had flowed. It was necessary "to efface by this work of expiation, the crimes which have crowned our sorrows," and France, "which has suffered so much," must "call upon the protection and grace of Him who gives according to His will, defeat or victory."[27]

The debate that followed on July 22 and 23 in part revolved around technical-legal questions and the implications of the legislation for state-church relations. The intransigent Catholics recklessly proposed to go much further. They wanted the Assembly to commit itself formally to a national undertaking that "was not solely a protestation against taking up of arms by the Commune, but a sign of appeasement and concord." That amendment was rejected, but the law passed with a handsome majority of 244 votes. A lone dissenting voice in the debate came from a radical republican deputy from Paris:

> When you think to establish on the commanding heights of Paris—the fount of free thought and revolution—a Catholic monument, what is in your thoughts? To make of it the triumph of the Church over revolution. Yes, that is what you want to extinguish—what you call the pestilence of revolution. What you want to revive is the Catholic faith, for you are at war with

the spirit of modern times. . . . Well, I who know the sentiments of the population of Paris, I who am tainted by the revolutionary pestilence like them, I tell you that the population will be more scandalized than edified by the ostentation of your faith. . . . Far from edifying us, you push us towards free thought, towards revolution. When people see these manifestations of the partisans of monarchy, of the enemies of the Revolution, they will say to themselves that Catholicism and monarchy are unified, and in rejecting one they will reject the other.[28]

Armed with a law that yielded powers of expropriation, the committee formed to push the project through to fruition acquired the site atop Butte Montmartre. They collected the moneys promised and set about soliciting more so that the building could be as grand as the thought that lay behind it. A competition for the design of the basilica was set and judged. The building had to be imposing, consistent with Christian tradition, yet quite distinct from the "monuments to vice and impiety" built in the course of the Second Empire. Out of the seventy-eight designs submitted and exhibited to the public, that of the architect Abadie was selected. The choice was controversial. Accusations of too much insider influence quickly surfaced, and conservative Catholics were distressed at what they saw as the "orientalism" of the design. Why could it not be more authentically French, they asked (which at that time meant true to the Gothic traditions of the thirteenth century, even as rationalized by Viollet-le-Duc)? But the grandeur of Abadie's domes, the purity of the white marble, and the unadorned simplicity of its detail impressed the committee—what, after all, could be more different from the flamboyance of that awful Opera House?[29]

By the spring of 1875, all was ready for putting the first stone in place. But radical and republican Paris, apparently, was not yet repentant enough. The Archbishop complained that the building of Sacré-Coeur was being treated as a provocative act, as an attempt to inter the principles of 1789. And while, he said, he would not pray to revive those principles if they happened to become dead and buried, this view of things was giving rise to a deplorable polemic in which the Archbishop found himself forced to participate. He issued a circular in which he expressed his astonishment at the hostility expressed toward the project on the part of "the enemies of religion." He found it intolerable that people dared to put a political interpretation upon thoughts derived only out of faith and piety. Politics, he assured his readers, "had been far, far from our inspirations; the work had been inspired, on the contrary, by a profound conviction that politics was powerless to deal with the ills of the country. The causes of these ills are moral and religious and the remedies must be of the same order." Besides, he went on, the work could not be construed as political because the aim of politics is to divide, "while our work has for its goal the union of all. Social pacification is the end point of the work we are seeking to realize."[30]

The government, now clearly on the defensive, grew extremely nervous at the prospect of a grand opening ceremony that could be the occasion for an ugly confrontation. It counseled caution. The committee had to find a way to lay the first stone without being too provocative. The Pope came to their aid and declared a day of dedication to the Sacred Heart for all Catholics everywhere. Behind that shelter, a much scaled-down ceremony to lay the first stone passed without incident. The construction was now underway. GALLIA POENITENS was taking shape in material, symbolic form.

The forty years between the laying of the foundation stone and the final consecration of the basilica in 1919 were often troubled ones. Technical difficulties arose in the course of putting such a large structure on a hilltop rendered unstable by years of mining for gypsum. The cost of the structure increased dramatically, and as enthusiasm for the cult of the Sacred Heart diminished somewhat, financial difficulties ensued. Abadie died in 1884, and his successors both added to and subtracted from his original design (the most notable addition was a very considerable increase in the height of the central dome). And the political controversy continued. The committee in charge of the project had early decided upon a variety of stratagems to encourage the flow of contributions. Individuals and families could purchase a stone, and the visitor to Sacré-Coeur will see the names of many such inscribed upon the stones there. Different regions and organizations were encouraged to subscribe toward the construction of particular chapels. Members of the National Assembly, the army, the clergy, and the like all pooled their efforts in this way. Each particular chapel has its own significance.

Among the chapels in the crypt, for example, is that of Jésus-Enseignant, which recalls, as Rohault de Fleury put it, "that one of the chief sins of France was the foolish invention of schooling without God."[31] Those who were on the losing side of the fierce battle to preserve the power of the church over education after 1871 put their money here. And next to that chapel, at the far end of the crypt, close to the line where the Rue des Rosiers used to run, stands the Chapel to Jésus-Ouvrier. That Catholic workers sought to contribute to the building of their own chapel was a matter for great rejoicing. It showed, wrote Legentil, the desire of workers "to protest against the fearsome impiety into which a large part of the working class is falling," as well as their determination to resist "the impious and truly infernal association which, in nearly all of Europe, makes of it its slave and victim." The reference to the International Working Men's Association is unmistakable and understandable, since it was customary in bourgeois circles at that time to attribute the Commune, quite erroneously, to the nefarious influence of that 'infernal" association. Yet, by a strange quirk of fate, which so often gives an ironic twist to history, the chapel to Jésus-Ouvrier stands almost exactly at the spot where ran the course of the "Calvary of Eugène Varlin." Thus it is that the basilica, erected on high in part to commemorate the blood of two recent martyrs of the right, unwittingly commemorates in its subterranean depths a martyr of the left.

Legentil's interpretation of all this was in fact somewhat awry. In the closing stages of the Commune, a young Catholic named Albert de Munn watched in dismay as the Communards were led away to slaughter. Shocked, he fell to wondering what "legally constituted society had done for these people," and concluded that their ills had in large measure been visited upon them through the indifference of the affluent classes. In the spring of 1872, he went into the heart of hated Belleville and set up the first of his *cercles-ouvriers*.[32] This signaled the beginnings of a new kind of Catholicism in France—one that sought through social action to attend to the material as well as the spiritual needs of the workers. It was through organizations such as this, a far cry from the intransigent, ultramontane Catholicism that ruled at the center of the movement for the Sacred Heart, that a small trickle of worker contributions began to flow toward the construction of a basilica on the hilltop of Montmartre.

The political difficulties mounted, however. France, finally armed with a republican constitution (largely because of the intransigence of the monarchists) was now in the grip of a modernization process fostered by easier communications, mass education, and industrial development. The country moved to accept the moderate form of republicanism and became bitterly disillusioned with the backward-looking monarchism that had dominated the National Assembly elected in 1871. In Paris the "unsubjugated" Bellevillois, and their neighbors in Montmartre and La Villette, began to reassert themselves rather more rapidly than Thiers had anticipated. As the demand for amnesty for the exiled Communards became stronger in these quarters, so did the hatred of the basilica rising in their midst. The agitation against the project mounted.

On August 3, 1880, the matter came before the city council in the form of a proposal—a "colossal statue of Liberty will be placed on the summit of Montmartre, in front of the church of Sacré-Coeur, on land belonging to the city of Paris." The French republicans at that time had adopted the United States as a model society, which functioned perfectly well without monarchism and other feudal trappings. As part of a campaign to drive home the point of this example, as well as to symbolize their own deep attachment to the principles of liberty, republicanism, and democracy, they were then raising funds to donate the Statue of Liberty that now stands in New York Harbor. Why not, said the authors of this proposition, efface the sight of the hated Sacré-Coeur by a monument of similar order?[33]

No matter what the claims to the contrary, they said, the basilica symbolized the intolerance and fanaticism of the right—it was an insult to civilization, antagonistic to the principles of modern times, an evocation of the past, and a stigma upon France as a whole. Parisians, seemingly bent on demonstrating their unrepentant attachment to the principles of 1789, were determined to efface what they felt was an expression of "Catholic fanaticism" by building exactly that kind of monument that the Archbishop had previously characterized as a "glorification of vice and impiety." By October 7 the city council had changed its tactics. Calling the basilica "an incessant provocation to civil war," the members decided by a vote of 61 to 3 to request the government to "rescind the law of public utility of 1873" and to use the land, which would revert to public ownership, for the construction of a work of truly national significance. Neatly sidestepping the problem of how those who had contributed to the construction of the basilica—which had hardly yet risen above its foundations—were to be indemnified, it passed along its proposal to the government. By the summer of 1882, the request was taken up in the Chamber of Deputies.

Archbishop Guibert had, once more, to take up the public defense of the work. He challenged what by now were familiar arguments against the basilica with familiar responses. He insisted that the work was not inspired by politics but by Christian and patriotic sentiments. To those who objected to the expiatory character of the work, he simply replied that no one can ever afford to regard their country as infallible. As to the appropriateness of the cult of the Sacred Heart, he felt only those within the church had the right to judge. To those who portrayed the basilica as a provocation to civil war, he replied: "Are civil wars and riots ever the product of our Christian temples? Are those who frequent our churches ever prone to excitations and revolts against the law? Do we find such people in the midst of disorders and violence which, from time to time, trouble the streets of our cities?" He went on to point out that while Napoleon had sought to build a temple of peace at Montmartre, "it is we who are building, at last, the true temple of peace."[34] He then considered the negative effects of stopping the construction. Such an action would profoundly wound Christian sentiment and prove divisive. It would surely be a bad precedent, he said (blithely ignoring the precedent set by the law of 1873 itself), if religious undertakings of this sort were to be subject to the political whims of the government of the day. And then there was the complex problem of compensation, not only for the contributors but also for the work already done. Finally, he appealed to the fact that the work was giving employment to six hundred families—to deprive "that part of Paris of such a major source of employment would be inhuman indeed."

FIGURE 117 *The Statue of Liberty in its Paris workshop before being shipped to New York.*

The Parisian representatives in the Chamber of Deputies, which by 1882 was dominated by reform-ist republicans such as Gambetta (from Belleville) and Clemenceau (from Montmartre), were not impressed by these arguments. The debate was heated and passionate. The government declared itself unalterably opposed to the law of 1873 but was equally opposed to rescinding the law, since this would entail paying out more than twelve million francs in indemnities to the church. In an effort to defuse the evident anger from the left, the minister went on to remark that by rescinding the law, the Archbishop would be relieved of the obligation to complete what was proving to be a most arduous undertaking and the church would be provided with millions of francs to pursue works of propaganda that might be "infinitely more efficacious than that to which the sponsors of the present motion are objecting."

The radical republicans were not about to regard Sacré-Coeur in the shape of a white elephant, however. Nor were they inclined to pay compensation. They were determined to do away with what they felt was an odious manifestation of pious clericalism and to put in its place a monument to liberty of thought. They put the blame for the civil war squarely on the shoulders of the monarchists and their intransigent Catholic allies. Clemenceau rose to state the radical case. He declared the law of 1873 an insult, an act of a National Assembly that had sought to impose the cult of the Sacred Heart on France because "we fought and still continue to fight for human rights, for having made the French Revolution." The law was the product of clerical reaction, "an attempt to stigmatize revolutionary France, to condemn us to ask pardon of the Church for our ceaseless struggle to prevail over it in order to establish the principles of liberty, equality and fraternity. We must," he declared, "respond to a political act by a political act." Not to do so would be to leave France under the intolerable invocation of the Sacred Heart.[35]

With impassioned oratory such as this, Clemenceau fanned the flames of anticlerical sentiment. The Chamber of Deputies voted to rescind the law of 1873 by 261 votes to 199. It appeared that the basilica, the walls of which had hardly risen above their foundations, was to come tumbling down. But it was saved by a technicality. The law was passed too late in the session to meet all the formal requirements for promulgation. The government, genuinely fearful of the costs and liabilities involved, quietly worked to prevent the reintroduction of the motion into a Chamber of Deputies that, in the next session, moved on to consider matters of much greater weight and moment. The Parisian republicans had gained a symbolic but Pyrrhic parliamentary victory. A relieved Archbishop pressed on with the work.

Yet somehow the matter would not die. In February 1897, the motion was reintroduced. Anticlerical republicanism had by then made great progress, as had the working-class movement in the form of a vigorous and growing socialist party. But the construction atop the hill had likewise progressed. The interior of the basilica had been inaugurated and opened for worship in 1891, and the great dome was well on the way to completion (the cross that surmounts it was formally blessed in 1899). Although the basilica was still viewed as a "provocation to civil war," the prospect for dismantling such a vast work was by now quite daunting. And this time it was none other than Albert de Munn who defended the basilica in the name of a Catholicism that had, by then, seen the virtue of separating its fate from that of a fading monarchist cause. The church was beginning to learn a lesson, and the cult of the Sacred Heart began to acquire a new meaning in response to a changing social situation. By 1899, a more reform-minded Pope dedicated the cult to the ideal of harmony among the races, social justice, and conciliation.[36]

But the socialist deputies were not impressed by what they saw as maneuvers of co-optation. They pressed home their case to bring down the hated symbol, even though almost complete, and even though such an act would entail indemnifying eight million subscribers to the tune of thirty million francs. But the majority in the Chamber of Deputies blanched at such a prospect. The motion was rejected by 322 to 196. This was to be the last time the building was threatened by official action. With the dome completed in 1899, attention switched to the building of the campanile, which was finally finished in 1912. By the spring of 1914, all was ready and the official consecration set for October 17. But war with Germany intervened. Only at the end of that bloody conflict was the basilica finally consecrated. A victorious France—led by the fiery oratory of Clemenceau—joyfully celebrated the consecration of a monument conceived of in the course of a losing war with Germany a generation before. GALLIA POENITENS at last brought its rewards.

Muted echoes of this tortured history can still be heard. In February 1971, for example, demonstrators pursued by police took refuge in the basilica. Firmly entrenched there, they called upon their radical comrades to join them in occupying a church "built upon the bodies of Communards in order to efface the memory of that red flag that had for too long floated over Paris." The myth of the incendiaries immediately broke loose from its ancient moorings, and an evidently panicked rector summoned the police to the basilica to prevent the conflagration. The "reds" were chased from the church amid scenes of great brutality. In commemoration of those who lost their lives in the Commune, an action artist, Pignon-Ernest, covered the steps below the basilica with shrouds bearing images of the Communard dead in the month of May. Thus was the centennial of the Paris Commune celebrated on that spot. And as a coda to that incident, a bomb exploded in the basilica in 1976, causing quite extensive damage to one of the domes. On that day, it was said, the visitor to the cemetery of Père Lachaise would have seen a single red rose on August Blanqui's grave.

Rohault de Fleury had desperately wanted to "place a cradle where [others] had thought to dig a grave." But the visitor who looks at the mausoleum-like structure that is Sacré-Coeur might well wonder what is interred there. The spirit of 1789? The sins of France? The alliance between intransigent Catholicism and reactionary monarchism? The blood of martyrs like Lecomte and Clément Thomas? Or that of Eugène Varlin and the twenty thousand or so Communards mercilessly slaughtered along with him?

The building hides its secrets in sepulchral silence. Only the living, cognizant of this history, who understand the principles of those who struggled for and against the embellishment of that spot, can truly disinter the mysteries that lie entombed there, and thereby rescue that rich experience from the deathly silence of the tomb and transform it into the noisy beginnings of the cradle.

NOTES

INTRODUCTION

1. Harsin (2002), 262 produces evidence to dispute the standard account. A recent summary of that account by Delattre (2000), 108–111 attributes it to Daniel Stern's (alias Marie d'Agoult) contemporaneous memoir, *Histoire de la Revolution de 1848*. Agulhon (1983) provides historical background to the revolution and its aftermath.
2. Flaubert, *Sentimental Education* (cited in Agulhon 1983), 39–40.
3. Guedalla, P. (1922), 163–164.
4. Exactly how Louis Napoleon came to power has been the subject of many riveting accounts, including, of course, that of Marx (1963). Agulhon (1983) is more discreet but evaluates historical opinion and the historical record with great care.
5. The most devastating evidence has been assembled by Casselle (2000). But the edited collections by Bowie (2001) and Des Cars and Pinon (1991) already strongly suggest this, and the most recent biography of Haussmann, by Carmona (2002), recognizes that Haussmann's *Mémoires* are less than reliable.
6. Janis (1986) presents Le Secq's photos of the demolitions in 1851–1852 in full, and much of Marville's photographic record is reproduced in De Thèzy (1994).
7. Cited in Hambourg (1981), 9.
8. Weeks (1999), 28 and Carmona (2002) confirm the account, which is based on Haussmann's *Mémoires*.
9. Loyer (1988), 67.
10. Steegmuller (1950), 168.
11. Flaubert (1979b), 134.
12. See accounts by Klein (1967) and Clark (1973a).
13. Baudelaire (1981), 104–107.
14. Baudelaire (1983b), 56–57.
15. Baudelaire (1981), 402–408.
16. Baudelaire (1947), 25–27.
17. Kemple (1995) provides a very interesting discussion of Marx's reliance upon and admiration for Balzac. See also Prawer (1978).
18. Daumier is discussed in Clark (1973a). A more conventional appraisal is given by Passeron (1979)

19. Schorske (1981).
20. Benjamin (1999). Among the many other compelling commentaries on this work, I find Frisby (1988), Gillock (1996), and Buck-Morss (1991) most useful for my purposes.
21. I cite Gaillard's (1977) work in particular because I am a great admirer of it and have drawn extensively upon her findings in what follows.
22. Scott (1988).
23. Rancière (1989).
24. The fullest theoretical statement is laid out in Harvey (1996). The theoretical framework that informed (but did not, I hasten to add, dictate) the form of the original Paris study (that which holds good in this version) was set out in Harvey (1982).

Chapter 1

1. Baudelaire (1965), 119–120.
2. Balzac, *History of the Thirteen* (HT), 311, 330.
3. Prendergast (1992), Marcus (1999), and Stierle (2001) are outstanding studies by literary critics that pay close attention to Balzac's understanding of urban life.
4. The first volume of the Pléiade *Collected Works* give Balzac's organization of the works as decided upon in 1845. The introductory essay is by Pierre-Georges Castex, and the chronology of publication and revisions of Balzac's works is laid out by Roger Pierrot.
5. Balzac, HT, 132.
6. Jameson (1982), 157.
7. Balzac, *The Peasantry*, 22; *The Wild Ass's Skin* (WAS), 268–269; 189.
8. Balzac, WAS, 137–138.
9. Balzac, HT, 179–184.
10. Balzac, HT, 180.
11. Balzac, HT, 82.
12. See Kemple (1995).
13. Balzac, *The Peasantry*, 38, 108; see also Scott (1985).
14. Balzac, *The Peasantry*, 215.
15. Clark's (1973b), 120–124 account of the rising hostility to Courbet's painting *Burial at Ornans* (which depicted class relations in the countryside) as it was moved from Ornans to be exhibited in Paris provides an interesting parallel. Clark comments that the Parisian bourgeois, when faced with an image that did not fit their preconceptions, were wounded and perplexed in ways they did not fully understand.
16. Balzac, *Lost Illusions* (LI), 170–182.
17. Balzac, HT, 33, 56, 151, 309–315: The Simmel (1971) reference is to his famous essay "The Metropolis and Mental Life."
18. Balzac, *César Birotteau*, 75.
19. Balzac, HT, 311, 325; see also Poulet (1959), 137.
20. Marx (1967), 151; Balzac, *Eugenie Grandet*.
21. Balzac, HT, 312–318
22. Balzac, HT, 64.
23. Balzac, *Cousin Bette* (CB), 428.
24. Balzac, *Old Goriot* (OG), 249.
25. Cited in Farrant (2001), 129.
26. Balzac, HT 309–310.
27. Balzac, HT, 312–313.
28. Balzac, HT, 318–320.

29. Balzac, HT, 321.
30. Balzac, HT, 322; on working conditions, see 318.
31. Balzac, HT, 324.
32. Balzac, HT, 325.
33. Balzac, HT, 318.
34. Balzac, HT, 31, 34, 181.
35. Balzac, HT, 178.
36. Balzac, HT, 112.
37. Balzac, HT, 34, 87, 128.
38. This contrast between ranging over space and being trapped in place is an important theme both economically and politically in this period. I shall later argue that the Commune (a revolution in a place) was largely destroyed by the superior capacity of the forces of reaction to command space, and to mobilize the rest of France to crush the revolutionary movement in Paris. This was also, as was noted in the introduction, a tactic that Thiers may have urged on Louis Philippe in February 1848.
39. Marcus (1999), 74.
40. Balzac, HT, 31.
41. This point is made strongly in Dargan (1985), Farrant (2001), and Stierle (2001).
42. The passages here are from Balzac, OG, 27–33.
43. Marcus (1999).
44. Balzac, HT, 366.
45. Balzac, HT, 305.
46. Balzac, *The Unknown Masterpiece.*
47. Balzac, *Cousin Pons* (CP), 148.
48. Benjamin (1999), 19.
49. Balzac, HT, 382
50. Poulet (1959), 106.
51. Balzac, HT.
52. Cited in L. Marx (1964), 164.
53. K. Marx (1973), 539; see also Harvey (1989), part III.
54. Balzac, *The Quest of the Absolute*, 173–174.
55. Balzac, WAS, 53–54.
56. Balzac, WAS, 198–199.
57. Quoted in Poulet (1959), 103–105.
58. Quoted in Poulet (1959), 99–100.
59. Balzac, HT, 32–33, 324.
60. Balzac, HT, 147.
61. Balzac, OG, 304.
62. Quoted in Poulet (1959), 126.
63. Balzac, *Colonel Chabert.*
64. Boyer (1994), 187–197; 372–379—I find Boyer's work very illuminating on many aspects of the problem of urban memory.
65. K. Marx (1963), 18.
66. This distinction is highlighted in Halbwachs (1992), Boyer (1994), and Benjamin (1968), particularly his "Theses on the Philosophy of History." The quotes that follow are from Benjamin and Boyer.
67. Balzac, HT.
68. Rossi (1982), 130.
69. Ferguson (1994) makes this point convincingly.
70. K. Marx (1967), chapter 1, does a famous job of dissecting the fetishism of commodities.

71. The figure of the flaneur in nineteenth-century Paris has exercised a peculiar fascination ever since Baudelaire highlighted it. Benjamin (1999) spends a great deal of time on it. Wilson (1992) provides a useful and critical overview coupled with an outline of its history.
72. Balzac, *The Physiology of Marriage*, 123–124.
73. Jameson (1995), 226.
74. Balzac, HT, 190.
75. Poulet (1959), 110. See also Balzac, *Louis Lambert*, 246.

CHAPTER 2

1. Clark (1984), 36.
2. Kantorowicz (1957).
3. Agulhon (1981).
4. Balzac, *The Peasantry*, 183.
5. Flaubert, *Sentimental Education*, 290.
6. Foucault (1984), 241.
7. Agulhon, (1981), 57.
8. César Daly's contributions have been examined at length by Becherer (1984).
9. The texts assembled by Ionescu (1976) are very helpful, and I have made considerable use of them in what follows.
10. Hill (1975); on the role of the French historians in the 1840s, see Agulhon (1983).
11. Rose (1978) is a powerful biography of Babeuf.
12. The texts on utopian thinking assembled by Corcoran (1983) are invaluable, and I make much use of them here. The collection of reflections and analyses assembled by the Société d'Histoire de la Révolution de 1848 is also excellent. Blanqui's life and works are considered at length in Dommanget (1926, 1957, 1970). Tristan (1843, 1982) provides both historical and political insights.
13. Benjamin (1999), 736.
14. Benjamin (1999), 25–26.
15. Durkheim (1958) goes to considerable lengths to rehabilitate Saint-Simon's reputation, in the face of the claims of August Comte (who worked as a student with Saint-Simon but later broke with him) to have been the source of the original ideas that founded contemporary social theory.
16. Text in Ionescu (1976), 153.
17. Texts in Ionescu (1976), 80, and Taylor (1975), 32.
18. Text in Ionescu (1976), 210.
19. Rancière (1989), in a brilliant and controversial text, reconstructs the thoughts and motivations of a select group of worker-writers and -poets who contributed to the worker presses that began to form in the 1830s and 1840s.
20. Bakunin's (1976) life of Leroux is a key source.
21. Baguley (2000) pays considerable attention to Louis Napoleon's engagements with utopianism in the 1840s and traces some of the effects in Second Empire policies.
22. There are two useful English editions of Fourier's works, published in 1971 and 1996; the introduction to the first, by Beecher and Bienvenue, provides useful background on his life and times. Beecher (2002) has a comprehensive biography of Considérant.
23. Beecher and Bienvenue, (1971), 36.
24. Johnson (1974), 66, provides a lot of background information on the various movements and publications while concentrating strongly on Cabet and the Icarians.
25. Cited in Corcoran (1983), 113; the collection organized by the Société d'Histoire de la Révolution de 1848 is a very rich source.

26. Sewell (1980).
27. Cited in Bakunin (1976), 99.
28. Rancière (1989).
29. Cited in Valette (1981).
30. Cited in C. Moses (1984), 92.
31. Cited in C. Moses (1984), 83, 111.
32. Vincent (1984), 144–146. There are many biographies and studies of Proudhon; I have mainly used Vincent (1984) and Hyams (1979).
33. Moss (1976) provides quite a lot of information on the associations, and Agulhon (1983) also gives them passing mention. The fundamental source is Gossez (1967).
34. See Vincent (1984), 141. Some of the speeches at the communist banquet are printed in Corcoran (1983), 72–79.
35. See Corcoran (1983), 188–196.
36. See Corcoran (1983), 81–82.
37. Johnson (1974), 107.
38. Rancière (1989), xxvi. The introduction to the English translation summarizes the responses of Johnson and Sewell to Rancière's argument.
39. Beecher and Bienvenue (1971), 33–34.
40. The attack on the utopians began with *The Communist Manifesto* of 1848.
41. Piore and Sable (1984); Harvey (1989), part II.
42. Becherer (1984).
43. Quoted in Marrey (1981, 193).
44. Pinon (1991).
45. Beecher and Bienvenue (1971), 2–7.
46. Marrey (1981), 203–204.
47. See Corcoran (1983), 193.
48. Benjamin (1999), 635.
49. The figure of Perreymond has been rediscovered in recent years (along with Meynadier, Lanquentin, and, of course, César Daly). Recent sources include Marrey (1981), Papayanis (2001), Moret (2001), Roncayalo (2002), and Des Cars and Pinon (1991). There is also a brief outline of his thought in Boyer (1994).
50. Marchand (1993) pays quite a bit of attention to Meynadier's ideas.
51. Ferguson (1994) uses the contrasts between Balzac and Flaubert to great effect.
52. Ferguson (1994), 95.
53. Flaubert, *Sentimental Education* (1964), 18, 257.
54. Ferguson (1994), 99.

CHAPTER 3

1. Ferguson (1994) makes the revolutionary tradition the main focus of her account.
2. Chevalier (1973), 45.
3. Marx (1963, 1964); Agulhon (1983); Dautry (1977).
4. There are several biographical accounts of Haussmann's life in addition to his somewhat unreliable *Mémoires*. The most complete (and therefore dullest) of these are Des Cars (1978) and Carmona (English translation 2002). Lameyre (1958) is more readable. For a lively recent account in English, see Weeks (1999).
5. Van Zanten (1994), 199–23.

6. There are several excellent accounts of the transformation of Second Empire Paris, such as Girard (1952, 1981) and Gaillard (1977); in English, the standard account by Pinkney (1958) has been thoughtfully supplemented by Jardine (1995). Marchand (1993) puts Haussmann's works in a longer term perspective in a very perceptive way.

CHAPTER 4

1. Leon (1976), 241; Clout (1977).
2. Girard (1952), 111.
3. Baudelaire (1983b), 73.
4. Plessis (1973), 110.
5. Miller (1981), 37.
6. This revolution in consumption patterns was strongly articulated according to income and class positions and pretensions, as contemporary commentators like Fournel (1858, 1865) clearly noticed.
7. Retel (1977).
8. Giedion (1941) provides a laudatory appraisal and, interestingly, Robert Moses (1942) wrote a thoughtful analysis of Haussmann's contributions, methods, and shortcomings early in his career as he in many ways replicated Haussmann's achievements in New York during the 1950s and 1960s (see Caro, 1974).
9. Haussmann, (1890–1893), vol. 2, 34.
10. Girard (1952), 118.
11. Greenberg (1971); Hazareesingh (1998).
12. Haussmann (1890–1893), vol 2, 202.
13. Schivelbusch (1977).
14. Zola (1954), 76–79.

CHAPTER 5

1. Autin (1984); Bouvier (1967); Zola (1991).
2. Harvey (1982), chapter 10, is the basis for this argument.
3. Tudesq (1956).
4. Marx (1967), vol. 3, 592; (1973), 156.
5. Dupont-Ferrier (1925); Levy-Leboyer (1976).
6. Autin (1984); Plessis (1982).
7. Autin (1984), 186.
8. Miller (1981), 28.
9. Lescure (1980), 19.
10. Zola (1991), 117–118.
11. Zola (1954a), 76.
12. Plessis (1982), 81.
13. Duchêne (1869).
14. Autin (1984), 249–256.
15. Hyams (1979), 154–71; Vincent (1984).
16. Kelso (1936), 102.
17. Workers Commission of 1867, *Rapports des délégations ouvrières* (1969), vol. 1, 126.

CHAPTER 6

1. Daumard (1965), 23–35. This work more generally is a fundamental source on the propertied interest in Paris during this period. Sutcliffe (1970) also is very helpful.

2. Daumard (1965), 137.
3. Gaillard (1977), 85–120.
4. Daumard (1965), 228.
5. Gaillard (1977), 136.
6. Gaillard (1977), 110–112.
7. See Pinkney (1958), 185–187; Sutcliffe (1970); 40–41; Gaillard, (1977), 27–30. Haussmann (1890–1893), vol. 2, 310, 371, also provides a parallel account. See also Daumard (1965), 215.
8. Halbwachs (1928).
9. Massa-Gille (1973), chapter 5; Sutcliffe (1970), 117.
10. Zola (1954a), 108.
11. Gaillard (1977), 121–127 and Daumard (1965), 267.
12. Gaillard (1977), 104–15; 127–44; Lameyre (1958, 152).
13. Girard (1981), 186; Gaillard (1977), 82.
14. Sutcliffe (1970), 118.
15. Girard (1981), 173–175; Sutcliffe (1970), 158; Daumard (1965).
16. Autin, (1984), 186; Lameyre (1958), 140–142; Gaillard (1977), 92; Halbwachs (1909).
17. Gaillard (1977).
18. Sutcliffe (1970); Gaillard (1977), 85–100.

Chapter 7

1. Gramsci (1971), 212–223; Zeldin (1958, 1963). A more benign view of Louis Napoleon can be found in Baguley (2000) and Carmona (2002) which seem to be part of a revisionist trend toward much greater appreciation of his contributions than was typically the case in the past.
2. Pinkney (1958); Massa-Gille (1973); Sutcliffe (1970).
3. Ferry (1868) is the key text. See also Sutcliffe (1970), 42.
4. A. Thomas (n.d.), 65.
5. Pinkney (1958), 178; the implications of debt financing are examined in Harvey (1982), 266–270.
6. Rougerie (1965), 129–134.
7. Gaillard (1977), 224–230, 269–273, 331–334; Kulstein (1969), 100.
8. Kulstein (1969); Zeldin (1958).
9. St. John (1854), 25.
10. Clark (1973a), 121; Rifkin (1979). Fournel's (1858, 1865) accounts are very rich with detail on street life.
11. Payne (1966); A. Thomas (n.d.), 174.
12. Dalotel, Faure and, Freimuth (1980); Kulstein (1969).
13. Bellet (1967).
14. Rifkin (1979).
15. Zeldin (1958, 1963).
16. Corbon (1863), 93; Duveau (1946); Rifkin (1979); Rancière and Vauday (1988).
17. Lefebvre (1974), 370.
18. Lazare (1869, 1870).
19. This is where Marx (1963) began his inquiry.
20. Haussmann (1890–1893), vol. 2, 371.
21. Gaillard (1977), 136.
22. Haussmann (1890–1893), vol. 2, 200.
23. Gaillard (1977), 331–332.
24. Haussmann (1890–1893), vol. 2, 197–202.

Chapter 8

1. Corbon (1863); Sewell (1980).
2. Rancière (1989).
3. Chevalier (1950), 75.
4. Scott (1988), chapter 6; Sewell (1980).
5. Daumas and Payen (1976); Chevalier (1950); Gaillard (1977); Retel (1977); Scott (1988).
6. Cottereau (1980); Girard (1981), 215–216; Gaillard (1977), 390; Duveau (1946), 252–269.
7. Cottereau (1988), 121.
8. Gaillard (1977), 380–391.
9. Chevalier (1950), 96; Gaillard (1977), 443.
10. Duchêne (1869).
11. Plessis (1982).
12. Gaillard (1977), 286.
13. Marx (1967), vol. 1, 342; Cottereau (1988), 146–148.
14. Du Camp (1875), vol. 6, 235.
15. Gaillard (1977); 378; 446.
16. Miller (1981).
17. Daumas and Payen (1976), 147.
18. Daumas and Payen (1976), 135; Zeldin (1958), 76.
19. Hershberg (1981) makes this point very strongly through a detailed analysis of the data for nineteenth-century Philadelphia.
20. Corbon (1863).
21. Foulon (1934); Lejeune (1977).
22. Cottereau (1988), 130.
23. Lejeune and Lejeune (1984).
24. Lepidis and Jacomin (1975), 230.
25. Cottereau (1988), 144.
26. Lejeune and Lejeune (1984), 102–103; Zola (1970), 176–177.

Chapter 9

1. McKay (1933).
2. Rougerie (1965, 1968b).
3. Hanagan (1980, 1982); Cottereau (1980), 70.
4. Sewell (1980).
5. Chevalier (1950); Gaillard (1977), Cottereau (1988), and Rancière (1989) all agree on the direction of this basic trend.
6. Retel (1977), 199–207.
7. Poulot's (1980) account is fascinating and Varlin's evidence comes in the Workers' Commission of 1867, *Rapport des délégations ouvrières*, (1869), vol. 1, 99.
8. A. Thomas (n.d.); Sewell (1980); Hanagan (1982); Duveau (1946)
9. Rougerie (1968a); Duveau (1946).
10. Gaillard (1977), 245–246.
11. A. Thomas (n.d.), 179.
12. Poulot (1980).
13. Duveau (1946), 236–248.
14. Chevalier (1950), 96; Fribourg (1872).
15. Lazare (1869, 1870), Cochin (1864), 83; Duveau (1946), 363; Gaillard (1977), 417.

16. Chevalier (1950); Pinkney (1958), 152.
17. Price (1981); Weber (1976); for a specific example see the memoires of Nadaud (1895).
18. Chevalier (1950), 233; Pinkney (1953; 1958), 157–161; Gaillard (1977), 405; Rougerie 1965).
19. Duveau (1946), 284–295; Gaillard (1977), 406–411.
20. Duveau (1946, 327); E. Thomas (n.d.), 200.
21. Simon (1861); Leroy-Beaulieu (1868).
22. Vanier (1960), 109; Dalotel (1981).

CHAPTER 10

1. Michelet (1981), 65; see also Gaillard (1977), 222–224, and Scott (1988), 147.
2. E. Thomas (1966).
3. E. Thomas (1966), chapter 1; Simon (1861).
4. Scott (1988); Miller (1981); McBride (1976, 1977–1978); Lejeune and Lejeune (1984).
5. E. Thomas (1966); Michel (1981).
6. F. Green (1965), 95.
7. Zeldin (1973), 307; Corbin (1978); Harsin (1985).
8. St. John (1854), 233–308; Lejeune and Lejeune (1984).
9. Harsin (1985); see also Poulot (1980).
10. Dalotel (1981), 134.
11. Scott (1988), 101; Cottereau (1980).
12. Rancière and Vauday (1988)
13. Dalatel (1981), 72.
14. Cottereau (1980), 25–27; Le Play (1983), 9; (1878), 5, 427–430.
15. Hellerstein (1976); McBride (1976), 21–22.
16. Michelet (1981).
17. Wilson (1992) gives a helpful critique of Pollock (1988), 62.
18. Le Play (1983), 9; Zeldin (1973), vol. 1, 293–303.
19. Berlanstein (1979–1980); Le Play (1983), 149; 274. Cottereau (1980) argues strongly for a broadly non-conflictual relation between feminism and socialism even in the face of Proudhon's exclusions. Rancière and Vauday (1988), however, suggest otherwise.
20. Corbon (1863), 65; McLaren (1978).
21. Poulot (1980); E. Thomas (1966); C. Moses (1984).

CHAPTER 11

1. Chevalier (1950), 50; Marx (1967), vol. 1, 269.
2. Fay-Sallois (1980); Chevalier (1950), 46–52; Girard (1981), 136; Gaillard (1977), 225.
3. Guerrand (1966), 85; Corbon (1863), 181; A. Thomas (n.d.), 179; Flaus (1949); Gaillard (1977), 129–31; Lameyre (1958), 174.
4. Poulot (1980), 146; Audiganne (1854), vol. 2, 379.
5. Engels (1935); Gaillard (1977), 209; Commission des Logements Insalubres de Paris (1866); Lazare (1869); Poulot (1980), 146.
6. Guerrand (1966), 105, 199.
7. Gaillard (1977), 233–267; Duveau (1946), 328–343.
8. Foulon (1934), 56–67.
9. Anderson (1970), 1975.
10. Hutton (1981).
11. Auspitz (1982).

12. Gaillard (1977), 281.
13. Girard (1981), 288–289; Gaillard (1977), 270.
14. Gaillard (1977), 416–423.
15. Foulon (1934), 20–26; Dalotel, Faure, and Freirmuth (1980); Michel (1981).
16. Duveau (1946); Le Play (1983).
17. Fay. Sallois (1980); Donzelot (1977).

Chapter 12

1. Van Zanten (1994), 211; Truesdell (1977) devotes a whole book to this question of spectacle. Sennett's (1978) book is by far the most interesting because it embeds an understanding of theatricality and spectacle within a more general understanding of how the capitalist city was evolving during these years. T. Clark (1984) uses the connections between commodification and spectacle to get at the sensibility deployed in the impressionist movement among the artists of the 1860s.
2. N. Green (1990), 77–80; Rancière (1988).
3. Benjamin (1973), 165–167.
4. Zola (1995), 76–77; on fashion see Vanier (1960).
5. Sennett (1978), 145–148.
6. Quoted in Bachelard, p. 192.
7. Baudelaire (1947), 52–53.
8. T. Clark (1984), 36.
9. Goncourt (1962), 53; see also Sennett (1978).
10. Haine (1996), 37; 162–163.
11. Goubert (1986), 74–76.
12. Vanier (1960), 178–180; Goncourt (1962), 53.
13. Benjamin (1973).
14. Benjamin (1973), 74.

Chapter 13

1. Gould (1995). See also Cobb (1975); Castells (1983); Ferguson (1994).
2. Daumard (1965, 1973).
3. Chevalier (1973); Haussmann (1890–1893), vol. 2, 200.
4. Marx (1963), 75; (1964), 47; Chevalier (1973).
5. Corbon (1863), 34–48.
6. Hugo (1976), 15.
7. Sewell (1980), 259.
8. Zeldin (1973), 481.
9. Duveau (1946), 218; Kulstein (1969); Corbon (1863).
10. Haussmann (1890–1893), vol. 2, 200.
11. Greenberg (1971), 80; Rougerie (1965), 75.
12. Gaillard (1977), 231.
13. Lefebvre (1974); Gaillard (1977); Greenberg (1971).
14. *Paris Guide* 1983 edition (1867), 170; M. Fried (1963).
15. Chevalier (1973), 300.
16. Quoted in Chevalier (1973), 198–199.
17. Margadant (1982), 106.
18. Corbon (1863), 102.
19. Reybaud (1869).

20. Copping (1858), 5.
21. Sennett (1978), 137.
22. Poulot (1980); Haine (1996); Sennett (1978), 215.
23. Gould (1995).
24. Cottereau (1988), 155; Berthier (1998); Haine (1999).
25. See Rifkin and Thomas (1988).

CHAPTER 14

1. Jordan (1995) covers these aspects of Haussmann's works particularly well.
2. N. Green (1990).
3. Reid (1991); Goubert (1986); Gandy (1999); Jordan (1995).
4. Trollope, quoted in Reid (1991), 38.
5. Pinkney (1958), 125–126.
6. Reid (1991), 30; Pinkney (1958), 132.
7. Quoted in Gandy (1999), 24.
8. Gandy (1999), 24.

CHAPTER 15

1. Rifkin (1979).
2. Charlton (1959), 2.
3. Corbon (1863), 83.
4. Charlton (1959), 10; Flaubert (1982), 25; Du Camp (1875); Goncourt (1962, 275; Delacroix (1980), 96.
5. Baudelaire is quoted in Klein (1967), 86; Hugo (1976), 1047.
6. Foulon (1934); Michelet (1981), 350; Flaubert (1976), 325.
7. Chevalier (1973), 269; Scott (1988); Le Play (1878).
8. Fortescue (1983); Zeldin (1973), 39.
9. T. J. Clark (1973a, 1973b); Rubin (1980).
10. Gildea (1983), 321.
11. Fox and Weisz (1980); Weisz (1983); Williams (1965).
12. Quoted in Zeldin (1958), 101; F. Green (1965), chapter 3.
13. Rifkin (1979); Hugo (1976); Tchernoff (1906), 517.
14. Marx (1963), 15.
15. Michael Fried (1969); Baudelaire (1981).
16. Rancière and Vauday (1988).
17. *Paris Guide* 1983 edition (1867), 33; Haussmann (1890–1893), vol. 2, 533; Vidler (1978), 84.
18. Vidler (1978), 91.
19. Zola (1954a).
20. Veuillot (1867), ix; Ferry (1868).
21. Goncourt (1962), 61.
22. Baudelaire (1947), 94.
23. Berman (1982), 155–164; Wohlforth (1970).
24. Wohlforth (1970); Marx (1973), 163.
25. Translation by David Paul, quoted in Benjamin (1973), 57.
26. Zola, (1954a), 78–79.

CHAPTER 16

1. Quoted in T. J. Clark (1973a), 16; and in Hertz (1985), 173–174.
2. St. John (1854), 91.
3. Rifkin (1979).
4. Tchernoff (1906), 506–526; Copping (1858), 80; T. J. Clark (1973a); F. Green (1965).
5. Copping (1858).
6. Quoted in Glacken (1967), 592; Gobineau (1853–1855); Biddiss (1970).
7. The myth of the noble savage is taken apart in Ellingson (2001).
8. Laurentie, quoted in Hazareesingh (1998), 127.
9. Chevalier (1973); Marchand (1993).
10. Gossmann (1974); Said (1979).
11. Hitzman (1981); Said (1979), 167.
12. Michelet (1981); Zola (1991).
13. Flaubert (1979a), 198–199.
14. Quoted in Chardak (1997); Dunbar (1978), 52.
15. T. J. Clark (1973b).
16. N. Green (1990).
17. Berman (1982), 153; Benjamin (1973); Vidler (1978).
18. Dommanget (1969).
19. St. John (1854), 11.
20. Hazareesingh (1998); Greenberg (1971), 24.
21. Haussmann (1890–1893), vol. 2, 202; St. John (1854), 14; Greenberg (1971); Gould (1995).
22. *Paris Guide* (1867), 30.
23. Chevalier (1973), 360–361.
24. Flaubert (1964), 334.
25. Lazare (1870), 60.
26. Cited in Lidsky (1970), 46.
27. Baudelaire, (1983b), 67; Flaubert (1979b), 49; Goncourt, from Becker (1969).
28. Hutton (1981), 66.
29. Audiganne (1854, 1865). See also Corbon (1863); Poulot (1980).
30. Vallés (1872–1873); Corbon (1863), 209; Lazare (1869, 1870, 1872).
31. Lepidis and Jacomin (1975), 285.
32. Hutton (1981); Dommanget (1926, 1969).
33. Corbon (1863), 110; Hyams (1979); *Procès-verbaux de la Commission Ouvrière de 1867* (1867), 28–33.
34. Marx (1967), vol. 3, 441.
35. Sewell (1980), 243–276.
36. Corbon (1863), 122–141.
37. Moilin (1869); Bernard (2001).
38. Lissagaray (1976), 393.
39. Quoted in Lidsky (1970), 45, 115; Thomas (1966), 182.
40. The most complete study is that of Thomas (1966).
41. Hertz (1983).
42. Agulhon (1981), 99.
43. A. Thomas (n.d.), 164; *Procès-verbaux de la Commission Ouvrière de 1867* (1867), 100; Moon (1975); C. Moses (1984).
44. Hyams (1979), 274.
45. D'Hericourt (1860); F. Green (1965), 95; E. Thomas (1966), 70–87.
46. Reff (1982); T. Clark (1984).

47. Agulhon (1981), 185; Hertz (1983).
48. Michelet (1981); Baudelaire (1983b), 531; *Procès-verbaux de la Commission Ouvriere de 1867* (1867).
49. Simon (1861); see also *Procès-verbaux de la Commision Ouvrière de 1867* (1867), 213–17; Scott (1988).
50. Dalotel (1981), 122; *Procès-verbaux de la Commission Ouvrière de 1867* (1867), 233.

Chapter 17

1. Marx (1963), 135.
2. Zeldin (1958), 10.
3. Thomas (n.d.), 192.
4. Lejeune (1977); Rougerie (1968b).
5. The battle for political consciousness is described in detail in Dalotel, Faure, and Freirmuth (1980).

Chapter 18

1. Jonquet (1890), 54.
2. Dansette (1965); Jonquet (1890).
3. Rohault de Fleury (1903–1909). This four-volume history of the building of Sacre-Coeur is a major source of information. It was privately printed and circulated, and very few copies exist. The library of the basilica has all four volumes, and others can be found in the Bibliothèque Nationale. A two volume assemblage of documents and commentaries was produced by Benoist (1992).
4. Rohault de Fleury (1903–1909), vol. 1, 10–13.
5. Ibid.
6. Guillemin (1956).
7. E. Thomas (1967).
8. Lissagaray (1976).
9. Bruhat, Dautry and Tersen, (1971), 75.
10. Marx and Lenin (1968); Cerf (1971).
11. Lazare (1872); Becker (1969).
12. Bruhat, Dautry, and Tersen (1971); Edwards (1971).
13. Lissagaray (1976), 75.
14. Guillemin (1971); Bruhat, Dautry, and Tersen (1971), 104–105; Dreyfus (1928), 266.
15. Rohault de Fleury (1903–1909), vol. 1, 88, 264.
16. Rohault de Fleury (1903–1909), vol. 1, 264.
17. Accounts of the Commune are many and varied. I have made extensive use of Bruhat, Dautry, and Tersen (1971); Lissagaray (1976), who was a participant; Rougerie (1971); Jellinek (1937); Edwards (1971). Du Camp (1878) provides a highly partisan account from a right-wing perspective, and Lidsky (1970) assembles a collection of writings from the period hostile to the Commune. The photography of the event and its aftermath has been the subject of interest in recent years; see Noel (2000), for a wonderful collection, as well as the Réunion des Musées Nationaux (2000). The myth of the *petroleuse* has been thoroughly investigated by E. Thomas (1966), and Rougerie (1965) examines in detail the records of all the trials of participants to find out who participated and to get some idea of motivations.
18. Foulon (1934).
19. Audéoud is quoted in Jellinek (1937), 339. Becker (1969), 28, in his selections from Goncourt's diary entries during the Commune period, gives the quote as being from Goncourt.
20. Rohault de Fleury (1903–1909), vol. 1, 13.
21. Becker (1969), 312.
22. Guillemin (1971), 295–296; Rohault de Fleury (1903–1909), vol. 2, 365.
23. Rohault de Fleury (1903–1909), vol. 1, 27.

24. Jonquet (1890), 85–87.
25. Pinkney (1958), 85–87; see also Woolf (1988).
26. Dansette (1965), 340–345.
27. Rohault de Fleury (1903–1909), vol. 1, 88.
28. Ibid.
29. Abadie (1988), 222–224.
30. Rohault de Fleury (1903–1909), vol. 1, 244.
31. Rohault de Fleury (1903–1909), vol. 1, 269.
32. Dansette (1965), 356–358; Lepidis and Jacomin (1975), 271–272.
33. Ville de Paris, Procès-verbaux (August 3, October 7, and December 2, 1880).
34. Rohault de Fleury (1903–1909), vol. 2, 71–73.
35. Rohault de Fleury (1903–1909) 71–76.
36. Lesourd (1973), 224–225.

Bibliography

Abadie, P. 1988, *Paul Abadie, Architecte, 1812–1884*. Paris.

Agulhon, M. 1981 (1979). *Marianne into Battle: Republican Imagery and Symbolism in France, 1789–1880*. Trans. J. Lloyd. London.

———. 1983 (1973). *The Republican Experiment, 1848–1852*. Trans. J. Lloyd. London.

Allison, J. 1932. *Monsieur Thiers*. New York.

Anderson, R. 1970. "The Conflict in Education." In *Conflicts in French Society*. Ed. T. Zeldin. London.

———. 1975. *Education in France, 1848–1870*. Oxford.

Audiganne, A. 1854. *Les Populations Ouvrières et les Industries de la France dans le Mouvement Social du XIXème Siècle*. Paris.

———. 1865. *Les Ouvrièrs d'à Présent et la Nouvelle Économie du Travail*. Paris.

Auspitz, K. 1982. *The Radical Bourgeoisie: The Ligue de l'Enseignement and the Origins of the Third Republic*. London.

Autin, J. 1984. *Les Frères Pereire*. Paris.

Baguley, D. 2000, *Napoleon III and His Regime*. Baton Rouge, La.

Bakunin, J. 1976. *Pierre Leroux and the Birth of Democratic Socialism, 1797–1848*. New York.

Balzac. H. de. 1951. *Old Goriot* (OG). Trans. M. Crawford. Harmondsworth, U.K.

———. 1955. *Eugenie Grandet* (EG). Trans. M. Crawford. Harmondsworth, U.K.

———. 1965. *Cousin Bette* (CBE). Trans. M. Crawford. Harmondsworth, U.K.

———. 1968. *Cousin Pons* (CP). Translated H. Hunt. Harmondsworth, U.K.

———. 1970. *A Harlot High and Low* (HHL). Trans. R. Heppenstall. Harmondsworth, U.K.

———. 1971. *Lost Illusions* (LI). Trans. H. Hunt. Harmondsworth, U.K.

———. 1974. *History of the Thirteen* (HT). Trans. H. Hunt. Harmondsworth, U.K.

———. 1976. *La Comédie Humaine*. Vol. 1. Paris (Pléiade edition).

———. 1977. *The Wild Ass's Skin* (WAS). Trans. H. Hunt. Harmondsworth, U.K.

———. 1994. *César Birotteau* (CBI). Trans. R. Buss. Harmondworth, U.K.

———. 1997a. *Colonel Chabert* (CC). Trans. C. Cosman. New York.

———. 1997b. *The Physiology of Marriage*. Baltimore.

———. 2001. *The Unknown Masterpiece*. Trans. R. Howard. New York.

———. N.d., *The Old Maid* (OM). London and New York, Chesterfield Society, *The Works of Honore de Balzac*. vol. 14.

————. de. N.d. *The Peasantry*. London and New York, Chesterfield Society, *The Works of Honore de Balzac*, vol. 20.

Bartier, J., et al. 1981. 1848: *Les Utopismes Sociaux*. Paris.

Baudelaire, C. 1947 (1869). *Paris Spleen*. Ed. and trans. L. Varese. New York.

————. 1981 (1845–1864). *Selected Writings on Art and Artists*. 2nd ed., repr. Trans. P. E. Charvet. London.

————. 1983a (1857). *Les Fleurs du Mal*. Trans. R. Howard. Boston.

————. 1983b. *Intimate Journals*. Rev. ed., repr. Trans. C. Isherwood. San Francisco.

Becherer, R. 1984, *Science plus Sentiment: Cesar Daly's Formula for Modern Architecture*. Ann Arbor, Mich.

Becker, G., ed. 1969. *Paris Under Siege, 1970–71: From the Goncourt Journal*. Ithaca, N.Y.

Beecher, J. 2002. *Victor Considerant and the Rise and Fall of French Romantic Socialism*. Berkeley, Calif.

Beecher, J. and R. Bienvenu, 1971. "Introduction." In C. Fourier, *The Theory of the Four Movements*. Trans. and ed. Beecher and Bienvenu. Boston.

Bellet, R. 1967. *Presse et Journalisme sous le Second Empire*. Paris.

Benjamin, W. 1968. *Illumination*s. Trans. H. Zohn. New York.

————. 1973. *Charles Baudelaire: A Lyric Poet in the Era of High Capitalism*. Trans. H. Zohn. London.

————. 1999. *The Arcades Project*. Trans. H. Eiland and K. McLaughlin. Cambridge, Mass.

Benoist, J. 1992. *La Basilique de Sacre-Coeur a Montmartre*. 2 vols. Paris.

Berlanstein, L. 1979–1980. "Growing Up as Workers in Nineteenth-Century Paris: The Case of Orphans of the Prince Imperial." *French Historical Studies* 11: 551–576.

Berman, M. 1982. *All That Is Solid Melts into Air*. New York.

Bernard, J-P. 2001. *Les Deux Paris: Les Représentations de Paris dans le Second Moitié du XIXème Siècle*. Paris.

Berthier, P. 1998. *La Vie Quotidienne dans La Comédie Humaine de Balzac*. Paris.

Biddiss, M. 1970. *Father of Racist Ideology: The Social and Political Thought of Count Gobineau*. New York.

Bouvier, J. 1967. *Les Rothschild*. Paris.

Bowie, K, ed. 2001. *La Modernité Avant Haussmann: Formes de L'éspace Urbain à Paris, 1801–1853*. Paris.

Boyer, C. 1994. *The City of Collective Memory: Its Historical Imagery and Architectural Entertainments*, Cambridge, Mass.

Braudel, F., and E. Labrousse, eds. 1976. *Histoire Économique et Sociale de la France*. Vol. 3. Paris.

Bruhat, J., J. Dautry, and E. Tersen. 1971. *La Commune de 1871*. Paris.

Canfora-Argandona, E., and R. H. Guerrand. 1976. *La Répartition de la Population: Les Conditions de Logement des Classes Ouvrières à Paris au XIX siècle*. Paris.

Casselle, P. 2000. "Commission des Embellissements de Paris: Rapport à l'Empereur Napoleon III Rédigé par le Comte Henri Simeon." *Cahiers de la Rotonde*, 23.

Castells, M. 1983. *The City and the Grassroots*. Berkeley, Calif.

Cerf, M. 1971. *Edouard Moreau*. Paris.

Chardak, H. 1997. *Elisée Reclus: Une Vie*. Paris.

Charlety, S. 1931. *Histoire du Saint-Simonisme*. Paris.

Charlton, D. 1959. *Positivist Thought in France During the Second Empire, 1852–1870*. Oxford.

Chevalier, L. 1950. *La Formation de la Population Parisienne au XIXeme Siècle*. Paris.

————. 1973 (1958). *Laboring Classes and Dangerous Classes*. Trans. F. Jellinek. Princeton, N.J.

Clark, T. 1984. *The Painting of Modern Life: Paris in the Art of Manet and His Followers*. London.

Clark, T. J. 1973a. *The Absolute Bourgeois: Artists and Politics in France, 1848–1851*. London.

————. 1973b. *Image of the People: Gustave Courbet and the 1848 Revolution*. London.

Clout, H. 1977. *Themes in the Historical Geography of France*. London.

Cobb, R. 1975. *A Sense of Place*. London.

Cochin, A. 1864. *Paris: Sa Population, Son Industries*. Paris.

Commission des Logements Insalubres de Paris. 1866. *Rapport Générale sur les Travaux de la Commission Pendant les Années 1862–1865*. Paris.

Copping, E. 1858. *Aspects of Paris*. London.

Corbin, A. 1978. *Les Filles de Noce: Misère Sexuélle et Prostitution aux 19eme et 20ème Siècles*. Paris.

Corbon, A. 1863. *La Secret du Peuple de Paris*. Paris.

Corcoran, P. 1983. *Before Marx: Socialism and Communism in France, 1830–48*. London.

Cottereau, A. 1980. "Etude Préalable." In D. Poulot, *Le Sublime*. Paris.

———. 1988. "Dennis Poulot's *Le Sublime*—a Preliminary Study." In A. Rifkin and R. Thomas, eds., *Voices of the People*. London.

Dalotel, A. 1981. *Paule Minck: Communarde et Féministe*. Paris.

Dalotel, A., A. Faure, and J. C. Freirmuth. 1980. *Aux Origines de la Commune: Le Movement des Réunions Publiques à Paris, 1868–1870*. Paris.

Dansette, A. 1965. *Histoire Religieuse de la France Contemporaine*. Paris.

Dargan, J. 1985. *Balzac and the Drama of Perspective*. Lexington, Ky.

Daumard, A. 1965. *Maisons de Paris et Propriétaires Parisiens au XIXème Siècle*. Paris.

———. ed. 1973. *Les Fortunes Françaises au XIXème Siècle*. Paris.

Daumas, M., and J. Payen, eds. 1976. *Evolution de la Geographie Industrielle de Paris et Sa Proche Banlieue au XIXème Siècle*. 2 vols. Paris.

Dautry, J. 1977. *1848 et la IIme République*. Paris.

Delacroix, E. 1980 (1926). *The Journal of Eugene Delacroix*. Trans. L. Norton, ed. H. Wellington. Ithaca, N.Y.

Delattre, S. 2000. *Les Douze Heures Noires: La Nuit à Paris au XIXeme Siècle*. Paris.

Des Cars, J., and P. Pinon, eds. 1991. *Paris-Haussmann: Le Pari Haussmann*. Paris.

De Thèzy, M. 1994. *Marville*. Paris.

D'Hericourt, J. 1860. *La femme affranchi*. Paris.

Dommanget, M. 1957. *Les idées politiques et sociales d'Auguste Blanqui*, Paris.

———. 1969. *Blanqui et l'opposition révolutionnaire à la fin du Second Empire*. Paris.

———. 1970 (1926). *Blanqui*. Reprint. Paris.

Donzelot, J. 1977. *La Police des Familles*. Paris.

Dreyfus, R. 1928. *Monsieur Thiers Contre l'Empire: La Guerre et la Commune*. Paris.

Du Camp, M. 1875. *Paris: Ses Organes, Ses Fonctions et Sa Vie dans la Seconde Moitié du XIXème Siècle*. 6 vols. Paris.

———. 1878. *Les Convulsions de Paris,* 4 vols. Paris.

Duchene, G. 1869. *L'Empire Industriel*. Paris.

Dunbar, G. 1978. *Elisée Reclus*. Hamden, Conn.

Dupont-Ferrier, P. 1925. *Le Marché Financier de Paris sous le Second Empire*. Paris.

Durkheim, E. 1958, *Socialism and Saint-Simon*. Trans. C. Sattler. Yellow Springs, Ohio.

Duveau, G. 1946. *La Vie Ouvrière en France sous le Second Empire*. Paris.

Edwards, S. 1971. *The Paris Commune*. Chicago.

Ellingson, T. 2001. *The Myth of the Noble Savage*. Berkeley, Calif.

Engels, F. 1935 (1872). *The Housing Question*. New York.

Farrant, T. 2001. "Du Livre Illustré à la Ville-Spectacle." In K. Bowie, ed., *La Modernité Avant Haussmann*. Paris.

Fay-Sallois, F. 1980. *Les Nourrices à Paris au XIXéme Siècle*. Paris.

Ferguson, P. 1994. *Paris as Revolution: Writing the 19th Century City*. Berkeley, Calif.

Ferry, J. 1868. *Comptes Fantastiques d'Haussmann*. Paris.

Flaubert, G. 1964 (1869). *Sentimental Education*. Trans. R. Baldick. Harmondsworth, U.K.

———. 1976 (1881). *Bouvard and Pecuchet*. Trans. A. J. Krailsheimer. Harmondsworth, U.K.

———. 1979a. *Flaubert in Egypt*. Trans. and ed. F. Steegmuller. Chicago.

———. 1979b. *Letters, 1830–1857*. Trans. and ed. F. Steegmuller. London.

———. 1982. *Letters, 1857–1880*. Trans. and ed. F. Steegmuller. London.

Flaus, L. 1949. "Les fluctuations de la Construction d'Habitations Urbaines" *Journal de la Société de Statistique de Paris* (May–June 1949).

Fortescue, W. 1983. *Alphonse de Lamartine: A Political Biography*. London.

Foucault, M. 1984. *The Foucault Reader*. Ed. P. Rabinow. Harmondsworth, U.K.

Foulon, M. 1934. *Eugène Varlin*. Clermont-Ferand.

Fourier, C. 1971. *The Utopian Vision of Charles Fourier: Selected Texts* Trans. and ed. J. Beecher and R. Bienvenu. Boston.

———. 1996. *The Theory of the Four Movements*. Ed. G. S. Jones and I. Patterson. Cambridge.

Fournel, V. 1858. *Ce Qu'on Voit dans les Rues de Paris*. Paris.

———. 1865. *Paris Nouveau et Paris Future*. Paris.

Fox, R., and G. Weisz. 1980. *The Organisation of Science and Technology in France, 1808–1914*. London.

Fribourg, A. 1872. *Le Paupérisms Parisien*. Paris.

Fried, M. 1963. "Grieving for a Lost Home," In L. Duhl, ed., *The Urban Condition*. New York.

Fried, Michael, 1969. "Manet's Sources: Aspects of His Art, 1859–65." *Artforum* 7, no. 7: 1–82.

Gaillard, J. 1977. *Paris: La Ville, 1852–1870*. Paris.

Gandy, M. 1999. "The Paris Sewers and the Rationalization of Urban Space." *Transactions, Institute of British Geographers* n.s. 24: 23–44.

Giedion, S. 1941. *Space, Time, Architecture*. Cambridge, Mass.

Gildea, R. 1983. *Education in Provincial France, 1800–1914*. Oxford.

Girard, L. 1952. *La Politique des Travaux Publics Sous le Second Empire*. Paris.

———. 1981. *Nouvelle Histoire de Paris: La Deuxième République et le Second Empire*. Paris.

Glacken, C. 1967. *Traces on the Rhodian Shore*. Berkeley, Calif.

Gobineau, A., Compte de. 1853–1855. *Essai sur l'Inégalité des Races Humaines*, Paris.

Gossez, R. 1967. *Les Ouvriers de Paris: L'Organisation, 1848–51*. Paris.

Gossman, L. 1974. "The Go-between: Jules Michelet, 1798–1874." *MLN* 89: 503–541.

Goubert, J.-P. 1986. *The Conquest of Water*. Oxford.

Gould, R. 1995. *Insurgent Identities: Class, Community and Protest in Paris from 1848 to the Commune*. Chicago.

Gramsci, A. 1971. *Selections from the Prison Notebooks*. Trans. Q. Hoare and G. N. Smith. London.

Green, F. 1965. *A Comparative View of French and British Civilization, 1850–1870*. London.

Green, N. 1990. *The Spectacle of Nature: Landscape and Bourgeois Culture in Nineteenth-Century France*. Manchester, U.K.

Greenberg, L. 1971. *Sisters of Liberty: Marseille, Lyon, Paris, and the Relation to a Centralized State, 1868–71*. Cambridge, Mass.

Guedalla, P. 1922. *The Second Empire*. New York.

Guerrand, R.-H. 1966. *Les Origines du Logement Social en France*. Paris.

Haine, W. 1996. *The World of the Paris Café*. Baltimore.

Halbwachs, M. 1909. *Les Expropriations et le Prix de Terrain, 1860–1900*. Paris.

———. 1928. *La Population et les Tracés des Voies à Paris Depuis un Siècle*. Paris.

Hambourg, M. 1981. "Charles Marville's Old Paris." In French Institute/Alliance Française, *Charles Marville: Photographs of Paris at the Time of the Second Empire on Loan from the Musée Carnavalet*. Paris and New York.

Hanagan, M. 1980. *The Logic of Solidarity*. Urbana, Ill.

Hanagan, M. 1982. "Urbanization, Worker Settlement Patterns, and Social Protest in Nineteenth Century France." In J. Merriman, ed., *French Cities in the Nineteenth Century*. London.

Harsin, J. 1985. *Policing Prostitution in Nineteenth Century Paris*. Princeton, N.J.

———. 2002. *Barricades: The War of the Streets in Revolutionary Paris, 1830–1848*, New York.

Harvey, D. 1982. *The Limits to Capital*. Oxford.

———. 1989. *The Condition of Postmodernity*. Oxford.

———. 1996. *Justice, Nature and the Geography of Difference*. Oxford.

Haussmann, G.-E. 1890–1893. *Memoires du Baron Haussmann*. 2 vols. Paris.

Hazareesingh, S. 1998. *From Subject to Citizen: The Second Empire and the Emergence of Modern French Democracy*. Princeton, N.J.

Hellerstein, E. 1976. "French Women and the Orderly Household." *Western Society for French History* 3: 378–389.

Hershberg, T. 1981. *Philadelphia: Work, Space, Family, and the Group Experience in the Nineteenth Century*. New York.

Hertz, N. 1983. "Medusa's Head: Male Hysteria under Political Pressure." *Representations* 4: 37–54.

Hill, C. 1975. *The World Turned Upside Down*. Harmondsworth, U.K.

Hitzman, A. 1981. "Rome Is to Carthage as Male Is to Female: Michelet, Berlioz, Flaubert and the Myths of the Second Empire." *Western Society for French History* 8: 378–380.

Hugo, V. 1976 (1862). *Les Misérables*. Trans. N. Denny. Harmondsworth, U.K.

Hutton, P. 1981. *The Cult of the Revolutionary Tradition: The Blanquists in French Politics, 1864–1893*. Berkeley, Calif.

Hyams. E. 1979. *Pierre-Joseph Proudhon: His Revolutionary Life, Mind, and Works*. London.

Ionescu, G. 1976. *The Political Thought of Saint-Simon*. Trans. and ed. G. Ionescu. Oxford.

Jameson, F. 1982. *The Political Unconscious*. London.

———. 1995. "Fredric Jameson on *La Cousine Bette*." In M. Tilby, ed., *Balzac*. London.

Janis, E. 1986, "Demolition Picturesque: Photographs of Paris in 1852 and 1853 by Henri Le Secq." In P. Walch and T. Barrow, eds., *Perspectives on Photography: Essays in Honor of Beaumont Newhall*. Albuquerque, N.M.

Jellinek, F. 1937. *The Paris Commune of 1871*. London.

Johnson, C. 1974. *Utopian Communism in France: Cabet and the Icarians, 1839–1851*. Ithaca, N.Y.

Kantorowicz, E. 1957. *The King's Two Bodies*. Princeton, N.J.

Kelso, M. 1936. "The French Labor Movement during the Last Years of the Second Empire." In D. McKay, ed., *Essays in the History of Modern Europe*. New York.

Kemple, T. 1995. *Reading Marx Writing: Melodrama, the Market and the "Grundrisse."* Stanford, Calif.

Klein, R. 1967. "Some Notes on Baudelaire and Revolution." *Yale French Studies* 39: 85–97.

Kulstein, D. 1969. *Napoleon III and the Working Class*. San Jose, Calif.

Lameyre, G.-N. 1958. *Haussmann, Préfet de Paris*. Paris.

Lavedan, P. 1975. *Histoire de l'Urbanisme à Paris*. Paris.

Lazare, L. 1869. *Les Quartiers Pauvres de Paris*. Paris.

———. 1870. *Les Quartiers Pauvres de Paris: Le XXème Arrondissement*. Paris.

———. 1872. *La France et Paris*. Paris.

Lefebvre, H. 1967. *La Proclamation de la Commune*. Paris.

———. 1974. *La Production de l'Espace*. Paris.

———. 1976 (1973). *The Survival of Capitalism*. Trans. F. Bryant. London.

Lejeune, M., and P. Lejeune. 1984. *Calicot: Xavier-Edouard Lejeune*. Paris.

Lejeune, P. 1977. *Eugène Varlin: Pratique Militante et Écrits d'un Ouvrier Communard*. Paris.

Leon, P. 1976. "La Conquête de l'Espace Nationale." In F. Braudel and E. Labrousse, eds., *Histoire Économique et Sociale de la France*. Vol 3. Paris.

Lepidis, C., and E. Jacomin. 1975. *Belleville*. Paris.

Le Play, F. 1878. *Les Ouvriers Européens*. 6 vols. Paris.

———. 1983. *Ouvriers de Deux Mondes*. Abridged ed. Paris.

Leroy-Beaulieu, P. 1868. *De l'État Moral et Intellectuel des Populations Ouvrières et Son Influence sur le Taux de Salariés*. Paris.

Lescure, M. 1980. *Les Sociétés Immobilières en France au XIXème Siècle*. Paris.

Lesourd, P. 1973. *Montmartre*. Paris.

Levy-Leboyer, M. 1976. "Le Crédit et la Monnaie: L'Évolution Institutionelle." In F. Braudel and E. Labrousse, eds., *Histoire Économique et Sociale de la France*. Vol. 3. Paris.

Lidsky, P. 1970. *Les Écrivains contre la Commune*. Paris.

Lissagaray, P.-O. 1976 (1876). *Histoire de la Commune*. Paris.

Lynch, K. 1964. *The Image of the City*. Cambridge, Mass.

Marchand, B. 1993. *Paris: Histoire d'une Ville*. Paris.

Marcus, S. 1999. *Apartment Stories: City and Home in Nineteenth Century Paris and London*, Berkeley, Calif.

Margadant, T. 1982. "Proto-urban Development and Political Mobilization during the Second Republic." In J. Merriman, ed., *French Cities in the Nineteenth Century*. London.

Marrey, B. 1981. "Les Réalisations des Utopistes dans les Travaux Publics et l'Architecture: 1840–1848." In Société d'Histoire de la Révolution de 1848 et des Révolutions du XIXème Siecle, *1848: Les Utopismes sociaux*. Paris.

Marx, K. 1963 (1852). *The Eighteenth Brumaire of Louis Bonaparte*. New York.

———. 1964. *Class Struggles in France, 1848–1850*. New York.

———. 1967. *Capital*. 3 vols. New York.

———. 1972. *Theories of Surplus Value*. 3 vols. London.

———. 1973. *Grundrisse*. Harmondsworth, U.K.

Marx, K., and F. Engels, 1952 (1848). *Manifesto of the Communist Party*. Moscow.

Marx, K., and V. I. Lenin, 1968, *The Civil War in France: The Paris Commune*, New York.

Marx, L. 1964. *The Machine in the Garden*. London.

Massa-Gille, G. 1973. *Histoire des Emprunts de la Ville de Paris, 1814–1875*. Paris.

McBride, T. 1976. *The Domestic Revolution*. New York.

———. 1977–1978. "A Woman's World: Department Stores and the Evolution of Women's Employment, 1870–1920," *French Historical Studies* 10: 664–683.

McKay, D. 1933. *The National Workshops: A Study in the French Revolution of 1848*. Cambridge, Mass.

McLaren, A. 1978. "Abortion in France: Women and the Regulation of Family Size." *French Historical Studies* 10, 461–485.

Meynadier, H. 1843. *Paris sous le Point de Vue Pittoresque*. Paris.

Michel, L. 1981 (1886). *The Red Virgin*. Trans. B. Lowry and E. Gunter. University, Ala.

Michelet, J. 1973 (1845). *The People*. Trans. J. McKay, Urbana, Ill.

———. 1981. *La Femme*. Paris.

Miller, M. 1981. *The Bon Marché: Bourgeois Culture and the Department Store, 1869–1920*. London.

Ministère de la Culture, de la Communication, des Grands Travaux et du Bicentenaire. 1988. *Paul Abadie: Architecte 1812–1884*. Paris.

Moilin, T. 1869. *Paris en l'An 2000*. Paris.

Molotch, H. 1976. "The City as a Growth Machine: Towards a Political Economy of Place." *American Journal of Sociology* 82: 309–32.

Moncan, P, and C. Mahout. 1991. *Le Paris du Baron Haussmann: Paris sous le Second Empire*. Paris.

Moon, S. 1975. "The Saint-Simonian Association of Working Class Women, 1830–1850." *Western Society for French History* 5: 274–280.

Moret, F. 2001. "Penser la Ville en Fourieriste: Les Projets pour Paris de Perreymond." In K. Bowie, ed., *La Modernité Avant Haussmann*. Paris.

Moses, C. 1984. *French Feminism in the Nineteenth Century*. Albany, N.Y.

Moses, R. 1942. "What Happened to Haussmann." *Architectural Forum* 77 (July): 1–10.

Moss, B. 1976. *The Origins of the French Labor Movement, 1830–1914*. Berkeley, Calif.

Nadaud, M. 1895. *Mémoires de Léonard, Ancien Garçon Macon*. Bourganeuf.

Noel, B, ed. 2000. *La Commune: Paris 1871*. Paris.

Papayanis, N. 2001. "L'Émergence de l'Urbanisme Moderne à Paris." In K. Bowie, ed., *La Modernité Avant Haussmann.* Paris.

Paris Guide. 1983 (1867). Paris.

Payne, H. 1966. *The Police State of Louis Napoleon Bonaparte.* Seattle, Wash.

Pinkney, D. 1953. "Migrations to Paris during the Second Empire." *Journal of Modern History* 25: 1–12.

———. 1958. *Napoleon III and the Rebuilding of Paris.* Princeton, N.J.

Piore, M., and C. Sable. 1984. *The Second Industrial Divide: Possibilities for Prosperity.* New York.

Plessis, A. 1973. *De la Fête Impériale au Mur des Fédérés, 1852–1871.* Paris.

———. 1982. *La Banque de France et Ses Deux Cents Actionnaires sous le Second Empire.* Paris.

Pollock, G. 1988. *Vision and Difference: Femininity, Feminism and the Histories of Art.* London.

Poulet, G. 1959. *The Interior Distance.* Trans. E. Coleman. Baltimore.

Poulot, D. 1980 (1870). *Le Sublime.* Paris.

Prawer, S. 1978. *Karl Marx and World Literature.* Oxford.

Prendergast, C. 1992. *Paris and the Nineteenth Century.* Oxford.

Price, R. 1975. *The Economic Modernization of France.* London.

———. 1983. *The Modernization of Rural France.* London.

Procès-Verbaux de la Commission Ouvrière de 1867. 1867. Paris.

Rabinow, P. 1989. *French Modern: Norms and Forms of the Social Environment.* Cambridge, Mass.

Rancière, J. 1988. "Good Times or Pleasure at the Barriers." In A. Rifkin and R. Thomas, eds., *Voices of the People.* London.

———. 1989. *The Nights of Labor: The Workers' Dream in Nineteenth Century France.* Trans. John Drury. Philadelphia.

Rancière, J., and P. Vauday. 1988. "Going to the Expo: The Worker, His Wife and Machines." In A. Rifkin and R. Thomas, eds., *Voices of the People.* London.

Reff, T. 1982. *Manet and Modern Paris.* Washington, D.C.

Retel, J. 1977. *Eléments Pour une Histoire du Peuple de Paris au 19eme Siècle.* Paris.

Réunion des Musées Nationaux. 2000. *La Commune Photographiée.* Paris.

Reybaud, L. 1869. "Les Agitations Ovrières et l'Association Internationale." *Revue des Deux Mondes* 81: 871–902.

Rifkin, A. 1979. "Cultural Movements and the Paris Commune." *Art History* 2: 210–222.

Rifkin, A., and R. Thomas, eds. 1988. *Voices of the People: The Politics and Life of "La Sociale" at the End of the Second Empire.* London.

Robb, G. 2000. *Balzac: A Biography.* London.

Rohault de Fleury, H. 1903–1909. *Historique de la Basilique du Sacré-Coeur.* 4 vols. Limited ed. Paris.

Roncayalo, M. 2002. *Lectures de Ville: Formes et Temps.* Marseille.

Rose, R. 1978. *Gracchus Babeuf: The First Revolutionary Communist.* Stanford, Calif.

Rossi, A. 1982. *The Architecture of the City.* Cambridge, Mass.

Rougerie, J. 1965. *Procès des Communards.* Paris.

———. 1968a. "Remarques sur l'Histoire des Salaires à Paris au Dix-neuvième siècle." *Le Mouvement Sociale* 63: 71–108.

———. 1968b. "Les Sections Françaises de l'Association Internationale de Travailleurs." *Colloques Internationales du CNRS.* Paris.

———. 1971. *Paris Libre.* Paris.

Rubin, J. 1980. *Realism and Social Vision in Courbet and Proudhon.* Princeton, N.J.

Said, E. 1979. *Orientalism.* New York.

Saint-Simon, H., Comte de. 1952. *Selected Writings.* Ed. and trans. F. M. H. Markham. Oxford.

———. 1975. *Selected Writings on Science, Industry and Social Organisation.* Trans. K. Taylor. London.

Saisselin, R. 1984. *The Bourgeois and the Bibelot.* New Brunswick, N.J.

Schivelbusch, W. 1977. *The Railway Journey: The Industrialization of Time and Space in the Nineteenth Century*. Berkeley, Calif.

Scott, J. C. 1985. *Weapons of the Weak: Everyday Forms of Peasant Resistance*. New Haven, Conn.

Scott, J. W. 1988. *Gender and the Politics of History*. New York.

Sennett, R. 1970. *The Uses of Disorder: Personal Identity and City Life*. New York.

———. 1978. *The Fall of Public Man: The Social Psychology of Capitalism*. New York.

Sewell, W. H. 1980. *Work and Revolution in France*. New York.

Simmel, G. 1971. "The Metropolis and Mental Life." In Simmel's *On Individuality and Social Forms*. Ed. D. Levine. Chicago.

———. 1978 (1920). *The Philosophy of Money*. Trans. T. Bottomore and D. Frisby. London.

Simon, J. 1861. *L'Ouvrière*. Paris.

Smith, W. 1991. *Napoleon III*. London.

Société d'Histoire de la Révolution de 1848 et des Révolutions du XIXème Siècle. 1981. *1848: Les Utopismes Sociaux*. Paris.

St. John, B. 1854. *Purple Tints of Paris*. New York.

Steegmuller, F. 1950. *Flaubert and Madame Bovary: A Double Portrait*. New York.

Stierle, K. 2001. *La Capitale des Signes: Paris et Son Discours*. Paris.

Sutcliffe, A. 1970. *The Autumn of Central Paris*. London.

Taylor, K. 1975. "Introduction." In Saint-Simon, *Selected Writings on Science . . .* Ed. Taylor. London.

Tchernoff, 1. 1906. *Le Parti Républicain*. Paris.

Thomas, A. N.d. *Le Second Empire, 1852–1870*. Paris.

Thomas, E. 1966 (1963). *The Women Incendiaries*. Trans. J. Atkinson and S. Atkinson. New York.

———. 1967. *Rossell (1844–1871)*. Paris.

Tilly, L. A., and J. A. Scott. 1978. *Women, Work, and Family*. New York.

Tristan, F. 1843. *L'Union Ouvrière*. Paris

———. 1982 (1840). *The London Journal of Flora Tristan*. Trans. J. Hawkes. London.

Truesdell, M. 1997. *Spectacular Politics: Louis-Napoleon Bonaparte and the Fête Impériale, 1849–70*. Oxford.

Tudesq, A.-J. 1956. "La Crise de 1847, Vue par les Milieux d'Affaires Parisiens." *Etudes de la Société d'Histoire de la Révolution de 1848* 19: 4–36.

Valette, J. 1981. "Utopie Sociale et Utopistes Sociaux en France vers 1848." *Société d'Histoire de la Révolution de 1848* 13–110.

Vanier, H. 1960. *La Mode et Ses Metiers*. Paris.

Vidler, A. 1978. "The Scenes of the Street: Transformations in Ideal and Reality, 1750–1871" In S. Anderson, ed., *On Streets*. Cambridge, Mass.

Ville de Paris, Conseil Municipal. 1880. *Procès Verbaux*. Paris.

Vincent, K. 1984. *Pierre-Joseph Proudhon and the Rise of French Republican Socialism*. Oxford.

Weeks, W. 1999. *The Man Who Made Paris Paris: The Illustrated Biography of Georges-Eugene Haussmann*. London.

Woolf, P. 1988. "Symbol of the Second Empire: Cultural Politics and the Paris Opera House." In D. Cosgrove, and S. Daniels, eds., *The Iconography of Landscape*. Cambridge.

Zola, E. 1954a (1872). *The Kill (La Curée)*. Trans. A. Texiera de Mattos. New York.

———. 1954b (1885). *Germinal*. Trans. L. Tancock. Harmondsworth, U.K.

———. 1970 (1876). *l'Assommoir*. Trans. L. Tancock. Harmondsworth, U.K.

———. 1991 (1891). *Money (L'Argent)*. Trans. E. Vizetelly, Stroud.

———. 1995 (1883). *The Ladies Paradise (Au Bonheur des Dames)*. Trans. Brian Nelson. Oxford.

Acknowledgments and Credits for Illustrations

Academic Press 35

Amgueddfa ac Orielau Cenedlaethol Cymru/National Museums & Galleries of Wales 54

Artography 6, 14, 17, 26, 42, 51, 83, 92, 94, 116 (bottom)

Ashmolean Museum, Oxford 2

Beth Lieberman 25, 36

Bibliothèque Nationale 13, 15, 21, 24, 27, 37, 40, 59, 63, 70, 71, 76, 77, 85, 95, 98, 99, 101

Collections d'Affiches, Alain Gesgon 118

Editions du Seuil 105

Editions de la Couverte 102

The Phillips Collection, Washington, D.C. 66

Photothèque des Musées de la Ville de Paris/Cliché Andreani 8, 43, 75A, 78, 79A, 79B, 91A; Bertheir, 9, 75B; Briant, 3, 4, 19, 32B, 33, 38, 46, 86A, 107A; Degraces, 18, 44, 84B, 114, 116; Giet, 89A, 89B; Habouzit, 11, 28A, 82, 84A, 86B, 108A; inconnu, 74A; Joffre, 16, 29, 30, 32A, 91B, 100, 104, 107B, 110, 111, 112, 113, 115; Ladet, 10, 28B, 31, 39, 57, 69, 73A, 81, 87, 103; Lifeman, 88; Pierrain, 5, 7, 52, 60, 65A, 108B; Trocaz, 34A, 72, 73B; Toumazet, 65B, 74B

Réunion des Musées Nationaux/Art Resource, NY 1, 22, 23, 67, 90B

Scala/Art Resource, NY 90A

Trustees of the British Museum 12

The Walters Art Museum, Baltimore 80

INDEX